IRISHMEN OR ENGLI

IRISHMEN OR ENGLISH SOLDIERS?

The times and world of a southern Catholic Irish man (1876–1916) enlisting in the British army during the First World War

Thomas P. Dooley

LIVERPOOL UNIVERSITY PRESS

First published 1995 by
LIVERPOOL UNIVERSITY PRESS
Senate House
Liverpool, L69 3BX
United Kingdom

British Library Cataloguing-in-Publication Data
A British Library CIP Record is available
ISBN 0-85323-590-2 (cased)
      0-85323-600-3 (paper)

Typeset by Books Unlimited (Nottm), NG19 7QZ
Printed and bound in the UK by Bell & Bain Limited,
Glasgow

In memory of my mother and father, and of the
grandparents I never knew

CONTENTS

LIST OF ILLUSTRATIONS

Plates

ACKNOWLEDGEMENTS

Without the help and influence of my mother (1907–1991) and my father (1904–1994), this book would not have been written. Their memories of Waterford city, the place of their birth, recalled during hours of enthralling conversation over the years, were inspirational.

I also wish to thank all those who have assisted and advised during research for this book, with particular mention of:

Professor Roy Foster for his encouragement, guidance and help, and the University of London Central Research Fund for its financial assistance.

The staff of Ealing Tertiary College Library (Acton centre) and particularly Barbara Marker.

The staffs of the Newspaper Library, Colindale; the British Museum; the Royal Artillery Institution Library, Woolwich; the Liddell Hart Centre for Military Archives, King's College; the National Army Museum; the Imperial War Museum; and the Public Record Office, Kew.

The staffs of the Irish National Archives, Four Courts; the National Library of Ireland; and Trinity College (manuscript room), University of Dublin.

The staff of Waterford Municipal Library and particularly Richard Fennessy.

Local Waterford historians Dan Dowling and Jack O'Neill and others using the 'Waterford Room' who provided much in the way of stimulating discussion, advice and local information.

The numerous Waterford residents, particularly Clive MacCarthy and William O'Meara, who provided hospitality and very useful information.

The small band of 'Ireland and the First World War' enthusiasts, particularly Terry Denman and Martin Staunton. During frequent meetings and telephone discussions they offered advice, information and shared source references.

I wish to thank the following for giving me permission to reproduce text, photographs, maps and illustrations in the book: The National Library of Ireland, the *Waterford News and Star*, Cork Examiner Publications, the Irish Ordnance Survey, the British Ordnance Survey, The British Library Newspaper Library, the Imperial War Museum, the National Army Museum, and the Liddell Hart Centre for Military Archives.

LIST OF ABBREVIATIONS

A/Cpl	Acting Corporal
A/CSM	Acting Company Sergeant Major
Amb	ambulance
amm	ammunition
AOH	Ancient Order of Hibernians
Batts	Batteries
Bde	Brigade
Bn	Battalion
Brig Gen	Brigadier General
Co	Company
Conn. Rangers	Connaught Rangers
Cpl	Corporal
Cos	Companies
CYMS	Catholic Young Men's Society
Divl	Divisional
DORA	Defence of the Realm Act
F Ambs	Field Ambulances
FTLU	Federated Trades and Labour Union
GAA	Gaelic Athletic Association
Howr	Howitzer
HQ	Headquarters
ILP	Independent Labour Party
in	inch
INL	Irish National League
IPP	Irish Parliamentary Party
IRA	Irish Republican Army
ISRP	Irish Socialist Republican Party
ITGWU	Irish Transport and General Workers Union
ITUC	Irish Trades Union Congress
L/Cpl	Lance Corporal
Leinster Regt	Leinster Regiment
Lt Col	Lieutenant Colonel
Lt Gen	Lieutenant General
Maj	Major
Maj Gen	Major General
MP	Member of Parliament
NCO	Non-Commissioned Officer
prs	pounders
Pte	Private soldier
R Dublin Fus	Royal Dublin Fusiliers

RE	Royal Engineers
RFA	Royal Field Artillery
RIC	Royal Irish Constabulary
R Innis Fus	Royal Inniskillin Fusiliers
R Irish Fus	Royal Irish Fusiliers
R Irish Regt	Royal Irish Regiment
R Irish Rifles	Royal Irish Rifles
R Munster Fus	Royal Munster Fusiliers
Sgt	Sergeant
Sig	Signal
Sqn	Squadron
TUC	Trades Union Congress
UIL	United Irish League
UTLC	United Trades and Labour Council
VC	Victoria Cross
Vet	Veterinary
YMCA	Young Men's Christian Association

INTRODUCTION

About 140,460 men, from north and south, enlisted in the British army in Ireland during the First World War. By the end of 1915 the 10th (Irish), the 16th (Irish) and the 36th (Ulster) Divisions had left for the front. The number of men killed while serving in Irish regiments has been estimated at 20,900.[1] Of this total about 3,900 Irish-born infantry, excluding officers, died while serving with the 16th (Irish) Division.[2] This display of 'affection and loyalty' by so many Irish Catholics has been described as one of the 'unexpected contradictions' which neither 'Sinn Feiners nor Unionists' could fully understand.[3]

Attempts to subvert Irish prisoners of war on a large scale were also unsuccessful. During December 1914 Irish prisoners were brought together at Limburg camp for the purpose of forming an 'Irish Brigade' to fight with the German army. But the men, when offered better rations and less fatigue work, submitted a petition requesting that the concessions should be shared by all British troops or withdrawn as 'in addition to being Irish Catholics, we have the honour to be British soldiers'. Only 53 men out of 2,500 prisoners of war were willing to join the brigade and Sir Roger Casement[4] concluded that nothing 'truly Irish [could] survive ... free entry into the British army'. The prisoners were 'not Irishmen but English soldiers' and 'more English than the English themselves'.[5]

But the reasons why Irishmen enlisted in the British army during the war and then remained loyal are far more complex than Casement's dismissal will allow. This study, an investigation into the phenomenon, assesses the credibility of Casement's judgement from three perspectives.

Firstly, the local community into which an identified recruit was born and in which he grew up, is investigated. The main social and economic factors conditioning his attitudes and making him susceptible to pressures to enlist are identified. How his community's Catholicism and nationalist traditions combined to undermine any labour challenge to the Irish Parliamentary Party or to John Redmond's war policy and how they intensified communal influences and reinforced John Redmond's authority over him, are also assessed.

Secondly, more immediate reasons for the man's decision to enlist are considered. The local effects of mobilisation and the consequences to him of war with Germany, the use of propaganda, organised recruiting campaigns, family and community pressures and the demands resulting from membership of the National Volunteers, are some of the 'triggers' considered.

And thirdly, having enlisted in the army, why he remained loyal to the 16th (Irish) Division and what, if anything, distinguished him from his British counterpart, are investigated. The man's place in the army as an institution and his

1 Callan, P. (1987), 'Recruiting for the British army in Ireland during the First World War', *Irish Sword*, XVII, pp. 42–56.
2 Denman, T. (1992), *Ireland's Unknown Soldiers: The 16th (Irish) Division in the Great War*, Dublin, pp. 183–85.
3 Robertson, N. (1960), *Crowned Harp*, Dublin, p. 56; Karsten, P. (1983), 'Irish soldiers in the British army, 1792–1922: suborned or subordinate?', *Journal of Social History*, XVII, pp. 31–64.
4 Sir Roger Casement (1864–1916), a Protestant Irish nationalist, was born in Dublin and raised in County Antrim. As a civil servant in the British foreign service, he earned an international reputation for his reports on human rights violations in the Belgian Congo and in South America. Awarded a knighthood in 1911, he was a member of the Gaelic League, a largely urban and ostensibly non-political organisation which did not take an overtly political stance until 1915. Founded in 1893, the League was non-sectarian and was dedicated to the 'de-Anglicisation' of Ireland through the revival and preservation of Irish as a spoken language. Casement joined the Irish Volunteers in 1913 and raised money to purchase arms. The Volunteers were created in response to the founding of the Ulster Volunteers, who pledged to resist home rule for Ireland. Convicted of high treason, Casement was executed in 1916.
5 Parmiter, G. de C. (1936), *Roger Casement*, London, pp. 185–215.

experiences during training in Ireland and England and on the western front are examined in this context.

There are inherent difficulties in such a study. Historians generally acknowledge that a range of factors motivated men to enlist but disagree on their individual significance. Some emphasise the economic factor.[6] In one view 'economics rather than sentiment' determined recruiting levels in Ireland to a greater extent than in Britain.[7] Another researcher has concluded that 'throughout the war, politics were much more important than economics in Ireland.'[8] Other explanations fall back on the stereotype or flirt with the esoteric. A 1915 Sinn Fein leaflet is typical of these frequently used devices. It accused British army recruiters of appealing to the Irishman's 'inherent valour'.[9] However, it is not made clear whether this valour, apparently unique to Irishmen, was genetically inherited, a spiritual attribute, or a product of environmental factors.

Crude generalisations also obscure significant local differences and variations in the behaviour of different social groups. It has been stated that the 'war-fever which swept middle-aged England ... and the consequent communal and family pressures on young men to join [the army]

scarcely affected Ireland outside Ulster.'[10] And despite John Redmond's[11] efforts, a 'unionist historian' has claimed the Irish 'masses' had little appreciation of the gravity of the issues at stake.[12] These statements are sufficiently general to reflect what *may* have been true in respect of the majority of people. But they take no account of the high enlistment rates in particular areas, especially among some urban populations. For various reasons, men in some communities and in some social groupings were more highly motivated to enlist than in others.

Problems associated with determining, with any degree of accuracy, the motivation of those Irishmen enlisting in the army are compounded by other difficulties. Firstly, there is a lack of direct evidence from other than a handful of articulate and literate men such as Tom Kettle,[13] Stephen Gwynn[14] and Willie Redmond.[15] The thoughts and feelings of ordinary men in the ranks have to be largely deduced from the writings and sayings of others. Rudyard Kipling, who toured the hastily erected training camps in England during 1915, noted that the average recruit, having chosen to do his bit, 'does it, and talks as much about his motives as he would of his religion or his love affairs'.[16]

And secondly, motivation is not amenable to a

---

6   Karsten (1983); Callan, P. (1984), 'Voluntary recruiting for the British army in Ireland during the First World War' (unpublished PhD thesis), University College, Dublin, pp. 365–366.

7   Fitzpatrick, D., 'The overflow of the deluge: Anglo-Irish relationships, 1914–1922' in O. MacDonagh and W. C. Mandle (eds.) (1986), *Ireland and Irish Australia: Studies in Cultural and Political History*, Beckenham, pp. 81–94.

8   Lucey, D. J. (1972), 'Cork public opinion and the First World War' (unpublished MA thesis), University College, Cork, p. 79.

9   Karsten (1983).

10   Fitzpatrick, D. (1977), *Politics and Irish Life 1913–1921*, Dublin, p. 109.

11   John Redmond (1856–1918), nationalist MP. A principal lieutenant of Charles Stewart Parnell when he was leader of the Irish Parliamentary Party, Redmond led the minority group who supported Parnell when the party split in 1890. He became leader of the re-united party in 1900. He was MP for Waterford city from 1891 until his death in 1918 and he pledged Ireland's support for the war, encouraging Irishmen to join the British army.

12   Townshend, C. (1984), *Political Violence in Ireland—Government and Resistance Since 1848*, Oxford, p. 279.

13   Thomas M. Kettle (1880–1916), writer and nationalist politician, was MP for East Tyrone 1906–10. Critical of what he regarded as narrow nationalism, he supported home rule and advocated that Ireland should absorb European influences. In November 1914 he joined the Royal Dublin Fusiliers and toured Ireland as a recruiting officer. He volunteered for active service and was killed on the western front.

14   Stephen L. Gwynn (1864–1950), grandson of William Smith O'Brien (1803–64) who supported repeal of the union, was a journalist, novelist, critic, poet and a Protestant nationalist politician and MP for Galway city (1906–1918). A strong supporter of John Redmond, he joined the ranks of the 16th (Irish) Division, was given a commission and served on the western front.

15   William Hoey Kearney Redmond, generally known as 'Willie' (1861–1917), was the younger brother, and supporter, of John Redmond. A nationalist MP from 1883, he represented East Clare from 1892 until his death. Joining the British army on the outbreak of war, he rose to the rank of major and was killed on the western front.

16   Kipling, R. (1915), *The New Army in Training*, London, p. 62.

reductionist analysis. The variables which go to make it up cannot be scientifically isolated, examined and labelled. They cannot be quantified or measured. Consequently, there is no guarantee that a group of men who were said to be motivated by patriotism, for example, actually shared the same experience. Nor is it certain that a man was able accurately to identify or describe the reasons for his own enlistment. An Irishman serving with a London Irish battalion thought that 'few men could explain why they enlisted, and if they attempted [to] they might only prove that they had done as a politician said the electorate does, the right thing from the wrong motive'.[17]

This nebulous condition is summed up in the opinion that men were not 'motivated by a clear view of their own interests; their minds [were] filled with the cloudy residues of discarded beliefs; their motives [were] not always clear even to themselves'. The historian's task therefore, is a difficult one.[18]

In recognising the difficulties, one historian has identified patriotism, the chance to escape dull routine, boyhood memories of imperialism and imperial wars, the need to retain the respect of social equals, a drive to emulate the action of relatives, and economic pressures as being a possible compound of motives.[19] Another has similarly concluded the factors impelling men to enlist were as 'diverse as the recruits themselves'. In his view, most of those volunteering were driven by a combination of external pressures and personal desires and loyalties.[20]

The long-standing 'nature or nurture' controversy is also relevant. The extent to which genetically fixed and inherited characteristics or changeable external environmental factors motivated a man to enlist raises unresolved issues.

Moreover, Freudian psychoanalysts might argue that a man's response to events in 1914 to 1918 was determined by his experiences during infancy.[21]

In this study the view is taken that environmental variables such as economic and political conditions and community relationships, rather than a genetically constructed personality or an inaccessible psychology, were mainly responsible for determining a man's decision to enlist. An attempt is made to reconstruct the external conditions which shaped attitudes and made men susceptible to pressures to enlist and, once enlisted, to remain loyal to the army.

For this purpose the case study approach has been adopted. There are four advantages to this method.

Firstly, a local study more accurately reflects those conditions which shaped an individual's decision to enlist. British studies reveal different recruiting patterns between regions, localities, communities and occupations. For instance, variations in national and local economic factors governing enlistment behaviour have been found to be 'extremely complex'.[22] Secondly, focusing on one identified man allows personal and family conditions, often pivotal in the decision to enlist, to be investigated. Thirdly, circumstances changed with time and a man's attitude, as well as the various external pressures on him, changed with them. A case study allows the changes to be traced. And fourthly, the integrated view of events necessary in understanding a specific case uncovers the intricate network of connecting circumstances and the interlinked human relationships which influenced a man's decision; it overcomes, to some extent, the disadvantages of periodisation and specialisation.

17 MacGill, P. (1915), *The Amateur Army*, London, p. 13. Patrick MacGill (1891–1961) was born in County Donegal and emigrated to Scotland when he was 14 years of age. An unskilled labourer and self-educated, he subsequently published several books. He served on the western front as a private with the London Irish Rifles.
18 Joll, J. (1984), *The Origins of the First World War*, Harlow, p. 206.
19 Beckett, I. F. W. and Simpson, K. (eds.) (1985), *A Nation in Arms—A Social Study of the British Army in the First World War*, Manchester, pp. 1–36.
20 Simkins, P. (1988), *Kitchener's Army: The Raising of the New Armies, 1914–16*, Manchester, p. 185.
21 Tosh, J. (1984), *The Pursuit of History*, Harlow, p. 74.
22 Winter, J. M. (1986), *The Great War and the British People*, Basingstoke, pp. 33–39; Simkins (1988), p. 107.

James English, the subject of this study, was one of the class described as the 'dark people … completely lost in the great anonymous sludge of history'.[23] But enough is known about him to assess his 'typicality' and attempt a classification.

From Waterford city, he was a practising Catholic. Representative of southern Ireland as a whole, in 1911 Waterford city's population was 92.2 per cent Catholic.[24] The majority of men making up the 16th Division's 48th Brigade were southern Irish Catholics. But the 47th and 49th Brigades were largely made up of men who, although Catholic, were from northern Ireland. Of the other two army divisions formed in Ireland, the 36th was predominantly Ulster Protestant and the 10th was about 70 per cent Irish and predominantly Catholic.[25]

Extrapolating from the limited evidence available, it has been calculated that over 50 per cent of men who enlisted in the Irish regiments were between the ages of 20 and 25 while 70 per cent of recruits were under 30.[26] And in one study only 20 per cent of those enlisting were probably married.[27] Having enlisted at the age of 38 and being married with five surviving children, James English was therefore 'typical' of a small category of recruits in these respects.

But in being employed as a general labourer,[28] he was representative of the Irish recruit nationally. In 1911, unskilled labour formed the second largest group of Irish workers. General labourers, agricultural labourers and factory labourers made up 22 per cent of the male working population between the ages of 20 and 45, the approximate age group from which men enlisted. An additional six per cent of males in the same age group were defined as 'non-producing' (unemployed). They were likely to be unskilled, making a probable 28 per cent of the total male population of this age group falling within the general labourer and labourer class.[29]

Unskilled men had traditionally provided the bulk of recruits for the army. A common observation is that made by a veteran of the Irish Guards who described the regular soldier in the Irish regiments as being

> mainly farm labourers, navvies and unskilled workers from the towns, some of them illiterate, most of them semi-literate. Like their fellows in other units of the British Army, most of them had taken the 'king's shilling' because they were unemployed.[30]

Another pre-war ranker thought his 'hungry, illiterate, hard-swearing' colleagues were 'hardly the cream of Ireland'.[31] It was this same class of people who filled the ranks of Kitchener's New

---

23 Snow, C. P. (1969), *The Two Cultures and a Second Look*, Cambridge, p. 26.

24 *Census of Ireland, 1911. Area, Houses, and Population: also the Ages, Civil or Conjugal Condition, Occupation, Birthplaces, Religion, and Education of the People. Province of Munster. County and City of Waterford* (British Parliamentary Papers, 1912–13 [Cd. 6050] CXV.1), p. vii.

25 Denman, T. (1987), 'The 10th (Irish) Division 1914–15: a study in military and political interaction', *Irish Sword*, XVII, pp. 16–25; Denman, T. (1987/1988), 'Sir Lawrence Parsons and the raising of the 16th (Irish) Division, 1914–15', *Irish Sword*, XVII, pp. 90–104.

26 Callan (1987).

27 Staunton, M. (1986), 'Kilrush, Co. Clare and the Royal Munster Fusiliers—the experience of an Irish town in the First World War', *Irish Sword*, XIV, pp. 268–70.

28 Confirmed by reference to James English's completed 1911 census return, (Census Returns), National Archives, Four Courts.

29 Percentages calculated using figures from the *Census of Ireland, 1911. Ages, Agricultural Holdings, Area, Birthplaces, Blind, Charitable Institutions, Conjugal Conditions, Deaf and Dumb, Education, Emigration, Health, Hospitals, Houses, Illiteracy, Infirmaries, Irish Language, Land Census, Lunacy, Marriage, Military in Ireland, Occupations, Outdoor Relief, Population, Prisons, Religion, Sick and Infirm, Workhouse Inmates, General Report* (British Parliamentary Papers, 1912–13 [Cd. 6663] CXVIII.1), pp. 9–15.

30 Nelson, J. E. (1973–74), 'Irish soldiers in the Great War, some personal experiences', *Irish Sword*, XI, pp. 163–79.

31 Lucy, J. F. (1992), *There's a Devil in the Drum*, Dallington, p. 41. John Lucy (1895–1962), the son of a cattle dealer, was born in Cork. Despite his nationalist tendencies, he and his brother joined the Royal Irish Rifles in 1912. He was badly wounded and his brother killed while serving on the western front. Lucy was commissioned from the ranks in 1917 and retired from the army in 1935. Appointed an officer in the Order of the British Empire, he died in Cork.

Armies[32] in Ireland. In Britain, the middle classes flocked to the colours and radically altered the social composition of the army. But this was less true of Ireland after an initially enthusiastic response. The effect of John Redmond's speech in the House of Commons on 3 August 1914, in which he committed Ireland's support to the war,[33] was claimed to have been 'instantaneous' and recruits poured in.[34] 'All trades, professions and classes' were found in the ranks and this mirrored, albeit to a lesser extent, the British experience.

There were reports that recruiters at Mallow were unable to cope with all of the 'old men and young sportsmen, students, car drivers, farm labourers, Members of Parliament, poets, [and] litterateurs' who wanted to enlist in 1914[35] and that the barracks at Buttevant could not accommodate the farmers and their sons who were enlisting. One observer thought enthusiasm for the war in Ireland in September 1914 'was equal to that in England'.[36] And T. P. O'Connor[37] recalled there was almost a fever for recruiting. Gallant young men 'rushed to the army' and nationalists sang

God Save the King for the first time in their lives.[38]

These assessments of the early reaction were exaggerated. For example, only one former and five serving nationalist MPs enlisted, and these included John Redmond's brother and son.[39] Dublin, with its tradition of providing men for the army, had one of the highest rates of recruitment in the United Kingdom up to the outbreak of war. Although 150 to 200 men joined every day during the first week of September 1914,[40] on 3 September 114 men enlisted, a total well below those for British cities with smaller populations.[41] By mid-1915 the labouring class was over-represented in the ranks and a government report admitted that the bulk of recruiting was from the landlord and the lowest classes.[42] In Kilrush, 80 per cent of those enlisting in the Royal Munster Fusiliers were classified as general labourers and 86 per cent of returned soldiers in Enniscorthy were employed as labourers.[43]

It was the urban poorer classes who filled the ranks of the Irish regiments. City born and reared, James English was a typical recruit in this

32 The New Armies, each made up of around 100,000 volunteers, were raised by Field-Marshal Lord Kitchener, Secretary of State for War, between August 1914 and June 1916. The armies were designated 'K1', 'K2', 'K3' etc. The 16th Division formed part of Kitchener's second army ('K2'). The new armies were expanded to eventually comprise a British army of some 5,704,000 men by 1918—'the largest and most complex single organisation created by the British nation up to that time' (Simkins (1988), p. xiv). See also Westlake, R. (1989), *Kitchener's Army*, Tunbridge Wells, pp. 9–13.
33 *Hansard* (Commons) 5th ser. LXV, 1828–29, 3 Aug. 1914.
34 Gwynn, S. L., 'Irish regiments' in F. Lavery (ed.) (1920), *Great Irishmen in War and Politics*, London, p. 172.
35 Dallas, G. and Gill, D. (1985), *The Unknown Army: Mutinies in the British Army in World War One*, London, p. 54.
36 Vane, F. F. (1929), *Agin the Governments*, London, pp. 247–48.
37 Thomas Power O'Connor (1848–1929) moved from Ireland to England in 1870 where he worked as a journalist and nationalist politician. Elected home rule MP for Galway in 1880, from 1885 to 1929 he represented the Scotland Division, Liverpool and was the only member of the Irish Parliamentary Party to sit for an English constituency. A supporter of the Land League (founded in Dublin in 1879 with the aim of protecting the tenant and abolishing landlordism), he advocated the extension of Irish land legislation to the British working class.
38 *Daily Chronicle*, 12 Feb. 1917.
39 Serving members who enlisted were Stephen L. Gwynn, John Redmond's brother 'Willie' Redmond and John Redmond's son William Archer Redmond. William A. Redmond (1886–1932), a nationalist MP and eldest son of John, represented Tyrone (1910–18) and Waterford city from 1918 to 1922 when he entered Dail Eireann as an independent. He attained the rank of captain and was awarded the DSO while serving with the British army on the western front. Daniel D. Sheehan and J. L. Esmonde were the other two serving members who enlisted and the former member was T. M. Kettle.
40 O'Flanagan, N. (1985), 'Dublin city in an age of war and revolution, 1914–22' (unpublished MA thesis), University College, Dublin, p. 36.
41 Simkins (1988), p. 66.
42 Karsten (1983).
43 Staunton (1986c); Codd, P. 'Recruiting and responses to the war in Wexford' in D. Fitzpatrick (ed.) (1988), *Ireland and the First World War*, Dublin, pp. 15–26.

respect. During the years 1914 to 1915, urban workers provided the greater percentage of recruits.[44] In January 1916, government sources calculated that over 55 per cent of recruits had come from the police districts of Belfast, Dublin, Cork, Derry, Limerick and Waterford. By October, nearly 50 per cent of available men in Dublin had enlisted and by 1918, 37 per cent of recruits from southern Ireland came from the Dublin Police District, the great bulk of whom were unskilled labourers.[45] The flow of volunteers from smaller centres boosted this urban bias to a probable 75 per cent. The Royal Munster Fusiliers for example, traditionally rural in character, was about 76 per cent urban in composition.[46]

Officials frequently deplored the poor response from small farmers, their families and urban shopkeepers. Eighteen months into the war an RIC report noted that the urban 'labourer and the cornerboys have gone ... and there remains none but shopboys and farmers' sons who are averse to enlisting'.[47] This assessment was confirmed by an army report in 1916 in which it was observed that the urban 'labouring classes have given most support to the war'.[48] To some extent this explains why the number of men enlisting was proportionately much less in Ireland than in Britain. Farmers, graziers, and their sons, grandsons, brothers and nephews were the largest single group of workers. They represented 30 per cent of the total manpower available for enlistment. Labourers, shepherds and servants contributed only 29 per cent to the rural manpower reservoir compared with 65 per cent in England and 54 per cent in Scotland.

There are a number of explanations for the cleavage between unskilled urban workers on the one hand and the urban middle classes and small farmers on the other. Noting in August 1915 that anti-recruiting efforts were only successful among 'drapers' assistants and shopmen generally', one contemporary thought the reason lay in an 'apathy much worse than any which existed in England'. In his opinion poor recruitment among farmers and their sons had nothing to do with religion or politics. They felt economic pressure less than other groups and had received most benefits from the state. Neither pro-German nor anti-English, they were simply 'apathetic'.[49] The Irish agricultural sector also experienced an early wartime boom and the profits to be had by remaining at home, combined with a policy of protecting agricultural occupations, resulted in an unwillingness to enlist.

However, it has been argued that Sinn Fein and Irish Republican Brotherhood[50] anti-war propaganda made special headway among farmers because of the long tradition of agrarian unrest and militant separatism in rural areas. Resistance to authority was weaker in the 'more anglicised, urban and working class communities' of towns and cities.[51] But tradesmen, government clerks, grocers' assistants, and drapers' assistants were among those taking part in the Easter

44 Garvin, T. (1981), *The Evolution of Irish Nationalist Politics*, Dublin, pp. 108–09.
45 O'Flanagan (1985), pp. 36, 56, 58.
46 Staunton, M. (1986), 'The Royal Munster Fusiliers in the Great War, 1914–19' (unpublished MA thesis), University College, Dublin, pp. 10–14; Staunton, M. (1989), 'Soldiers who died in the Great War 1914–19 as historical source material', *Stand-To*, 27, pp. 6–8; Staunton (1986c); Callan (1987).
47 Dallas and Gill (1985), p. 56.
48 Denman (1992b), p. 134.
49 J. O. Hannay (George A. Birmingham), 'Ireland and the war', *Nineteenth Century and After*, LXXVIII (Aug. 1915), pp. 393–402. Reverend James Owen Hannay (1865–1950) was a Church of Ireland clergyman who objected to his Church's stand on unionism and believed it should accept the reality of Irish nationalism. An active member of the Gaelic League, he aroused the suspicion and wrath of Catholic priests and withdrew from the league's executive in 1906. He was a prolific writer, using George A. Birmingham as a pseudonym. He was an army chaplain on the western front between 1916 and 1917.
50 Founded in 1858 and originally called the Irish Revolutionary Brotherhood, the organisation's aim was the overthrow of British rule in Ireland and the creation of an Irish republic. The IRB regarded itself as the government of the Irish Republic 'virtually established', and the Irish Republican Army gave its allegiance to the IRB. After a failed insurrection in 1867, the IRA was re-established for the Easter Rising, 1916. All those connected with the republican movement were popularly referred to as fenians after that movement was founded in New York at the same time as the IRB.
51 Karsten (1983).

Rising[52] and it is clear that militant separatism was potentially as strong among some middle-class and white-collar urban workers as it was among some rural communities.

The better-off small farmer and his family also traditionally regarded recruitment into the army as a drop in social status. The army was not a favoured occupation for farmers' sons with 'prospects' and 'gone for a soldier' was a disgrace if it applied to a farmer's son.[53] When charged with assaulting a soldier on leave, a respectable farmer observed that 'it was all the scruff and corner boys that were in the army and that only for being rowdies, they would not be in it at all'.[54] A repugnance towards the army on social grounds was also evident among the urban middle classes. During a recruiting campaign in Waterford, Stephen Gwynn publicly acknowledged the frequently expressed fear that if a man 'of education' joined the army he would find himself in company that he did not like.[55] 'Gentlemen' volunteers often found army life 'shockingly different' and were ill at ease in socially inferior units. 'Foul language, night urinal buckets, unappetising food and the personal habits of the lower working class put sensitive recruits through a purgatorial existence.'[56] Lord Roberts[57] had recognised this as a barrier to recruitment in 1899. In recommending improved barracks accommodation he observed that

> single men will no longer consent to be herded together in a common sleeping room. Education inculcated self-respect, and the self-respecting man will not endure being always exposed to the society of men of a lower level than himself …. He can put up with them at drill, on parade, and in the performance of his duty generally, but they are intolerable to him during meals, in his leisure hours, and, above all, at night.[58]

A Yorkshire-born Oxford graduate who enlisted in the 6th Battalion Connaught Rangers at the beginning of the war, found life intolerable. He recalled sharing sleeping accommodation with

> about a dozen seedy, ragged, lousy unshaven tramps who lurched in and lay on their cots smoking, spitting, quarrelling, making water all over the room … hiccuping and vomiting. It was after three before the last of them settled into a repulsive noisy slumber among his rags.[59]

Finally, James English could neither read nor write and 'signed' his 1911 census return with an 'X'. In severely circumscribing knowledge and understanding, illiteracy undermined a man's confidence and autonomy. It determined his place and status in society and reinforced social deference. The ability to write just his own name was a simple yet fundamental gesture which carried a man across the threshold which separated a literate and an oral culture. Crossing it was like passing from one world into another.[60]

A poor standard of education may have been a key element in a man's decision to enlist in the British army. It has been noted that the occupa-

52 Murray, R. H. (1916), 'The Irish enigma again (III)—the Sinn Fein rebellion', *Nineteenth Century and After*, LXXIX, pp. 1203–20.

53 Gwynn, S. (1919), *John Redmond's Last Years*, London, p. 140.

54 Staunton (1986c).

55 *Waterford Standard*, 27 Mar. 1915.

56 Beckett, I., 'The nation in arms, 1914–18' in Beckett and Simpson (eds.) (1985), pp. 99–125.

57 Field-Marshal Frederick Sleigh Roberts, VC, first Earl of Kandahar, Pretoria and Waterford (1832–1914), was the youngest son of General Sir Abraham Roberts of Waterford. His mother was from Tipperary. He was appointed commander-in-chief, Ireland in 1895 and resigned as commander-in-chief of the British army in 1905.

58 Roberts to the under-secretary of state for war, 6 July 1899 (Roberts Papers, 8310–162), National Army Museum [hereafter NAM].

59 Staniforth, J. H. M., letters, 12 to 18 Oct. 1914 (Staniforth Papers), Imperial War Museum [hereafter IWM]; Denman, T. (1989), 'An Irish battalion at war: from the letters of Captain J. H. M. Staniforth 7th Leinsters, 1914–18', *Irish Sword*, XVII, pp. 165–73.

60 Logan, J., 'Sufficient to their needs: literacy and elementary schooling in the nineteenth century' in M. Daly and D. Dickson (eds.) (1990), *The Origins of Popular Literacy in Ireland*, Dublin, pp. 113–37.

tional background of British army recruits contrasted consistently with those of Sinn Fein and
Irish Republican Army (IRA) members. The
IRA was largely made up of people from the
lower middle class—those with a 'modest stake'
in society such as small farmers and shop assistants and it was officered by well-educated and
well-born people.

Ireland had the highest illiteracy rate in the
United Kingdom. In 1891, 3.4 per cent of Scottish males were illiterate. In 1901, the figure for
England and Wales was 2.8 per cent. But in
Ireland it was 13.2 per cent. The Irish figure for
males and females combined was 16.4 per cent.[61]
From the evidence available, and despite the
findings in one study that the 'vast majority of
local recruits could read and write in English',[62]
it is postulated that the illiteracy rate for New
Army recruits was about 30 per cent. James
English was therefore typical of a large category
of Irish recruits in this respect. This contention
is made on five grounds.

Firstly, as the evidence already reviewed suggests, between 70 and 80 per cent of the ranks
were made up of unskilled workers. There was a
proportionately greater number of illiterate men
in this class of worker than in any other. The
1911 census, for instance, shows that 29 per cent
of unskilled male workers resident in Thomas's
Avenue, the street in which James English lived
when he enlisted, could neither read nor write
and four per cent could read only.

Secondly, it is probable that the proportion of
illiterate men joining the army was greater than
those who were literate. This is a reasonable
assumption for two reasons. Literate men had a
scarcity value. They were more likely to be
settled in relatively satisfactory and stable jobs
and less likely to find the army attractive. And
the army also drew heavily on the unemployed
for recruits. These men were more likely to be
among the illiterate.

Thirdly, the evidence for deciding literacy was
unsatisfactory and makes any conclusions unsafe.
For the purposes of the census, people who could
write their name were deemed able to read and
write and therefore literate. A person's ability to
read only was apparently assessed by the enumerator who completed the census form on his
behalf. How far a man's ability to write his name
should be taken as evidence that he was literate
raises problems of definition. The impossibility
of establishing the precise relationship between a
man's capacity to sign his name ('alphabetism'
being suggested as a better word) and true literacy, defined as the ability to use the written word
as a means of communication, has been noted by
at least one historian.[63]

The fourth ground is linked to the third and
relates to the unreliable nature of the evidence
provided by the census. People exaggerated their
reading ability and it has been suggested the real
standard of literacy fell below that claimed in the
1911 census.[64] Although it has been contended
that inflated literacy levels were compensated for
by those who under-estimated their skills, there
is direct evidence of the unreliability of the census returns. A Waterford general labourer who
signed his name with a mark in the 1901 census
was returned as being unable to read or write.
His age was recorded as being 34 and that of his
wife as 27. In the 1911 census the same man
signed his name and was returned as able to read
and write. His age was recorded as being 38 and
his wife's as being 40. It is possible that the man
learned to write his name in the intervening 10
years but how far he should be considered literate
is questionable. In this respect the 1911 census
enumerator, a local Royal Irish Constabulary
(RIC) police officer, completed the return on his
behalf. The returns for other residents on the
same street who claimed to be able to read and
write, were also completed by the enumerator but
signed by the residents. Moreover, the discrep-

61 Akenson, D. H. (1970), *The Irish Education Experiment*, London, pp. 376–77.
62 Staunton (1986c).
63 Stone, L. (1969), 'Literacy and education in England, 1640–1900', *Past and Present*, **42**, pp. 69–139.
64 Lee, J. (1973), *The Modernisation of Irish Society 1848–1918*, Dublin, p. 13.

ancy in ages, although understandable when dealing with people who did not know their date of birth, must inevitably throw doubt on the accuracy of the census returns.[65]

Finally, pre-war Irish recruits were of such a poor educational standard that high numbers of non-Irish non-commissioned officers (NCOs) had to be used in the Irish regiments. When in 1901 attempts were made to enlist men of an educationally higher calibre there was a 'notable decline' in the number of recruits. A regulation in 1911 made it possible for a man who could neither read nor write in English to join an Irish regiment.

As an unskilled Catholic and urban worker, James English was therefore typical of the bulk of Irish recruits in the 16th Division. Being 38 years of age, married and with children made him less typical but none the less representative of a large number of recruits. How far his illiteracy was typical is uncertain but about 30 per cent or more of recruits are likely to have been in this category.

However, because the locality in which a man was born and raised could make the group to which he belonged unique in many aspects, the concept of a 'typical' Irish recruit has limitations. The Waterford city recruit, therefore, was 'atypical' in several respects.

65 The Waterford resident was John Dooley and his wife was Mary Ellen. In 1901 they lived at 10 Wheelbarrow Lane (Thomas's Avenue). In 1911 they lived at 3 Harrington's Lane. The enumerator in 1911 was Constable Timothy Collins. The claim that the enumerator completed the returns is made on the basis that the forms all appear to have been completed in the same handwriting and the writing is different from any of the signatures belonging to the residents but very similar to that of Constable Collins (Census Returns, 1901 and 1911, National Archives, Four Courts).

CHAPTER 1

The Social and Economic Background

I

Born in July 1876, the nature of the society in which James English grew up explains to some extent his enlistment in the 16th (Irish) Division. He belonged to a subordinate social group. Other classes shaped his world and controlled the events which conditioned his mental attitudes. These classes supported John Redmond's war policy and encouraged recruitment. James English also belonged to a close community and his decision to enlist was partly the result of communal pressures.

II

At the turn of the nineteenth century Waterford port was rural in character and survived by servicing its rich agricultural hinterland. It exported horses, pigs, sheep, cattle, hams, bacon, some fresh meat, poultry and fish. A large part of its export trade was also made up of oats, meal, corn, eggs, condensed milk, butter, lard and porter.

City society was structured according to a graduated class system. Like Cork, Waterford could be described as

> merely a country town filled with half-rich and pauper-poor, and small merchants and petty tradesmen who ... fatted the priests and kept the monks and nuns and starveling beggars alive, and made those half-rich happy in their half-wealth.[1]

A huge gap in wealth and lifestyle separated the lower from the upper classes. Just as in Britain, the deep gulf between the working classes and the rest of society was the major accepted fact of life.[2] Dublin was a particularly brutal manifestation of this social cleavage,[3] but it was as vividly evident in provincial cities like Waterford. A 1905 newspaper report noted how in 'usually dull, dead' Waterford there was extravagance as well as much poverty: 'wealth and poverty, gaiety and rags, music and weeping, sobriety and drunkenness, religion and immorality' were all represented.[4] Unlike the industrialised British cities, however, Waterford society was still traditional and homogeneous. Attitudes were parochial and there was no militant class-consciousness.

James English was an unskilled labourer and four characteristics distinguished members of this class from the rest of society. Firstly, their earnings were below the tax threshold and they made no financial contribution to the state. The wealthier classes funded public works and government assistance to the poorer classes. Secondly, they formed a pool of unemployed or under-employed labour and lived precariously close to pauperism. Thirdly, a great many of the labouring class were illiterate or, at best, semi-literate. Finally, any movement into the skilled 'aristocracy of labour' was restricted by barriers

1 O'Faolain, S. (1985), *Bird Alone*, Oxford, pp. 297–98.
2 Marwick, A. (1965), *The Deluge: British Society and the First World War*, London, pp. 20–26.
3 O'Brien, J. (1982), *Dear, Dirty Dublin*, California, p. 161.
4 *United Irishman*, 4 Nov. 1905.

as formidable as those between the working and upper classes.[5] Lack of class mobility meant there were no prospects of satisfying social and economic aspirations. One contemporary sombrely recorded that the movement of this class of worker from the day of his marriage was downward.[6]

The group which had the greatest impact in shaping James English's environment was an amalgam of people from the different classes which monopolised wealth, social status and political power. There were historical divisions within this grouping of clergy, businessmen, professionals, landed gentry and aristocrats. Some were Old and others New English landowners.[7] Some were unionists and others home rulers. Some were Catholic and others were Protestant. But their common interests were more pronounced than their differences.

Considered a 'progressive spirit', the fifth Marquis of Waterford bred livestock of high quality and actively encouraged innovative farming as well as the improvement of local stock. He was acclaimed as the leading man of the county by members of the Waterford Farming Society at the 1876 Waterford agricultural show.[8] A descendant of the New English Beresford family which had married into the powerful Old English Catholic Le Poer family, he inherited the great tracts of land in Waterford county granted to the Le Poers in the twelfth century[9] and was one of the few enlightened unionists to support local

government reform plans for Ireland in October 1891.[10] In 1904, Lord Waterford's estates in Ireland comprised about 109,000 acres and in 1910, an agent was managing his estate from an office in Parnell Street, Waterford city.[11]

When agrarian disturbances ended the agricultural shows in 1880, it was the sixth marquis, then president of the Waterford Agricultural Society, who with city businessmen, including Sir W. G. D. Goff and his son Herbert, formed a limited company for the purpose of encouraging local business and trade by financing a revival of the Waterford agricultural show in 1902. Landowners and tenants were encouraged to buy shares in the company and a 13-acre site at Newtown opposite Goff's Glenville residence was purchased and developed by the company and named St Patrick's Park[12] (see Map 1).

Sir W. G. D. Goff, descendant of a New English family whose lands had been confiscated by Charles II because it had supported Cromwell in the English Civil War and were subsequently restored,[13] gave his occupation as 'baronet' in the 1911 census when he was 72 years of age. But, essentially a man of commerce, he was representative of the upper middle class. He was chairman of the board of directors of Davis, Strangman and Co. Ltd, one of two local breweries of which his son Herbert was also a director. At various times Goff was also vice-chairman of the Waterford and Tramore Railway, a director of the Waterford Steamship Co. Ltd, a director

5 Murphy, M. (undated), 'The working classes of nineteenth century Cork', *Cork Historical and Archaeological Journal*, 85, pp. 26–51.
6 MacSweeney, A. M. (1915), 'A study of poverty in Cork city', *Studies*, pp. 93–104.
7 The 'Old English' were descendants of the 12th-century Anglo-Norman conquerors who mainly inhabited the towns and the Pale. Strongbow, for example, had occupied Waterford and married there. Henry II used Waterford to land his army in 1171 and King John granted the city a charter in 1206, visiting the city in 1211. The 'Old English' generally retained their Catholic faith and came to be identified as 'Irish' in England. The 'New English' were the Protestant landowners introduced during the Tudor plantation schemes in the late sixteenth and early seventeenth centuries.
8 *Waterford News*, 22 Sep. 1876.
9 *Burke's Peerage and Baronage* (1980), London, pp. 2758–63; Beckett, J. C. (1981), *The Making of Modern Ireland*, London, pp. 40–55; Beckett, J. C. (1976), *The Anglo-Irish Tradition*, London, Chapter 2; Foster, R. F. (1988), *Modern Ireland 1600–1972*, London, Chapter 3; *Waterford Standard*, 4 May 1904.
10 Shannon, C. B. (1973), 'The Ulster Liberal Unionists and local government reform, 1885–98', *Irish Historical Studies*, 18, pp. 407–23
11 Ward, Lock & Co. (1904), *A New Practical Descriptive and Pictorial Guide to Waterford and Wexford*, London; Porter, F. (ed.) (1910), *Thom's Directory of the City and County of Waterford 1909–1910*, Dublin, Waterford city street list section.
12 *Waterford Standard*, 5 Mar. and 20 Aug. 1902.
13 Davis-Goff, A. (1990), *Walled Gardens —Scenes from an Anglo-Irish Childhood*, London, pp. 235–55.

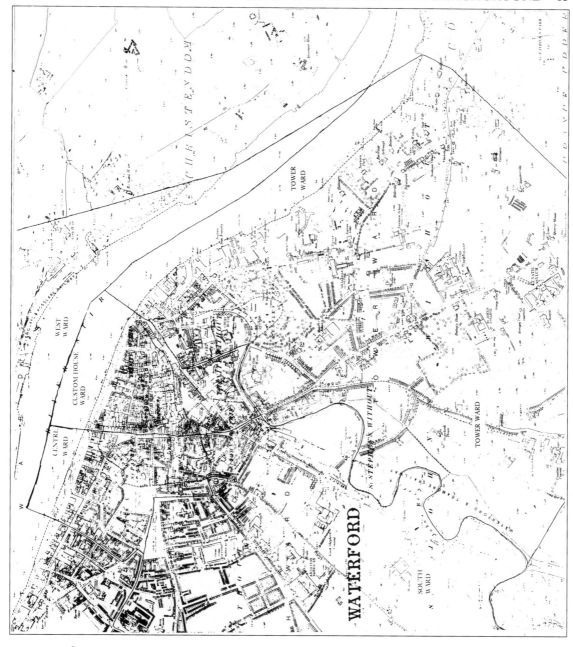

Map 1: Ordnance
survey map of
Waterford city and
immediate environs,
1905 (Scale:
approx. 4½ inches
to 1 mile)

(Source: Reproduced from
an edition by Phoenix
Maps, Dublin. Based on
the Ordnance Survey by
permission of the
Goverment [Permit No.
6017])

of the Southern Steam Trawling Company, a shareholder in the Waterford and Duncannon Steamboat Co. and a trustee of the Waterford Savings Bank. In addition to his business interests, he was a director of the Waterford Chamber of Commerce. As a member of the Harbour Board he supported Joseph Strangman's nomination for the auditorship of the board.[14]

A Protestant unionist, Goff was one of the largest employers of labour and an elected member of the corporation. He was appointed city high sheriff in 1869 and in 1900. He also held the shrievalty of county Waterford and was a magistrate.[15]

The number of wealthy Protestants in the professional occupations and among the leaders of commerce and industry was disproportionate to their total number. Most of them lived in Tower Ward (see Map 1) where nearly 70 per cent of residents were houseowners. About 35 per cent of these householders occupied inner-city sites, about 25 per cent lived in the John's Hill area, while residential sites along the Newtown and Dunmore Roads both within Tower Ward and beyond the city boundaries were favoured by the wealthiest. Ballinakill House near The Little Island was built in the late sixteenth century or early seventeenth century as the seat of the Dobbyn family, and the nearby Faithlegg House was built in 1783 by Cornelius Bolton MP.[16] Only about three per cent of houseowners, the lowest percentage for the city, resided in Centre Ward, the most densely populated area and where some of the city's poorest inhabitants lived.

The labouring class inhabited a world distinctly separate from that in which the wealthy Catholics and Protestants lived. In 1876 Lord and Lady Waterford were among the many aristocratic guests at Kilkenny Castle when the Marquis and Marchioness of Ormonde celebrated their return from a wedding tour. The supper room 'recalled to mind an oriental tale of fabulous riches, so resplendent was it with celebrated Ormonde gold service, each piece a work of art, and all combined more in value than a king's ransom'.[17] During the same year a new ice-skating rink was opened[18] and a wing of City Hall was converted into a 1,000 seat theatre. The local gentry boasted of it being 'one of the handsomest to be found in any part of the kingdom out of London and equal to most in that city for comfort, convenience and artistic merit.'[19]

Sir W. G. D. Goff and his wife lived at Glenville, an Italianate mid-nineteenth-century house about one and a half miles from Waterford and overlooking the River Suir. Here they were attended by a groom, a parlour-maid, a cook, a housemaid, a kitchen-maid and a general servant. The property was large enough to encompass the main house, a walled garden, a couple of fruit gardens, landscaped gardens, three ponds, two gate lodges, a coachman's house, a tennis court, good stabling, small kennels and enough paddocks and grazing for a few hunters and 'a cow or two'. Herbert Goff lived in the adjacent Maypark property with his family and eight servants.

In 1884, Goff purchased the racing yawl *Neptune* and entered it for cross-channel races. And in 1899 his yacht *Iver* was considered one of the prettiest of the summer fleet in British waters.[20] During the same year, emulating the wealthy of Dublin among whom the elation of car travel was making life more exciting than ever,[21] he created wonder among many who had never seen a motor car by driving his new Paris-built vehicle around

14 Coyne, W. P. (ed.) (1902), *Ireland, Industrial and Agricultural*, Dublin, pp. 483–84; *Thom's Directory*, p. 48; Egan, P. M. (1894), *Egan's Guide to Waterford*, Kilkenny, pp. 454U–54V; *Waterford Standard*, 16 Dec. 1891, 20 Aug. 1902, 18 Nov. 1914.
15 *Waterford News*, 7 Jan. 1899, 28 Jan. 1899, 12 Jan. 1900; *Thom's Directory*.
16 Bence-Jones, M. (1988), *A Guide to Irish Country Houses*, London, p. 17 and entry under Faithlegg House.
17 *Waterford News*, 28 Apr. 1876.
18 *Waterford News*, 12 July 1876.
19 *Waterford News*, 8 Jan., 14 Apr. and 21 Apr. 1876.
20 *Waterford News*, 6 June 1884, 28 Jan. 1899.
21 Curriculum Development Unit (1973), *Dublin, 1913—A Divided City*, Dublin, pp. 28–30.

the Quay. The owner of the first car registered in Waterford, his number plate WI1 was retained in the family for many years.[22]

Gerald Purcell Fitzgerald, a Catholic descendant of the powerful Old English family, occupied an ancestral castle on the 311-acre Little Island located approximately three miles outside of the city. The island and much of the surrounding country had belonged to his family since 1280. Confiscated after the Battle of the Boyne, part of their land, including The Little Island, was later restored to them. No doubt spurred on by the various land acts, Fitzgerald secured The Island for his family and held on to his local prominence by buying out the rights of tenant farmers. The Little Island reverted back to being a demesne[23] and Fitzgerald rebuilt and restored the interior of the castle during the 1900s in 'luxurious' style, including the installation of central heating.[24] The building was remodelled, modernised and had large wings added to it.

Wealthy local merchants mixed socially with aristocrats, and Waterford newspapers carried regular and frequently detailed advice and comments on the cross-channel movements of the British and Irish aristocracies. In 1876 the *Waterford News* reported fully on the visits of the Marquis of Huntington and the Lords Frederick and Edward Cavendish with their wives to the Duke of Devonshire's 40,000-acre estate at Lismore. On one occasion Lord Southampton, having travelled all night from England, joined Lord and Lady Waterford, George Malcolmson the local businessman, and Herbert Goff at a meet of the Waterford hounds. And the Marquis and Marchioness of Waterford attended balls at Mrs Malcolmson's.[25]

III

Although lay and clerical city leaders shared common interests and generally conducted their affairs harmoniously, disagreements did occur. But these were relatively minor. In 1902 Father William B. O'Donnell complained that of 45 senior Great Southern and Western Railway Company employees only two were Catholic, and Catholic shareholders threatened retaliatory action unless there was a satisfactory explanation.[26] Charitable offers sometimes foundered on uncharitable prejudices. In 1891 the Ferrybank parish priest refused to allow a local Protestant woman to give poor children Christmas tea for fear they would be required to sing *God Save the Queen* and Protestant hymns.[27] And in 1912 W. G. D. Goff was refused the use of City Hall for a meeting of Waterford unionists, the mayor telling him he could use it for 'any purpose except that of holding an anti-Home Rule meeting'.[28] During the 1904 Catholic university debate Dr Richard A. Sheehan, Bishop of Waterford and Lismore, claimed Catholics were entitled to look for finances from the government if only because 'our non-Catholic fellow-countrymen are greatly richer, as a body, than we are'.[29] Although potentially divisive, however, this statement reflected no more than the truth.

Sometimes the interest of the smaller businessman, who dominated the corporation, conflicted with those of the wealthier classes and resulted in some quarrelling. In 1888 the mayor told a nationalist gathering that he wanted to see Waterford free of those 'hard, grasping and arrogant monopolies'—the toll bridge, the railway companies and the Harbour Board.

The toll bridge, known locally as 'Timbertoes',

---

22 *Waterford News*, 14 Jan. 1899; Davis-Goff (1990), p. 221.
23 An unidentified newspaper cutting, 'The Fitz-Geralds of The Island' (ILB 94141), National Library of Ireland (hereafter NLI).
24 Anonymous article from an unidentified journal, 'The Island, Waterford', Waterford Municipal Library.
25 *Waterford News*, 21 Apr. 1876, 14 Jan. 1899; *Waterford Standard*, 5 Mar. 1902.
26 *Waterford Standard*, 20 Aug. 1902.
27 *Waterford News*, 23 Dec. 1891.
28 Letters written by W. G. D. Goff, 30 May 1912 and Mayor M. Kirwan, 31 May 1912, published in the Union Defence League's *Irish Facts* (July 1912).
29 *Waterford News*, 5 Feb. 1904.

was owned by a company incorporated by act of parliament in 1786. It was the only link between the north and south of the city and was a profitable investment, bringing in regular dividends of 12 per cent and with an accumulated reserve fund of between £10,000 and £12,000 in 1905.

Railway companies paid a fixed sum of £2,000 or more annually in lieu of tolls. Hotels with buses paid between £100 and £200. Carrying and shipping firms were charged from about £1,000 upwards and jarveys paid 6d each way. Pedestrians had to pay a halfpenny for each crossing. The toll was increased for men on horseback and up to 2d was charged for traps and other vehicles depending on their loads. A payment per head for animals herded across the bridge, including stock shipped by rail, was also demanded.[30] The toll was burdensome for businesses but for a labouring man earning the average 14 shillings a week it could impose severe restrictions on his movements and those of his family. One return journey a day on foot just for himself would take four per cent of his week's wages. The bridge was finally purchased by the corporation in 1907 and the tolls were lifted.

In condemning the monopolies, the mayor denounced the Waterford, Dungarvan and Lismore Railway Company for burdening the community with an annual tax of £14,000 without giving it any representation on the board.[31] Rapid growth and the expansion of railways in Ireland generated conflict in the scramble for profits and ownership. The powerful local Malcolmson family, for instance, had at considerable cost successfully fought off a takeover of the Waterford and Lim-erick Railway Company by the Great Southern and Western Railway Company in 1866,[32] although the board was subsequently infiltrated by outsiders such as the notorious Dublin businessman William Martin Murphy.[33]

Initially, men such as Malcolmson had interests in shipping as well as railway companies, thus creating a monopoly across the transportation industry. But friction between the two sectors increased with a growing divergence in ownership. Railway companies were frequently in competition with shipping lines, the interests of which were generally the same as those of the Harbour Board. As well as having substantial interests in shipping, for instance, W. G. D. Goff was also a member of the Waterford Harbour Board.

Proposals to link Cork and Waterford by rail to a new Rosslare to Fishguard railway-controlled steamer route provoked a bitter dispute during 1890. Apparently referring to the Waterford Steamship and the Clyde Shipping Companies, it was argued the route would benefit Waterford's citizens by breaking that 'saucy monopoly', the 'steamring'.

The Waterford Steamship Company ran 13 steamers to Bristol, Liverpool and Irish ports. According to *Egan's Directory*, it was founded by Waterfordmen, maintained by Waterfordmen and owned by Waterfordmen.[34] Reorganised and registered as a new company in 1836 under the chairmanship of Joseph Malcolmson it subsequently fought damaging but successful battles with competing shipping lines and railway companies.[35] Shipping routes between Waterford and other ports in the United Kingdom were there-

---

30 Statement on the Waterford Toll Bridge, by Feely, J. J. (May 1905), (Redmond Papers, 15,245[6]), NLI; *Munster Express*, 15 Feb. 1913; *Waterford News*, 2 Jan. 1892; McCarthy, M. J. F. (1902), *Priests and People in Ireland*, London, pp. 490–91; Walsh, J. J. (1968), *Waterford's Yesterdays and Tomorrows*, Waterford, pp. 10–11, 88.
31 *Waterford News*, 14 Sep. 1888. The mayor was Captain Toole.
32 O'Neill, J. (1986), 'Waterford's five railways', *Irish Railway Record Society*, 16, pp. 106–19.
33 *Egan's Guide to Waterford*, p. 454H. William Martin Murphy (1844–1919) was a businessman who constructed railways in the United Kingdom and financed their construction in Africa and South America. MP for St Patrick's Division of Dublin between 1885 and 1892, he also constructed tramways and purchased newspapers, including the *Irish Independent*, and other interests in Ireland.
34 *Egan's Guide to Waterford*, pp. 454G-54H; O'Donnell, M. (1986), 'The Waterford steamship company in the 1880s, *Decies*, 16, pp. 106–19.
35 *Waterford Standard*, 20 Nov. 1901; McNeill, D. B. (1971), *Irish Passenger Steamship Services*, Vol. 2, Newton Abbot, pp. 80–96.

after shared between the Waterford Steamship and Clyde Shipping companies.

It was claimed competition between the proposed Rosslare rail and steamer route and the 'steamring' would result in reduced rates for all freight and produce great benefits for the labourer. The railway would 'scatter immense sums among his class'. In an apparent reference to Goff, it was argued that even the 'steamring' would continue to thrive but

> without becoming millionaires screwing colossal fortunes out of the hard earnings of the masses, to be squandered in palatial residences, having gate lodges roofed in copper, in magnificent steam-yachts and luxurious 'cuisines' superintended by French cooks at fabulous salaries.[36]

Generally, however, lay and clerical leaders of all denominations subscribed as fervently as their British counterparts to the prevailing philosophies of *laissez faire* and the divine origins of the existing social order. Anomalies and ill-effects produced by the economic system were attributed to 'English mismanagement and discrimination'.[37] It was a system in which the labourer's contribution was passive and which also minimised central and local government intervention. Landowners and entrepreneurs such as Goff had the role of creating employment. The corporation's decision to provide jobs by draining the Kilbarry bogs during the depression in the 1880s[38] was a rare incidence of intervention.

IV

Between 1901 and 1911 Waterford's population increased more than that of any other southern Irish city except Dublin and the task of adequate job creation was made more difficult. The number of jobs created failed to match the increase in population. The number of unemployed of working age rose dramatically between 1881 and 1901. Unemployment continued to rise steadily, although by 1911 the number of unemployed males had actually fallen.

One consequence was the overwhelming signs of poverty which a visitor in 1871 judged to be due to a scarcity of enterprise. Indifferent citizens had failed to exploit the steam links with Britain. 'The fault', he concluded 'lies much at the door of the Waterford merchants and moneyed classes themselves.' He also complained of mud being allowed to accumulate in the inner harbour[39] and five years later the Waterford and Limerick Railway Company was still protesting that the mud was seriously affecting trade by preventing loading and unloading at their wharves.[40] In a similarly critical 1905 report, the writer thought the city's people were

> easy-going, light-hearted, frank, generous, but too much given to trivial amusements, and too apt to let things drift. They do not seem to think for themselves, and like to follow the example of their neighbour whether it be right or wrong.

They were not business people, and in this respect 'Waterford resembles a country town in the West of Ireland'.[41]

However, some local businessmen were conscious of the need for investment. In 1876 Malcolmson asked the chief secretary for £100,000 to build a dry dock.[42] But by the 1880s Malcolmson's shipbuilding works at the Neptune Yards had collapsed, throwing some 400 high-class mechanics out of work. Harland and Wolff had deprived the city of its only major non-agricultural industry and ended an important Waterford

36 *Waterford News*, 8 Feb. 1890.
37 MacMahon, J. A., OFM (1981), 'The Catholic clergy and the social question in Ireland, 1891–1916', *Studies*, LXX, pp. 263–88.
38 O'Connor, E. (1989), *A Labour History of Waterford*, Waterford, p. 79.
39 Anonymous (1871), 'A visit to Waterford', *The Irish Builder* (15 Sep.), pp. 236–37.
40 *Waterford News*, 21 Apr. 1876.
41 *United Irishman*, 4 Nov. 1905.
42 *Waterford News*, 8 Jan. 1876.

shipbuilding tradition.[43] Malcolmson also with-drew from active control of the Waterford Steamship Company[44] which took over the Neptune Works as a repair yard until the company's failure in 1912.

By 1903 the president of Waterford's workers' organisation, the Federated Trades and Labour Union (FTLU), was concerned that Waterford was 'going back year after year and nearly all her industries had vanished'. Even educated lads had no outlet for their energies.[45] In the same year there were attempts to create new industries. On one occasion prominent Irish merchants and some 'English Capitalists' discussed the formation of a syndicate to convert closed-down corn mills along the Rivers Suir and Barrow into factories for clothes, boots, linen, cotton and wool wear manufacturers.[46]

In 1904 a desperate councillor suggested the mayor convene a meeting for the purpose of establishing a ready-made clothing factory.[47] The FTLU hoped to create work by obtaining King Edward VII's support for their plans that the city be made a military headquarters again, that an admiralty training ship be stationed in the Suir and that a dockyard be constructed for repair purposes.[48] These plans all remained unfulfilled but there were some successes.

Martin J. Murphy of Tramore, a county councillor elected MP for Waterford East in a 1913 by-election, had generated 'tens of thousands of pounds' worth of business in Waterford since he took over the Tramore racecourse in the 1890s. The city was an emporium out of which the Tramore traders drew the commodities con-sumed by thousands of visitors.[49] Local bottlers opened a new glass factory at Bilberry, and W. G. D. Goff, local builder George Nolan, and Graves and Co. (timber merchants and roofing manufacturers) combined to invest more than £5,000 in a new brick factory at Bilberry in 1898 with the intention of replacing bricks imported at heavy cost from England.

Equipped with the most modern machinery and using nearby quarries, the factory produced 20,000 bricks a day. Initially 17 hands and a supervisor were employed but this was later increased to about 100 hands when bricks were being exported.[50] George Nolan also built the Waterford branch of the Ulster Bank in The Mall in 1902.[51] The Southern Steam Trawling Company, with its registered office on The Quay, was formed in the same year by Sir W. G. D. Goff and five other men, three of them from Waterford, with a capital of £65,000 in £1 shares.[52]

Goff was one of a group who formed the Waterford and Duncannon Steamboat Company in 1907 for allegedly 'philanthropic' purposes, the objective being to benefit the people of Wexford and Waterford. None the less a dividend of five per cent was declared in November 1914.[53] The O'Connell Street basket factory employed dozens of young girls and exhibited at the 1900 Irish Industries exhibition at Mansion House, London.[54]

Bishop Sheehan was also concerned about local unemployment. His remedy was to advise young men not to expect high wages too soon or while learning their job or trade and to develop 'steadiness and perseverance' in doing their

43 *Waterford News*, 26 Jan. and 9 Feb. 1912: Sir James Harland entered into partnership with G. W. Wolff in 1862 and together they laid the basis of what became the largest shipbuilding firm in the world. By 1914, the firm was Belfast's biggest employer.
44 *Waterford Standard*, 20 Nov. 1901.
45 *Waterford Standard*, 10 June 1903.
46 *Waterford Standard*, 2 May 1903.
47 *Waterford News*, 8 Jan. 1904.
48 *Waterford Standard*, 9 Apr. 1904.
49 *Waterford News*, 9 Mar. 1900.
50 *Waterford News*, 23 Apr. 1898; O'Neill, J. (1986), 'Waterford, 1913 and now' in *Waterford News and Star* (Christmas supplement).
51 *Waterford Standard*, 5 July 1902.
52 *Waterford Standard*, 20 Aug. 1902.
53 *Waterford Standard*, 18 Nov. 1914.
54 *Waterford News*, 30 Mar. 1900.

work.[55] A strongly partisan local attitude arose from the Irish industrial movement in 1893,[56] and in 1905 a visitor hoped that the city's Industrial Development Association would 'send a thrill of industrial life through the now slumbering Urbs Intacts'.[57] In 1912 the *Waterford News* promised its readers it would publish the names of those people who had developed the 'bad habit' of going out of town to buy commodities which could be bought in town, thereby depriving the city of trade and jobs.[58]

As ground landlord, the Marquis of Waterford was approached when the Dungarvan brewery, the only surviving industry in town, was in danger of closure and of throwing many out of work. He responded by spending thousands of pounds in overhauling and remodelling the buildings and procuring new steam engines and boilers. Efforts were made to encourage local trade and generate new jobs. A new mineral water plant was installed and extensive bottling undertaken. Corks were cut on the premises and local barley was purchased. John Purcell Fitzgerald of The Island was also reported as spending 'very large sums' in reclaiming waste lands on his property so as to provide employment. This was considered to be the 'best form' of relief for poor labourers.[59]

An inadequately skilled local labour force and the introduction of modern technology compounded the problems. The supervisor of the newly opened brick factory, for example, had to be brought in from Wales. And, despite the existing pool of cheap labour, businessmen found it necessary to employ labour-saving technology in order to compete effectively with rivals. A 1907 advertisement announced that Hearne and Co.'s powerful furniture-making machines could do as much work in one minute as a man could do in three hours. Moreover, the best tradesmen were employed from Liverpool, London, Manchester and Belfast.

David MacDonald, city councillor and barm manufacturer, was conscious of the repercussions of new technology on the local labour market. He installed the most up-to-date machinery in his company's Bridge Street premises without reducing the number of workers employed. He also claimed to have revived the barm manufacturing industry locally when every other factory of its kind had been ruined in southern Ireland. About 90 per cent of the materials used by his company were of home manufacture. A new building was constructed by Paddy Coston, a local builder, using Bilberry bricks, and the heads of 20 local families were employed.[60]

The opening up of the Chamber of Commerce to a more representative membership helped in the search for fresh ideas and new industries. It had been monopolised by a clique of 25 but in 1908, when subscriptions were reduced, membership increased to 80 people and included drapers, ironmongers, bakers, grocers and hoteliers.[61]

However, although a small privileged group managed the local economy, the people most vulnerable to its vicissitudes were those employed in the 'unspecified commodities' and domestic service categories.

V

These were the two predominant categories of worker in 1911. The majority of workers included were unskilled, the largest single male category being the general labourer and the largest single female category being the domestic indoor servant.

An observer unkindly noted that labourers

55 *Waterford Standard*, 8 June 1904.
56 Riordan, E. J. (1920), *Modern Irish Trade and Industry*, London, pp. 265–75.
57 *United Irishman*, 4 Nov. 1905.
58 *Waterford News*, 9 Feb. 1912.
59 *Waterford News*, 12 Feb. 1915. A report from the newspaper files of 10 Feb. 1865.
60 *Waterford News*, 8 Jan. 1904.
61 Cowman, D. (1988), *The Role of Waterford Chamber of Commerce 1787–1987*, Waterford, pp. 50–52.

were 'men without any definite trade, ready for anything and good for nothing'.[62] Generally they moved between temporary or seasonal jobs in the building industry and the distributive trades, usually as quay workers. Only limited employment was available in other mainly agricultural-based industries. The city's prosperity and the volume of work available depended on its provisions trade with Britain.

Waterford had been a port of importance in the early nineteenth century and provided work for most of the unskilled. A fleet of locally owned, deep-sea merchantmen traded with Newfoundland, North and South America, Africa and the West Indies. But the majority of Waterford registered ships were small coastal and cross-channel craft. In 1876 trade was considered to be 'quite marvellous' and proof of the city's progress. Merchandise carried by the Clyde Shipping Company covered a third or a quarter of the city's quays. The latest of the company's ships, plying between the city and other ports in the United Kingdom, was equipped with an 'elaborate' smoking room, passenger berths and a 'richly and a handsomely' ornamented saloon and was capable of carrying 900 tons of freight.[63]

During the late 1870s and the 1880s an agricultural depression combined with a harvest failure to produce high levels of unemployment. Nor could Waterford take advantage of markets created by the expansion of urban populations elsewhere in the United Kingdom. Shortfalls in food supplies were met by cheap products carried in refrigerated transportation from the New World. The 'people's refreshment room' in King's Street, just one of Waterford city's soup kitchens, issued 40,000 rations in a three month period in 1879.[64] At the turn of the century large numbers of labourers still relied on the docks for work. They were generally recruited on a daily basis, only a few being guaranteed stable and permanent employment with local firms.

The great bulk of Waterford's foreign exports was transported to London, Bristol and Liverpool then transferred to larger vessels for shipping to colonial and overseas markets. But the provisions trade with Britain accounted for most traffic. Steamers carrying live and dead stock to Britain left the quays daily. Frequently, a live cargo would consist of up to 500 head of sheep and 1,000 head of cattle.

Although pig dealers might find it profitable, the export of live stock could have profound repercussions on local employment, however. In the 1890s bacon curing was one of the few significant industries in the city. The four Waterford bacon curing firms employed about 850 people and supported over 150 pig buyers. One of the smaller Waterford firms, with 150 employees, could kill up to 3,500 animals a week, while Henry Denny and Son employed about 400 people. The extent to which these factories dominated the city can be gauged by considering Map 2. When the quantity of live pigs being shipped in the cross-channel trade restricted the number of hogs available to the local curers, they laid off staff and reduced paid working time.[65]

Employment in any of the bacon factories generally meant security for a man's working life but the bacon industry had been a local institution for nearly two centuries and the privilege of working in it was usually inherited. At the time war was declared, many workers were the fourth- or fifth-generation members of families who had worked in the industry.[66]

However, by the 1900s the Irish had lost ascendancy in the British market to the Danes and the bacon trade only employed 2,000 poorly paid workers. In 1898 Waterford's Chamber of Commerce noted that low bacon prices could hardly have been 'remunerative either to the

62   Lyons, F. S. L. (1973), *Ireland Since the Famine*, London, p. 102.
63   *Waterford News*, 29 Dec. 1876.
64   O'Connor (1989), p. 79.
65   *Waterford News*, 12 Jan. 1900; O'Connor (1989) p. 69; Riordan (1920) pp. 79–82.
66   O'Neill, J. (1984), 'The sights, the sounds and the smells of Waterford', *Waterford News and Star* (Christmas supplement).

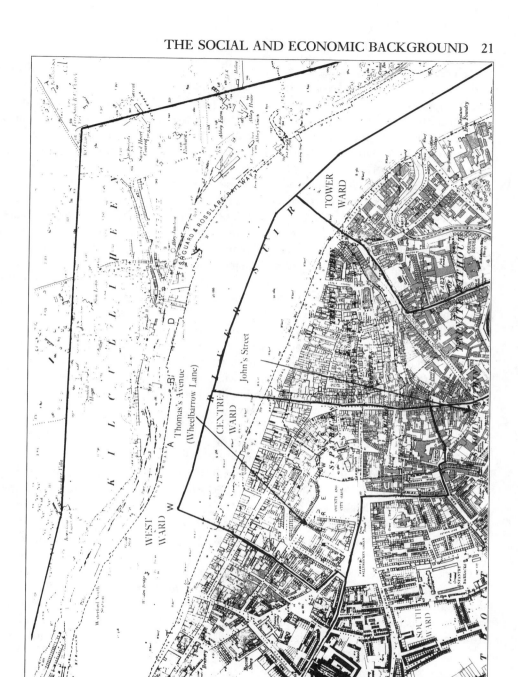

Map 2: Ordnance survey map of Waterford city centre and Ferrybank, 1905 (Scale approx. 6½ inches to 1 mile)

(Source: Reproduced from an edition by Phoenix Maps, Dublin. Based on the Ordnance Survey by permission of the Government [Permit No. 6017])

trade or to the farmers' and, when contrasted with the Danish industry, Irish trade was 'absolutely deplorable'.[67]

In Waterford, difficulties were aggravated by a bitter, drawn-out and frequently violent dispute between the Ballybricken pig buyers and the curers from 1892 to 1897. And despite the introduction of new refrigeration plant and pudding and sausage producing machinery by at least one local bacon factory,[68] by 1904 city councillors were expressing a concern that Waterford's economy depended almost completely on a 'decaying' bacon industry. This decline in the city's staple industry and a loss of traffic to the railways when the Rosslare to Fishguard route opened, destroyed labourers' jobs on the quays.

By the time of the 1911 census there was a significant decline in the number of vessels visiting the port and in July 1912 the Waterford Steamship Company sold its vessels and goodwill to the Clyde Shipping Company. The number of men employed in harbour and dock services dropped by about 51 per cent between 1881 and 1911. Large numbers of quay labourers had to find work elsewhere. James English, entering the labour market around 1891 when he was 15 years old, took up residence at No. 5 Thomas's Avenue (previously named Wheelbarrow Lane—see Map 2) about 1904, and is likely to have experienced the insecurity associated with the changing work patterns.

For the bulk of the labouring class, poorly paid and living in poverty and insecurity, the alternative to drink or carrying on in the hope that some 'unexpected force'[69] might provide escape from their social and economic deprivation, was emigration. And this was officially encouraged. A local advertisement in 1876 offered a free passage to New Zealand and Queensland and an assisted passage to Canada for eligible migrants.[70] Those willing to go were paid £5 per head. However, some of the wealthier classes were offended by this treatment of the poorer Irish.[71]

James Connolly[72] explained the Irish labourers' failure to organise collectively and change their conditions as an acceptance of leadership by their 'economic oppressors'.[73] Men such as Sir W. G. D. Goff and James English, however, were locked into a traditional class system built around the central pillars of 'place' and 'duty'. Leading citizens like Goff genuinely sought, in the light of their own values, to ameliorate the harshness of the existing system. And there is no evidence to suggest that men like him or James English saw this system as being anything other than a naturally fixed and God-given social order. The poor simply 'accommodated' to their poverty.

VI

Perhaps the greatest obstacle frustrating other routes of escape through self-improvement was the labourer's illiteracy. The number of illiterate residents in Thomas's Avenue was significantly greater than the Irish average. There is a clear correlation with the residents' unskilled occupations.

However, Sir Robert J. Paul, vice-chairman of the Waterford Farming Society, thought the labourer's malaise originated in his drunkenness. In 1876 he observed that 'intemperance was fast

---

67 *Waterford News*, 14 Jan. 1899.
68 *Egan's Guide to Waterford*, pp. 451–54H.
69 Thompson, P. (1975), *The Edwardians*, London, pp. 183–220.
70 *Waterford News*, 7 Jan. 1876.
71 Gwynn, S. (1926), *Experiences of a Literary Man*, London, p. 33.
72 James Connolly (1868–1916) was a socialist and trade union organiser. An unskilled labourer and a self-educated Marxist, he was highly regarded as a theorist. Scots born of a Scottish father and an Irish mother, he went to Dublin in 1896 and founded the Irish Socialist Republican Party and edited the *Workers Republic*. He left Ireland in 1903 but returned in 1910. He was Belfast organiser for the Irish Transport and General Workers Union and co-founder of the Irish Labour Party and Trade Union Congress, and was executed in 1916 for his part in the Easter Rising.
73 Connolly, J. (1897), 'Patriotism and labour', *Shan Van Vocht*, reproduced in Connolly, J. (1987), *Collected Works*, Vol. 1, Dublin, pp. 310–14; Greaves, C. D. (1961), *The Life and Times of James Connolly*, London, p. 93.

creeping into' the labourer's social condition and although paying a fair day's wages, employers were not getting a fair day's work in return. It was the employer's business to help workers to improve their moral and social conditions. The labourer and Ireland would never be prosperous until they struck at the root of intemperance, a 'great evil on the increase'.[74]

Others also attributed a lack of discipline and thrift and what they saw as the low quality of the labouring class, to drunkenness. Bishop Sheehan mounted a continuing crusade against the 'drink curse'. He claimed that Waterford had more public houses in proportion to its population than any other part of the country, and also by far the greatest number of people taken to court for drunkenness or drunken and disorderly conduct.[75] But when he opposed an increase in licensed premises in 1899, he was gently reminded of the prevalence of 'shebeening' in the city. A working man could obtain drink at all times in Waterford's backstreets and in some isolated dwellings.[76]

However, the bishop and his parish priests maintained their campaign. In 1902 he spoke of drunkenness as an 'evil ... so great, so far reaching, so deeply rooted in our country' that an average family of five spent five shillings a week on drink.[77] This represented 35 per cent or more of family income if, as was usual, just the man was working. The bishop traced the cause to many factors but primarily to wretched homes, squalor and discomfort and to 'wicked' national customs. Drunken and demoralised men and women, young boys and young girls, lived in wretched houses in the city's lanes and alleys. In 1905 a correspondent was of the opinion that in no other Irish city was there 'so much apparent indifference to drunkenness'. A temperance movement was badly needed.[78] By this time, the con-sensus had shifted and alcoholism was generally considered to be the product of widespread unemployment and the consequence of social deprivation rather than vice versa. Still, the distinction between cause and effect was not easy to draw. In 1899 Mayor Henry Grainger, a draper from Barronstrand Street, noted that he entered many homes where there was 'appalling poverty ... the sole cause being drink'.[79]

Cardinal Logue, Archbishop of Armagh and Primate of All Ireland, remarking on the 'thoughtless ... luxurious lives and wasting wealth' of the rich side by side with their brothers' suffering want and misery in the slums of the cities, thought it was the consequence of the economic system and contact with the materialistic English who had renounced Catholic principles. The misery was a product of 'soulless individualism'.[80] Certainly, sections of the British working class were just as disadvantaged. The work of Booth and others established that the 'drink' problem was not peculiarly Irish.

Contrasting with Logue's view were those of others who saw Catholicism as the cause of poverty and apathy. In a polemical and hostile work which casts doubt on its objectivity, one visitor recorded that if Waterford were freed of the burdens of Catholicism it had the potential to be one of the wealthiest cities in Ireland. Next to Dublin it was the 'most priest-infested territory in Ireland'. This accounted for it being a city of 'imbeciles', and in it 'dirt [was] triumphant [and there were] filthy women ... bareheaded and barefooted ... drinking, snuffing, smoking, spitting'.[81] Plunkett's more reasoned view was that Irish Catholics were characterised by a listlessness and apathy in regard to economic improvement which amounted to a form of fatalism. This generalisation was clearly not applicable

74 *Waterford News*, 22 Sep. 1876.
75 *Waterford News*, 21 Jan. 1893 and the supplement on 25 Nov. 1893.
76 *Waterford News*, 7 Jan. 1899.
77 *Waterford Standard*, 5 Mar. 1902.
78 *United Irishman*, 4 Nov. 1905.
79 *Waterford News*, 7 Jan. 1899.
80 MacMahon (1981).
81 McCarthy (1902), pp. 87–88, 488–490.

to the Catholic middle classes, and one study has concluded that if religion did influence economic performance then that influence was limited.[82] More probable explanations for the inertia apparent in so many of the labouring class in Ireland and Britain were enervating ignorance, poverty and the fruitlessness of any ambitions. Like alcoholism, however, the condition was magnified in Ireland because poverty and unemployment were more extensive and the lack of education more widespread.

Whether he was a Catholic and drank or not, the labourer was often precariously poised on the verge of destitution. Regularly pawning belongings at the beginning of the week and redeeming them at the end of it was common practice and in 1909 there were seven pawnbrokers clustered in the poorer areas of Waterford. He and his family were under the constant threat of pauperism, the relief of which was provided by the wealthier, ratepaying classes who financed the poor law system and provided charity to supplement support from families, church, religious orders and neighbours. The poor law served to accentuate the labourer's dependence on the wealthier classes. A respectable man would do anything to avoid pauperism. Paupers formed a distinct group of stigmatised second-class citizens deprived of their most important rights,[83] and under severe economic conditions the fear of pauperism might well have propelled a man to enlist.

The English poor law system, extended to Ireland in 1838,[84] was considered inappropriate and criticised by many. However, it advanced the concept of Irish local government bodies being elected by a wider franchise, as all ratepayers were entitled to vote representatives on to the Board of Guardians. A need to cater for the destitute was also obvious. The Waterford city workhouse was opened in 1844, and in 1847 the provision of outdoor relief was allowed.[85] But it was costly. In 1887 some guardians were 'astounded' that £3,500 had been given in outdoor relief over 12 months. They were also concerned that the system of outdoor relief was not only being abused but that it 'sapped the energy' of many by giving out unearned money, that it encouraged begging which was an epidemic in Ireland and that it lessened the 'moral status' of people, making them 'idle and lazy'.

But others defended it. It was 'cruelty to force the poor into the workhouse' where self-support was almost unknown. And because of a dislike of the workhouse, people would not seek relief when they needed it.[86] Enforcement of the workhouse regime humiliated inmates. In 1895 a man who had absented himself from the Waterford union workhouse without leave was sentenced to one month in hard labour after the court was told he had taken up living with a woman of 'very bad character'. Another man was charged with refusing to break the regulation quantity of stones and sentenced to 14 days in prison.[87]

However, although the indignity of having to seek relief may have been deeply felt, the workhouse was a vital facility for labourers and their families when times were hard. At the time of the census in 1881 about five per cent of the Waterford Poor Law Union population were either workhouse inmates or receiving outdoor relief. In 1911 this had dropped to four per cent. Even so, poor relief provision in Cork, Limerick and Waterford in 1910 exceeded that of Dublin.[88]

82 Connolly, S. J., 'Religion, work-discipline and economic attitudes: the case of Ireland' in T. M. Devine and D. Dickson (eds.) (1983), *Ireland and Scotland 1600–1850*, Edinburgh, pp. 235–44.
83 Marshall, T. H. (1970), *Social Policy*, London, pp. 18–20.
84 Ireland was divided into 130 Poor Law Unions, each of which had its own electoral divisions. Each union was centred on a market town where a workhouse was built for the relief of the distressed. Workhouses were administered by a Board of Guardians. In 1847 the Irish poor law was separated from the British system and the number of unions increased to 162.
85 Kinealy, C., 'The workhouse system in County Waterford, 1838–1923' in W. Nolan and T. P. Power (eds.) (1992), *Waterford: History and Society*, Dublin, pp. 579–95.
86 *Waterford News*, 1 July 1887.
87 *Waterford News* supplement, 26 Jan. 1895.
88 Larkin, E. (1989), *James Larkin, Irish Labour Leader*, Winchester, p. 45.

The distance between 'respectability' and pauperism could be very short indeed. In 1902 the families of militiamen called up for annual training ended up in the workhouse. The Board of Guardians resented being unable to recover any money for providing this support and constantly sought ways to reduce costs. Some guardians complained of inmates being a burden upon the ratepayer from the time of their birth until their death. One debate ended in an eight to three decision not to provide the £8 required to give the institution's healthy children an annual day trip to Tramore because it would discriminate against the 'poor and squalid' children of the city who did not have excursions. One disgusted guardian provided £4 for the trip out of his own pocket.[89]

The traditions of charity and paternalism, in bolstering the sense of obligation and dependence on others, further eroded the labourer's autonomy and reinforced the concept of his 'childlike' quality.

There were several charitable institutions in Ballybricken. In 1865 it was reported that 'without the slightest pressure' being required, within a fortnight of the mayor setting up a relief fund following severe weather, unemployment and the spread of an infectious disease, a fund of £330 had been created. A further £693 was subsequently raised. It was observed that few communities could boast of a 'more charitable public than that which inhabits and surrounds' the city, and the number of endowed institutions would do 'credit to the largest and most prosperous cities in the island'. This was a boast repeated in 1915 when it was claimed that Waterford had more 'philanthropic institutions' than any other city in Ireland.[90]

In all of them, according to the *Waterford News*, the inmates were amply catered for and they were visited by many charitable citizens.[91] The city's privately endowed institutions were backed up by a wide range of church organisations, such as the premises near Barrack Street managed by the Little Sisters of the Poor in 1887, which supported over 100 'poor old persons of both sexes' without cost or rates. The sisters lived with the poor, feeding and attending them without the assistance of servants. Their chapel could accommodate a further 100 people, and a new wing could take an additional 60.[92]

Landowners fulfilled their paternal responsibilities through a variety of activities. In 1876 the Earl and Countess of Bessborough dispensed a customary Christmas bounty among their poor tenantry. The *Waterford News* reported that in consequence 'many a fireside has been made happy'.[93] And when praised by a priest in a 'charity sermon' for his 'liberality and kindness' in giving grants and donations towards the building of a school and church for his local Catholic tenantry in 1876, the Marquis of Waterford replied that it was no more than his duty to do so.

Less happily, however, another priest complained that for some 'unexplained reason' the marquis had turned down a request for a site on which to build a Catholic church at Dunmore East. None the less, it was hoped that his lordship would, 'like many nobles and landed proprietors in Scotland and England ... take a deep and intelligent interest in the cause of popular education' in those areas of his estates where local funds were insufficient.[94] However, in language which reflected contemporary journalistic style rather than the subservience suggested, a new school in Kilmacthomas was said to have 'the approval, the approbation of the Lord of the Soil—the noble and popular marquis of Waterford—who has ever shown himself anxious to promote the true interests of his tenants'.[95]

89 *Waterford Standard*, 5 July 1902.
90 *Waterford News*, 12 Feb. 1915. A report from the newspaper files of 10 Feb. 1865.
91 *Waterford News*, 1 Jan. 1915.
92 *Waterford News*, 1 July 1887.
93 *Waterford News*, 29 Dec. 1876.
94 *Waterford News*, 20 Oct. 1876.
95 *Waterford News*, 8 Jan. 1876.

For the 1892 August bank holiday Lady Waterford and Lady Gwendoline O'Shee were among the ladies who arranged a special train at half the usual fare to transport visitors from the city to Woodhouse near Stradbally. Cars and carriages supplied by the local gentry carried the visitors from the station to Woodhouse where there was a bazaar, concert, wax works, *tableaux vivants* and luncheons and teas supplied at 'abnormally low prices'. The purpose was to raise funds for 'local wants'.[96]

Fitzgerald of The Little Island was reported as being a 'good landlord' in 1865. He gave the parish priest flannel and warm clothing for distribution to the poor of Ballygunner parish and provided £13 each year in weekly payments to a few old and infirm poor people. He was also commended for providing a 'good education' for the children of his tenants and the poor of the parish.[97]

Frequent reference is found to the charitable works of Sir W. G. D. Goff in the *Waterford News*. This is not surprising as the proprietor, C. P. (Banquo) Redmond, although a Catholic nationalist, was his friend, supporter and a fellow member of the cycling club. Goff is reported to have 'done for Waterford more than any of its citizens and is beloved by all who know him'. As an employer of labour he was reputably 'highly appreciated' by his many workmen. As 'one of the most liberal-minded gentlemen in the city ... his well-stocked purse has always been open when the wants of the people, irrespective of class or creed, were in question'. Regarded as a 'leading philanthropist and generous employer',

he donated the Goff cycle track to the People's Park and gave a 'heap of resources' to the various funds connected with amateur sports in Ireland.[98] When appointed city high sheriff in 1900, he returned his £100 salary on the grounds that nobody occupying the position should be paid out of ratepayers' funds.[99] And he gave over a field at Glenville for hockey games.[100]

Before the 'plan of campaign'[101] was implemented in November 1886, Lord Waterford was one of many landowners who freely granted 'substantial reductions' of rent in 1885 when a combination of agricultural depression and a flood of imported foreign cattle, wheat and butter had an 'appalling effect' on the Waterford markets. The city corporation also reduced its urban rents by 20 per cent and its agricultural rents by 25 per cent following the 'immense' fall in prices.[102]

Where rent reductions or the actions of a landlord or his agent were considered less than generous, the local press waged campaigns on behalf of the tenant. In 1886 Claude De Lacy, Fitzgerald's newly arrived agent from England, served writs on some 'old and respectable tenants' on The Island. They owed just one year's rent and his action was condemned as an 'impudent step' and an 'extreme course on the eve of the harvest'. The writs, it was claimed, amounted to 'death sentence[s]'.[103]

City lay magistrates could also be considerate on occasion. In January 1915 eight hackney cab drivers who were summoned for leaving their horses unattended at Waterford North Station, were given reduced fines of one shilling as business was bad.[104]

96 *Waterford Standard*, 20 July 1892.
97 *Waterford News*, 12 Feb. 1915. A report from the newspaper files of 10 Feb. 1865.
98 *Waterford News*, 7, 28 Jan. 1899.
99 *Waterford News*, 16 Feb. 1900.
100 *Waterford Standard*, 3 Jan. 1914.
101 The 'plan of campaign' was published on 23 Oct. 1886 in the *United Ireland* (a newspaper founded by Charles Stewart Parnell in 1881, which became the official organ of the Land League and the Irish Parliamentary Party. It ceased publication in 1898). It was a plan to force landlords to accept a reduction in rent at a time of depression in the prices of dairy produce and cattle which left many tenants in arrears with rent. It signalled the second phase of the land war. The first phase, lasting from 1879 to 1882, had been a violent struggle between tenants led by the Land League and landlords. The more conciliatory third phase (1891–1903) involved the transfer of land to tenants through various acts of parliament.
102 *Waterford News*, 4 Dec. 1885.
103 *Waterford News*, 6 Aug. 1886.
104 *Waterford News*, 22 Jan. 1915.

Other wealthy citizens dispensed charity in a number of ways. The occupant of The Grange in Tower Ward occasionally entertained children from the workhouse national school, providing them with a 'sumptuous feast' and amusement.[105] In 1901, £375 more than the stipulated £1,000 was raised to secure the £5,000 Carnegie gift for the construction of a free library[106] on a Lady Lane site given for the purpose by a local citizen. Donors sent in objects daily to fill the library. The 'gentry and merchants of the city and county' were reported as being 'most energetic in their efforts to secure its success'.[107] The library elicited rare praise from a writer in the *United Irishman*. It was good, and all the readers—'practically all of the[m] working-class—conducted themselves like gentlemen'.[108]

The Quay coffee shop was started by 'philanthropic ladies, clergymen and other good citizens' in May 1914 to provide coffee, tea, cocoa and more substantial fare at moderate prices for quay workers and others of the working classes at all hours.[109] A local newspaper was concerned at the lack of cover for jarveys when it rained. Noting it was 'pitiable to see the drivers of jaunting-cars subjected to a soaking', the paper suggested building a shelter for them when public funds became available.[110]

Paternalism was so embracing it effectively supplanted the employee's individual rights. All the staff of the *Waterford News* were 'greatly indebted' to Banquo Redmond for allowing them to have a whole day off during a busy season. It was a 'concession' which was 'much appreciated'. The day out, arranged by Redmond, included a trip to Lord Waterford's demesne at Curraghmore and an afternoon at Carrick-on-Suir where everyone joined in singing *For He's a Jolly Good Fellow*.[111] No employees paid rent on Fitzgerald's island and food produced on the farm was provided free. A £2 bonus was distributed after the harvest. Workers were allowed a day off to attend the Tramore races and were sometimes transported by boat for a picnic at Dunmore. Entertainers, including magicians, were hired to perform for workers in the castle's 'big hall'.[112]

A number of major employers gave their employees time off to visit a 1902 Cork exhibition. Two thousand citizens, including 'an enormous number of the working classes', travelled in three excursion trains. They were accompanied by the mayor, the high sheriff, many other members of the corporation, Fathers Patrick F. Flynn, William B. O'Donnell and Tom Furlong as well as other priests, and the Waterford Temperance Fife and Drum Band.[113] And a deputation from the cycle club received a generally good response from local shopkeepers and employers when it asked for half-day closing to allow people to attend the cycle races. Representatives from the whole of the United Kingdom competed and Sir W. G. D. Goff presented the challenge shield.[114]

The London-born general manager of the gasworks claimed employees were fairly paid and well treated. Some were housed on the firm's three-acre site. Staff were taken on an annual picnic to Curraghmore, and permanent hands were given a suit of Irish tweed at Christmas.[115] As well as offering secure, relatively well-paid jobs with reasonable chances of promotion, railway companies ensured the acquiescent loyalty of their staff by providing houses which were

105 *Waterford News*, 1 July 1887.
106 *Waterford Standard*, 20 Nov. 1901.
107 *Thom's Directory*, p. 36.
108 *United Irishman*, 4 Nov 1905.
109 *Waterford News*, 21 May 1915.
110 *Waterford News*, 8 Oct. 1915.
111 *Waterford News*, 23 Aug. 1901.
112 Information provided by the author's father who lived or worked on The Island for many years as a young boy and adult.
113 *Waterford Standard*, 20 Aug. 1902.
114 *Waterford News*, 12 May 1894.
115 *Egan's Guide to Waterford*, pp. 454L–54M.

generally better than those normally occupied by working men.

An employer's authority was sometimes enforced by a strict disciplinary code which could include a system of fines for misdemeanours or carelessness. The indenture of one Wexford shop assistant prohibited 'fornication or matrimony', dice, cards, or other unlawful games, or visiting taverns, ale-houses or playhouses. A fine of ten shillings was imposed for each day of absence.[116] Tough disciplinary procedures enforced by the Midland and Great Western Railway resulted in a father and son being dismissed when the son gave oil to a Waterford and Limerick Railway fireman.[117] Fitzgerald's steward on The Island held daily report sessions in the castle gunroom. At these he dealt with matters of discipline. When resident on The Island, Fitzgerald enforced attendance at Sunday mass by interrogating any of his employees or tenants who were not at Ballygunner Church.[118]

Too late to affect the older generation's attitudes, the Liberal government's welfare legislation reduced to a significant extent reliance on the poor laws and on charity and it subverted the old paternalistic order. The Old Age Pensions Act, 1908 provided a non-contributory pension for married couples and single persons.[119] But the unpopular 1909 budget antagonised the propertied classes by financing social legislation, as well as Royal Navy dreadnoughts, through increased income tax, a super tax and indirect taxation. It was condemned as being calculated to destroy the Irish brewing and distilling industry and over-tax the average Irishman. The hierarchy spoke out against it and William Martin Murphy launched a concerted attack on it in the *Irish Independent*.[120]

W. G. D. Goff, Michael O'Sullivan, a local bottler and James English's employer, and the separatist councillor Patrick W. Kenny were present when the Waterford Chamber of Commerce debated the resolution that Ireland would be 'unduly and prejudicially affected' by the new taxes. Goff and O'Sullivan were concerned about the effects on the distilling industry and Goff condemned the budget. The government was accused of failing to develop Irish industries, provide employment or discourage emigration. The poor, it was claimed, would suffer. There would be a cutback in employment and in subscriptions to hospitals and other institutions.[121]

The Irish Parliamentary Party (IPP) initially opposed the budget. Its financial backers were adversely affected by the taxes, and the payment of old age pensions put Ireland in the position of costing more than it contributed to the exchequer. During the 1911 discussions on home rule, financial issues rather than the Ulster question therefore dominated.[122] Health insurance for those between the age of 16 and 60 who were earning less than £160 a year came into operation in January 1913. The worker, employer and the state made a contribution which entitled employees to free medical treatment, sickness and disability benefit, and a maternity grant. Unemployment insurance only covered some categories of workers and did not extend to James English. However, a labour exchange was set up in Lady Lane in 1910 under the Labour Exchanges Act of 1909.

Improved education opportunities also created a route by which a labourer's children might escape inherited economic and social deprivation, even though he might not himself. Following the Technical Instruction Act 1889 and the Agriculture and Technical Instruction (Ireland) Act of 1899, the permanent Waterford Central Technical Institute was opened in Parnell Street in 1906. Bishop Sheehan was chairman of the

116 Anonymous (1978), 'Conditions of employment a century ago', *The Past*, **12**, pp. 31–32.
117 O'Neill (1986a).
118 Information provided by the author's father.
119 Evans, J. (ed) (1978), *Social Policy 1830–1914*, London, pp. 161–72, 272–80.
120 Miller, D. W. (1973), *Church, State and Nation in Ireland 1898–1921*, Dublin, pp. 250–52.
121 *Waterford News*, 28 May 1909.
122 Jalland, P. (1986), *The Liberals and Ireland*, Brighton, pp. 44–47.

technical instruction committee on which W. G. D. Goff also had a place. Goff's wife was appointed to the ladies' committee. The institute's courses gave men and women the opportunity of handling tools and learning trade processes. At a cost of five shillings per term for each subject,[123] a determined labourer equipped with a rudimentary education might breach hitherto insurmountable barriers and join the artisan class.

For the illiterate labourer, however, the habit of deference was intensified by the narrowness of his mental and physical horizons. Families, generally one to a room, led cluttered lives in the small houses of over a hundred lanes which 'spread like blood vessels in all directions'.[124] The development of the bicycle from the 1880s onwards lifted many of the lower classes out of their isolation, and a fully equipped cycle factory, employing six people, was operating in Railway Square by 1894. But their cost put cycles beyond the reach of many labourers. The *Urbs Intacta*, produced locally, was priced at £3 19s 9d in 1909 and imported cycles cost £3 10s.[125]

The lack of mobility helped to create close and generally static communities. James English's parents, James and Catherine *née* O'Keeffe, were both from Green's Lane, Ballybricken. Neither a formally recognised city division nor a parish, the term 'Ballybricken' was sometimes used to describe Trinity Without Parish, the terms 'Within' and 'Without' describing a parish's position in relation to the old city wall. Or the name was loosely used to describe the area around Ballybricken Green or that part of Trinity Without Parish which included Centre Ward and the urban area of South Ward. Trinity Catholic Church (see Map 2) was more commonly referred to as Ballybricken Church and men from Ballybricken considered themselves, and were generally described as, Ballybricken men rather than as Waterfordmen.

Ballybricken families generally knew one another or were related to each other. Private affairs soon became public business and James English's parents were one instance of a tendency for people to marry others from the same street or from nearby. If someone died, it was the next door neighbour who called the priest, consoled the bereaved and laid out the corpse.[126] Community life revolved around institutions such as the numerous street bands.

VII

The king encouraged local bands[127] and neither election meetings nor much else could be done without them.[128] Rivalry between the Waterford bands was sometimes more than artistic. In 1884 when the Morgan Street Fife and Drum Band met the John Street Band in Thomas Street, the resulting fight needed the mayor and two constables to end it, but not before several windows and a house door were completely smashed.[129]

The bands had large memberships and attracted many followers, generating a range of social activities. The Robert Emmet Independent Band, founded in the 1870s, changed its name to the Erin's Hope Prize Flute Band in 1899 and won prizes in competitions all over Ireland. Boxing matches were held in the band's room on Saturday evenings. Venues for band promenades were shared out. While the Erin's Hope Prize

123 Waterford Central Technical Institute, *Central Technical Institute, Prospectus of Classes, Session 1907–08* (Ir 370), p. 23, NLI.
124 Wymberry, E. (*c.* 1991), *Well! Well!: Memories of Waterford in the 1950s*, Waterford, pp. 16–23. Conditions had changed little since the turn of the century and Wymberry's description conveys an accurate image of Waterford in the 1890s and early 1900s.
125 *Thom's Directory*, pp. 105, 114, 134, 143.
126 Wymberry, E. (*c.* 1989), *Well!: Recollections of Waterford in the 1940s and '50s*, Waterford, pp. 8, 72–75. Information from the present author's father (born May 1904) and mother (born Nov. 1907) confirmed the situation described by Wymberry was much the same as that at the turn of the century.
127 *Waterford Standard*, 20 Aug. 1902.
128 Gwynn (1926), pp. 297–99.
129 *Waterford News*, 28 Mar. 1884.

Band played on Ballybricken Hill, the Barrack Street Brass and Reed Band, founded as the Amateur Band in 1870, performed in the People's Park. Contests were frequent and on one occasion in 1905, huge crowds gathered at the Court House to watch Ballybricken bands raise funds for a new church organ by outplaying contestants from Wales.[130]

However, the bands relied on subscriptions from the city's businessmen and religious leaders, who would contribute from less than 3s to £1 when called on to do so by a band's committee.[131] The corporation also provided work for them. The Parnell Independent Band was paid £20 to play on 20 occasions during the summer of 1892[132] and the corporation voted to increase this to £40 for the Barrack Street Brass Band in 1915.[133]

Other small pleasures alleviated the otherwise frugal existence of the labourer and his family. Groups of young people travelled on cycles around the county and sometimes beyond, competing in Irish dances which frequently took place in private homes. Contests were also held in the Theatre Royal which provided other entertainment at affordable prices. Visiting companies, on occasion comprising 25 artistes with two large truckloads of scenery, put on shows at the theatre. In 1904 they included *The Taming of the Shrew* and *The Merry Wives of Windsor*. Boxes were priced at £1 10s, the circle 3s, stalls 2s, a reserved seat 2s 6d, the pit 1s and gallery seats were 6d.

Special trains also took people to the Tramore beaches. And although the annual hunt balls, with tickets costing £1 for gentlemen and 15s for ladies,[134] were well beyond the reach of the labouring class, they might watch films which were introduced into the city in 1912 when a skating rink, built in 1910, was converted into the Rink Picture Palace.

Films, considered 'the best and most up-to-date pictures together with a splendid orchestral accompaniment', were also shown at the Theatre Royal during intervals between theatrical company engagements[135] and could be afforded by most people. Running for three nights and a matinee performance, the films included *Dante's Inferno* which, costing over £50,000 to produce, comprised 100 scenes considered to be 'a marvel of the film maker's art'.[136] In August 1913 a new cinema opened in Broad Street[137] and by October the Theatre Royal was showing films every night to an increasingly appreciative audience.[138] The Coliseum replaced the Rink Picture Palace in October 1915.[139]

But pleasures could be simpler. James English's wife, Catherine, enjoyed smoking a 'jaw-warmer', a colloquialism for the locally produced, shortened clay pipe. And clean, open country visible from Ballybricken Hill was within easy reach. Long walks, sometimes with the children, would be taken as relief from oppressive city slums. This amenity gave Irish towns like Waterford and Mallow an advantage over the industrialised British towns.[140]

Traditionally, contact with the world outside of Waterford was mainly with England. Fast schooners and brigs continually crossed the channel and they frequently transported young Waterfordmen looking for work. Although few Waterfordmen had been to other Irish cities, most, because of unemployment, knew Liver-

130 Combined Area Residents' Association (hereafter CARA) (1991), *Ballybricken and Thereabouts*, Waterford, pp. 100–06; *Waterford News*, 1 Oct. 1915; *Munster Express*, 20 Sep. 1913.
131 *Waterford Standard*, 8 May 1915.
132 *Waterford News*, 2 July 1892.
133 *Waterford News*, 7 May 1915.
134 *Waterford Standard*, 13 Jan. 1904.
135 *Munster Express*, 20 Sep. 1913.
136 *Munster Express*, 30 Aug. 1913.
137 CARA, *Ballybricken and Thereabouts*, pp. 88–91; *Munster Express*, 1 Aug. 1913.
138 *Munster Express*, 29 Oct. 1913.
139 *Waterford Standard*, 6 Nov. 1915.
140 Lankford, S. (1980), *The Hope and the Sadness*, Cork, pp. 74–75.

pool, Manchester and London better than they knew Dublin, Cork or Limerick.[141]

James English was therefore part of a close community in which corporate opinion could sometimes overwhelm individual judgement. The Ballybricken pig buyers, central to the commercial activity of Waterford, also played a major role in the city's social and political life. They were influential in the formation of local opinions. Their attitudes and the popular views of the wider Ballybricken community had a major impact on James English's attitudes towards Germany, the war and enlistment.

The argument that wars are inherent in the capitalist system is inconclusive and too abstract to be meaningful. But for the Ballybricken pig buyers and some of the privileged and wealthy in Waterford, the war and consequent military enlistment served their interests and offered a solution to the expensive and potentially disruptive social problems created by large numbers of unemployed and paupers.

VIII

There was an anti-German mood among some business people which undoubtedly contributed to moulding public opinion. The provisions trade, and particularly bacon curing, had been under threat since at least 1887 when Germany prohibited the importation of swine and the raw products from swine. By the early 1900s Waterford traders were complaining about the exclusion of their ham products from Germany. No doubt Ballybricken's pig dealers shared this antagonism. David MacDonald, the barm manufacturer, was also mindful of the dangers from trading rivals, the Germans in particular. He attacked the bread baked from imported German

yeast as being unhealthy and harmful and claimed his company's barm bread was more nutritious. By buying Irish, large numbers were employed at home and money was spent in the country which would otherwise find its way to 'our friends the Germans'.[142]

James English's own employer, Michael O'Sullivan, was involved with the other principal bottlers in opening a glass factory at Bilberry during 1900 in the face of what they identified as a German threat, although 20 years previously, Irish glass products had cost nine times those of Belgian imports. The factory was hailed as providing much needed employment. An attempt to keep the plant going by using apprentices instead of adult workers resulted in a labour dispute which shut it down in February 1904. But it was operating at 'full blast' in April and it was hoped to give the 'German dumpers' a fight.[143] However, Irish glass bottle factories were soon forced to shut down because of cheaper German imports.[144]

The depth of any anti-German mood and the extent to which it may have been communicated to the labouring class cannot be gauged with precision. Although its scope is uncertain, it seems reasonable to conclude that this mood was one element in the decision of some men to enlist. At least one British recruit enlisted because he thought war was the 'only effective course to protect the trade interests of the nation and counteract the unemployment caused by the dumping of cheap German manufactured goods.'[145] But a contemporary thought the anti-German fervour was more apparent among the British than the Irish.[146]

James Connolly's suggestion that there was a conspiracy among Irish and English capitalists and a 'half-educated' English working class to smash the superior German industrial competi-

141 Wymberry (1989), p. 8; the present author's father was one of those who worked a passage on a schooner to Bristol in search of work in the 1920s without having seen much of Ireland other than Waterford county.
142 *Waterford Standard*, 5 July 1902; *Egan's Guide to Waterford*, pp. 454I-54J.
143 *Waterford News*, 16 Mar. 1900 and 1 Apr. 1904; *Waterford Standard*, 20 Feb. 1904.
144 Riordan (1920), pp. 166–67.
145 Simkins (1988), pp. 168–69.
146 Hannay, J. O. (1916), 'Ireland in two wars—recruiting in Ireland today', *Nineteenth Century and After*, LXXIX, pp. 173–80.

tors and steal their trade,[147] is not sustainable. Apart from the problems of verification, many Irish capitalists and leaders frequently saw British competitors and the British government as being their main protagonists. However, they did play a major role in creating a popular pro-war movement in support of Redmond's policy.

Suspicions and doubts among businessmen and community leaders about the British government's Irish economic and employment policies surfaced continually in a number of minor ways. In 1882 the secretary of state for war was asked pointedly if a new rule requiring military clothing made in Ireland to be sent to London for inspection and approval, resulted in a loss of contracts to Irish firms.[148] And in 1890 a Cork MP wanted to know why troops in Ireland had to obtain canteen and other supplies from the London army and navy co-op stores when it put a few officers who had interests in these stores in a position to obtain 'pecuniary advancement ... over claims of local traders'.[149] This wariness of government intentions was reflected locally. Differences in pay between Irish and British letter-carriers had been challenged, for instance.[150] And in 1890 the government was asked if an existing vacancy for a postmaster at Waterford would be filled by promotion within Ireland, as the Irish were not given the same opportunities as the English and Scots to fill appointments elsewhere in the United Kingdom.[151]

In 1896, Laurence C. (Charlie) Strange, a local solicitor and councillor, identified technical advances as being the cause of a great many artisans and unskilled labourers being unable to obtain employment with reasonable wages. He called on the government, whose duty he thought it was to provide the jobs necessary for a man to support himself and his family, to intervene and create the necessary work.[152] As early as 1876, a Waterford correspondent had recognised the value of education in industry. 'Education sir,' he noted, 'is the watchword of the 19th century.' Successful economic expansion in the United States was due to knowledge and, he argued, the Germans had defeated the French in 1871 because of superior education. It was also essential for the Irish if they were to keep up with other races.[153]

However, in a meeting convened to discuss the Catholic university question in 1904, attended by W. G. D. Goff and Bishop Sheehan among others, the mayor complained that Waterford was unable to obtain sufficient funds from the government to erect and equip a technical school to 'compete against the foreigners and prevent the dumping down of all things "Made in Germany"'. He called for an Irish education as broad as that of Germany.[154]

Bishop Sheehan also complained of the inadequacy of government funds for technical education. In a published letter he wrote that while 'wealthy England gets from imperial sources close on £1,000,000', Ireland gets only £55,000 and mostly from Irish funds.[155] As early as 1884 it was formally acknowledged that impoverishment and decay in Waterford, as well as the lack of regular employment, was partly due to an excessive imperial tax burden.[156]

This long-standing popular belief was confirmed by the Royal Commission's report on financial relations between Great Britain and Ireland in 1896. A letter from the Irish Financial

147 Connolly, J., 'The war upon the German nation', *Irish Worker* (29 Aug. 1914), reproduced in Connolly (1987), Vol. 1, pp. 418–24.
148 *Hansard* (Commons) 3rd ser. CCLXVIII, 24, 27 Mar. 1882.
149 *Hansard* (Commons) 3rd ser. CCCXLIII, 551, 15 Apr. 1890.
150 *Hansard* (Commons) 3rd ser. CCLXIII, 1910, 15 Aug. 1881.
151 *Hansard* (Commons) 3rd ser. CCCXLIII, 1831, 1 May 1890.
152 *Waterford News*, 9 May 1896.
153 *Waterford News*, 20 Oct. 1876.
154 *Waterford News*, 5 Feb. 1904.
155 Unidentified newspaper cutting (Redmond Papers, 15,227), NLI.
156 *The Third Report of the Royal Commission for Enquiry into the Housing of the Working Classes in Ireland* (British Parliamentary Papers 1884–5, XXX1.187, 203, 313) [Cd. 4547, 4547–1, 4402–III], pp. xv–xvi.

Reform League was published in a Waterford newspaper during the 1899 municipal elections calling on every candidate to pledge himself to help in carrying out the commission's findings.[157]

In seconding a Chamber of Commerce resolution condemning the 1909 budget, Patrick W. Kenny, an independently-minded and forthright man, protested against all British government taxation in Ireland and noted that opposition to the 'people's budget' of 1909 had brought together men of all creeds, trades and classes. He had spent most of his life in Australia where, he claimed, there was home rule in the 'fullest sense' and no toleration for the kind of fiscal oppression Ireland suffered. Declaring that nothing better could be expected from any British government, Liberal or Conservative, he urged members to combine for home rule. Resentment against what many believed to be British exploitation of the Irish economy, as well as concepts of political freedom, underpinned nationalist politics.

Nationalism and the Catholic faith were two important cultural elements which helped to integrate the Ballybricken community, conditioned its response to Redmond when he called on men to enlist and helped to secure the loyalty of men to the 16th (Irish) Division.

157 *Waterford News*, 14 Jan. 1899.

CHAPTER 2

The Religious and Political Background

I

Religion and politics could not easily be separated out at Westminster or in any country within the United Kingdom.[1] Political divisions generally followed religious lines and the claim that religion was a badge of Irish nationality which strongly affected social behaviour and political attitudes[2] is therefore justified on one level. A Catholic Old English family such as the Fitzgeralds of The Little Island and Catholic city merchants and professionals such as Banquo Redmond or Charlie Strange, shared with labourers the nationalist identity and the strong communal bond of a Catholicism which had survived the plantations and centuries of persecution. But at another level, the class structure made social and political attitudes more complex. As well as religion and nationality, class was a major variable in the politics of the United Kingdom.

Although uniquely Irish in character, still traditional and far less abrasive than that in the industrial British city, Waterford society none the less replicated the British class structure. Fitzgerald of The Island had more in common with a New English Protestant aristocrat such as Lord Waterford, and Catholic nationalists such as Charlie Strange or Banquo Redmond had more in common with a Protestant unionist such as W. G. D. Goff, than they had with the low-born and illiterate James English. The middle and upper classes, whether Catholic or Protestant, shared a dominant social status as well as political and economic power. Class was therefore as important as religion and nationality. Nationalist politics, by focusing on the differences between Irishman and Briton, obscured these aspects of a common heritage and also disguised the distinctions existing between Irishmen.

Not only was Waterford's economy locked into that of Britain's, but because of its cultural affinity it was frequently described as a 'British' city. Irish towns like Waterford were 'essentially a variant on British provincial culture'. Claims that the Irish 'really were a little bit British'[3] and that any modern Irishman without English blood was a 'genetic freak'[4] have substance.

James English's family name, although hibernicised and common in Munster, was, like those of Fitzgerald, Redmond and Strange, of Norman or twelfth-century English extraction.[5] And as has been seen, Lord Waterford inherited connections with the Norman and Catholic Le Poer family. For constitutional nationalist leaders, there was the added danger of becoming 'mesmerised by the legislative process' and forgetting the divisions that did exist between Irishman and Briton.[6] In Daniel D. Sheehan's opinion, for example, John Dillon was an English radical first and an Irish nationalist afterwards, while T. P.

---

1 Turner, J. (1992), *British Politics and the Great War: Coalition and Conflict 1915–1918*, London, p. 22.
2 Daly, M. E. (1981), *Social and Economic History of Ireland Since 1800*, Dublin, p. 125.
3 Garvin (1981), pp. 103–09.
4 McConville, M. (1986), *Ascendancy to Oblivion*, London, pp. 53, 120–21.
5 MacLysaght, E. (1982), *More Irish Families*, Dublin, pp. 91–92.
6 Lyons (1973), pp. 29–30.

O'Connor was so long out of Ireland he had lost touch with genuine Irish opinion and was more a Liberal in his political actions.[7] The paradoxical result of this intricate web of counterbalancing loyalties was to make Waterford society relatively homogeneous despite the potential for dissension. But confusion about national roots and loyalties could also create a dilemma.

Sean O'Faolain considered that in 1900 he was born 'in a place that did not exist'. Ireland, 'politically, culturally and psychologically [was] just not there. All that was there was a bastard piece of the British Empire'.[8] O'Faolain's observation that anglicisation caused a problem of identity is borne out in the instance of the daughter of a Waterford First World War veteran who commented, 'any good I ever got, I got from England … I got feck all from this country'.[9] It was a comment uncannily similar to that frequently made by James English's daughter, Margaret.

It is therefore probable that some Irishmen experienced emotions similar to the patriotism which motivated so many Britons to enlist. And Irishmen did share, to some extent, an enthusiasm for the empire and a belief in the need to defend it. Irish as well as British politicians thought of themselves as superior to the black races and this was the basis of much of their support for the Boers.[10] John Redmond was proudly conscious of Britain as the centre of a great empire in which Ireland held an honoured place[11] and he found no contradiction in declaring that Irish roots were in the imperial as well as the national.[12] Sean O'Faolain recalled that he

had … no consciousness of my country as a

separate cultural entity inside the Empire. Not that this bothered me in the least. … I was tremendously proud of belonging to the Empire, as were at that time most Irishmen. I gloried in all its trappings, Kings, Queens, dukes, duchesses, generals, admirals, soldiers, sailors, colonists, and conquerors, the lot.

The Easter Rising came as a shock. It suddenly presented him with a country whose birth was

supposed to wipe out all those social values that I had … lived by … Gordon of Khartoum, the Relief of Lucknow, the Charge of the Light Brigade, Irish-born Wellington, the Munster Fusiliers, the glory of the flag, the belly stirring rumble of the preliminary drum roll of God Save the King, Lord Kitchener, the Angel at Mons, but above all the dream of every well-bred imperial boy of one day becoming A Gentleman.[13]

'Servitor imperialism' (the imperialism of second-class citizens) has been advanced as one explanation of why Irishmen of James English's class were attracted to imperialism. Identification with the empire served to 'expiate some of the inferiority associated with peripheral social origins; it may [have given] individuals from disadvantaged groups the first opportunity to escape from a self-assessment as victim to one of conqueror'. Walter Bagehot thought imperialism distracted the 'masses' from immediate problems by an appeal

to some vague dream of glory, or empire, or

7 Sheehan, D. D. (1921), *Ireland Since Parnell*, London, p. 153.
8 O'Faolain, S. (1976), 'A portrait of the artist as an old man', *Irish University Review*, 6, pp. 10–18. A writer and teacher, and the son of an RIC constable, O'Faolain's attitudes towards the British army, his nationalism and the changes they underwent were fairly common. His first reaction to the Easter Rising was one of rage against those who had betrayed Irish soldiers fighting in France. By the end of Easter week he had taken the side of the insurgents. A member of the IRA for six years, he supported Eamon De Valera in 1921. He worked and lived in the USA and Britain for the period 1926 to 1933 during which time his nationalist views underwent reassessment and change. Becoming more practical and less abstract and idealistic, his questioning of the 'nationalist myth' became 'relentless' (McCartney, D. (1976), 'Sean O'Faolain: a nationalist right enough', *Irish University Review*, 6, pp. 73–86).
9 Dunne, S. (1991), *In My Father's House*, Dublin, pp. 11–12.
10 Edwards, O. D., 'Ireland', in O. D. Edwards et al. (eds.) (1968), *Celtic Nationalism*, London, pp. 124–126.
11 Lyons (1973), p. 261.
12 Bew, P. (1987), *Conflict and Conciliation in Ireland 1890–1910*, Oxford, p. 19.
13 O'Faolain (1976).

nationality. The ruder sort of men ... will sacrifice all they hope for, all they have themselves, for what is called an idea—for some attraction which seems to transcend reality, which aspires to elevate man by an interest higher, deeper, wider than that of ordinary life.[14]

Pride in empire and service in the army were synonymous in the minds of many Irishmen, but a latent conflict of loyalties existed. Attitudes were far from simple. The same man could applaud the imperial feats of the Irish in the British army but just as readily denounce it as the occupying force of an alien power, events and changing circumstances determining which of these conflicting views was uppermost. Willie Redmond, for example, having condemned imperial military campaigns as enlarging an 'over-bloated empire', later announced his pride in the 'Irishmen in South Africa [who] are fighting as gallantly [in the British army] as Irishmen always have done'. By 1907 he was also advocating schemes for imperial defence.[15] It was an incongruity in attitudes mirrored by several nationalists who served in the army[16] and it was commented on by soldiers and outside observers.

In Stephen Gwynn's opinion, 'mingled with nationalists' attitude of estrangement from the forces ... there was a deep-seated pride in the exploits of Irish troops, and no man felt this more strongly than [John] Redmond'.[17] A New Army recruit remembered how men enlisting in the army had the 'entirely Hibernian faculty of being able to combine a most fanatical and seditious brand of Nationalism with a genuine and ardent enthusiasm for the British Empire.'[18] In 1914 Corporal Michael O'Mara, an Irish guardsman from Waterford, wrote:

in deadly combat we are Irishmen [and also] we are British soldiers and proud of the name ... it is sufficient to show that though loving and fighting for the Empire to which he is proud to belong, the Irish soldier still cherishes his true nationality and glories in the name of Ireland.[19]

And John Lucy recorded how, when he enlisted, his mind was 'slightly troubled' because he would have 'preferred to have pledged [his] body to the cause of Ireland, still in thraldom' but, although wishing England had been 'kinder to my countrymen', he 'felt bound in honour to England too, for [he] had attested on oath, and [he] was a British soldier as well as being an Irishman and a Catholic'. Even when a hard and experienced veteran soldier, he felt his

only true love was Ireland—that lovely and tyrannical [woman] who made full claim on all my being, although I did not own a single acre of her green fields. More imperious than any empire, she is always demanding, always insistent.[20]

Patrick MacGill also betrayed confusion when he wrote, 'we British are one of the most military nations in the world'. Apparently unaware of the contradiction, he then smugly observed that he and the colonel were the 'only two *real* Irishmen' in the London Irish battalion to which he belonged.[21]

A British journalist visiting Newtown Mount Kennedy during 1917 praised its 'magnificent record of Imperialism and enthusiasm'. Out of 100 able-bodied men, 95 had joined the colours and gone 'very gladly to fight for a British King'. Whenever one of them was mentioned in despatches there was 'great rejoicing'. There was no

14 Hechter, M. (1974), *Internal Colonialism*, California, pp. 234–43. The Bagehot quotation is from Hechter, p. 241.
15 Denman, T. (1992a), ' "A voice from the lonely grave" ': the death in action of Major William Redmond MP, 7 June 1917', *Irish Sword*, **XVIII**, pp. 286–96.
16 Fitzpatrick, 'The overflow of the deluge' in MacDonagh and Mandle (eds.) (1980).
17 Gwynn, S. (1919), pp. 106–08
18 Hay, I. (1915), *The First Hundred Thousand*, London, p. 174.
19 *Evening News* (Waterford), 26 Oct. 1914.
20 Lucy (1992), pp. 319–20.
21 MacGill (1915), p. 15. The italics are MacGill's own.

bitterness, no spread of the Sinn Fein doctrine and no anti-English feeling. But though the local people were content and loyal, they were not 'denationalised'. They were as conscious of their nationhood and as devoted to their religion as people in western Ireland.

The journalist thought a difference in response to recruiting between these villagers and people in the west was probably due to the local connection with Major Willie Redmond, MP, that 'gallant and chivalrous soldier'. It was the writer's opinion that 'the Irish will follow their leaders to the end when their leaders have all those rare personal qualities that seize the imagination and inspire loyalty and affection'.[22]

Folklore and ballads, glorifying Irish military prowess in the British army as well as military achievements of the 'Wild Geese' and rebels at home, perpetuated the confusion in national identity. P. J. Power, MP for East Waterford, attempted an unconvincing explanation of this convoluted loyalty when, although condemning Britain's role in the Boer War, he conceded that Irishmen in the army 'must do their duty to the colours ... our race is a martial race, and ... the army will always have attractions for people of Celtic blood'.[23]

Attitudes towards nationality, imperialism and the army were ambiguous and capricious, making generalised statements unsafe. But a range of experiences would have moulded a man's opinion about the army, and Waterford, as a garrison town, had a long association with the military which undoubtedly contributed to determining the attitudes of its population.

II

The local garrison comprised a combined cavalry and artillery barracks and a separate infantry barracks, both located in Ballybricken (see Map 1). In 1849 the Duke of Wellington recommended that after providing an efficient garrison and reserve to ensure Dublin was 'securely occupied', troops should be dispersed around Kilkenny. Waterford was one of the towns which formed part of this chain of military garrisons designed to 'suppress rebellion'. The artillery barracks accommodated 5 officers, 121 men and 62 horses and the infantry barracks could house 16 officers, 417 men and 8 horses.[24]

In 1885 Joseph Chamberlain referred to the British system in Ireland as being 'founded on the bayonets of 30,000 soldiers encamped permanently in a hostile country'. By 1904 over 34,000 troops were garrisoned in the country, more than 25,000 of them being located in the south.[25] The sense of occupation by an alien force was heightened by a system of rotating the mostly British troops to prevent too great an attachment to the local population. And the patronising and imperialist attitude of many of the British officer class towards the native Irish was underscored by frequent references to their 'childlike' and 'simple' characteristics.[26] Inevitably, there was friction between British soldiers and local residents, especially at times of political tension.

Violent clashes between soldiers and Waterfordians were frequent in pubs and in Ballybricken's streets. In 1885, after brawling between soldiers and residents, the stoning of troops and the killing of a local man, the magistrate recommended removal of the 24th Regiment (the South Wales Borderers)[27] and the secretary of state for

22 *Daily Chronicle*, 20 Mar. 1917.
23 *Hansard* (Commons) 4th ser. 89, 240, 15 Feb. 1901.
24 Duke of Wellington to Lord John Russell, 12 Dec. 1849 (WO 30/113, PRO); Harris, R. G. (1989), *The Irish Regiments: a Pictorial History 1683–1987*, Tunbridge Wells, p. 284.
25 Bates, M. D. (1965), 'The barracks and posts of Ireland—1', *An Cosantoir*, XXV, pp. 19–27. There were 33,173 men, 95 warrant officers and 1,318 officers.
26 Muenger, E. A. (1981), 'The British army in Ireland 1886–1914' (unpublished PhD thesis), University of Michigan, pp. 4–5, 73–77 and Chapter III.
27 *Waterford News*, 17 July 1885.

war later confirmed its replacement.[28] In 1897 bad feeling was still evident when a delegate to the Irish Trades Union Congress (ITUC) in Waterford objected to the Irish paying for the excessive military presence in a 'peaceful' Ireland.[29] And a citizen was shot dead by a soldier firing from the wall of the barracks after a serious mêlée in about 1902.[30]

The Boer War deepened hostility against the army and enlistment was generally discouraged by nationalists. It was an issue raised by members of the FTLU in 1899[31] and during a visit to Waterford in 1901, Willie Redmond was introduced as someone who 'told the British government to its teeth, what he and his colleagues thought of the war in South Africa'. Willie Redmond spoke of admiring the Boer struggle. 'England,' he proclaimed, 'was in her death grips in South Africa now (cheers) and she had her enemies on the continent and at home, and never ... had Ireland such a chance as she had to-day for securing her liberty.'

A local speaker accused the 'British bully' of establishing 'murderous concentration camps (groans)'. There were cheers when he referred to 10,000 Boers knocking 200,000 British soldiers into a 'cocked hat'. Britain, he said, was a nation which could reward a man like Lord Kitchener with £30,000 for 'treating people as if they were dogs and not human beings'.[32] This probably referred to a gift of the same amount made to

Lord Kitchener for his part in the Sudan campaign of 1896–98. A local councillor spoke disparagingly of the militia being sent out to 'shoot the poor Boers'.[33] Anti-British feeling was aggravated when the city was proclaimed and the proprietor and editor of the *Waterford Star* arrested in 1902. Having published reports on United Irish League (UIL)[34] proceedings, both were convicted of 'inciting intimidation' and the editor was sentenced to two months in prison.[35] In 1904, while on a visit to Waterford, John Redmond told his constituents that 'Ireland was occupied by a hostile force.'[36]

In 1906 Stephen Gwynn did what he could to discourage recruiting[37] but in 1907 Tom Kettle, who had distributed anti-recruiting leaflets during the Boer War, dismissed the Sinn Fein anti-enlisting programme as an inadequate vehicle for achieving independence. He commented 'I ... wondered whether you could do much by preventing a couple of thousand wastrels a year from joining the absurd British Army'.[38] But the relationship between Irishmen and the army was not clear-cut. An officer observed that 'popular as the army was, for it brought trade and profit, it never touched the heart of the people',[39] and in the view of one historian, the British 'garrison', winning friends among shopkeepers, publicans and girls, was treated with 'indulgence if not affection'.[40] On the whole, rural youths may have been hostile towards the army but it was arguably so popular

28 *Hansard* (Commons) 3rd ser. 299, 923, 16 July 1885.
29 Clarkson, J. D. (1970), *Labour and Nationalism in Ireland*, New York, footnote on p. 206.
30 These recollections contained in a 1937 newspaper cutting relating to the Waterford Historical Society (ILB 94141), NLI.
31 *Waterford News*, 17 Nov. 1899.
32 *Waterford News*, 13 Dec. 1901.
33 *Waterford Standard*, 5 July 1902.
34 The United Irish League, an agrarian organisation, was founded by William O'Brien, MP, in January 1898. Under the slogan 'the land for the people', it called for the redistribution of large estates among the small farmers. It grew quickly and by 1900 claimed to have 462 branches and between 60,000 to 80,000 members. It also had its own newspaper, edited by O'Brien. John Redmond assumed the presidency of the UIL in 1900 on reunification of the Irish Parliamentary Party which had split in 1890 over the continued leadership of Charles Stewart Parnell. The UIL became the party's constituency organisation and in 1901 it had around 100,000 members.
35 *Hansard* (Commons) 4th ser. 107, 447–48, 1 May 1902.
36 *Waterford Standard*, 9 Jan. 1904.
37 Gwynn, S. (1926), p. 301.
38 Redmond, J. E. et al. (1907), *The Irish Party and its Assailants—its Policy Vindicated: A record of Achievement* (A pamphlet of speeches), p. 53, (Ref. Ir 300), NLI.
39 Muenger (1981), pp. 77–84.
40 Fitzpatrick, 'The overflow of the deluge' in MacDonagh and Mandle (eds.) (1986).

among urban working-class youths that Sinn Fein had to propagandise against it.[41]

Nationalist disapproval of the army carried little force with pre-war 'green redcoats' who were mostly poor, apolitical and saw themselves as joining 'the army' rather than 'the British army'. The decision to enlist was more frequently a matter of practicalities than of ideologies. Nor was Bishop Sheehan deterred from becoming chaplain to the military in Cork early in his career.[42] Many families contributed generations of men to the military.[43] In 1878 Irishmen constituted about 22 per cent of the army's manpower and were widely distributed throughout the infantry regiments. By 1913 this had decreased to nine per cent. But it was one of the few institutions which reflected the idea of Ireland being truly part of a United Kingdom.[44]

At the Waterford celebrations of the re-unification of the IPP in 1900, a county councillor observed that 'Irish blood was being freely poured out in defence of the Crown of England' in South Africa. And when Redmond declared 'we have given to Great Britain, to the British Army, some of her bravest soldiers, and her most able and successful generals', there was cheering.[45] A memorial in Waterford's Christ Church records that Sir W. G. D. Goff's son, William Ernest, aged 28, was killed in action in South Africa the following month.

The Irish militia, although small in numbers, was one vehicle through which service with the British military achieved respectability in the eyes of nationalists. Willie Redmond held a commission with the 3rd Battalion Royal Irish Regiment (the old city of Wexford militia) before resigning it to take part in the Land League movement[46] and being imprisoned.[47] A strong supporter of the militia throughout his life, he saw it as being an indigenous force. He told the House of Commons that it was made up of men of 'the same religion and of the same habits as the people'.[48] However, raised in 1793, the Waterford militia had strong Anglo-Irish connections and the colours of the old regiment were 'religiously kept' at Dromana, the seat of Henry Villiers-Stuart.

In 1886 the actual strength of the militia, including permanent staff, was approximately 355. This fell short of the authorised strength by about 50 per cent.[49] Militiamen annually undertook six weeks' training, and their embarkation at the city's quays on a river steamer bound for Duncannon Fort added to the generally active military presence.

In 1900, as reports of casualties at Ladysmith were being received, the 3rd Royal Irish Regiment left Waterford by steamer for Aldershot[50] and Willie Redmond claimed militiamen were being pressurised into serving abroad. Later,

41 Garvin (1981), p. 121.
42 *Waterford News*, 2 Jan. 1892. This edition contains a brief biography of Bishop Sheehan. He was appointed bishop of the diocese of Waterford and Lismore in December 1891 at 47 years of age. From Bantry, he was ordained in 1868. First appointed as gaol chaplain, he was then appointed to the curacy of St Patrick's and chaplain to the military in Cork before becoming bishop.
43 Harris, H. (1968), *The Irish Regiments in the First World War*, Cork, p. 1.
44 Hanham, H. J., 'Religion and nationality in the mid-Victorian army' in M. R. D. Foot (ed.) (1973), *War and Society*, London, pp. 159–81.
45 *Waterford News*, 27 Apr. 1900.
46 The Land League was founded in 1879 as a reaction to the worsening conditions experienced by tenant farmers during the depression of the late 1870s. It was supported by the Irish Republican Brotherhood, the fenians and the Irish Parliamentary Party. This linking of the revolutionary, the agrarian and the constitutional elements came to be known as the 'new departure'. According to its constitution, the league was a 'moral force' rather than a 'physical force' movement, the most powerful weapon employed by the league being the 'boycott'. However, during the violent phase of the land war (1879–82), the tenants were led by the Land League. Its primary aim was to secure the three 'F's—Fair rent, Free sale and Fixity of tenure—for tenants. It brought together people of different classes, religions and political persuasion. The league was suppressed by the government in 1881 but the Land Act of the same year met the three Fs and the league's demands.
47 Redmond, W. (1917), *Trench Pictures from France*, London, p. 14.
48 Denman (1992a).
49 *Waterford News*, 6 Aug. 1886.
50 *Waterford News*, 12 Jan. 1900.

however, about 320 officers and men of the Waterford militia left for garrison duty in Plymouth, thereby releasing regulars for the South African war. Their departure caused considerable excitement. 'Fully six thousand people' surged around the quays to see them off [51] and in 1903 the wives, children and permanent staff of the part-time soldiers were given a treat at the city's infantry barracks.[52]

A resident recalled the scarlet-coated British soldiers and how the 'big money they always spent so freely made the district a busy and lively thoroughfare'. Military bands, orders barked out on the barrack square and shrill trumpet calls enlivened the streets and made locals 'walk with a brisker pace and a more upright gait'.[53] The business which garrisons brought to towns is considered by one authority to have been a more significant factor than nationalism in determining Irish attitudes towards the army.[54]

As well as adding to local prosperity, garrisons enriched local social and sporting life and there were many romances and marriages. In Waterford, the Garrison Cricket Club, which was represented on the city's Cricket League,[55] played fixtures with The Island XI,[56] a reference to Fitzgerald's Little Island. Banquo Redmond, whose newspaper was later to denounce Waterford's 'shoneenism', was appointed a committee member at the first general meeting of the newly formed cricket club in 1887,[57] nearly three years after the Gaelic Athletic Association (GAA) was

founded and banned cricket as a 'denationalising plague'.[58] And in 1909, P. F. Murphy, secretary of the Christendom Cricket Club, and of the Waterford Cricket League, was also the honorary secretary of the GAA's Waterford Commercial Football Club, as well as being president of the Catholic Club. A captain serving with the 72nd Battery Royal Field Artillery in Waterford before the war, who was an 'ardent follower of the Waterford hounds', wrote to the mayor giving an account of how men of the battery were faring in the war. The letter was published in the *Waterford News* under the title 'Waterford Battery in Action'.[59]

But conflicts of interest continually surfaced. In 1899 city councillors petitioned Lord Roberts to increase the garrison numbers for a 'commercial or pecuniary purpose'.[60] The United Trades Club, founded about 1878 and renamed the Federated Trades and Labour Union in the 1890s to reflect the unionisation of the unskilled worker, demanded that the names of those involved be published. It considered the councillors' action 'reprehensible' and inconsistent with the duties of nationalist municipal representatives. The editor of the *Waterford News* refused to print individual names as all members of the corporation were in favour of the decision on the 'not unreasonable ground that a large sum would annually accrue to the city'.[61]

However, troops were withdrawn from Waterford and Wexford and relocated in Kilkenny and Clonmel. This followed a spate of incidents in

---

51 *Waterford News*, 11 May 1900.
52 *Waterford Standard*, 10 Jan. 1903.
53 CARA, *Ballybricken and Thereabouts*, pp. 123–26.
54 Muenger (1981), pp. 77–79.
55 *Thom's Directory*.
56 *Waterford News*, 22 May 1903.
57 *Waterford News*, 1 July 1887.
58 Mandle, W. F. (ed.), 'The I.R.B. and the beginnings of the Gaelic Athletic Association' in A. O'Day (Intro) (1987), *Reactions to Nationalism*, London, pp. 95–115. The Gaelic Athletic Association, an amateur sporting association, was created in 1884 for the purpose of preserving and cultivating Irish national pastimes. It was anti-British in outlook and banned its members from participating in non-Gaelic games. Those serving in the crown forces were also banned from membership.
59 *Waterford News*, 5 Feb. 1915.
60 By the turn of the century the city's barracks accommodated fewer troops than the number for which it was originally designed. The artillery barracks could accommodate 54 men, officers and NCOs and 66 horses and the infantry barracks about 228 men, officers and NCOs and 18 hospital patients in addition to 6 horses. These figures are taken from a plan of the artillery barracks corrected to July 1909 and a plan of the infantry barracks corrected to Mar. 1903 (PRO WO 78/3085); in 1911 there were only 125 personnel living in the barracks. In addition there were 45 family members (*Census 1911*).
61 *Waterford News*, 14 Jan. 1899.

which Willie Redmond and local authorities were involved in refusing the army a range of services and facilities. The loss of about £2,000 annually persuaded the Wexford corporation to ask for the reintroduction of troops, but this was refused. Withdrawal of the troops, however, is more likely to have been the consequence of a policy of rationalisation rather than a response to local opposition. Concern about difficulties created by the scattering of garrisons had been long-standing and the new Rosslare to Fishguard connection was part of an improved mobilisation scheme.

In 1912 Colonel W. B. Hickie argued that the existing troop disposition was based on obsolete thinking and he made a number of recommendations.[62] However, the debate about the Irish role in mobilisation remained inconclusive. The use of militia and volunteers to create a special reserve in Britain to support any British expeditionary force, and a territorial force for use in home defence, did not extend to Ireland. Procrastination and subterfuge by influential figures in the War Office who did not trust the Irish with their own home defence force delayed a final decision. Mobilisation in August 1914 therefore involved sending British and Irish regular troops stationed in Ireland to the front and replacing them with British territorials for home defence in Ireland.[63]

Apart from its own garrison, Waterford was an important centre for troops in transit to or from the Fermoy, Clonmel and Kilkenny barracks. Before the Rosslare to Fishguard link was completed, it was common for troops to be seen loading and unloading ammunition and kit on the Waterford quays. The city's population therefore was accustomed to the sight of army personnel and there was a closeness to, and familiarity with, army life. This may well have made it easier and more acceptable for men to enlist, as well as providing an incentive.

Attitudes of Waterford citizens towards Field-Marshal Lord Roberts exemplify the ambivalent posture of many towards the army. Roberts was a committed unionist and cooperated with Henry Wilson, General Rawlinson, Bonar Law and Sir Edward Carson during the Curragh 'mutiny'.[64] He was prepared to declare the home rule bill unconstitutional if the king signed it and, denigrating the new territorial force in Britain, he worked to introduce conscription into the United Kingdom.

An important patron for the young Henry Wilson, Roberts supported the signing of the Ulster covenant[65] and suggested the name of a commander for the Ulster Volunteer Force.[66] And Wilson, a friend of General Hubert Gough who led the group of officers involved in the Curragh incident, assisted Roberts in preparing

---

62 Hickie, W. B. (c. 1912), 'A suggestion for the better distribution of regular infantry battalions in the Irish Command' (Hickie Papers, 8095), NLI.

63 Muenger (1981), Chapter VI.

64 The Curragh 'mutiny' occurred in March 1914 shortly before the third home rule bill, which was strongly opposed by unionists, was due to come into force. It was intended to use the army to protect arms depots in Ulster and officers were told they would be dismissed if they refused to carry out the orders. Fifty-six officers at the Curragh military camp decided to resign rather than move against the Ulster opponents of home rule. General Sir Hubert De La Poer Gough (1870–1963), who said if the issue had to be decided in open conflict he would rather fight with than against Ulster, chaired the meeting. He communicated the officers' decision to the County Longford-born General Sir Henry Wilson (1864–1922) who supported it. Wilson, a staunch unionist, a supporter of the Orange Order and MP for County Down in 1921, was assassinated by republicans in June 1922. Andrew Bonar Law (1858–1923) became leader of the Conservatives in 1911 and in 1912 had assured unionists he would support Ulster's resistance to home rule. Sir Edward Carson (1854–1935), Dublin-born leader of the Irish Unionist Party, led the government's fight against the 'plan of campaign', signed the Ulster covenant and threatened that Ulster would establish its own government if home rule was granted.

65 Copies of 'Ulster's solemn league and covenant' which bound the signatories to use 'all means which may be found necessary to defeat the present conspiracy to set up a home rule parliament in Ireland', were distributed throughout the province and signed by more than 200,000 people on 28 September 1912 in a ceremony which evoked an atmosphere of religious devotion.

66 Beckett, I. F. W. (ed.) (1986), The Army and the Curragh Incident 1914, London, pp. 5–6, 54–55, 225–26. The Ulster Volunteer Force was founded in January 1913 for the purpose of resisting the implementation of home rule. Finance was provided by Ulster businessmen and landed gentry. Sir Edward Carson was a leader and subscribed £10,000. Aid also came from England; Rudyard Kipling provided £50,000 and a poem.

his pro-conscription speeches.[67] Appointed as commander-in-chief, Ireland in 1895 he repeatedly put the view that in the event of mobilisation, the Irish militia should be sent to Britain for duty and replaced by British regulars and militia because of the 'possibility of disaffection'.[68]

However, Roberts had close links with Waterford. His great-grandfather designed many of the city's major buildings, including the Protestant and Catholic cathedrals, City Hall, the leper hospital and the Chamber of Commerce, and he was also responsible for the design, in part, of Lord Waterford's seat at Curraghmore. His grandfather was a well-known local clergyman and his father was in the Waterford militia before joining the regular army. Roberts himself lived in Waterford for some years as a boy and married in the city's St Patrick's Church in 1859.

Under a heading 'General Roberts of Waterford', the *Waterford News* praised the general's march at the head of 10,000 from Kabul to Kandahar in 1881 and his 'brilliant victory'. Although there were no Irish regiments on the march, the newspaper noted that Irish soldiers served in the British regiments which participated. The report concluded: 'the Afghan hero is a Waterford man by birth .... The son of the abused Celt did the work, and again the "Sassenach" gets the profit and the glory'.[69]

The corporation unanimously agreed to confer the freedom of the city on him in 1893. Cornelius Redmond, the strongly nationalist father of Banquo, was among those attending the ceremony in City Hall and the mayor boasted that 'our country has given many brilliant generals and gallant soldiers to the British Army'. In acknowledgement, Roberts replied that he was 'proud of being an Irishman'. While resident in the city he stayed with F. G. Bloomfield of Newpark, the Conservative so heavily defeated by Richard Power, the Parnellite candidate, when he contested the city seat in the general election of 1885. Among those attending a dinner in his honour at the County and City Club were W. G. D. Goff, Herbert W. Goff, Sir R. J. Paul and A. E. Graves.[70]

A Waterford soldier serving with Roberts in the Boer War was disturbed by British tactics: 'it is our awful fate to witness and hear the cries of the women and children looking on at their houses and homes and all their belongings burned. I am fairly sick of it. ... The fellows in the regiment are going wild over it.' But when he read of a proposal to erect a memorial to Roberts in Waterford he was 'glad to hear of it' and hoped it would be successful.[71]

When Lord Roberts died of natural causes in France during November 1914, the corporation proposed a motion of condolence. Believing that it was 'just retribution' that Roberts should have 'fallen in this war which through Carson he has done so much to bring about', Councillor Edward Walsh none the less observed he was a 'distinguished Irishman, he was a brave soldier, he was a father of the men who fought with him, and in every way he was a man the world might well be proud of'.[72]

The unionist *Waterford Standard* probably reflected the view of many local nationalists when it opined that Waterford people 'felt particular pride in the grand old man of the Army'. On news of his death, flags were flown at half-mast on City Hall and on shipping in the harbour. The Harbour Board passed a resolution of sympathy: 'we have always been proud of him as a great soldier and as a man who has done a great deal for the country and army and navy. ... He was a great Irishman'.[73]

---

67 Jeffery, K. (ed.) (1985), *The Military Correspondence of Field Marshal Sir Henry Wilson 1918–1922*, London, pp. 1–17.
68 Muenger (1981), pp. 286–87, 339, 377.
69 *Waterford News*, 4 Feb. 1881. In fact, although he was brought home at the age of two years, Roberts was born in Cawnpore, India, where his father was a lieutenant-colonel commanding the 101st Royal Bengal Fusiliers, which subsequently became the 1st Battalion Royal Munster Fusiliers.
70 *Waterford Standard*, 18 Nov. 1914.
71 *Hansard* (Commons) 4th ser. 89, 240, 15 Feb. 1901.
72 *Waterford Standard*, 2 Dec. 1914.
73 *Waterford Standard*, 18 Nov. 1914.

Roberts's name was subsequently evoked to promote enlistment during the First World War. Lieutenant Lynch, a Waterford man, when recruiting in the city told his audience that Lord Roberts was the last local man to win a Victoria Cross and Waterford needed another one.[74] And in December 1915, Redmond referred to Roberts as 'that great Waterford soldier ... [who] made the name of Waterford in military circles all over the world ever honoured and known'.[75]

Therefore, despite an ambiguous hostility towards the army in some quarters, a number of Irish recruits, like their British counterparts, were probably driven to enlist by an 'intense, almost mystical patriotism, and [by the] inarticulate elitism of an imperial power's working class'.[76]

However, cultural and political differences separating Irishman and Briton could be underestimated as well as over-emphasised. In 1900 Willie Redmond told members of the House of Commons that soldiers in the Irish regiments were mostly from the south, Catholic and nationalists. He warned them, 'you must not imagine because these men have entered your army that they are not in sympathy with us [the IPP], because they are.'[77] And Augustine Birrell, the Irish chief secretary between 1907 and the Easter Rising, recognised that the loyalty of men like James English could not be taken for granted. Giving evidence to the enquiry into the rebellion he said:

> The spirit of what to-day is called Sinn Feinism is mainly composed of old hatred and distrust of the British connection, always noticeable in all classes, and in all places, varying in degree, and finding different ways

of expression, but always there as the background of Irish politics and character.[78]

Thus, a pre-war British army Irish recruit pledged loyalty to Queen Victoria but told the recruiting officer, 'if she or her leaders ever turns with cruelty on the Irish race, I will be the first that will raise my sword to fight against her'.[79] And Irish nationalist sensibilities could be easily offended. When in October 1914 T. P. O'Connor was reported as saying that Irishmen should take up arms until there was 'a triple steel-clad fortress behind which stood the millions of the British race', he was rebuked in an editorial for inferring that the Irish were subsumed in a greater British race.[80]

There were two key differences between recruits such as James English and his British counterpart. These were his Catholicism and his Irish nationalist traditions.

III

Religion was central to the personal lives of 'most Irishmen' throughout the period after the famine.[81] In 1907 a visitor observed, 'no one can visit Ireland without being impressed by the intensity of Catholic belief there, and by the fervour of its outward manifestation'.[82] And Lieutenant Lyon of the Leinster Regiment, a Protestant born in County Longford and educated in a Jesuit school, noted that among all denominations there was a great respect for 'the cloth'.[83] However, Catholicism and Protestantism differed in their consequences as well as in their teachings.

Sean O'Faolain's experiences of his Catholi-

74 *Munster Express*, 24 July 1915.
75 *Waterford Standard*, 4 Dec. 1915.
76 Keegan, J. (1978), *The Face of Battle*, Harmondsworth, pp. 219–221.
77 Denman (1992a).
78 *Report of Royal Commission on the Rebellion in Ireland, Evidence and Appendix* (British Parliamentary Papers, 1916 [Cd 8311] XI.185), p. 5.
79 Karsten (1983).
80 *Evening News*, 20 Oct. 1914.
81 Lyons (1973), p. 17.
82 Miller (1973) p. 1.
83 Lyon, W. A., typescript memoirs, Vol. 1, p. 11 (Lyon Papers, 80/25/1), IWM.

cism was shared by a great many. Reared as a 'very pious Irish Catholic boy', he described his faith as filling him from the age of four onwards with a 'profound mistrust of the reality of material phenomena; an early fear that all life may be a dream and all this physical world a deception'. It was an attitude which he thought could not be wholly eradicated and in guaranteeing to get him through 'this unpleasant world to [his] happy destination in the next', his faith failed to 'develop the character of men as social animals'.[84]

Catherine English recalled the time when city lives were ordered by religious duty. When the bells rang in the priory, Bridge Street, for instance, the 'richer' people responded by taking food to the monks. On an altar in her home, an oil lamp burned day and night before a statue of the Sacred Heart. Women of the period had a great faith and total trust in God which helped them immensely.[85]

Catherine said the rosary with her children and went to mass daily. She wore a scapular which bore a medal of the Sacred Heart and also wore a cincture of what is thought to have been the Third Order of Saint Francis. A habit in which she was to be buried was paid for weekly. Miracles and revelations confirmed the faith and the Waterford, Limerick and Western Railway Company ran regular pilgrimage trains from Waterford to Knock.[86] The community was superstitious. Catherine's daughter, Margaret, remembered how she was known locally as a blessed and lucky woman. Her neighbours and the local fish women came to her for the 'handsome', a ritual involving her spitting on a silver threepenny coin which was then returned to them and brought them luck.

A religion-dominated culture meant that considerable authority was exercised by Catholic priests. For those with a commitment to their faith, the priest's role as confessor, absolver and indispen-sable intermediary was central to their spiritual existence, a position of authority naturally spilling over into secular matters. James English was a practising and an apparently devout Catholic, and his decision to enlist is likely to have been affected by his religious beliefs in two respects.

Firstly, his faith was exploited for propaganda and recruiting purposes. And secondly, the views of Bishop Sheehan and the local priests had a significant impact on his attitudes. Father Patrick Francis Flynn, a priest in Ballybricken from about the early 1880s and parish priest from 1890 to 1914,[87] and Father Thomas F. Furlong who succeeded him, would have been most influential. But the views of other priests such as Father William B. O'Donnell, the parish priest of St Patrick's in 1914 and 1915 who actively engaged in recruiting campaigns, were also important.

The religious role and status of priests made them social leaders and people lived in awe of them. Their special place in society was acknowledged by the Waterford and Tramore Railway which permitted free travel to members of all religious orders in Waterford. And when Fitzgerald of The Little Island refurbished his ancestral home in 1900, Bishop Sheehan and Fathers Tom Furlong and W. B. O'Donnell as well as Lord and Lady Waterford were invited to the celebrations. They admired Fitzgerald's 'magnificent paintings' and participated in an afternoon's coursing after which prizes were given out by Lady Waterford. According to the *Waterford News*, on a day 'the like of which was never witnessed before in such close proximity to Waterford', they were entertained in the castle.[88]

A labourer's illiteracy created dependence on the clergy in practical matters but priests were also attributed with the mystique, power and authority which those with a wider education generate among unschooled people.[89] Many

84 O'Faolain (1976).
85 Lankford (1980) p. 44.
86 O'Neill (1986a).
87 CARA, *Ballybricken and Thereabouts*, pp. 7–8; *Waterford News*, 12 May 1894.
88 *Waterford News*, 30 Mar. 1900.
89 Fitzpatrick (1977), pp. 88–89.

priests cultivated a paternalistic attitude and there were references to 'our simple people' or observations that 'the people require to be treated ... like children'.

In the view of Lord Cowper, lord lieutenant between 1880 and 1882, priests exercised an 'extraordinary influence over the people'.[90] And during discussion of the draft 1898 Local Government Act, which handed over power to the nationalists by abolishing the grand jury and introduced proportional representation and female suffrage to the United Kingdom, Chief Secretary Gerald Balfour argued forcefully for the exclusion of the clergy from office because of the Catholic priests' 'unique spiritual hold' over their flock.[91] Although observations by W. P. Ryan[92] and James Hannay were no doubt coloured by their quarrels with the hierarchy, and in Ryan's case by his socialist beliefs, they are none the less valid opinions. Priestly power is a theme which dominates Ryan's *The Plough and the Cross*. In it, it is observed 'the clergy are ... powerful, and the people ... docile'.[93] In 1907, along with the 'political boss', Hannay considered priests one of 'the twin tyrannies which are crushing our lives out'.[94]

A recruit in the Royal Dublin Fusiliers, born of Irish parents in the slums of London's Canning Town, was shocked at the violent authority wielded by an indigenous Irish priest in Cork. He recalled how the small priest challenged a 'big, broad', poverty-stricken man of well over six feet for not attending Sunday mass or taking holy communion. After an exchange of angry words the priest slapped the man's face and 'kicked the poor bloke right up his arse and this fellow just stood and took it from the little holy man'.[95] And an officer in the Irish Guards found the threat to write to a soldier's parish priest an adequate deterrent in the case of misdemeanours.[96]

James English's daughter Margaret recalled Father Tom Furlong as being 'stern' in the confessional. At mass he frequently scolded the 'Barrack Street men' for being 'loafers, idlers and cursers'. Everyone was expected to show the priest due respect. Men doffed their hats in the streets and women covered their heads. People were publicly condemned from the altar for offences such as leaving children outside the pub when they were inside drinking, and they either corrected their behaviour or were subjected to censure by their neighbours. Those arriving late for mass and those women whose heads were not covered, commonly with a shawl, would be sent home.

According to one authority, the 'vast majority' of priests were generally sons of well-off tenant farmers who shared a common belief that social classes were fixed in accordance with the will of God[97] and they therefore reinforced the status quo. But Canon Tom Furlong's old friend Father Kavanagh of New York was a Ballybricken man who frequently visited the hill.[98] However, priests generally opposed any changes in the social order in which they held a central place, the bishops resisting compulsory education, for instance. But, as has been seen, Bishop Sheehan pushed for government funding of technical education, and in 1909 an expatriate County Waterford man blamed 'native landlordism and the rule of British capital-

90   Woods, C. J. (1968), 'The Catholic Church and Irish politics 1879–1892' (unpublished PhD thesis), Nottingham University, pp. 80, 112–13.
91   Gailey, A. (1984), 'Unionist rhetoric and Irish Local Government Reform 1895–9', *Irish Historical Studies*, 24, pp. 52–68.
92   William Patrick Ryan (1867–1942), born in County Tipperary, worked for a time as a journalist in London under T. P. O'Connor. A renowned socialist, he returned to Ireland in 1905 as editor of the *Irish Peasant*. In it, he criticised the Catholic Church for its paternalism and its opposition to nationalist movements. The Church used its influence to have the paper closed down.
93   Ryan, W. P. (1910), *The Plough and the Cross*, Dublin, p. 33.
94   Fitzpatrick (1977), p. 101.
95   Roworth, J. W., 'Experiences of "E. Casey" ', unpublished MS (Roworth Papers, 80/40/1), IWM.
96   Nelson (1973–74).
97   O'Shea, J. (1982), *Priest, Politics and Society in Post-famine Ireland*, Dublin, pp. 13–16, 119–21.
98   *Waterford News*, 16 Apr. 1915.

ists' as well as the lack of brotherhood for having driven thousands of 'unskilled, uneducated and penniless' Irish abroad.[99] But in 1894 Waterford city was one of 30 out of the 118 municipal bodies which, empowered to act as local attendance authorities, had done nothing effectual in enforcing the Irish Education Act of 1892.[100] By January 1900, however, the school attendance committee had initiated a number of prosecutions. In one case a fine of 3s 6d with costs was imposed and attendance orders made.[101]

In 1901 Father P. F. Flynn, a member of the school attendance committee, claimed that there had been a great improvement in attendance. A new school for 300 children had been built and other convent schools enlarged.[102] None the less, Bishop Sheehan complained that in 1909 1,500 out of 5,000 children on the city's school rolls never attended. 'Mooching' was routine and children sometimes had the impression no one cared.[103] The bishop's concern was less for the failure to equip them for responsible, independent adulthood, than for the moral dangers to which they were exposed by roaming the streets. 'The parents were the securities before God of the morals of those children, and God would call them to dread account one day for the manner in which they had filled this great responsibility.'[104]

His Catholic faith, the authority it gave to priests and their social and political attitudes were therefore important aspects conditioning the labourer's willingness to enlist in response to the urging of his religious leaders. But nationalist politics also had an influence which was three-fold.

Firstly, like his Catholicism, it further cemented community homogeneity, strengthening common loyalties and exposing him to a variety of communal pressures.

Secondly, it generated a sufficiently powerful personal and local loyalty to John Redmond and the constitutionalist cause for the labourer to respond as an individual, or as part of a social group, to Redmond's call to arms. And it had the potency to override other loyalties and interests which might otherwise have militated against enlistment. The grip of Parnellite politics on Waterford city, it has been claimed, prevented the formation of an independent labour movement, postponed the rise of labour for 20 years and ensured the future ascendancy of Redmondism.[105]

And thirdly, by distracting attention away from the problems of the urban labourer, nationalist politics helped to perpetuate the poor economic and social conditions which were partly responsible for his enlistment.

IV

The first problem in assessing how far nationalist feelings had an impact on his decision to enlist, is deciding to what extent, if at all, James English experienced nationalism. The claim that the 'working-class Catholic population having little to lose, was almost unanimous in its desire for Home Rule'[106] is too general and too imprecise to be convincing.

Unskilled labourers lacked the leisure time, the

99 Wheatley, J. (1909), *The Catholic Workingman*, Glasgow. The Irish-born son of migrants, Wheatley progressed from the Lanarkshire pits to become a successful businessman, county and city councillor, an Independent Labour Party MP and a minister in the first Labour government in 1922 (Howell, D. (1986), *A Lost Left: Three Studies in Socialism and Nationalism*, Manchester, pp. 12–13, 227–287).
100 Akenson (1970), pp. 344–49. The 1892 act made education for children between 6 and 14 years of age effectively free and compulsory. However, it was 'riddled with absurdities and inadequacies'. The act extended to some towns only and did not apply to rural areas. A variety of conditions also allowed many children to be exempted.
101 *Waterford News*, 12 Jan. 1900.
102 *Waterford News*, 19 Apr. 1901.
103 Information from the author's father who was a regular 'moocher'.
104 *Waterford News*, 21 May 1909.
105 O'Connor, E. (1979), 'The influence of Redmondism on the development of the Labour Movement in Waterford in the 1890s', *Decies*, 10, pp. 37–42.
106 Muenger (1981), pp. 26–29.

political sophistication and the educational wherewithal to formulate their own concept of nationalism or to fully comprehend its implications. The general standard of education was considered to be so low in Clare that, according to a police report, the views of the people were 'drawn from the local paper, the priest and the national schoolmaster'. 'Incuriosity', it has been claimed, was one of the foundations of organised nationalism.[107]

Generally, the attitude of Irish labourers is unlikely to have been very different from that of unskilled British workers. A contemporary Staffordshire labourer thought that all they wanted was 'enough money as they could get a drink. And then I think the rest of their pleasure was getting kids ... it was drink and then come in— and bed. That was it'.[108] Recent evidence also suggests a 'good deal' of the working class in the 1880s and 1890s were 'largely apolitical, apathetic and resigned to a life which combined the constant dread of unemployment and poverty with fear of outside forces threatening traditional patterns of life'.[109] In the view of one writer, pre-war Irish recruits were 'no more political than are most of the very poor of any other land'.[110] Allowing for W. P. Ryan's bias, there are still reasonable grounds for his observation that when a nationalist procession, representing 'some living and hopeful idea', passed through poor Dublin areas in 1912, it was in 'awesome contrast' to

the inertia and weariness and cold, clammy hopelessness of those street and quayside crowds .... They look like people who have no healthy interests, no fresh and natural desires, nothing that the wildest imagination could call dreams; people who go through life as a narrow, burdensome, unintelligible pilgrimage; they have lost the capacity of sympathy, understanding, and hope.[111]

Arthur Griffith[112] considered that 'Ireland will never be freed by day-labourers'[113] and claims that the Irish were 'exceptionally politicized' have been contested. Fewer people took part in politics than in religious life. At the time of the IPP split there was no shortage of cash but the party's finances were critical as it was the Church to which people donated 'immense gifts'. Nor was there a wholesale rejection of British ideology or institutions. In 1895 Archbishop Croke[114] complained that 'the country is notorious and indeed, shamefully apathetic. There is no desire for Home Rule.'[115] And in the opinion of one historian, nationalism 'was above all a rural preoccupation'. The organisational urge which lay at the centre of Irish nationalism was more likely to be manifested in the intense corporate life of a rural parish than in the town. Rural life was intricately structured and it incorporated political clubs which provided music, dances, lectures and plays as 'barricades against boredom'. The 'transient, characterless quality' of urban populations made the clubs redundant in the towns.[116]

107 Fitzpatrick (1977), pp. 90, 92.
108 Thompson (1975), pp. 241–42.
109 Levy, C., 'Education and self-education: staffing the early ILP' in C. Levy (ed.) (1987), *Socialism and the Intelligentsia 1880–1914*, London, pp. 135–210.
110 Karsten (1983).
111 Ryan, W. P. (1912), *The Pope's Green Island*, London, p. 276.
112 Arthur Griffith (1871–1922), journalist, politician and active Gaelic League and Irish Republican Brotherhood member, was also a Sinn Fein leader. It was he who advocated a dual monarchy for Ireland and the rest of the United Kingdom, with Ireland as self-governing and economically self-sufficient, her industries being protected by tariffs. These ideas were adopted as Sinn Fein policy.
113 Clarkson (1970), p. 283.
114 Thomas William Croke (1824–1902). As Archbishop of Cashel between 1875 and 1902, he supported land agitation and other forms of nationalism. He was a Land League supporter and devised a plan whereby the 'plan of campaign' could continue despite condemnation by the Vatican. The government considered prosecuting him as author of the 'no tax manifesto', a published letter in which he condemned the payment of taxes as they were used to suppress nationalism.
115 O'Day, A. 'The Irish Problem' in T. R. Gourvish and A. O'Day (eds.) (1988), *Later Victorian Britain 1867–1900*, London, pp. 229–49.
116 Fitzpatrick, D. (1978), 'Geography of Irish nationalism 1910–1921', *Past and Present*, 78, pp. 113–44.

But urban communities could also be prone to localised nationalism. Ballybricken, with a community structure quite different from that of Tower Ward or Ferrybank, had the local traditions, heroes, associations and institutions which were the vehicles of nationalism.[117] Nor was there the kind of abrupt transition between the urban and surrounding rural communities which allows each to be treated as a discrete entity of its own.[118] Ballybricken's resident population was relatively stable, thus allowing a sense of community to exist. Although 73 per cent of the city's population were city or county-born in 1911, 97 per cent of Thomas's Avenue residents were from the city.[119]

City dwellers had as much need to relieve boredom as country residents. The several city bands, with names redolent of a nationalist culture, served this purpose. The Thomas Francis Meagher Brass and Reed Band, which became known as the Sinn Fein Band, and the T. F. Meagher Fife and Drum Band commemorated the city's own Young Ireland hero. The Erin's Hope Prize Band recalled the abortive fenian landing at Dungarvan. The Charles Stewart Parnell Band, the John Mitchel Fife and Drum Band and the Wolfe Tone Fife and Drum Band all echoed Ireland's nationalist traditions.

The city's network of nationalist organisations included branches of the UIL, the Irish National Foresters,[120] the Ancient Order of Hibernians (AOH),[121] the Gaelic League and a battalion of the Irish Volunteers.[122] They combined social with political and military functions and were sufficiently embracing to smother any embryonic independent labour movement or any opposition to Redmond and the Irish party.

The Ballybricken labourer was more politically conscious than his British counterpart and labourers in some other Irish urban or rural areas. Recollections that James English was an ardent 'Redmondite' and was 'for the English' undoubtedly reflected the extent of Redmond's and the IPP's grip on local politics and of James English's understanding of what constitutionalism and Redmond's war policy meant. Catherine English followed an established tradition by voting for Redmond's son in the 1918 elections.

The process by which an illiterate urban labourer constructed his version of nationalism combined several elements.

V

Waterford's parish priests were politically active. So were their curates on occasion. Fathers P. F. Flynn and W. B. O'Donnell played significant political roles in Ballybricken. Although even the poorest men sometimes formed independent opinions, priests were important local agents for transmitting nationalist ideas. The altar was used as a political platform and there were accusations of 'spiritual intimidation' and of 'the ignorance of simple-minded parishioners ... [being] shamefully and criminally abused'.[123] From 1890 onwards priests were considered to have more influence than any other body of men in choosing parliamentary representatives,[124] and they were the chief professional group in elec-

---

117 Edwards, 'Ireland' in Edwards et al. (eds.) (1968), *Celtic Nationalism*, London, p. 70.
118 Garvin (1981), Chap. V.
119 Of the 22 families resident in Thomas's Avenue (Wheelbarrow Lane) at the time of the 1901 census, seven were still there in 1911. But the families moving tended to stay in Ballybricken: for example, John Dooley and his family moved the short distance to Harrington's Lane (Census returns, National Archives, Dublin).
120 Founded in 1877 as a benefit society, the Irish National Foresters' leaders included members of the Irish Republican Brotherhood and other nationalist organisations. To qualify for membership, applicants had to be Irish by birth or descent.
121 An important part of the nationalist political machinery in Ulster, the Ancient Order of Hibernians was founded in 1641 but took its modern form as a Catholic reaction in 1838 to Ulster's Orange Order which was revitalised in its opposition to Catholic emancipation and repeal of the union. The Ancient Order of Hibernians gave its support to the Irish Parliamentary Party.
122 The Irish National Volunteers (more properly termed the Irish Volunteers) was formed in November 1913 as a reaction to the Ulster Volunteer Force, founded in January of the same year. The INV numbered about 180,000 by August 1915.
123 O'Shea (1982), pp. 48–51.
124 Gwynn (1926), pp. 270–79, 291–95.

tioneering, sometimes initiating and practically directing campaigns.[125]

Local and national newspapers were important media for creating and disseminating political opinion. In 1886 the active nationalist Harry D. Fisher, editor of the *Munster Express* and the *Waterford Daily Mail*, described how the press found its way into the remotest corners of the land where the teaching of orators 'were powerless'. It educated the masses of people in the history of their country and led them to understand the significance of liberty.[126]

The press significantly contributed to forming the opinions of workers who could read and of those who exercised influence or authority over the labourer. They would have transmitted news, views and ideas to the illiterate at places of work, in the streets in which they lived, in pubs and at social gatherings. That people knew each other through a 'general loquaciousness' which pervaded the country and cut across social lines with 'cavalier ease and familiarity' is a fair assessment.[127] News-carrying country-folk were regular visitors to the frequent Ballybricken fairs. News and gossip travelled rapidly and widely. Roving Ballybricken pig buyers were well-known carriers of news. They were politically conscious, and portraits of John Mitchel and T. F. Meagher[128] were hung in their association rooms in Ballybricken Green.

In 1877 there were nine local newspapers. Three were described as neutral, one as independent, three as conservative and two as liberal. Cost put some of them out of the range of literate labourers, the *Waterford News* for example being priced at 3d. But they were probably purchased and passed around among fellow-workers and neighbours. Three of the papers survived into 1914, by which time two further news-sheets were added. Priced at 1d, the older established newspapers were now described as nationalist with the exception of the unionist *Waterford Standard and General Advertiser*.

Proprietorship sometimes included more than one paper and was generally retained in family hands throughout the period.[129] The owners were at some stage city councillors, were Redmondite in sympathy and had strong nationalist traditions. Unimpressed with this pedigree, however, in 1905 a writer for the *United Irishman* reported that 'the ink, paper, and ideas of the Waterford Press are all of foreign manufacture'. The city badly needed a pressman with 'plenty of courage, tact and grit'.[130]

Cornelius Redmond founded the *Waterford News* in September 1848 and exhaustively reported the trial of Thomas Francis Meagher. He subsequently served as mayor and his proudest boast was that his grandfather had been executed by British troops as a rebel on Vinegar Hill in 1798. An 'enthusiastic supporter' of Daniel O'Connell[131] he also had the confidence of Meagher, who gave the *News* many manuscripts, some of them appearing in the early editions of

125 O'Shea (1982), pp. 50, 146–50.
126 *Waterford News*, 6 Aug. 1886.
127 Muenger (1981), p. 23.
128 John Mitchel (1815–75) and Thomas Francis Meagher (1822–67) were both Young Irelanders, a nationalist movement intended to establish 'internal union and external independence'. The experience of the famine (1845–49) radicalised some nationalists and in 1848 Young Ireland initiated an uprising which quickly collapsed. T. F. Meagher was born in Waterford city. Sent to France as an emissary of Young Ireland, he returned with the tricolour which was later adopted as the national flag. Mitchel and Meagher were convicted of treason for their part in the 1848 rising and transported to Tasmania. Both escaped, Mitchel subsequently returning to Ireland and Meagher going to the USA where he died.
129 *The Newspaper Press Directory* (London). An annual publication, reference has been made to all volumes between 1874 and 1916.
130 *United Irishman*, 4 Nov 1905.
131 Daniel O'Connell (1775–1847), popularly known as the 'liberator', was an outstanding 'mob orator' and founded the Catholic Association which fought elections. In 1830 he was the first Catholic in modern history to sit in the House of Commons. Founder of the Repeal Association, the aim of which was to force the repeal of the union, he split it in 1844 when he argued that Ireland should be part of a federal United Kingdom. Young Ireland militants, led by T. F. Meagher, seceded from the association and weakened it.

the paper. In 1898 Cornelius's son, known as Banquo and who had inherited the newspaper, founded the *Evening News*, the only daily newspaper and cheap at a halfpenny. The newspapers passed out of family control in 1907.[132]

During 1848 the offices of the *Waterford Chronicle* were searched for rebels and its proprietor arrested on suspicion of harbouring John O'Mahony[133] and subsequently of helping him to escape.[134] He was held at Ballybricken prison where, according to local newspaper reports, 'respected citizens ... [were] confined for loving their country'. Among those imprisoned was Thomas Fitzgerald Strange, father of Charlie, and a former owner of the *Waterford Chronicle* under whom Cornelius Redmond had served his apprenticeship. Descended from one of the oldest and most respectable local Norman families, Thomas Strange was a lawyer closely associated with Meagher. He lost business as a result of his imprisonment but the fact of his being subsequently elected mayor by 'rebels and Tories' alike[135] demonstrated the phenomenon whereby members of Waterford's elite could take opposite political positions and yet remain consistent in class attitudes.

A popular medium of mass-communication, the cinema was also used to transmit the nationalist message. Films with nationalist themes were being made in Killarney by 1910 and included titles such as *Ireland the Oppressed*.[136] A film of the 'great Home Rule demonstration' at Limerick in October 1913, was shown in the Theatre Royal. An 'epoch-making' demonstration, the theatre expected it to draw big audiences.[137]

Demonstrations and addresses by local men, national figures and Members of Parliament were frequent. Processions in Waterford passed through the city's major streets to Ballybricken Green where generally thousands of people pressed into the open space to hear their speeches. If James English was not drawn into the demonstrations, which seems improbable given the location of his residences (see Map 2), he is unlikely to have remained unexposed to, or unaffected by, their purpose and content.

O'Connell had cultivated the tradition of extreme rhetoric when addressing monster meetings, balancing the threat of violence against the lack of intention. By 1879, the home rule party's technique of presenting a modest policy in Britain but condemning the evils of foreign rule and stirring memories of ancient conflict through fiery rhetoric when in Ireland, added power to the nationalist message being expressed in songs, newspapers and books. This tradition of using 'fly-blown', 'historical' and sometimes extreme rhetoric when it suited them was a device to which all nationalist politicians resorted.[138]

But in the mixture of excitement and enthusiasm generated by zealous and constantly reiterated calls to fight for 'freedom', and by the burning torches, flaming tar barrels and the stirring national airs hammered out in the darkness by bands, labourers no doubt found relief from their pressing boredom and from their fears as

132 *Waterford News*, 23–30 Sep. 1938.
133 John O'Mahony (1815–77) was a Young Irelander who supported the rising of 1848. After its collapse he attempted to organise another one. He started the fenian movement in the USA in 1858 at the same time as the Irish Republican Brotherhood was founded in Dublin. The fenians came to connote dedication to the use of physical force in securing the independence of Ireland and the establishment of an Irish republic. Although the fenians served as an auxiliary of the Irish Republican Brotherhood, supplying it with officers, volunteers and arms, 'fenianism' came to include the Brotherhood. The fenians led an abortive rising against the British in 1867.
134 Series of newspaper cuttings (1932–1954), relating to Waterford Historical Society (ILB 94141) NLI.
135 *Waterford News*, 28 Jan. 1899.
136 Hickie, D. J. and Doherty, J. E. (1980), *A Dictionary of Irish History Since 1800*, Dublin.
137 *Munster Express*, 18 Oct. 1913.
138 Foster (1988), pp. 415, 458.

well as possibly the promise of a better future for their children. Men listening to Parnell thought 'the hour had come'[139] and the lack of any detailed political, social or legislative programme was not an obstacle to their passion.

According to the *Cork Examiner*, the Easter insurgents had acquired their knowledge of modern Irish history from ballad poetry,[140] and George Russell was 'convinced Irish enmities are perpetuated because we live by memory more than by hope'.[141] Oral traditions, popular ballads, songs and legends contributed significantly to the development of Irish nationalism. Frequently reworked and used as political propaganda, they presented versions of history which mirrored, interpreted and created the popular mind[142] and gave the illiterate urban labourer access to Irish history. They were an essential part of the politicisation process.

Waterford's own legendary figure, 'Meagher of the Sword', had strong connections with Ballybricken and his name was constantly evoked to stir nationalist passions. Meagher's revolutionary activities, his transportation to Tasmania, his subsequent escape to the United States, his and the Irish Brigade's participation in the American Civil War and his mysterious death provide the stuff of which legends are made. Arthur Griffith thought he appealed to the popular imagination in Ireland more than any other nineteenth-century Irish patriot except Robert Emmet.[143]

The fenian movement also provided Waterford people with experiences from which to fashion legends. The authorities considered Ballybricken to be 'where ... all the active Fenians of Waterford reside' and James English's parents, living in Green's Lane (see Map 2), were part of the community out of which the local movement emerged after a secret meeting in Francis Street. Several pig buyers joined the

fenians and John Dillon, a pig buyer with wide business contacts, was made the Waterford head of centre. Kneeve's Lane, in which his premises were located, entered local folklore as Dillon's Lane. Waterford was proclaimed and arrests followed. An itinerant ballad singer was seized while singing *The Fenian Men* to an audience of about 200 and the resident magistrate reported fenian arms were 'passing under our eyes along the quays of Waterford continually'. John Dillon was arrested and subsequently immortalised in a ballad denounced by the resident magistrate as 'treasonable rhymes':

> Poor Dillon, he was taken,
>   Says the Shan Van Vocht;
> For makin' a few pikes
> To fight for Ireland's rights—
> Poor Dillon he was taken,
>   Says the Shan Van Vocht

A man from Mayor's Walk was stabbed to death when crowds outside the gaol were charged by sabre-swinging mounted police, and young men singing fenian songs were the centre of incidents in Newgate Street, Barrack Street and Ballybricken. John A. Blake, MP for the city between 1857 and 1869, denounced the conditions under which men were held without trial. The findings of a county grand jury committee supported Blake and prominent Waterford unionists expressed misgivings about the way prisoners were treated.

Considerable local sympathy was generated for those arrested as fenian suspects and the intervention by Sir Robert Paul in 1866 to secure the release of a Dunmore East man was recalled by a resident in 1939. In November 1868 an estimated 2,000 to 3,000 people held a torchlight rally in Ballybricken in support of an arrested fenian suspect. And thousands joined the funeral

---

139 Edwards, 'Ireland', in Edwards et al. (eds.) (1968), pp. 177–78.
140 Edwards, O. D. and Pyle, F. (eds.) (1968), *1916: The Easter Rising*, London, p. 258.
141 *The Irish Times*, 19 Dec. 1917.
142 Thuente, M. H. 'The folklore of Irish Nationalism' in T. E. Hachey and L. J. McCaffey (eds.) (1989), *Perspectives on Irish Nationalism*, Kentucky, pp. 42–60.
143 Griffiths, A. (ed.) (1916), *Meagher of the Sword, Speeches of Thomas Francis Meagher in Ireland 1846–1848*, Dublin, pp. iii–xviii.

cortege of a local man, also arrested in 1866, who spent 18 months in prison before dying from broken health in November 1874.[144]

James English therefore grew up at a time when for many in his community the incidents and the personalities of 1848 and 1867 were vivid and frequently recalled memories.

VI

Waterford city voters were more nationalist than those in the county. In 1876 the two county parliamentary seats were held by the Conservative, Lord C. Beresford and the home ruler, Sir John Esmonde. Following the death of Esmonde, and amid 'apathy' and 'utter indifference', *The Nation* took up Isaac Butt's[145] appeal for those few who were enfranchised to elect a home ruler in the 'sacred cause of their country'. Whereas the city had elected two home rulers, Richard Power and Major O'Gorman, the county had chosen 'insincere or half-hearted Members ... [who are] of little value to Ireland'.[146]

The Catholic bishop and his clergy pledged support to any candidate who, in order of priority, was a tenant righter, a home ruler, a denominational educationalist, was for Sunday closing and who was an Irishman. The resolution ruled out one candidate who was a retired, wealthy merchant from London and also Gerald C. Purcell Fitzgerald of The Little Island who alien-

ated the clergy with his opposition to Sunday closing. James Delahunty, a former 'zealous' city MP, was elected.[147]

Among the 61 home rule MPs elected in April 1880 were Richard Power and Edmund Leamy for the city which was at that time a two-seat constituency. The home ruler and former city MP John A. Blake, and the Liberal H. W. Villiers-Stuart took the county seats. When Parnell[148] made his first visit to the city on Sunday 5 December 1880, within weeks of the government's decision to start proceedings against him, a large force of police and troops was drafted in. Special trains and steamers brought crowds into the city. Ships in the quays were draped in bunting and evergreen and principal streets were extravagantly decorated. In John Street, the birth place of James English, a green banner welcomed 'Parnell, Ireland's future President' and another hanging outside the station proclaimed 'Hail to the Chief'. He arrived to the sound of fog-signals and among the prominent citizens who met him were the mayor, Thomas F. Strange (now law adviser to the corporation), Alderman Richard Power, Cornelius Redmond, MPs Richard Power and Edmund Leamy and Fathers Tom Furlong and Patrick F. Flynn.

In Ballybricken Green, from a monster platform packed with priests and local politicians, Parnell told the crowd of an estimated 40,000, 'we will work by constitutional [means] so long as it suits us. We refuse to plunge this country

144 Upton, S., *Waterford and the Fenians*, a lecture delivered to the Waterford Historical Society and serialised in the *Waterford News*, 24 Mar.–25 Apr. 1939; *Waterford News*, 8 Oct. 1915 (reprint of Oct. 1865 report); *Waterford News*, 11 Feb. 1916 (reprint of Feb. 1866 report); *Waterford News*, 25 Feb. 1916 (reprint of Feb. 1866 report); Luanaigh, D. (1983), 'Suspected importation of fenian guns through the port of Waterford', *Decies*, **22**; Newspaper cuttings (ILB 94141), NLI.

145 Isaac Butt (1813–79) was a strong unionist who, as a result of the famine, became a federalist and advocated a parliament in Dublin to legislate on purely Irish matters. As a barrister, he defended members of Young Ireland after the '48 rising and members of the Irish Republican Brotherhood (fenians) between 1865 and 1867. He was president of the Amnesty Association, created in 1868 to campaign for the release of fenians who were imprisoned in harsh conditions after the 1867 rising. In 1870 he founded the Home Government Association with the intention of achieving a federal system of government. It contained Catholics and Protestants, Orangemen and repealers, Liberals and Conservatives and a few fenians and Young Irelanders. It was succeeded in 1873 by the Home Rule League, also founded by Butt. In the general election of 1874, the league secured 59 seats—the first step in the evolution of the Irish Parliamentary Party.

146 *Waterford News*, 22 Dec. 1876.

147 *Waterford News*, 29 Dec. 1876.

148 Charles Stewart Parnell (1846–91) unsuccessfully stood for the Home Rule League in 1874 but won the Meath seat in 1876. He joined the obstructionists in parliament and became leader of the 'new departure' in 1879. He was president of the Land League and leader of the Irish Parliamentary Party between 1880 and 1890. He introduced 'boycotting' in 1880. With the suppression of the Land League, he was imprisoned in October 1881 and released in May 1882.

into the horrors of civil war' but if there was a chance of success wouldn't they consider it their 'highest duty to give their lives for the country that gave them birth?'

The striking feature of the procession which made its way to Ballybricken was its rural character. Farmers led it, followed by agricultural labourers carrying a huge banner with a harp without the crown and inscribed 'The labourer claims his rights'. In the addresses there were calls for the abolition of 'iniquitous land laws' which had kept the Irish in 'miserable and deplorable servitude'. The bishop of Waterford and Lismore called for constitutional agitation and the Tramore parish priest referred to the Irish Party as 'a powerful engine which ... will overthrow this iniquitous land system'. He was happy to know that 'religion and patriotism is [sic] always together'.

Responding to Parnell's call for support from the municipalities as 'one of the most potent weapons we can use', city men enthusiastically embraced the cause. An alderman pledged himself and 'the men of Ballybricken' to the fight being led by 'General Parnell'. And in his speech, Edmund Leamy addressed the problems faced by rural labourers but neglected any reference to the city labourers whom he represented. However, representatives of the city's trades, most carrying banners, did take part and included in the procession were painters, coach-makers, printers, hairdressers, bakers, salters, coopers, tailors, carpenters and joiners, and victuallers.

A *Waterford Standard* editorial cynically observed that tenant farmers, 'contented and prosperous under the generous landlords', were 'conspicuous by their absence' from the celebrations. 'If it had not been for the tradesmen, shopkeepers and shop assistants from the city and surrounding districts, the show would have been very meagre, indeed.' And Parnell, 'the great agitator ... whose teachings have set the whole country ablaze', took the opportunity to join Lord Waterford's Curraghmore hounds.[149]

However, leading citizens had strong interests in the county. In 1876 gentlemen from the city made up 51 per cent of Lord Waterford's Curraghmore hunt and the money subscribed by them was 'vastly in advance' of that subscribed by county members.[150] A Tramore farmer whose interests were auctioned off in the Court House following his refusal to pay no more rent than the Griffith valuation[151], occupied a farm owned by a Ferrybank man.[152]

The absence of city labourers in the procession symbolised the coupling of nationalist politics to the land issue and the diversion of attention away from their own plight. Town dwellers pointed out they had nothing equivalent to the 1870 land act[153] to protect them and no entitlement to compensation for any improvements made by them. The lack of improvements was the cause of the 'wretched conditions' of the smaller tenements. Like the rural tenant, city tenants were also subject to rent-racking. Rents in the suburbs had increased by 50 per cent in the last six months. And in just one day during January 1881 the court of petty sessions processed 68 evictions.

But the mayor denounced the tenants' tactic of offering landlords reduced rents in pursuit of their own version of the 'three Fs'. He argued that if a city tenant did not like his house, he could leave it and find a cheaper one. But a farmer put the sweat of years into his farm and if he was put off it, all he had was the workhouse. None the less tenants established a Town Tenants League, claiming landlords had entered into 'co-partnerships' to boycott those tenants

149   *Waterford Standard*, 8 Dec. 1880; *Waterford News*, 14 and 21 Oct. 1939 (reprint of contemporary reports).
150   *Waterford News*, 8 Jan. 1876.
151   Griffith valuation referred to 1852 legislation under which land was valued at 25–30 per cent less than its letting value, for the purpose of regulating taxation not for fixing value. During the land war, the Land League insisted tenants should pay no more rent than that fixed by this valuation and if rejected by the landlord, then rents should be withheld entirely.
152   *Waterford News*, 22 Apr. 1881.
153   The Landlord and Tenant (Ireland) Act 1870 attempted to give legal status to the three Fs and to compensate rural tenants for disturbance in occupancy and for improvements, but the act proved a failure in practice.

searching for cheaper rented property. Although admitting conditions were worse for the urban than the rural labourer, priests generally failed to support the league and it was ineffective. By 1913 leadership of the organisation had been appropriated by the city's oligarchy. The posts of president and vice president were both held by councillors.[154]

If the city's leaders were unsympathetic in their response to the urban labourer's problems, they were at the forefront of political agitation in the county. Councillors, leading citizens and MPs attended and promoted Land League demonstrations. Joseph Fisher, proprietor of the *Munster Express* and the *Waterford Daily Mail* and president of the city's Land League branch,[155] Cornelius Redmond and MP Richard Power were on the platform when city MP Leamy seconded a resolution accusing the county MPs of 'masquerading' and calling upon them to do their duty in support of the nationalist cause.[156]

A large column of city-based troops and police evicted tenants on Lord Waterford's estates in May 1881 and the city's newspapers reported how bells were rung to summon a crowd of hundreds to obstruct them.[157] In a rousing speech, Joseph Fisher denounced Lord Waterford to about 500 league supporters outside the city Court House when the interests of five farms on the Curraghmore estate were auctioned off.

Pressed on why the city as well as the county had been prescribed when there had been just one case of serious assault and one case of intimidation during the six months since January 1881, Chief Secretary Forster replied that the headquarters of any system of intimidation in the county would be in the city itself. Richard Power

disagreed: 'There was not in Ireland a city so quiet ... . The government by their acts were seeking to drive people into open revolt.'[158] In July Power complained that prescription had damaged the city's trade. Forster admitted no arrests had been made in Waterford since the city was prescribed but would not agree to lift the prescription.[159]

During early August 1881 the Marquis of Waterford spoke against the land bill. He thought it sanctioned 'confiscation without compensation [and] took away the rights of one class and gave large advantages to another'.[160] On 20 September the Carrick-on-Suir branch of the Land League resolved to prevent hunting in Waterford county and this was followed by two violent incidents in October during which Lord Waterford's Curraghmore hunt was ambushed and stoned.

From 1877 to 1886 poor law unions provided the battle ground for a struggle between landlords and tenants[161] and in 1881 Joseph Fisher engineered the passage of a resolution by the Waterford Board of Guardians condemning Lord Waterford. On 11 October at a hunt meeting in the Imperial Hotel which included Henry Denny, Joseph Strangman, W. G. D. Goff and Sir Robert Paul, the marquis announced his resignation as hunt master. Paul exposed the incomprehension of landowners when he remarked that agitators causing the trouble must have been outsiders. Local people spoke in the 'warmest manner' of Lord Waterford and it was difficult to believe that 'such a change could have come over their natures in one year'.[162]

However, General Sir Hubert Gough, subsequently commander of I Corps, of which the 16th Division formed part, recalled the bitterness

154 *Waterford News*, 14 Jan. 1881; *Munster Express*, 15 Feb. 1913; O'Shea (1982), Chapter 5.
155 Curtis Jr, L. P., 'Stopping the hunt, 1881–1882: an aspect of the Irish land war' in C. H. E. Philpin (ed.) (1987), *Nationalism and Popular Protest in Ireland*, Cambridge, pp. 349–402.
156 *Waterford News*, 14 Jan. and 22 Apr. 1881.
157 *Waterford News*, 27 May 1881.
158 *Hansard* (Commons) 3rd ser. CCLXII, 1227–1830, 24 June to 1 July 1881.
159 *Hansard* (Commons) 3rd ser. CCLXIII, 640–41, 12 July 1881; 844–45, 14 July 1881.
160 *Waterford News*, 5 Aug. 1881.
161 Kinealy, 'The workhouse system in County Waterford' in Nolan and Power (eds.) (1992).
162 *Waterford News*, 14 Oct. 1881.

of the land war in Waterford county. His Catholic mother, like Lord Waterford, had hereditary connections with the De la Poer family and he spent his childhood at the family home at Gurteen Le Poer, Kilsheelan. Brought up in a religiously liberal but anti-home rule atmosphere, Gough remembered the violent ambushes launched by tenants and the seizure of their cattle by landlords. His uncles and cousins always carried revolvers on these raids.[163]

Following Parnell's arrest on 13 October, tension in the city was high with arrests made for tearing down government proclamations. The Kilmainham treaty[164] not withstanding, there was rejoicing in Waterford's streets after Parnell's release in May 1882. Pictures of Parnell, Michael Davitt,[165] the Waterford-born Thomas Sexton[166] and of Archbishop Croke were hung out in several streets with green flags and banners. Scores of candles illuminated house windows at night. A huge procession led by five bands paraded through the city. The largest bonfire on record burned in Ballybricken Green and smaller ones were lit in other places.[167]

A meeting to elect officers to the Waterford branch of the Irish National League (INL)[168] took place in November 1884. About 200 people enrolled and paid subscriptions. Mayor W. J. Smith was elected president and Charlie Strange was elected vice president. The 26-year-old Strange, a partner with his cousin in a city law business, was the youngest alderman in Ireland when elected in 1888. Also a member of the National and Literary Club, he had spoken in a debate where the majority voted in favour of Irish separation or self-government.[169] By 1886 Father Patrick F. Flynn was presiding at Ballybricken branch meetings of the INL. Distributing copies of the 'plan of campaign' appearing in the *United Ireland*, he called on league members to stand united during the campaign.[170] In 1888 another priest was vice president.[171]

At the time of the 1885 general election Waterford was a single-seat constituency contested by Richard Power and the Conservative F. G. Bloomfield from Newpark. In a farewell speech to his former constituents, Edmund Leamy offered his special thanks to 'the men of Ballybricken'. He recalled having gone as a stranger to various parts of Ireland but in every place he went where the Ballybricken men had been in the course of their trade he had always received a kindly welcome because they had spoken well of him. Dismissing Bloomfield as a

---

163 Gough, H. (1954), *Soldiering On*, London, p. 23.

164 Imprisoned in Kilmainham Gaol in October 1881 for opposing the 1881 Land Act, Parnell subsequently agreed to cooperate with the government in implementing the reforms and to use his influence to contain violence and end the land agitation campaign. Some nationalists considered this reversal of policy a betrayal.

165 Michael Davitt (1846–1906) was a journalist, nationalist MP, agrarian agitator and trade unionist with strong socialist leanings. Evicted from their smallholding, his family moved to Lancashire where he worked as a child labourer and had his arm severed at the age of 11 years in a machine accident. He joined the Irish Republican Brotherhood and was chief arms purchaser for the fenians. In 1870 he was sentenced to 15 years in prison but was released in 1877. He joined Parnell in launching the 'new departure' in 1879. In 1881 he was imprisoned in Portland Gaol and was subsequently imprisoned on several other occasions.

166 Thomas Sexton (1848–1932), a nationalist MP as well as high sheriff and mayor of Dublin, played prominent roles in the Land League and the 'plan of campaign'. He was imprisoned with Parnell in 1881 and was a signatory to the 'no rent manifesto' which was issued from Kilmainham Gaol by the leaders of the Irish Parliamentary Party and called on supporters of the Land League to withhold payment of rents in opposition to the 1881 Land Act.

167 *Waterford News*, 28 Oct. 1938 (reprint of a contemporary report).

168 The Irish National League, or National League, was founded by Parnell in 1882 and was built on the framework of the Land League which it replaced after that organisation was suppressed. It was the constituency organisation of the Irish Parliamentary Party. In 1884, Catholic priests were made ex officio delegates to the league's conventions. The league's principal functions were to organise conventions at which candidates for general elections were chosen, and to provide financial support for the IPP. Local branches of the league prosecuted the 'plan of campaign'. The league split during 1890–91 as a result of the division within the IPP over Parnell's involvement with Katharine O'Shea. The Parnellites, led by John Redmond after Parnell's death, held control of the league, while the anti-Parnellites founded the Irish National Federation. The rise of the United Irish League brought about the reunification of the IPP in 1900 and the UIL replaced the INL as the constituency organisation.

169 *Waterford News*, 28 Mar. 1884.

170 *Waterford News*, 21 Nov. 1884; *Waterford News*, 26 Nov. 1886.

171 *Waterford News*, 14 Sep. 1888.

'Protestant Tory', Leamy considered the election issue a 'plain and simple one; we must either govern ourselves and remain on friendly terms with our former conqueror, or they must try and govern us, and we must remain the determined and implacable enemies of the British Empire'.[172]

In Power's opinion, Bloomfield was 'only a poor Orangeman from the North'. Denying that the House of Commons had a 'debilitating' effect upon the patriotism of Irish members, Power's political programme consisted of nothing more than a promise to 'destroy every vestige of alien legislative rule in this country'. Fully backed by the priests, he took the seat on a 65 per cent turnout, winning 90 per cent of the votes.

The 1885 reform act, which added over half a million mainly small farmers and agricultural labourers to the voters' register, and a determined effort by the city's Parnell supporters ensured similar sweeping wins in the county. Charlie Strange and Banquo Redmond acted as Jasper D. Pyne's volunteers when he stood for West Waterford. Pyne's Conservative opponent Sir Richard F. Keane, described by a priest as being the representative of a 'harsh and cruel class ... put forward by a tyrannical and desperate set', obtained just nine per cent of the votes cast. Strange and Redmond also acted as volunteers for Patrick J. Power who stood for East Waterford against the Conservative Captain W. G. De la Poer.[173] Power won the constituency with 91 per cent of the votes cast. Both city and county were now solidly nationalist and all three candidates were returned unopposed in the July 1886 general election.

Nationalist politics generated enough excitement to fill the vacuum between elections. The unveiling of relics belonging to T. F. Meagher in August 1886 was the occasion for an extravagant liturgy in celebration of a local and national hero. The relics included a sprig of green worn by Meagher at Fredericksburg, his unsheathed sword, a presentation sword, a medal presented to him when he resigned command of the Irish Brigade, the guide flag of the 5th Regiment of the Irish Brigade and a girdle and sash worn by him. Special trains, one 27 carriages long, brought contingents to the ceremony from Cork, Limerick, Ross, Clonmel, Carrick-on-Suir and Piltown.

The familiar evergreens, flags (some green and bearing the harp without the crown), bunting and triumphal arches decorated the city streets. John Street and Michael Street 'surpassed all other localities' in the abundance of their decoration. In Ballybricken, portraits of Emmet, Wolfe Tone and O'Connell[174] were exhibited. Led by the Thomas Francis Meagher Band, a procession of between 35,000 and 40,000 made its way to Ballybricken. The Waterford branch of the GAA took part. Members of the Young Ireland Society carried the relics and a painting of Meagher in a wagonette. Representatives from the Pig Buyers Association carried a banner of Meagher. And the United Trades Club as well as the Temperance Hall and the National and Literary Club had 'many beautiful portraits of Ireland's illustrious sons' displayed on their walls. Labourers were drawn into the celebrations. Quay porters were prominent in the procession and carried a banner with the message 'The labourer is worthy of his hire'.

In Ballybricken the mayor ritualistically raised each relic to the 'wildest and most enthusiastic cheering'. Edmund Leamy, now the MP for Cork North East, called for a statue of Meagher to be erected. Richard Power MP claimed to speak for the many present who had known Meagher personally when he observed 'our memories are far

172 *Waterford News*, 20 Nov. 1885.
173 *Waterford News*, 4 Dec. 1885.
174 Robert Emmet (1778–1803) and Theobald Wolfe Tone (1763–98) were members of the United Irishmen, founded in Belfast and in Dublin during 1791, to seek parliamentary reform. Driven underground, it was reconstituted as a secret, oath-bound society dedicated to establishing a republic. It led a revolt in 1798 which was suppressed with great savagery. Emmet's unsuccessful attempt to organise a further rebellion in 1803, for which he was executed, spelt the death of the movement. O'Connell approved of the liberal principles of the United Irishmen and their call for reform and Catholic emancipation. But he disagreed with the open rebellion of 1798.

reaching'. Meagher, with 'a brave heart and a noble mind, [had been] ready to sacrifice everything in the cause of Irish nationality ... . Waterford will never forget him'. It was a theme he picked up again at a banquet in City Hall. 'They had memories', he declared, 'of '98 and memories of '48, aye, and immortal memories of '67' upon which there was loud cheering, again and again renewed as 'every person in the room' rose to his feet.

Stephen Farrell, a tailor, replied to the toast on behalf of the United Trades Club. His words reveal the extent to which local labour politics was driven by nationalism. Men like Farrell, Strange, Fisher and Redmond were drawn together from across the class divide. The status quo and traditional class relations went unchallenged. Farrell said he was only a working man, but

> without working-men they would have no nation ... [and] Meagher's memory would not be celebrated ... . It was working-men [who] swelled the demonstration of '48. The patriots of Ireland would degenerate were it not for the co-operation of Irish working-men, and by working-men he included every man who earned his bread by the sweat of his brow.[175]

Farrell had been a member of the Trades Guardians Association, Waterford's first trade council, formed in 1862 following three industrial disputes. Trade councils were voluntary bodies with no full-time officers and they emerged in the absence of a national labour structure. They co-ordinated the actions and represented the views of their member unions. Unskilled workers were not represented. The association's objective was to 'earn social acceptance' for its members. Considered a centre of fenianism, however, police raided Trades Hall in Ballybricken and arrested Farrell. The association was wound up in about

1868 when the Trades Union Congress was formed in Britain and Irish unions accepted it as representing their industrial interests. Intimately tied to nationalist politicians and politics, Irish trade councils viewed the political struggle as a separate issue.

Waterford's second trade council, the United Trades Club which was created in the same conservative mould as the TUC, was formed about 1878. Membership was restricted to skilled men and it cultivated relations with politicians, employers and the Chamber of Commerce. The 'big worlds' of unskilled male and female urban labour remained untouched[176] and quay workers who struck for improved unloading rates were sacked and replaced. Although Farrell publicly commented that 'there was no such thing as picking out a tradesman from a labouring man', he subsequently presided over a conference to set up an Artisans Trades Association, giving credence to the report that before the arrival of Larkin and Connolly the skilled trades 'just tolerated' the unskilled worker.[177]

Now, he and labour leaders who were also nationalists, actively supported the 'plan of campaign'. Five city bands and one from Tramore attended a demonstration at Knockboy (Ballygunner) in January 1887. The priest acting as chairman having proclaimed Irish nationality and independence to be a 'great, a glorious, a national, a patriotic ... a holy and sacred cause', Charlie Strange urged farmers to go to jail if necessary. And the city mayor, claiming that home rule 'will make the poor labourer and tradesman happy and contented and save the farmer from that mortal coil of landlordism', encouraged farmers to join the INL.[178]

Some 10 years before the Local Government Act of 1898 destroyed grand juries, 'the last bastion of Anglo-Irish ascendancy',[179] city nationalists also took the lead in protesting the removal

175 *Waterford News*, 6 Aug. 1886.
176 D'Arcy, F. A. and Hannigan, K. (eds.) (1988), *Workers in Union*, Dublin, pp. 1–7.
177 Malone, A. E. (1918), 'Four years of Irish economics, 1914–1918: Irish labour in wartime' in *Studies*, pp. 319–327.
178 *Waterford News*, 7 Jan. 1887.
179 Gailey (1984).

of Sir Thomas Grattan Esmonde from the shrievalty of Waterford county. While the official grand jury, containing establishment figures such as Sir R. J. Paul, a grand juror for about 45 years,[180] Sir R. Keane, W. C. Bonaparte Wyse, Joseph Malcolmson and Colonel Hillier, was being sworn in at the Court House, Sir Thomas Esmonde held his own grand jury meeting in the council chamber. It included county and city councillors and the county MPs. Charlie Strange, appointed by Esmonde as sub-sheriff, acted as secretary.

Sir Thomas's unofficial grand jury denounced the use of taxation to provide extra police as 'taxation without representation' and protested against the arbitrary action of government in replacing him as county high sheriff. His removal was believed to have been because of his political opinions and the representative character of the grand jury selected by him. At a meeting at Kilmacthomas, held under the pretext of its being a football match to avoid it being proclaimed, Charlie Strange, Banquo Redmond and Mayor Richard Power addressed the crowds. Strange warned that a coercion act was expected within weeks.

He also addressed the crowds at a monster demonstration at Lismore where there were pro-tests at the 'despotic action of an alien and hostile government'.[181] Many people from the city, including several councillors, Charlie Strange and Banquo Redmond, were also present with the county MPs at Newtown when in September T. M. Healy[182] attacked 'root and branch', the existing system of government in Ireland.[183]

The city played host to national figures who had been arrested during the land war. Among the street decorations when the freedom of the city was conferred on William O'Brien[184] and T. D. Sullivan[185] in September 1888, were banners proclaiming 'Ireland A Nation', 'Remember Mitchelstown', 'Heroes of Tullamore' and 'In Memory of Mandeville'.[186] About 700 quay porters and labourers preceded by the T. F. Meagher Brass Band led the procession which included tradesmen from the United Trades Club, various contingents of labourers from the county, representatives from INL branches, salters, members of the Pig Buyers Association and 500 men from city and county branches of the GAA wearing green jerseys.

Fathers P. F. Flynn, W. B. O'Donnell and Tom Furlong were among those present on the platform in Ballybricken and at the banquet in City Hall. Banquo Redmond, Charlie Strange and Harry Fisher were also in attendance.

180 *Waterford Standard*, 20 July 1982.
181 *Waterford News*, 18 Mar. 1887.
182 Timothy Michael Healy (1855–1931), a nationalist MP born in Cork, emigrated to Newcastle-upon-Tyne when he was in his teens. He referred to Parnell as the 'uncrowned king of Ireland'. He was imprisoned for treason and played a prominent role in the 'plan of campaign'.
183 *Waterford News*, 23 Sep. 1887.
184 William O'Brien (1852–1928), a nationalist MP and strong supporter of the Land League, edited *United Ireland*, which he described as 'an insurrection in print', from 1881 to 1890. One of Parnell's principal lieutenants in the IPP, he was a leader in the 'plan of campaign' and was imprisoned with Parnell in 1881. He wrote the 'no rent manifesto' and was a leading organiser of the Irish National League. He was subsequently imprisoned several times. He founded the United Irish League, which later replaced the Irish National League as the Irish Parliamentary Party's constituency organisation. By 1900 he was convinced the solution of the land question and any demand for Irish self-government lay in all groupings, unionists and nationalists and landowners and tenants, being brought together. His emphasis was now on conference and conciliation and on this basis he founded the All For Ireland League and spoke on army recruiting platforms during 1914 and 1915.
185 Timothy Daniel Sullivan (1827–1914). A nationalist MP, he was the uncle of T. M. Healy. He supported Young Ireland, the Home Government Association, the Home Rule League and the Land League and he was a leader in the 'plan of campaign'. Imprisoned in 1888, he was the author of a number of popular nationalist ballads, including *God Save Ireland*—a song of the Manchester martyrs.
186 In 1887 William O'Brien organised a rent strike near Mitchelstown, Cork and he and John Mandeville were ordered to appear in court. In the resulting disorder, three people were killed and this became known as the 'Mitchelstown massacre'. O'Brien and Mandeville were imprisoned in Tullamore Gaol. Refusing to wear prison garb, Mandeville was kept naked in his cell and died soon after his release in July 1888, his death being attributed to ill-treatment in prison.

O'Brien remarked that the Waterford men were 'full of fight', and that the IPP had an organisation that nothing could shatter and a leader whom 'we can trust to the death'. Richard Power MP observed that Balfour had failed to 'strike terror into the Irish heart' by proclaiming Waterford. T. D. Sullivan praised Waterford's 'magnificent demonstration of Irish patriotism and Irish resolution'. Mayor Richard Power, a coal merchant who had used his coal boats to transfer fenian men and munitions when he was an alderman, expressed his pride that 'we have got into our ranks men who belonged to the physical force party'. In a reference to the 'new departure', he noted these 'honest, sincere, dangerous and desperate men' had been won over to constitutional methods.

Charlie Strange praised the Ballybricken men for their support. In their addresses, the Pig Buyers Association described how the Ballybricken men had laboured in the cause of Irish nationality and the United Trades Club thanked O'Brien for his efforts on behalf of our 'oppressed and expatriated people'. Banquo Redmond, honorary secretary of the GAA, explained that the organisation had no political objective but that 'no true Irishman exists who would not be ready to dare anything in order to obtain ... freedom'.[187]

In November, police attempting to prevent the public celebration of the Manchester martyrs'[188] anniversary cleared the streets and disrupted mass when they entered the Catholic cathedral. From the pulpit, an angry priest urged people to restrain 'those giddy boys who hoot and cheer' but not to go home when ordered to do so by the police. They had a right to walk their own quays and streets. 'The whole thing was a scandalous proceeding got up at the instigation of a few stupid bigoted Protestants.'[189]

The visit of John Dillon[190] in December was largely a repetition of O'Brien's and Sullivan's reception. A priest's reference to police 'beating and bludgeoning' people on the city's streets during the Manchester martyrs celebrations was taken up by Dillon at a meeting in the Theatre Royal. Father Flynn demanded home rule: 'nothing short of an Irish Parliament will satisfy the legitimate aspirations of the Irish people.' He had 'respect and confidence in Parnell and his associates ... [and] Waterford men were ... determined to face every suffering in the holy cause of Ireland'.

Addresses were delivered on behalf of 40 city and county INL branches by Fathers W. B. O'Donnell, Tom Furlong and five other priests. Stephen Farrell speaking for the United Trades Club, and representatives from several other city organisations including the Pig Buyers Association, also gave addresses. In an editorial the *Waterford News* commented:

> Waterford County and City is armed and up. The League branches are so consolidated, drilled and disciplined that fifty Lord Waterfords would be no match for them. The Plan of Campaign drawn up at the convention was admirable and complete.[191]

But although nationalist issues created political unity, on the industrial front labour militancy threatened to smash both the status quo and the city's social homogeneity.

---

187 *Waterford News*, 14 Sep. 1888.
188 The 'Manchester martyrs' were three fenians executed for the murder of a police sergeant during the rescue of fenian leaders in police custody in Manchester on 18 September 1687. The executions, the anti-Irish reaction and the doubtful evidence upon which the men were convicted, caused widespread indignation in Ireland.
189 *Waterford News*, 30 Nov. 1888.
190 John Dillon (1851–1927) was a nationalist MP and a leading agitator in the Land League. He advocated the use of the boycott, was a signatory to the 'no rent manifesto' and was a leading figure in the 'plan of campaign'. Prosecuted in 1879, he was also imprisoned in 1881, 1887 and 1888.
191 *Waterford News*, 22 Dec. 1888.

VII

British New Unionism,[192] although representing a tiny fraction of unskilled workers, radicalised sections of Irish labour. The National Union of Dock Labourers and the National Union of Gas Workers extended their activities to Irish centres and to other groups of workers. The Amalgamated Society of Railway Servants initiated strikes which spread to the smaller systems and in 1890 porters on the Waterford and Limerick Railway struck to win an extra two shillings a week and a 10-hour day. Both the National Union of Dock Labourers and the National Seamen's and Firemen's Union organised branches and strikes in Waterford during 1889 and 1890.

Swept up in the tide of militancy, Waterford's United Trades Club was renamed the Federated Trades and Labour Union and set up strike support committees. But it still mirrored local social and power structures and the preoccupation with nationalist politics. Stephen Farrell was the president and city MP Richard Power was honorary vice president. Partly a social club and partly a trades council, its membership of 300 in 1890 included ratepayers and artisans as well as labourers. Nevertheless, it was the only Irish body other than the Dublin Trades Council to send a delegate to a conference of the British Labour Electoral Association founded by the TUC in 1886 to press the political interests of labour.

A confident, unskilled labour movement and 12 industrial disputes made 1890 one of the most industrially disturbed years in Waterford's experience. There was unrest among dockers, seamen, railway labourers, coal porters, carters, timber heavers and builders' labourers. However, it was the Waterford branch of the Amalgamated Society of Pork Butchers, formed in 1890 by men from Waterford, Limerick and Cork, and featuring T. F. Meagher on its banner, which entered into the biggest, most successful and most important dispute.

Although inspired by militant New Unionism, the reason for the pork butchers' success was their appeal to community rather than class solidarity. Strike leaders did not challenge the status quo. They fought an 'old-fashioned campaign, making a moral appeal for middle class support'.[193] The FTLU pledged its support, asked for that of the clergy, INL branches and other associations, and called a public meeting. Subscriptions were received from a range of people including Ballybricken priests, and Harry Fisher offered the use of columns in the *Munster Express* to acknowledge them. There was solid support from the city's skilled and unskilled workers and the Pig Buyers Association. One man applauded the strike because 'it put life and animation into the men. They were a long time ridden over by the employers and it was about time that they should do something'.[194]

General sympathy was qualified, however. New Unionism was perceived as a threat to the existing order and it invoked hostility. Despite the admitted justice of their cause, Father P. F. Flynn had reservations about addressing a public meeting in support of the strike because the butchers had adopted a Limerick-proposed programme refusing 'lay or clerical interference' which did not 'fall in with what [he thought was] right and proper, and prudent ... a strike or misunderstanding of this kind ... can never be remedied or settled unless by arbitration or interference on the part of some friendly person'. But they were his own people and he was 'so bound up in their interests spiritual and temporal', that whatever concerned them 'of necessity' concerned him. In a speech which was highly

---

192 'New Unionism' is a collective description for the spread of a new type of trade union in the 1880s. The new unions differed from the 'old' in that they catered largely for unskilled and poorly paid workers. They tended to have low entrance fees and subscriptions and depended on aggressive strike tactics to win concessions from employers. They were often 'general' rather than elitist and recruited workers across a range of employment.
193 O'Connor (1989), p. 91
194 *Waterford News*, 8 Feb. 1890.

approved of by many, he told the butchers that they would receive sympathy only when their cause was put to arbitration. And he advised the people of Ballybricken to conduct themselves 'as men of intelligence, as men of common-sense and prudence'. He was happy to be one of the priests and citizens called to a meeting by the mayor to settle the strike.[195]

However, with a coercion act in force nationalist rather than labour politics continued to dominate. In February 1890 Charlie Strange's attempt to escape the surveillance of police while on his way to meet with the local INL branch secretary in Dungarvan led to an 'exciting' 10-mile chase. A priest ignored the warning by police that he was chairing an illegal meeting and presided over the selection of a West Waterford representative.[196]

In June Father Flynn and other local priests, the mayor, justices of the peace and councillors rallied to the support of Harry Fisher of the *Munster Express* and of Banquo Redmond, who had taken over the *Waterford News* from Cornelius in 1887, when they were arrested. Prosecuted for intimidation after they published resolutions passed by branches of the INL, Redmond was sentenced to terms of imprisonment on three charges, one of which related to what A. J. Balfour described as a serious case of boycotting.[197]

By the end of 1890 the threat posed by militant New Unionism had receded in Waterford. There were rifts within the FTLU and the influential National Union of Dock Labourers left it. The rupture was exacerbated by the split in the IPP. Ninety-one per cent of FTLU members voted to endorse MP Richard Power in his support of Parnell. This overwhelming commitment to nationalist politics by the city's only indigenous labour organisation demonstrated a loyalty to Parnell which was transferred to John Redmond when he stood for the constituency.

195 *Waterford News*, 8 Feb. 1890.
196 *Waterford News*, 1 Mar. 1890.
197 *Hansard* (Commons) 3rd ser. CCCXLV, 1375–76, 1495–96, 1500–02, 19–20 June 1890.

Plate 1

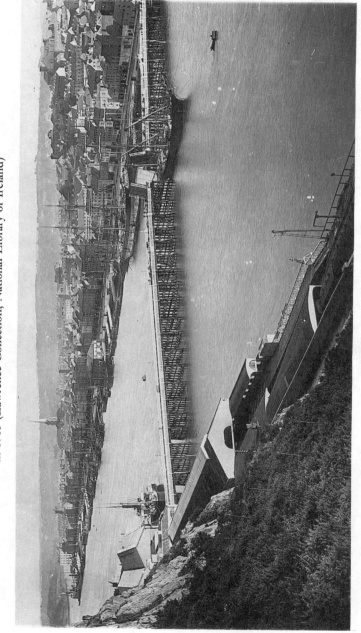

Waterford city, *c.* 1903, showing 'Timbertoes'—the wooden bridge replaced by the 'John Redmond' bridge in 1913 (Lawrence Collection, National Library of Ireland)

Plate 2

The Waterford quays, c. 1903 (Lawrence Collection, National Library of Ireland)

Plate 3

Broad Street, Waterford, looking towards the Quay, *c.* 1903. Michael Sullivan's (referred to as O'Sullivan's in the text) Wines and Spirits shop is on the left hand of the picture next to Power's Grocers (Lawrence Collection, National Library of Ireland)

Plate 4

The Mall, Waterford, during King Edward VII's visit, 1904 (Lawrence Collection, National Library of Ireland)

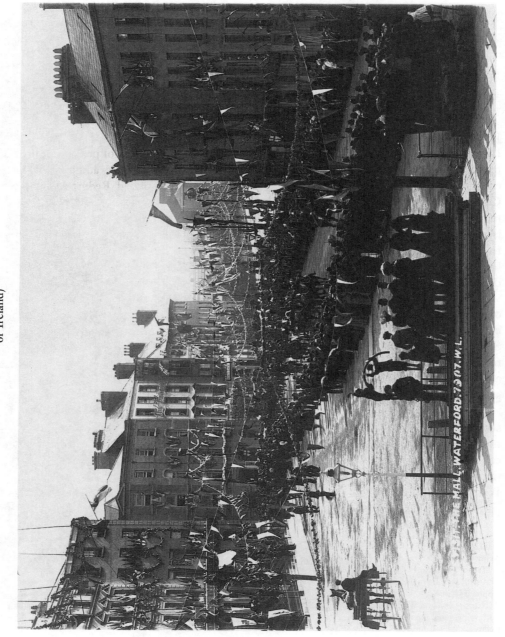

CHAPTER 3

The Redmond Factor

I

John E. Redmond, MP for Waterford city from December 1891 until his death in 1918, was a major influence on James English's decision to enlist. On 3 August 1914 he told the House of Commons that British troops could safely be removed from Ireland which would be defended by 'her own sons'. His manifesto urging Irishmen to join the British expeditionary force was published in newspapers on 16 September and four days later, at Woodenbridge, he told a parade of volunteers to 'account for yourselves as men, not only in Ireland itself, but wherever the firing line extends'. At the Dublin Mansion House on 26 September, he publicly supported Prime Minister Asquith's call for army recruits and asked for an 'Irish brigade' to form part of the expeditionary force and fight abroad.

By the time war was declared Redmond had secured an unrivalled authority in Waterford and the impact of his statements would have been considerable. Building on local Parnellite traditions, which in the view of John Dillon made Waterford the Redmond 'stronghold',[1] his campaign for the seat on Richard Power's death in

1891, was conducted when the IPP was divided.[2] It was hard-fought and violent but his victory over Michael Davitt, his anti-Parnellite opponent, set the tone of politics locally for the whole of James English's adult life. The McCarthyite press dubbed Redmond's campaign a 'foul conspiracy' formed by the 'Bolton–Strange–Manning–Ballybricken combination'.[3] Redmond acknowledged the 'enormous' contributions of Charlie Strange, Banquo Redmond of the *Waterford News*, the *Munster Express* newspaper (managed by Harry D. Fisher),[4] and M. A. Manning, the brother of the city's mayor who supervised a team of young men working day and night, sometimes until three or four o'clock in the morning.[5] And Redmond's association with the Ballybricken pig buyers became legendary. But the support of unionists such as Charles P. Bolton of Halfway House and of the Conservative *Waterford Standard*[6] ensured his success.

Some local Conservative voters declared an intense dislike of Davitt's policies, and John Dillon thought Waterford's 'Tory employers of labour ... worked for Redmond as vigorously as any of his nationalist friends'.[7] F. G. Bloomfield of Newpark thought Davitt's published election

1 Dillon to O'Donnell (Australian National League), 15 Jan. 1892 (Davitt Papers, 9323–4) Trinity College, Dublin (hereafter, Trinity).
2 The IPP split in 1890 followed Parnell being cited as co-respondent in the divorce of Captain O'Shea from his wife Katharine who had been Parnell's mistress since 1880. John Redmond assumed leadership of the Parnellite wing on Parnell's death in 1891. Opponents of Parnell followed Justin McCarthy and in the Waterford press they were variously described as 'anti-Parnellites', 'McCarthyites' and 'Federationists' (after the setting up of the Irish National Federation in opposition to the Irish National League). Both wings contained various factions but the success of the United Irish League forced the reunification of the IPP under John Redmond's leadership in 1900. However, the party never regained its Parnellite solidarity.
3 *Waterford Standard*, 2 Dec. 1891.
4 Letter from J. E. Redmond to the *Irish Independent* and published in the *Waterford News*, 2 Jan. 1892.
5 *Waterford News*, 2 Jan. 1891.
6 *Waterford News*, 2 Jan. 1892.
7 Dillon to O'Donnell, 15 Jan. 1892 (Davitt Papers, 9323–4), Trinity.

address 'sufficient to prevent any man who had the prosperity and happiness of Ireland at heart' from supporting him. He condemned the McCarthyite alliance with Gladstone's Liberal government and considered that any form of home rule would lead to civil war, clerical interference in politics and bankruptcy, as well as 'clerical dictation ... over the minds of the illiterate'.[8] Another local man refused Davitt his support and that of 13 other voters because of Davitt's claim that he had the support of priests. Those Irishmen who had become priests sacrificed their 'manhood' and, in his opinion, the country was labouring under the 'curse' of its 'Romish prelates and priests'.[9]

On his arrival in Waterford Redmond went to the pig buyers' rooms at Ballybricken where portraits of Davitt and Gladstone had been hung upside-down. There he told the gathering that he and his colleagues 'had long been familiar with the patriotism and stirling spirit of the Pig Buyers Association and the people of Ballybricken'. During the campaign Charlie Strange and others addressed crowds of thousands throughout the city. Redmond and the mayor canvassed the workers at the FTLU and the workingmen's clubs.[10] Addressing employees at all four bacon curing factories and at Strangman's brewery, Redmond told them 'all the organised bodies of labourers in the city [were] strongly on his side'.[11] After an address to 'many thousands' in Ferrybank, he led a procession back to his committee rooms. And Edmund Leamy spoke to employees at Cox Brothers' timber yard on Redmond's behalf.

Davitt 'sincerely' regretted the contest was being fought and he was 'certain' the Parnellite candidate would be beaten.[12] None the less, the McCarthyite campaign got underway on Sunday 13 December amid 'scenes of great disorder'. A procession led by Michael Davitt, William O'Brien and Father P. F. Flynn, was attacked by a city mob. Davitt was struck with a stick and badly injured, the Lismore Board of Guardians condemning the 'cruel assault' as 'shameful' and calling on the Waterford city electors to return the 'father of the Land League'.[13] At the federation's meeting police baton-charged the brawling crowds. Father Flynn, acting as chairman, promptly accused them of breaking up the meeting and a defiant Davitt decided to fight the seat personally. He told the crowd:

> I came to support the Nationalist candidate, but after the cowardly manner in which I have been treated ... I will fight him [Redmond] for Waterford. ... I will rely upon the artizans and labourers of Waterford to send me to Parliament to represent the Nationalist convictions.[14]

Father Flynn officially proposed Davitt as a candidate, handled his election accounts,[15] issued handbills declaring support for him and chaired several federation meetings. Potentially Davitt, with his empathy for the unskilled worker, offered the Waterford labourer an alternative to Redmond's conservatism. Although he had faced opposition from Parnell, Davitt was strongly inclined towards labour politics and he laid the foundation of the ITUC in 1891. However, he identified with British as well as Irish workers, and after 1882 he concentrated on his work in Britain in the belief he was also serving the Irish urban and rural worker as well as the tenant

---

8 Bloomfield to Davitt, 21 Dec. 1891 (Davitt Papers, 9471), Trinity.
9 'Would-be supporter' (Waterford) to Davitt, 19 Dec. 1891 (Davitt Papers, 9471), Trinity.
10 *Waterford Standard*, 16 Dec. 1891.
11 *Waterford Standard*, 16 and 19 Dec. 1891.
12 Davitt to McCarthy, 2 Dec. 1891 and Davitt to Redmond, 11 Dec. 1891 (Davitt Papers, 9367), Trinity
13 Kinealy, 'The workhouse system in County Waterford' in Nolan and Power (eds.) (1992).
14 F. S. L. Lyons was of the view that Davitt's acceptance of the candidacy was a pre-arranged response rather than an 'uncharacteristic' reaction to the assault (Lyons, F. S. L. [1975], *The Irish Parliamentary Party 1890–1910*, Connecticut, pp. 33–34). However, correspondence in the Davitt Papers (Trinity) suggests that Davitt genuinely had no planned intention to stand for the constituency himself.
15 A copy of the accounts and correspondence between Flynn and Davitt are on file (Davitt Papers, 9471), Trinity.

farmer.[16] But ultimately, despite the lure of international socialism, Davitt was a committed Irish nationalist and home ruler.

Taking place a year after the unprecedented industrial unrest of 1890, Redmond believed the campaign would be won by the 'labouring vote'[17] and he summed up the demands of labour as being for nothing more than 'some state regulation of ... hours'. However, he saw even this as being difficult to achieve as Irish labour was in competition with foreigners who did not set maximum hours. But he did agree that a legal limit of eight hours should be set in 'dangerous and exhausting occupations'. For the remainder of the campaign he concentrated on attacking the legitimacy of Davitt's claim to represent the working man. Davitt, standing as a labour as well as an anti-Parnellite candidate, recognised the difficulties in appealing to Waterford's working classes. He aimed to win over the conservative voter, calculating that any labour candidate needed the support of the city's business people because Waterford workers were 'not likely to separate themselves from Factionism in order to uphold the interests of labour'.[18]

The Redmondite undermining of Davitt's labour credentials was unremitting and provided the focus of the campaign. Accusing him of having 'lived upon a fictitious reputation', Redmond claimed to be as much a labour candidate as Davitt who theorised and produced 'crude and impossible notions' while the IPP did 'solid and practical work'. His own family had 'spent their energies—aye, and their fortune – in giving employment to the working classes' while Davitt had done nothing except start strikes in Dublin and other places which led to 'misery and failure'. Redmond dramatically declared he would 'have had his right hand cut off' before opposing a true labour man.

Edmund Leamy dismissed Davitt's labour programme as a 'red herring' and Charlie Strange condemned him as a coward and a liar. He was accused of preferring 'loud-mouthed and pompous work rather than ... disseminate the cause of Home Rule in England'. In The Mall, lit up by burning tar barrels, Waterford's constituents were told little would ever be done for working men and labourers until they were able to look after their own affairs through a parliament in College Green. Home rule 'as quickly as possible' was the 'real remedy'.

The president of the Cork United Trades Council, brought to Waterford by Redmond, told a gathering in The Mall that Davitt was trying by 'false means to win the votes of the working men of Waterford by pretending that he was standing in the labour interest'. A telegram from the United Trades Council of Dublin was produced denouncing Davitt as a 'bogus labour candidate' and calling on Waterford labour to support Redmond. Names of artisans appearing on a welcoming address for Davitt were declared to be forgeries and lists of trades people who supported Redmond were promulgated.

Waterford labourers were claimed to be 'solid on the side of the principles of Parnell' and to support Redmond 'to a man'. The president of the Coach Builders Society and the coach builders themselves were said to have pledged their support to him. The salters from all four bacon curers had allegedly gone 'unsolicited' to the Parnellite committee rooms and given £20 towards Redmond's election expenses. And when Davitt visited the Cox brothers' yard, all but four or five of the workers were reported as having walked away cheering for Redmond.

Davitt defended his work on behalf of labour but his arguments, as well as his campaign, received a meagre media coverage. The extent of his published defence appears to be the statement that he had organised a Dublin strike of bricklayers' labourers which had resulted in a 2s and 2s 6d rise in weekly pay.[19]

---

16 Moody, T. W., 'Michael Davitt' in J. W. Boyle (ed.) (1978), *Leaders and Workers*, Dublin, pp. 47–55.
17 *Waterford Standard*, 23 Dec. 1891.
18 Davitt to Dillon, 3 Dec. 1891 (Davitt Papers, 9403), Trinity.
19 *Waterford Standard*, 16, 19 and 23 Dec. 1891.

McCarthyites were subjected to constant intimidation. The presence of priests prevented John Dillon and William O'Brien being manhandled on one occasion, and a Parnellite crowd which followed MPs William O'Brien, T. J. Condon and David Sheehy from mass in the cathedral was only kept under control by Banquo Redmond and Councillor David Hyland. While canvassing 'in some of the streets inhabited by the lower classes', O'Brien and Condon were reported to have been 'accorded anything but a pleasant reception'. No meeting could be held when Davitt visited Barnes's bacon factory because the feeling against him was 'so strong' and Dr Tanner MP had to be protected by working men when a young man offered to fight him. McCarthyite campaign bills were destroyed or pasted over by the sheriff's official announcements.

In Davitt's opinion, the campaign was a 'very ugly one. [Waterford] is the Parnellite stronghold and feeling ... is being worked upon in the most wicked way by Redmond and his friends'.[20] According to him, the Pig Buyers Association was 'dead against' him and they intimidated the voter 'to [the] utmost'. The 'boys of Ballybricken ... knew how to make things lively for whoever would dare to try to wrest the political rule of Waterford from their hands'. Davitt complained that all the city's employers gave Redmond's campaigners free access to employees while only one employer allowed him the same opportunity. Nor could he hold an outside meeting without disruption. There were threats of violence against his canvassers and helpers. On polling day the

'formidable pig buyers were everywhere. They swarmed in the booths ... [and] took charge of the illiterates and "educated" them'. He accused the Redmondites of coercing the labour voter by threats of beatings and dismissal from work.[21]

Davitt condemned those encouraging such proceedings as 'becoming the deadliest enemies of Ireland'.[22] One supporter in County Leitrim considered him 'too honourable for the blackguards [he] had to encounter'[23] and Father Flynn, who doubted that Davitt would ever again want to return to Waterford,[24] denounced the use of intimidation.[25] But Charlie Strange, Redmond's election agent, denied any had occurred.[26]

Despite his difficulties, Davitt told a voter the election would be a 'close one' with less than a 100 majority for the winner.[27] However, Redmond polled 59 per cent of the votes on a 76 per cent turn-out.[28] Defending Redmond against the accusation that he won the election through a combination of 'toryism and terrorism', the *Waterford News* thought the ability to attract Conservatives was a

> hopeful sign for the future ... . Nationality is our objective. We want a nationality that will inflame with a ... love of country – a nationality which may embrace Catholic, Protestant and Dissenter; a nationality to include every man who makes Ireland his home.[29]

In defending his seat in the July 1892 and the 1895 general elections, Redmond's campaigns were straight Parnellite versus anti-Parnellite nationalist contests but with promises made to

20   Davitt to Mrs Byles, 19 Dec. 1891 (Davitt Papers, 9338), Trinity.
21   Davitt, 'Why I was beaten at Waterford', newspaper cutting in scrapbook kept by Davitt (Davitt Papers, 9621), Trinity.
22   Davitt to Miss Mander, 17 Dec. 1891 (Letter, 24,531), NLI.
23   Edward Golan (the name is barely decipherable and may be incorrect) of master's office, Mohill workhouse, Leitrim to Davitt, 30 Dec. 1891 (Davitt Papers, 9471), Trinity.
24   Flynn to Davitt, 8 Mar. 1892 (Davitt Papers, 9471), Trinity.
25   *Waterford News*, 2 Jan. 1892.
26   *Waterford Standard*, 30 Dec. 1891.
27   Davitt to Mayor P. M. Egan of Kilkenny, 22 Dec. 1891 (Letter, 13,157), NLI.
28   *Waterford News*, 2 Jan. 1892. 3,004 of the electorate cast a vote. According to *Whitaker's Almanack*, 3,973 were on the electoral roll.
29   *Waterford News*, 2 Jan. 1892. For the possible figure of 170 Conservative voters supporting Redmond, see *Waterford News*, 9 July 1892.

the labourer in return for his vote. In 1892 Redmond retained the seat with 57 per cent of the votes on a 73 per cent turn-out and bonfires were lit to celebrate his victory. An effigy of David Sheehy, his opponent, was burned in The Mall and Redmond was presented with a commemorative silver afternoon fruit service by the ladies of Ballybricken.[30] He was seen off from the station by all the city bands and a crowd estimated at 5,000.[31]

Redmond opened his 1895 election campaign during a visit to Waterford in October 1893. He was greeted by exploding rockets and vessels decked out in coloured lights. Thousands gathered to meet him and he told his 'staunchest friends', the Ballybricken Pig Buyers Association, that with their support he was bound to win. Although dock and city labourers lit up the city streets with tar barrels carried on their shoulders, it was home rule and not their plight which dominated the political agenda. The 'magnificent demonstration' was taken to confirm an 'unswerving loyalty to the principles of Charles Stuart [sic] Parnell' and that the 'sons of the city of Meagher [were] as deeply imbued with the true spirit of nationality as they were in '48 and '67'. Redmond told the crowds:

> we expect the time is near at hand when the call 'to arms' will again be sounded within the city walls of our ancient city, and the sons of the men who followed Meagher in '48 and who fell into line with the brave men of '67, will flock to your standard.

Banquo Redmond promised him that the city would return him at the next election and 'silence for ever the West Britons who howl for your defeat' and Charlie Strange moved a resolution declaring that John Redmond and his party 'have alone kept the banner of Independence flying and that it is alone through their action that any good

has been secured'.

An address on behalf of labourers spoke of Waterford being 'faithful and loyal to true and brave men down to our illustrious Meagher of the Sword' and assured Redmond that he had no 'truer hearts to the cause … nor more loyal supporters … than … the Quay and Dock Labourers'. At a meeting attended by, among others, victuallers, pork butchers, representatives of the FTLU and the city's Independent Hackney Drivers and Owners Association, he was told the working class would ensure he remained the city's MP. Redmond replied that nothing had made him feel so 'proud and happy' as his reception by the labourers and working men of the city.

Redmond told the town labourers they had made the Land League, suppressed in 1881 and replaced by the Irish National League (INL), a power over the last 15 years when the farmers were 'too selfish and too cowardly to take a prominent part' in it. He was 'the first to admit that the labourers in the towns have, during the whole course of this agitation, derived little or no benefit from the sacrifices that they have made'. Like similar movements in the past, the city's labourers had been the 'most self-sacrificing and bravest Nationalists in the country' and their lack of benefits 'ought to be changed'. 'I think', he declared, 'the time has come when responsible politicians in Ireland should turn their attention to the case of the labourers, when their interests should no longer be allowed to sink into insignificance compared to the interests of the farmers.'

With only nine Parnellites in the House, however, little could be done. But if returned with an increased number of members,

> then I say to you that amongst the first business we will put our hands to will be an endeavour to do something to raise the lot of the labourers of Ireland and enable them to

---

30 *Waterford News*, 23 July 1892.
31 *Waterford News*, 2, 9, 16, 23 and 30 July 1892. These editions contain detailed reports of the campaign.

reap some benefit for their sacrifices and their bravery in the past.[32]

The promises were empty rhetoric, however. His real interests lay with the skilled worker and the wealthier classes, one historian describing the IPP as 'obesely bourgeois'.[33] The party, 'ostensibly dedicated to a programme of social reform', realistically did little.[34] And James Connolly, noting that 'Mr Redmond's heart bleeds for the poor of Ireland' observed that neither he nor anyone else fought for the inclusion of Ireland in the Meals for Necessitous School Children Act.[35]

But, presenting himself as a nationalist candidate whose policies were in labour's best interests, Redmond again successfully defended the seat. He won 58 per cent of the votes cast. The reunification of the IPP under his leadership was celebrated in the city and brought it status. He promised to make 'the voice of Waterford heard and respected in the foreign senate to which I was sent'. People from Kilkenny, Tipperary, Cork, Limerick and Wexford arrived by motor transport, steamers and trains and thousands joined the procession to Ballybricken Green where Redmond called for unity within Ireland and within his constituency and for an increased membership and re-organisation of the UIL.

Redmond told the crowds, 'you will have reason to be proud of the record of your native city ... you, the true men of Waterford, who, all during the century, have given such signal proof of your devotion to faith and fatherland'. But home rule and land ownership linked with inequitable financial relations, not the urban labour issue, were again the 'great vital question[s]'.

According to Redmond, Englishmen were afraid of an Irish parliament because they thought of nationalists as 'Revolutionaries,

Anarchists [and] Socialists. I cannot help smiling,' he said, 'because I know it would be a sober, steady, and conservative body, anxious to maintain the property of every man and of every class, anxious to promote the prosperity of Ireland ... . I believe in discipline'. In his view, if the British ruling class could be convinced it would not mean anarchy or socialism in Ireland, 'we would obtain Home Rule very soon'.[36]

Pledges of loyalty came from the United States as well as from Ireland. A loving cup from the Waterford men and women of New York was presented to Redmond to commemorate his assuming leadership of the IPP at a ceremony attended by, among others, Father W. B. O'Donnell, FTLU president Stephen Farrell, Banquo Redmond and Harry Fisher who, as well as being honorary secretary to the loving cup presentation committee, was also co-secretary of the demonstration committee for Redmond.[37]

Redmond's right to hold the Waterford city constituency was never again challenged and by the time he called for Waterfordmen to enlist in the 16th Division, his political ascendancy and authority in the city were well consolidated. In 1915 a Local Government Board officer in Dublin corresponding with Redmond on the need to cancel funding for new housing, wrote:

> your influence is so great in Waterford that it only needs a word from you to make the corporation understand that, while the completion of their scheme is assured, they must wait until money is available.[38]

Of Waterford county, a police report noted in 1916 that the majority of farmers had purchased their holdings under the land acts and consequently showed no interest in politics and gave little to political funds. The county was 'strongly

32 *Waterford News*, 23 July 1892.
33 Lee (1973), p. 152.
34 Lyons, F. S. L., 'Decline and fall of the Nationalist Party' in Edwards and Pyle (eds.) (1968), pp. 52–61.
35 Connolly, J. (1913), 'British labour and Irish politicians', *Forward* (3 May); Connolly, J. (1911), 'Mr. John E. Redmond, M.P.: his strength and weakness', *Forward* (18 Mar.). Both reproduced in Connolly (1987), Vol. 1, pp. 349–63.
36 *Waterford News*, 27 Apr. 1900.
37 *Waterford News*, 12 Jan. and 27 Apr. 1900.
38 Robinson to Redmond, 10 Aug. 1915 (Redmond Papers, 15,261 [6]), INL.

Redmondite and the people are prepared to follow their leaders and accept any "Home Rule Bill" as a matter of sentiment'.[39]

This Redmondite hegemony was secured in a number of ways.

II

Firstly, Redmond cultivated a core of committed local IPP loyalists who oversaw his interests and consolidated his influence. The energetic and ubiquitous Charlie Strange was an important example of this technique. In March 1892, shortly after the first issue of the *Irish Independent*, in which Redmond had at least 150 shares, Charlie Strange and Banquo Redmond encouraged members of the workingmen's club to establish an 'Independent Shares Club' and visited 'great numbers' of prominent Waterford citizens to persuade them to buy shares in the newspaper.

Redmond sought help from Strange in having his own nominee elected as mayor. However, acknowledging that there was no one he would do more for than Redmond, Strange refused to help his nominee because the man was a 'sweat and a liar'. Strange subsequently complained that Redmond's name had been used to denounce his own candidacy for the mayoralty.[40]

Father William B. O'Donnell became a close supporter of Redmond. When Redmond visited the city in 1904, Father O'Donnell proposed the resolution that citizens of Waterford 'express our unabated confidence in our city member ... and the Irish Party'. Men of 'class, men of intelligence and position and stake within the city'

supported Redmond, he said. Redmond and the IPP had the necessary 'fighting qualities' to push through land acts and to obtain a university.[41]

As early as 1902, Redmond had declared his opposition to any Irish visit by King Edward VII. Even though Ireland was 'part of the heart of this [British] Empire', he said the Irish would absent themselves from the coronation. Edward had been warned by his ministers that 'he could not ... put his foot upon Irish soil'.[42] But Irish attitudes towards the monarch could be as ambivalent as their opinions about the army. In 1892, the Lismore Board of Guardians condemned two army officers for not allowing Irish soldiers to wear shamrocks on their uniforms on St Patrick's Day but offered Queen Victoria their condolences on the death of the Duke of Clarence. When Waterford's local leaders split over the royal visit to the city in May 1904 and created problems for Redmond, Father O'Donnell was central in managing Redmond's own visit in 1905.

Plans for the king's visit generated fierce debate and dissension, the West Waterford UIL branch condemning the 'shoneen' city council for agreeing to it.[43] Father Flynn was unable to accept the corporation's invitation to be on the reception committee. But in contrast to his revolutionary calls for home rule in the 1880s, and no doubt impressed with the pope's reception of the monarch in Rome[44] and also probably remembering the bitter differences with Redmond supporters in pre-unification days, he called on Waterford people to give a 'sincere, fitting and enthusiastic' reception to the king. It was the 'duty of Irish subjects' to meet the royal family and he hoped Waterford would be a credit to the

39 Mac Giolla Choille, B. (1966), *Intelligence Notes 1913–16*, Dublin, p. 216.
40 Strange to Redmond, 28 Nov. 1893 (Redmond Papers, 15,238 [11]), NLI. The man to whom Strange refers is identified as 'Murphy' and probably refers to P. A. Murphy, or to Martin J. Murphy of Tramore who was elected MP for East Waterford in a 1913 by-election. He did run for mayor at some point and was beaten by two votes (*Waterford News*, 12 Jan. 1900). A strong supporter of Redmond, his letters to Redmond generally started with the salutation 'Dear Chief'.
41 *Waterford Standard*, 9 Jan. 1904.
42 Redmond, J. E. (1902), *Mr Redmond's Speech* (a pamphlet printed for private circulation) (Ir 32341 p. 22), NLI.
43 O'Connor (1989), pp. 109–10.
44 Oldmeadow, E. (1940), *Frances Cardinal Bourne*, Vol. 1, London, pp. 203–04. The idea that King Edward had a special interest in Ireland was 'widely held' according to Robertson (1960), pp. 1–36. Wall chalkings sometimes proclaimed 'The King has been to Holy Mass. He is a Roman Catholic'.

'patriotic feeling that everyone should have' when receiving the king and queen.[45]

The president of the FTLU declared himself as 'strong a nationalist' as anyone but he thought the king meant good for Ireland, and the city and its working people would gain considerable benefit from the visit. W. G. D. Goff, noting that the corporation was 'overwhelmingly nationalist' told its members they were not yielding 'one iota' by welcoming the king and the visit was likely to bring trading benefits.[46]

In the *United Irishman*, Arthur Griffith was scathing in his criticism of the FTLU and the corporation: 'hypocrites and fools that they are, they think an address to the king will establish shipbuilding.'[47] To the Irish nationalist, the 'loveliness and beauty' of the lit-up ships was a 'distressing sight' because it was 'bestowed on the British monarch'.[48] During the visit and in reply to several addresses pledging loyalty, the king regretted 'the industrial wealth of Waterford and the employment available for the labouring population [was] not more plentiful'.[49] But neither the visit nor the king apparently did much to improve conditions. However, a legacy of discord was one by-product and Redmond relied on his local loyalists to help him deal with it.[50]

Alderman Thomas Whittle, referring to a 'cleavage' in Waterford's local national forces because of the king's visit, suggested that Redmond should defer his own visit to the city. The 'royalists' intended to engineer his stay to escape the 'censure which their defiance of ... [Redmond] and the party and their betrayal of the national cause ... merits'. Whittle was running for mayor and the opposing faction was determined to defeat him. Both parties were concerned about how the visit would affect the contest. Bishop Sheehan was keen for it to proceed

although he would not advise Redmond on what to do in case 'anything unpleasant' occurred.

However, Father O'Donnell thought he might be able to get the two parties to unite in the common cause and 'induce them to sink their petty politics'. He considered the dispute a legacy of the IPP split rather than a simple disagreement over the king's visit. This reflected the position in the national party in which personal rivalries remained acute after reunification. He noted 'a great deal of bitterness' between the Parnellites and the McCarthyites but Redmond agreed with his recommendation to proceed with the visit and say nothing about the king during it.

The priest acted as Redmond's manager. According to Banquo Redmond, O'Donnell could be relied upon: 'the dogs will lie quietly for him.' Arrangements were tightly planned and managed, Father O'Donnell consulting Redmond on details such as the addresses, resolutions, times and dates which would meet Bishop Sheehan's request that his priests be present at receptions and meetings, what bands would be attending and which city representatives should be invited.

Redmond also built a close working relationship with Bishop Sheehan, frequently providing a link between the Irish and English hierarchies. The bishop, who showed a keen interest in education and spoke at a meeting on the university question at the Theatre Royal,[51] asked him to oppose the bill promoted by the Protestants of Waterford requesting the transfer to them of the city's model schools. These had been established in 1846 as part of the training system for teachers and had then been opposed by the Catholic hierarchy. And he liaised between Bishop Sheehan, Archbishop Logue, Cardinal Bourne of Westminster and the Home Office regarding the

45 *Waterford News*, 25 Mar. 1904.
46 *Waterford Standard*, 10 June 1903, 9 Apr. 1904.
47 Clarkson (1970), footnote on p. 262.
48 *The United Irishman*, 4 Nov. 1905.
49 *Waterford Standard*, 4 and 7 May 1904. These editions contain very full and detailed reports of the visit.
50 W. B. O'Donnell to Redmond, 15 and 29 Oct. and 14 Nov. 1905; Whittle to Redmond, 20 Oct. 1905; C. P. (Banquo) Redmond to John Redmond, 28 Oct. 1905 (Redmond Papers, 15,245 [10]), NLI.
51 *Waterford Standard*, 30 Jan. 1904.

factory and workshop bill to which the Catholic hierarchy was opposed.[52] Cardinal Bourne asked Redmond to form part of a deputation to see the prime minister.[53] Bourne and Redmond also worked closely on considering English education legislation and its effects on Catholic schools.

Not everyone in the hierarchy was satisfied with Redmond's role. The Bishop of Limerick accused the IPP of being 'puppets of the English Liberals' in the matter of education. In his view the party was contaminated through contact with liberal, secularist politics and opinion in England. He suggested that if they should

> come over to Ireland and enquire why the fine generation of young Irishmen that is growing up is turning away from them *en masse* for the Gaelic League, or Sinn Fein, or some other policy, they would learn some salutary truths.[54]

On a local level, however, Redmond could draw on a bank of goodwill. He had, for instance, represented the interests of the De La Salle Training College to Balfour in 1897 and Brother Thomas told him:

> I have ... confidence in your influence with the government to obtain what you request. Personally I feel grateful to you for the interest you have shown in our College and for the efforts you are making to relieve it of its difficulties.[55]

Secondly, Redmond loyalists instilled a wider allegiance and deepened Redmond's power-base through the city's network of institutions which they controlled. As elsewhere in the country, IPP activists infiltrated organisations which either

had nationalist objectives or which could be used to feed nationalism and these were added to the 'cluster of party auxiliaries'.[56] At the end of 1899 there were just two Irish towns which had any significant UIL presence while County Waterford had four branches.[57] Redmond was initially slow to commit himself to the UIL. When he recognised it as the official nationalist organisation in June 1900, however, the IPP set out to capture it.

Waterford city's branch was inaugurated on 9 December 1901. Those present included the mayor, Charlie Strange, Banquo Redmond, Harry Fisher, Father W. B. O'Donnell, P. J. Power, MP for East Waterford, John Redmond's brother Willie and several councillors. Father O'Donnell, his reference to 'our talented and patriotic' leader drawing 'immense cheering', moved the first resolution and said 'I assured him [Redmond] ... we would have a flourishing branch ... amongst us before his return'. He saw men before him who would 'stand shoulder to shoulder with their fellow countrymen in the coming struggle for self-government in Ireland'. Many joined and paid their subscriptions.[58]

Institutions ostensibly remote from politics were drawn into the IPP's vortex by the network of Redmond supporters. Local branches of Catholic organisations such as the Catholic Young Men's Society (CYMS) were mobilised in support of the Gaelic League, the leading officials of which were also officers in the local UIL branch. By 1913 the top four posts of the local UIL branch were held by Mayor Thomas Whittle who was also on the Board of Guardians, an alderman, a councillor and Father Tom Furlong who was vice president.[59] Furlong was

52 Bishop Sheehan to Redmond, 3 Jan. 1902 and 21 June 1907; Redmond to Sheehan, 6 June 1902 and 1, 5 Aug. 1907; Archbishop Logue to Sheehan, telegram 3 Aug. 1907 (Redmond Papers, 15,227), NLI.
53 Cardinal Bourne to Redmond, 18 July 1907 (Redmond Papers, 15,172), NLI.
54 Miller (1973), pp. 172, 176.
55 Brother Thomas to Redmond, 23 Dec. 1897 (Redmond Papers, 15,238 [8]), NLI.
56 Fitzpatrick (1977), pp. 100–01
57 Bull, P. J. (1972), 'The reconstruction of the Irish parliamentary movement 1895–1903: an analysis with special reference to William O'Brien' (unpublished PhD thesis), Cambridge, pp. 204, 320.
58 *Waterford News*, 13 Dec. 1901.
59 *Munster Express*, 15 Feb. 1913.

also spiritual director of the CYMS, president of the CYMS literary and dramatic class, president of the CYMS cycling club and a committee member of the Waterford branch of the Gaelic League.

P. A. Murphy, a local solicitor, was an officer of the local AOH, president of the Catholic Club and subsequently a provisional committee member of the city's Volunteer battalion. Edward Walsh was a councillor, city high sheriff in 1915, a member of the Board of Guardians and he took over the *Munster Express* in 1907. John Redmond was president of the National and Literary Club and David Hyland, its vice president and a staunch Redmondite, was also a city high sheriff. John Redmond and Fathers Flynn and O'Donnell, as well as a host of leading gentry, were governors of the Waterford County and City Infirmary. All three, and Bishop Sheehan, were also ex officio members of the Fanning charitable institution.

Na Fianna Eireann, the name of a republican youth movement euphemistically translated as the National Boy Scouts, was an example of a nationalist organisation which, presenting a potential threat to this local Redmondite hegemony, was viewed initially with suspicion and then won over. Founded in 1909 by Countess Markievicz and Bulmer Hobson, it was a movement distinct from the Scout Association of Ireland and the Waterford branch was established in 1912.[60] In November 1914 contingents from *Na Fianna Eireann* as well as RIC members and recruits from the barracks, attended the memorial service for Lord Roberts which was synchronised with one held in St Paul's Cathedral, London.[61] In March 1915 a circularised appeal for support was necessary as the boys had themselves provided their own equipment and were required to defray all other expenses.[62] The following month the *Munster Express* complained that some who 'do not understand the nature [of the movement] are inclined to discourage its progress'. As a result it had experienced 'many difficulties and reverses'. In calling for recruits, the movement's aims were set out as being for the 'unity of all classes and creeds in the cause of nationality and freedom'.[63] The appeal apparently worked and subscriptions were received from staunch Redmondites. Hearne and Co. subscribed £1 for example. Edward Walsh himself and the firm of E. Walsh, each subscribed five shillings.[64]

Most, if not all, of the city's major institutions, overtly political or otherwise, were therefore under the control of Redmondite loyalists. Unionists such as W. G. D. Goff also played a role in this process, so the institutions fulfilled a secondary function of reinforcing the *status quo* and deepening Waterford's political and social cohesion.

Thirdly, connections with government meant that Redmond could extend his influence through patronage. In a letter from the owners of the *Waterford Mirror* he was asked to nominate their candidate as a member of the land courts under the 1896 act. Their man 'although a Conservative' was said to be a warm Redmond supporter. The owners of the *Mirror* claimed to have cast three Conservative votes for him at the last two general elections. Requests for him to exercise his influence also came from outside of the city. A man stating he was a consistent supporter of Parnell and a 'considerable' subscriber of funds, asked Redmond to use his influence in obtaining one of four positions as resident magistrate. And an army major-paymaster asked him

60   *Munster Express*, 3 Apr. 1915. According to D. J. Hickey and J. E. Doherty (1980), the branch was founded by 1911. The organisation's stated objective was to 're-establish the independence of Ireland' and its members had to declare: 'I promise to work for the independence of Ireland, never to join England's armed forces, and to obey my superior officers.'
61   *Waterford Standard*, 21 Nov. 1914.
62   *Munster Express*, 27 Mar. 1915.
63   *Munster Express*, 3 Apr. 1915.
64   *Waterford News*, 21 May 1915.

to arrange privately an increase in his pension through the secretary of state for war.[65]

Patronage could also be exercised at local level. A *Waterford News* employee was promoted to sub-editor of the *Irish Independent* soon after the 1891 by-election. Charlie Strange, Banquo Redmond and M. A. Manning were at the send off[66] and it seems probable that this appointment was a reward for the consistent support the newspaper had given Redmond. It was also an opportunity for Redmond to tighten his control of the *Independent* by manning it with loyal staff.

Fourthly, the IPP enhanced its reputation with the less well-off majority of voters by claiming the Liberal government's social legislation as its own. By 1912, 22 per cent of people receiving pensions in the United Kingdom were in Ireland.[67] And in February 1915 the party declared the pensions act was one of the 'most beneficent measures ever passed in Ireland'. It allowed men and woman to live at home instead of ending their days in the workhouse, 'one of the most loathed and hated of British institutions'. Over 203,000 people received the pension in Ireland at a cost of approximately £11,720,000. Shopkeepers and the community in general benefited. It was claimed there had been a reduction in the number of workhouse inmates and in the local rates. And £979,295 in insurance money was paid out in Ireland between 1913 and 1915.[68]

Fifthly, Redmond was an effective constituency MP. Irish reliance on their MPs was accentuated by the population's estrangement from a remote and inefficient Dublin government. It was Redmond who got things done, not Dublin. In the process he consolidated local contacts and personal loyalties. The demonstration committee

for Redmond in 1895 compared the local franchise in Ireland unfavourably with that in England. An act of 1834 granted the municipal franchise to all ratepayers and gave greater powers. In England the sheriff was elected but in Ireland he was nominated by the lord lieutenant. O'Connell saw the differences as demonstrating the 'Sham' nature of the union and as supporting calls for repeal. When there was local pressure for a wider enfranchisement, Redmond demonstrated his influence in Westminster and his value to Waterford. He steered the Waterford corporation bill, which widened the local voting qualification, through parliament in 1896. Charlie Strange told him 'the tradesmen in Waterford are extremely pleased at the franchise move and I think it brings home to their mind more fully than anything of late the advantage of being in touch with their member.'[69] And he thanked Redmond for all of his 'local public works'.[70]

Redmond's contacts with his constituents operated at all levels. The Waterford harbour bill 1893 affected the water and poor rates and the Board of Guardians asked him to represent their interests in the House. He took charge of a bill relating to the leper hospital, W. G. D. Goff's solicitor drafting it in accordance with Redmond's suggestions. The work was completed in close consultation with several people, including Bishop Sheehan. He successfully piloted it though parliament while having to deal with McCarthyite opposition in Waterford city and county.[71]

There was stiff city opposition to the railway amalgamation bills of 1899 as they stood and Redmond arranged a deputation consisting of, among others, Charlie Strange, the local builder

65 *Waterford Mirror* to Redmond, 11 Aug. 1896; F. O'Carroll to Redmond, 26 Feb. 1894; major-paymaster to Redmond, 3 May 1894 (Redmond Papers, 15,238 [11]), NLI.
66 *Waterford Standard*, 9 Dec. 1891.
67 O'Flanagan (1985), p. 92.
68 *Report of Standing Committee of the United Irish League* (Dublin, 1915), attached as a supplement to the *Waterford News*, 5 Feb. 1915.
69 Strange to Redmond, 19 Mar. 1896 (Redmond Papers, 15,238 [7]), NLI.
70 Strange to Redmond, 18 Mar. 1896 (Redmond Papers, 15,238 [7]), NLI.
71 Thomas Took to Redmond, 1 Mar. 1893; W. G. D. Goff to Redmond, 28 Mar. 1894, 28 Feb. 1896; W. G. D. Goff's solicitor to Redmond, 19 Nov. 1894 and 15 Mar. 1895 (Redmond Papers, 15,238 [11]), NLI.

George Nolan and representatives from the Harbour Board and Chamber of Commerce to meet the Irish secretary, Gerald Balfour, and press for guarantees to protect the city's trade.[72] More dubious requests involved people who wanted to safeguard their personal stakes. A correspondent with shares in both city breweries asked him to oppose a parliamentary bill because it would damage his interests.[73]

The success by Redmond in obtaining a £38,000 grant which helped to finance the abolition of the toll bridge and the construction of a new bridge after a long campaign in which Banquo Redmond was prominent, was considered something of a *coup*. A corporation resolution thanked him for his 'able and successful efforts'.[74] The bridge was opened in 1913 and in their address at a home rule demonstration the following January, the Waterford Asylum Attendants and Nurses Benefit Society noted Redmond's 'untiring efforts' for the betterment of Waterford's citizens and improvements in the city. They made particular reference to his 'great work' in helping to abolish the toll bridge, 'so long a burden on the community and a tax especially severe on the poorer classes'.[75]

Redmond willingly dealt with the problems of his less exalted constituents. He took up a fisherman's request for a reduction in the cost of a licence and having interviewed the mayor about a need to speed up the morning mails, he drafted a memorandum to the postmaster-general. Minor problems concerning the Barrack Street telegraph office were also raised with the postmaster-general. Redmond investigated the case of a Waterford man's son who was dismissed as a porter by the London Post Office. He agitated for the release of a sick prisoner and received a letter of thanks from a stonemason of John Street for 'the interest you have taken on behalf of my son, towards his release'. And he was requested to support local activities such as the Temperance Society.[76]

There were also opportunities for Redmond to strengthen his Ballybricken links. In February 1892 Ballybricken men visited John Daly and James Egan in Portland prison[77] and Redmond assured them the efforts of the IPP to have the men released would 'never cease'. Charlie Strange acted as solicitor for the Waterford branch of the revived Amnesty Association which Redmond inaugurated in October 1893. During a visit in January 1895, Redmond, knowing 'how deep and intense is the feeling' of the city on the amnesty question, reported that he had himself visited Portland prison to see John Daly and had pressed for his release.[78]

The practice of visiting the city at least once a year to give an account of his stewardship, kept Redmond in contact. On one occasion he took the opportunity to give a lecture on Irish leaders from Swift to Parnell at the Theatre Royal.[79] Generally these visits were accompanied by torchlight processions, band music and large

72 Report from the Commissioners for Improving the Port and Harbour of Waterford, 7 Feb. 1899 (Redmond Papers, 15,238 |10|), NLI.

73 R. S. Lee to Redmond, 27 Apr. 1895 (Redmond Papers, 15,238 |11|), NLI.

74 J. J. Feely, Town Clerk's Office, 'Statement on Waterford toll bridge', May 1905; C. P. (Banquo) Redmond to John Redmond, 13 June 1905; copy of corporation resolution, 4 July 1905; chief secretary to Redmond, 4 July 1905 (Redmond Papers, 15,245 |6| and |7|), NLI.

75 *Munster Express*, 31 Jan. 1914.

76 A sample of letters taken to represent Redmond's constituency work: unidentified Waterford constituent to Redmond, 22 Mar. 1893, 19 Nov. 1894; J. N. White to Redmond, 30 Mar. 1893; Maurice Quinlan to Redmond, 19 May 1894; William Collins to Redmond, 30 Sep. 1895; R. S. Lee to Redmond, 27 Apr. 1895; G. E. White to Redmond, 23 Apr. 1895; father of Henry Wyse to Redmond, Feb. 1896 (Redmond Papers, 15,238 |11|), NLI.

77 Daly and Egan were arrested during a dynamiting campaign in England in the 1880s. The dynamiters were directed by the fenians and attempts were made to blow up civic buildings, railways, docks and barracks. James Francis Egan and John Daly (1845–1916), a fenian and active member of the Irish Republican Brotherhood in the 1867 rising, were arrested at Birkenhead in possession of explosives in 1884. Egan was sentenced to 20 years' imprisonment and Daly to life. But public agitation led to Daly's release in 1896.

78 *Waterford News*, 27 Feb. 1892; 21 Oct. 1893; 26 Jan. 1895.

79 *Waterford News*, 3 Dec. 1898.

demonstrations of loyalty. An assertive policy on home rule and the land and university questions following reunification focused public attention. In 1904 Redmond told his constituents that English politicians believed concessions on the land issue would kill the demand for home rule. 'It was time to undeceive them ... the movement for Home Rule would now once more come to the front.' And he attacked the Irish government as being inefficient and extravagant.[80]

By 1915 the home rule movement was well established in Irish communal life. It was the single most dominant issue and Redmond's constituency work was neglected as he pressed it in his capacity as leader of the IPP. On opening the new bridge in 1913, he admitted he would have liked to have done more for the 'material benefit' of Waterford but had found the home rule issue 'all-engrossing'.[81] As the leading nationalist in the fight for home rule, Redmond was bound to attract the loyalty of men who believed in it. For individuals in Waterford this loyalty to Redmond and the IPP no doubt deepened as he became engaged in a progressively fiercer struggle to achieve it.

III

By the time he opened the new bridge in February 1913, the 'almost entirely illusory'[82] 1912 home rule bill had passed its third reading in the House of Commons and the occasion was used to celebrate its passage as well as the opening of the bridge. Redmond arrived to the sound of exploding fog-signals and the welcome of a crowd estimated at 25,000. Among the corporation members and prominent citizens greeting him at the station were the mayor, Martin J. Murphy, W. G. D. Goff, Bishop Sheehan and Father Tom Furlong.

The corporation expressed 'full and absolute confidence in [his] wise and able leadership'. The city branch of the UIL confirmed its 'unswerving loyalty' to Redmond and Councillor William Fitzgerald considered him 'victor in the mighty struggle for freedom, begun in the dark and evil days, [which] has been brought at last to a successful close'. Congratulating him on his 'great generalship', the Pig Buyers Association declared itself 'proud to be represented in the English Parliament by a man of such wonderful genius and tact'. Despite Redmond's being busy, the opening of the bridge demonstrated that the 'welfare of Waterford [and] its citizens has never been neglected'. The Town Tenants League took the opportunity to remind Redmond that in the 'valued struggle for Home Rule' much had been done for the tenant farmers. But the town dwellers now wanted the right to purchase homes.

Redmond responded to the optimistic mood. The ominous significance of the Ulster Volunteer Force, founded in January, and a protest against the House of Lords' rejection of the home rule bill by the president of the local branch of the AOH, were lost in the euphoria. Through all the addresses Redmond noted the 'spirit of absolute confidence that we are now at the end of this long and weary struggle and at the goal for which our fathers worked and died'. Home rule, considered by Daniel Sheehan to be 'poor and paltry a thing',[83] was claimed to be the harbinger of a better future.

> We all believe and know that in a few short months an Irish Parliament will be sitting in College Green [and there will be] the blending of all creeds and classes of Irish people into one body whose one aim will be the welfare and prosperity of the country.

At a banquet in City Hall he referred to the 'atmosphere of depression and decay' having disappeared from Waterford. 'Today there is a buoyant spirit and a new confidence.' The crowd

---

80 *Waterford Standard*, 9 Jan. 1904.
81 *Munster Express*, 15 Feb. 1913.
82 Lyons, 'The decline and fall of the Nationalist Party' in Edwards and Pyle (eds.) (1968).
83 Sheehan (1921), p. 239.

which unyoked the horses from Redmond's carriage and dragged it to the Imperial Hotel sang *A Nation Once Again* and a torchlit procession accompanying him to the station included the Barrack Street Band, the Portlairge War-pipes, the Erin's Hope and the T. F. Meagher's Fife and Drum bands.[84]

Redmond's optimistic predictions did not match reality and the Irish Volunteers were founded in 1913. An estimated 50,000 people crowded into Waterford for a home rule demonstration attended by Redmond and his wife during January 1914. In Redmond's view this, the 'most remarkable Nationalist demonstration' ever held in Munster, disproved the

> slander employed by [the] Tory press ... that the masses of the Irish people are apathetic on this great question of self-government. [Here there were] Nationalists of all classes, from the sturdy working man to the commercial magnate and owner of many acres.

The city streets and a platform erected in Ballybricken Green were gaily decorated. Arches spanned the streets and mottoes declared 'Waterford is loyal to Redmond and Ireland's cause', 'We must get Home Rule' and 'Waterford stands for unity and Ireland'. In a 'touching and impressive' exhibition of patriotism by the 'poorer people' of Ballybricken, busts and photographs of John Redmond, Parnell, Devlin[85] and Dillon were displayed in windows and over doors in 'beautiful and artistic' settings. Among the decorations was a scroll: 'Historic Ballybricken pledges allegiance to Redmond.'

Addresses were given from the platform on which 50 Catholic clergy, including Father Tom Furlong (vice president of the UIL), and dignitaries from seven other counties were gathered. The corporation again pledged its 'full and absolute confidence' in Redmond. County council members declared that future Irish men and women would hold his memory 'in priceless heritage for leading Erin out of the darkness' and the Board of Guardians thanked him for 'leading our oppressed people from political slavery to legislative freedom'.

The UIL were convinced that on his next visit Redmond would come as 'premier of a Home Parliament'. He had 'striven to wrench the shackles of slavery from the limbs of Erin'. Unable to attend, Bishop Sheehan wrote that Redmond by his 'patriotism, skill, and unflagging devotion, has brought our country to the very threshold of freedom'. Many more addresses similarly fulsome in their praise were offered from a host of nationalist and civic organisations.

Redmond told his constituents the struggle was almost at an end. 'We have fought and we have won,' he claimed, 'but we have yet to reap the fruits of victory.' He considered talk of civil war nonsense. The enemies of home rule would not intimidate Asquith: 'Lift up your hearts. Ireland's long travail is at an end. You are about to witness the rebirth of Irish freedom, prosperity, and happiness.'[86] In March the Curragh incident finally wrecked Asquith's Ulster policies and Redmond acceded to a six-year exclusion period for Ulster. Nationalist newspaper staff were alleged to have intimidated worshippers in Waterford's Protestant cathedral. Prayers were offered up in 'these times of difficulty'[87] and a unit of the Irish Volunteers was established.

By May there were five Volunteer units in Waterford with a membership of 1,075 mainly made up of clerks, shop assistants and superior artisans.[88] In June the city battalion accompanied by the Erin's Hope Band marched to Kilmacow. As they stood drawn up in front of the Catholic church, the parish priest told them that they,

---

84 *Munster Express*, 15 Feb. 1913.
85 Joseph Devlin (1872–1934), nationalist MP and leading member of the Ancient Order of Hibernians, built up a strong working-class support in his Belfast constituency. As leader of Ulster's nationalists, he accepted the home rule act of 1914 and encouraged army recruitment during the war.
86 *Munster Express*, 10, 31 Jan. 1914.
87 *Hansard* (Commons) 5th ser. LIX, 886, 9 Mar. 1914.
88 Mac Giolla Choille (1966), pp. 81–82, 109, 110.

coming from the city of Thomas Francis Meagher, would do their duty for 'faith and fatherland'.[89] By July ex-NCO instructors were reportedly dismissed from Wexford branches because they had served the king and there was the fear of a general massacre of Protestants if war erupted in Ulster.[90] And Redmond sent T. M. Kettle to buy arms for the Irish Volunteers in defiance of the government's arms proclamation. A martial spirit suffused all sections of the population, including the unfranchised and the labourers.[91]

On the evening of Friday 24 July coastguards reported sighting a suspicious vessel off Tramore. Amid rumours that arms were to be landed for the Volunteers, police patrolled the coast and the banks of the River Suir as far as Passage East. A cruiser and three destroyers arrived off Tramore during the night. Police, 'armed to the teeth', were seen leaving the city and a force of them was stationed overnight on The Island as Gerald Purcell Fitzgerald had 'recently identified himself with the Volunteer movement'. On Sunday 26th the warships anchored off Dunmore East and the local newspapers reported a 'scene of slaughter' in Dublin's Bachelor's Walk after the Howth gun-running incident.[92] With reference to the Curragh 'mutiny', it was observed: 'the troops which the government would not draft into Ulster because they feared they would not consent to act against Ulster have been ready enough to kill the people in Dublin amongst whom they live.'

Flags were flown at half-mast at Hibernia Hall in O'Connell Street, and also on municipal buildings on the orders of the mayor. The 'most intense indignation prevailed' throughout the city where the 'brutal occurrence' in Dublin was the sole topic. Redmond had seized leadership of the Volunteers[93] and the commanding officer of the city's battalion sought his permission to form a procession. 'Practically every man, woman and child in the city' turned out for the monster demonstration on Tuesday 28 July. The procession, led by a wagonette containing the mayor, P. A. Murphy, councillors and priests and with the rear brought up by a contingent of *Na Fianna Eireann* in uniforms and with flags, marched through the principal streets to Ballybricken Green where P. A. Murphy addressed the crowds on behalf of the mayor. A member of the local Volunteers committee, he demanded punishment for those who perpetrated the killings in Dublin and congratulated the Volunteers on the landing of arms at Howth. He insisted on either the reinstatement of the Dublin Metropolitan Police officers who were dismissed for refusing to fire on the crowds or that the same justice be meted out to the Curragh army officers, and he supported Redmond's call for the proclamation prohibiting the import of arms to be withdrawn.

Before dismissing the Volunteers, their commander called on non-members to enrol at once: 'after Sunday's business any Irishman not in the ranks of the Volunteers was not for but against Ireland.' He urged the Volunteers to be proud of their Dublin compatriots who had 'faced the loaded rifles and fixed bayonets of the army of occupation in Ireland'. They did not want trouble, but he 'solemnly warn[ed] [the authorities] that any attempt made to take from the city

89 *Munster Express*, 6 June 1914.
90 Anonymous secret report, 'Report on Irish Nationalist Volunteers', *c.* July 1914 (Paget Papers, MS 51250), British Museum.
91 Fitzpatrick (1977), pp. 102–06.
92 German weapons were purchased by the Ulster Volunteer Force and landed at Larne during April 1914 without government intervention. In response, Sir Roger Casement was among those who planned the purchase from Germany of guns for the Irish National Volunteers and *Na Fianna Eireann*. The weapons were landed at Howth, County Dublin, on 26 July 1914. Troops of the King's Own Scottish Borderers were despatched to Howth and this led to their being stoned in Bachelor's Walk, Dublin. They opened fire and three people were killed and at least 38 injured. There was widespread indignation in England and Ireland at what was seen as uneven justice in favour of the Ulster Volunteer Force.
93 John Redmond, fearing the Volunteers would be used to prevent the passage of the third home rule bill, demanded half the seats on the organisation's provisional committee. To avoid splitting the movement, his demands were conceded in June 1914, despite opposition from the more radical members.

of Waterford Volunteers any rifle or ammunition … while the Ulster Volunteers were allowed to retain their arms, would be resisted to the bitter end.'

At their weekly meeting, the Board of Guardians spoke of murder in 'cold blood' and demanded even-handed justice. Edward Walsh, owner of the *Munster Express*, called for rapid self-government with no more 'dallying with the present Home Rule Bill or pandering to the Ascendancy Party'. A unionist guardian thought the Dublin incident 'enough to make Unionists almost turn their coats inside out'.[94]

On the eve of the First World War, therefore, Redmond and his Waterford constituents were driven even closer together by the threat to home rule and the possibility of civil war. Despite deadlock over the House of Lords' amendment to the home rule bill excluding the northern counties permanently, his personal influence and prestige never stood so high in Ireland.[95] And the Gaelic revival, operating through the city's clerical and lay institutions, had been easily harnessed by Redmond's supporters to further enhance his prestige and authority. In one view, 'impoverished' men like James English would not have been immune to its tendency to rejuvenate national pride.[96]

IV

In sport, Waterford had the Waterpark Celtic Association Football Club, the GAA Waterford Commercial Football Club, the De la Salle Gaelic Football Club, the De la Salle Athletic Association, the president of which was Brother Thomas who was so confident in Redmond's influence, and the Gracedieu Hurling and Football Club.

Fixtures were constantly advertised throughout the period.

Thousands flocked to Aglish on foot, on bicycles and in wagonettes, cars and carts, amid flying banners and the sound of horns, to watch the match between Erin's Hope (Dungarvan) and Blackwater Ramblers (Lismore) to decide the GAA Waterford football championship in 1899.[97] And in Christendom, on the north side of the city, a 'very large assembly' watched a Gaelic football game between Limerick Commercials and the local slate-quarry miners.[98] Waterford battled with Kerry hurling and football teams in Cork[99] and special trains brought spectators from Kilkenny to watch the De la Salle College team (the Geraldines) meet the T. F. Meagher's at the sports ground in a match to decide the senior hurling championship of East Waterford.[100] During March 1915 the Waterford team met Kerry in hurling and Irish football in the Wolfe Tone memorial tournament.[101]

The Waterford branch of the Gaelic League was also active at the turn of the century and in 1904 it organised its second *feis*. Opening it, Father Tom Furlong told the 'very large attendance' that the Gaelic League movement was

> a good one and a truly patriotic one, having for its objectives the revival and preservation of the ancient language of Ireland, and the revival and promotion of the industries of the country, and the restoration and preservation of the Irish song and the Irish dance, and … it was a movement that not only promoted the national and material, but also the moral, welfare of the country.

Bishop Sheehan spoke of the 'marvellous advance' of the Gaelic movement in a very short period. 'The child of today,' he observed, 'knows

94 *Munster Express*, 1 Aug. 1914.
95 Gwynn, D. (1932), *The Life of John Redmond*, London, pp. 323–25.
96 Lyons (1973), pp. 226–27.
97 *Waterford News*, 17 Nov. 1899.
98 *Waterford Standard*, 20 Aug. 1902.
99 *Waterford Mail*, 13 June 1906.
100 *Munster Express*, 15 Feb. 1913.
101 *Munster Express*, 27 Mar. 1915.

ten times as much about the Gaelic movement as the man or woman did three or four years ago.' The *feis* was only a small part of a 'far reaching and very diversified' movement which had 'invaded the homes ... overflowed into the schools ... found its way into the church and ... contributed in a large way to our national life'. Through the league, Irish people had recovered the folklore which he thought had contributed to developing 'a deep national feeling among us'. All the city's Catholic schools were represented when prizes were presented for competitions in the Irish language, singing, playing the pipes and dancing the jig and the reel.[102]

In 1915, however, the *Waterford News* gave a more circumspect assessment of the Gaelic League's impact on the city. The *feis* that year was considered to have been a 'brilliant success' with the majority of the estimated 3,000 spectators coming from 'every class' of citizen. There was a 'big muster' of the city's leading citizens and practically all the clergy. Canon Tom Furlong was on the platform with other priests who filled the top offices of the local league branch. Patrick W. Kenny was also present. But according to a *Waterford News* editorial such an attendance was unusual. Most of those attending past *feiseanna* had been residents of the county.

> No doubt Portlairge [Waterford] in the past did not put forth the vigorous efforts to combat the strong influence of the foreigner: the Sassenach had more scope here probably than in any other city in Ireland; and shoneenism laid a heavy hand on our middle classes until they became more English than the English themselves ... . Centuries old customs and manners of the imported type are not easily rooted out. But we are gaining ground and gaining it rapidly too.[103]

Still, as Bishop Sheehan had noted, the *feis* was only one element of the revival and by 1908 the teaching of Irish had been introduced into the national schools. There was a considerable barrier of ignorance to overcome, however. In 1911 only 7.7 per cent of the city's population spoke Irish and every one of these persons was bilingual. Only 4 per cent of the residents of Thomas's Avenue could speak Irish (see Appendix J). James Connolly, taking the labourer's point of view, sought to give the debate a realistic perspective.

> You cannot teach starving men Gaelic; and the treasury of our national literature will and must remain lost forever to the poor wage-slaves who are contented by our system of society to toil from early morning to late at night for a mere starvation wage ... . Celtic lore would hold but a secondary place in their esteem beside a rasher of bacon.[104]

None the less, the *Waterford News* and *Munster Express* had regular Gaelic League news columns in Irish. 'Fairly well attended' Irish classes were held in the Gaelic League rooms at 29 Barronstrand Street[105] and Irish dance lessons were offered at Hibernia Hall and by the Irish National Foresters in the hall, Rose Lane.[106] People of James English's generation would have been less directly influenced by the league's activities but his daughter Margaret, born in 1907, spoke Irish fairly well by the time she left school and was also a prize and medal winner in many Irish dance competitions. For a small fee, she and about six other girls received nightly dance instruction in a private house on the Yellow Road to the music of the 'fiddle' and the 'melodeon'.

Interest in Irish culture was such that in the first meeting of the *oireachtas* committee at the beginning of 1916, an extensive preliminary pro-

102 *Waterford Standard*, 8 June 1904.
103 *Waterford News*, 2 and 9 July 1915.
104 Connolly, J. (1898) 'The Language Movement', *Workers' Republic*, reproduced in Connolly (1987), Vol. 1, pp. 340–41; Allen, K. (1990), *The Politics of James Connolly*, London, pp. 22–23.
105 *Waterford News*, 25 Feb. 1916.
106 *Waterford News*, 11 Feb. 1916.

gramme was drawn up for the festival. GAA fixtures and war-pipe band and solo contests were to be held on the sports field while City Hall, Temperance Hall, the technical school, the CYMS building and St Joseph's schools would be used for industrial and art exhibitions and for singing and dancing contests. It was planned to run special trains from Dublin, Cork, Tralee, Athlone, Limerick and other main centres.[107] St Patrick's Day was another occasion which would have generally heightened nationalistic awareness, whether or not a man directly participated in Irish cultural or Gaelic League activities.

The Gaelic League had successfully campaigned to have St Patrick's Day declared an official public holiday and in 1913 the procession and public meeting held in City Hall was one of the largest seen in years.[108] The 1914 festivity, organised by the Waterford branch of the Gaelic League, was typical. Celebrated in a 'fitting and patriotic manner', mass was said in the cathedral every hour until noon when there was high mass. About 300 CYMS members, wearing green rosettes and accompanied by the Barrack Street Brass and Reed Band, marched in procession from the hall in Parnell Street to high mass. The sermon was given in Irish and a procession which included bands, school pupils, GAA club members and the representatives of several national bodies, started from City Hall and paraded the streets. An Irish language meeting was held in City Hall. Priests and councillors called for the teaching of Irish in schools and for support of the Gaelic League.[109]

In 1915 some of the St Patrick's Day services and prayers as well as the rosary were said in Irish and the organist in the cathedral played 'national music'. The procession, under the direction of the Gaelic League, included a uni-

formed guard of the Irish National Foresters and a contingent of *Na Fianna Eireann* who 'were the centre of attraction with their handsome uniforms and equipment, their flag, war pipes and bannerettes'. Hearne and Co. lent the horses, car and drapery for a *tableau*. Redmondite National Volunteers paraded in 'trim uniforms and equipment'. When the Irish Volunteers split after John Redmond's Woodenbridge speech on 20 September 1914 the majority of members followed him to form the National Volunteers. The remaining separatist element retained the 'Irish Volunteers' title. Students and representatives from the GAA clubs and city and county branches of the AOH, also took part. Several bands accompanied them. A public meeting chaired by the mayor in City Hall was addressed by several priests, Patrick W. Kenny, who called for the resuscitation of the Irish language, and Edward Walsh the city high sheriff.[110]

John Redmond acknowledged the strength of the developing Irish-Ireland movement and the potential Sinn Fein threat. In 1907 he wrote,

> there are, everyone recognises, new forces stirring in the country. The Gaelic League, with all its developments, its intellectual and industrial revival, all should make for strengthening the National forces instead of being turned, as some of the opponents of the Irish Party seek, into causes of fresh discord and dissension, by representing us as opponents.[111]

However, Waterford reflected the accuracy of the view that Catholic Ireland was virtually a one-party nation by 1914.[112] The Redmondite monopoly of political power reinforced the city's homogeneity and stifled any diversity of political expression.

107 *Waterford News*, 25 Feb. 1916.
108 *Waterford Standard*, 19 Mar. 1913.
109 *Munster Express*, 21 Mar. 1914.
110 *Waterford Standard*, 24 Mar. 1915; *Munster Express*, 20 Mar. 1915.
111 Redmond, J. E., 'Letter from Mr J.E. Redmond, M.P.' in Redmond et al. (1907), pp. 3–6.
112 Fitzpatrick (1977), p. 85.

V

The Waterford parliamentary seat was never contested between 1895 and 1918. Because he did not reach voting age until 1897, James English was therefore effectively deprived of his franchise. He had no opportunity to cast his ballot or to vote for anyone other than Redmond. However, this statement is subject to qualification. It is not clear whether in a practical rather than a legal sense he would have been able to exercise his right to vote anyway. Although the franchise had been extended to illiterate urban labourers by the Representation of the People (Ireland) Act 1868, two factors operated to limit its effect.

Firstly, in practice the legislation excluded large numbers of unskilled workers. When the British and Irish reform acts were passed, nobody then in parliament wanted to extend the franchise beyond the 'respectable working class' (artisans) to the 'residuum'. The acts were therefore hedged about with restrictions which effectively deprived an estimated 20 to 30 per cent of the potential electorate of the franchise.[113]

The poorer and more mobile unskilled workers were the most disadvantaged and probably formed the bulk of the 60 per cent of Waterford city males over 21 years who were excluded from the electorate in 1911. Not a single lodger appeared on the electoral register for the city in 1910.[114] By not paying rates landlords could deprive tenement residents of the vote. Redmond claimed 40 tenants on 'one whole side' of Alexander Street in Centre Ward who had 'voted solid' for him in 1891, were not registered for the 1892 election. Men who had lived in the same houses for years and had voted in 1891 were not included in the 1892 electoral rolls. And in his speech of thanks to about 2,000 supporters outside City Hall, Redmond alleged that 'whole Streets' had been 'absolutely disenfranchised' chiefly because of non-payment of rates.[115]

Secondly, the influence of priests could inhibit any free choice. Some parishioners would follow their priests anywhere. However, Parnellism remained strong in urban areas despite anti-Parnellite campaigning by priests. In contrast to the city, rural Waterford was solidly anti-Parnellite. It has been argued that less sectarian and clerical pressure was the reason for this,[116] but there was as much pressure applied by priests on the urban as on the rural voter. A significant difference in the educational standards of voters was the most probable explanation. There were far fewer illiterate urban voters. Nine per cent of Waterford city voters were illiterate in 1895 compared with 25 per cent in West Waterford in 1910.[117]

The greater number of more sophisticated urban voters were less susceptible to priestly pressure and it has been shown that during the 1891 and 1892 elections, Parnellites were less likely to win votes in those urban districts with the greater number of illiterate voters. Here the influence of the priests was probably decisive.

Illiterate voters had to declare their choice of candidate orally to presiding officers. This would have been within the intimidating presence of priests who, in acting as personation agents,[118] gave their services free.[119] The clerical influence in the 1891 and 1892 polls has been described as resembling that of the pre-secret ballot days. Priests standing at the polling booths instructed voters on the appropriate choice of candidate as

113 Dunbabin, J. P. D., 'Electoral reforms and their outcome in the United Kingdom, 1865–1900' in Gourvish and O'Day (eds.) pp. 93–125; Walker, B. M. (1973), 'The Irish electorate, 1868–1915, *Irish Historical Studies*, XVIII, pp. 359–406.
114 *Return Showing the Number of Persons who Voted as Illiterates in each Constituency of the United Kingdom at the General Election of January, 1910, and the Total Number of Votes polled in each Constituency* (British Parliamentary Papers, 1910 (283) LXXIII.673), p. 19.
115 *Waterford News*, 9 July 1892.
116 Garvin (1981), pp. 84–88.
117 Percentages calculated using figures in *Return Showing the Number of Persons who voted as Illiterates in the January 1910 Election* and *Return showing Number Voting as Illiterates in the 1895 General Election* (British Parliamentary Papers, 1896 (84) LXVII.307).
118 Woods (1968), pp. 381–82.
119 Flynn to Davitt, 14 Mar. 1892 and Davitt to Flynn, 15 Mar. 1892 (Davitt Papers, 9471), Trinity.

they went in. Redmond supporters claimed that illiterate voters went 'in scores' to their committee rooms asking for instructions on the voting process in the 1891 Waterford by-election.[120] But the Centre Ward vote went against Redmond.

Local priests, and especially Father Flynn, were intensely involved in the political struggle and Charlie Strange thought one reason for the defeat in Centre Ward was that clergy at the booths were 'most demonstrative' in their support of Davitt. Other reasons were that 'certain local traders' had applied pressure on their employees and also some anti-Redmond Ferrybank voters used a Centre Ward polling booth. None the less Strange objected to calls for the disfranchisement of illiterate voters.[121]

In February 1892, Father Flynn founded the anti-Parnellite *Waterford Star*, the first edition being planned to appear on 2 April,[122] with help from the city branch of the INL. He raised £80 and appointed an editor and manager from the *Clonmel Nationalist*.[123] Michael Davitt donated £30 from the unused balance of his Waterford election fund, the remaining £153 16s 2d being given to the evicted tenants fund.[124]

The move, according to the *Waterford News*, was 'a gasping, frantic effort' by Father Flynn, the 'Alpha and Omega of the Waterford Federation, to set up a party of Political Trickery in the city'.[125] When the *Waterford News* accused Father Furlong of having 'defended the scurrility of Mr Tim Healy',[126] he wrote to the paper: 'You might well leave, I think, to the Orange papers the policy of discrediting the priests of Ireland, or you may become more Orange than the Orange-

men themselves.' And when Father Furlong told the chairman (Father Flynn) that a *Waterford News* reporter was at a federation meeting, the reporter was asked to leave. Outside, Redmond supporters gave a 'lusty cheer'.[127]

The priests' activities were not restricted to the city. Fathers Flynn and Furlong were accused of 'working the women and children in Passage up to a terrible state of excitement' against the county Parnellites.[128] Another priest warned his parishioners: 'beware of the wolf in sheep's clothing'[129] and asked them to pray for the conversion of the Parnellites.[130] A drop in Redmond's proportion of the 1892 ballot and the reduced number of people voting was explained by the Parnellites as partly due to the increased activity of priests. There were priests at almost every polling booth to 'watch their interests' and their presence was considered to have had a 'considerable influence on the voters'.[131]

Out of eleven polling booths used in the 1892 election, only two polled an anti-Redmond majority. Significantly, the majority of those using the Ballybricken newsroom booth, where Father Flynn acted as the 'Whig agent', voted for Redmond. The newsroom was the headquarters of the politically conscious and articulate members of the Pig Buyers Association, whose address to Redmond on his arrival in Waterford read in part, 'if they [the anti-Parnellites] will not have peace then let us give them war ... we loved our chief, we hate the men who betrayed him'. But at the O'Connell Street booth, the majority of men from the lanes of Centre and Custom House Wards voted for David Sheehy. Nor did the

120 *Waterford News*, 2 Jan. 1892.
121 *Waterford Standard*, 30 Dec. 1891.
122 Flynn to Davitt, 24 Mar. 1892 (Davitt Papers, 9471), Trinity.
123 Flynn to Davitt, 11 Mar. 1892 (Davitt Papers, 9471), Trinity.
124 Handwritten notes and copy of the election account from the city sheriff's office (Davitt Papers, 9471), Trinity.
125 *Waterford News*, 18 Jan. and 20 Feb. 1892, 12 May 1894.
126 Following the split in the IPP in 1890, Healy, along with John Dillon and William O'Brien among others, joined Justin McCarthy in setting up the Irish National Federation. Healy was expelled from the federation in 1895 and in 1896 Dillon became the leader when McCarthy resigned.
127 *Waterford News*, 25 June 1892.
128 *Waterford News*, 16 July 1892.
129 *Waterford News*, 30 July 1892.
130 *Waterford News*, 6 Aug. 1892.
131 *Waterford News*, 9 July 1892.

priests, absent from the booth, deem it necessary to police the voters. Redmond also failed to attract the Ferrybank voters.[132]

Although limited in the exercise of his parliamentary franchise, local politics offered a possible avenue of expression for labourers like James English. However, Redmondite nationalism permeated and suffocated local as well as national politics.

VI

The Local Government Act of 1898 has been assessed as a 'purely English necessity for an "English crisis" '[133] which imposed on the 'humblest and poorest tenants' restrictions similar to those of the parliamentary franchise.[134] But it gave the urban underprivileged an opportunity to create a political culture free of Redmond, the IPP and a nationalist tradition which took little account of the labourer's interests. According to Daniel Sheehan, the act 'broke for ever the back of landlord power' and in enfranchising the workers in town and country it gave 'into the hands of the people for the first time the absolute control of their own local affairs'.[135]

The first opportunity for James English to use his vote came in the January 1899 municipal elections when he was 22 years of age. However, using a familiar tactic, Redmond's supporters usurped the role of local labour representatives and far from freeing the labourer, the act has been described as laying the political framework for an 'instinctive parochialism' in Irish society.[136]

Charlie Strange, known for his socialist views, combined the roles of radical and conservative Redmondite nationalist. In 1896 he told Redmond that he was an 'avowed socialist' and that he did not want 'to disguise from myself the fact that the majority of the artisans of Waterford look on me as being peculiarly their friend'.[137] But he identified his socialism with the interests of the conservative skilled worker and his reaction to the threat posed by a militant labour movement was no different to that of Father Flynn's or of others in his class. His concerns were the preservation of social hegemony and the achievement of nationalist goals. When heavily involved in Redmond's 1891 and 1892 election campaigns, he gave a lecture on poverty and its causes. In his view,

> the greatest curse a country ever suffered under was the system of strikes, for eventually the capitalist would gain more capital as a consequence and would ultimately be able to use that increased capital to oppress and repress the artizan more than ever before.

He dabbled in theory but did not take a serious interest in practical labour politics. Men such as Strange diverted attention away from the political possibilities for the labourer at a time when labour movements in the United Kingdom and other developed countries were discovering a latent power. There were those who argued that 'bourgeois intellectuals' like Strange were decisively responsible for the degeneration of socialist parties. However sincere their commitment to the cause of proletarian emancipation, their 'whole training, outlook and style of life were in fact inimical to it'.[138]

While enthusiastically helping to organise Redmond's 1891 campaign, Strange published letters, articles and addresses on socialism.[139] And during a period when he was a member of the

132 *Waterford News*, 2, 9 and 20 July 1892.
133 Gailey (1984).
134 *Waterford Standard*, 20 Aug. 1902.
135 Sheehan (1921), pp. 51, 176.
136 Gailey (1984).
137 Strange to Redmond, 18 Mar. 1896 (Redmond Papers, 15,238 [7]), NLI.
138 Beetham, D., 'Reformism and the "bourgeoisification" of the labour movement' in C. Levy (ed.) (1987).
139 *Waterford Standard*, 9 Dec. 1891.

Independent Labour Party (ILP)[140] and later of Connolly's Irish Socialist Republican Party (ISRP), Strange advised Redmond to use his influence and 'calm down' the leader writer of the *Independent*, suggesting the way he 'fulminates his thunderbolts against those who come under the general and not well defined ... head "Socialist" [was] likely to lose a few votes' for the Parnellites.[141]

Yet when addressing workers and when it suited him, Strange could sound like a convinced and convincing radical. About three months before he was so prominently active in Redmond's 1895 campaign, as one of a delegation from the FTLU he addressed a meeting of rural labourers at Ring. A speaker had condemned the workhouse, the only recourse to unemployed labourers, as 'degrading' and argued for some other form of relief. Strange broadened out the theme.

> The bloated aristocracy ... were taking and keeping everything and putting the labourer in what they called their proper condition. ... [Labourers had to] ... set up a spirit of independence which would enable them to look on themselves as being entitled to the good things of this world just the same as every other individual in it ... why was it they should be living in this condition of poverty and destitution when other people who did absolutely nothing were living in a condition of enjoyment and wealth.

In an apparent reference to the International Workingmen's Association, he told the workers of the need to organise. He belonged to an international association of four million who would get their rights in spite of 'anything the marquis of this or the earl of that might say to the contrary'. It was spreading across Europe and would become the dominant power. Within 15 years an organisation started by a handful of men now had 41 representatives in the German *Reichstag*, 25 members in the French House of Representatives and it had 'completely obliterated the Liberal party in the Belgian Parliament'.[142]

When Keir Hardie, a founder member and president of the Independent Labour Party, and the first British Labour MP, visited Waterford during his tour to organise Irish branches of the ILP in 1894, Charlie Strange called on workers to form a united movement. But only 50 workers turned up at the inauguration of the city branch despite encouragement by the FTLU. Charlie Strange, who kept up correspondence with Redmond throughout the period, was nominated by the ILP branch to fight the 1895 and 1896 municipal elections. However, the Waterford branch soon became a 'middle class debating society'.[143] On the formation of the ISRP, the Waterford ILP members, including Strange, switched allegiance and the ILP collapsed in less than two years. Success in mobilising working-class support for the Labour Party in the United Kingdom at this time varied widely according to local conditions,[144] so the Waterford experience was not exceptional.

The ISRP's programme was to 'wean the Irish worker from a dumb acceptance of the *status quo*' and move him leftwards.[145] But after two years less than 50 people had enrolled in the party and weekly attendance at meetings hovered at around 20. In May 1897 Charlie Strange wrote to Dublin 'speaking in a very hopeless manner of the prospects of socialism in Waterford, and declining to

---

140   The Independent Labour Party, inaugurated in Britain on 13 January 1893, resulted from the desire of local labour parties and trade unions to build a parliamentary party with a programme of labour reform. Its principal object was to secure the collective ownership of the means of production, distribution and exchange. In 1900 the ILP took part in a conference out of which emerged the Labour Representation Committee. This laid the ground for the founding of the Labour Party in 1906. Ireland did not have its own labour party until 1912 when the Irish Labour Party and Trades Union Congress was founded by James Connolly and James Larkin thus politicising the Irish Trades Union Congress which had been founded in 1894.
141   Strange to Redmond, 18 Mar. 1896 (Redmond Papers, 15,238 [7]), NLI.
142   *Waterford News*, 23 Mar. 1895.
143   O'Connor (1989), p. 99.
144   Turner (1992), pp. 31–32.
145   Lyons (1973), p. 274.

help in holding a meeting'. In Cork the ISRP was condemned by the bishop in a letter read in all churches, and branches outside of Dublin soon folded.[146] In 1897 Strange won a seat in Centre Ward but not as a nominated labour representative.

On the industrial front, however, the labour movement was more successful. Although membership of the FTLU, which now included societies representing general labourers, factory workers, brewery men and bottling store operatives, had peaked at 700 in 1892 and by 1894 was down to 400, the city's first modern Trades and Labour Council was formed under the presidency of Patrick J. Leo in 1895. With 13 affiliates representing 350 members, it projected the 'moderate, deferential mentality of contemporary trade unions'.[147]

Charlie Strange was elected vice president and delegate to the 1895 Irish Trades Union Congress. At the time Strange was not only campaigning for Redmond in the general election but his law firm was also handling Redmond's election accounts.[148] A year later Strange reported to Redmond that the council, though non-political, was dominated by men who had 'strong socialist leanings' and was mainly composed of delegates 'who were formerly very much opposed to us [an apparent reference to the Parnellite wing of the IPP] as well as many men who have always been with us'.[149] The FTLU and the Trades Council were soon in disagreement and the city's labour movement entered the 1899 municipal elections divided.

Nationalism and the personality-centred, community approach to local politics weakened any industrial radicalism. Redmond worked closely with clerics and local labour leaders to settle industrial disputes. And local labour leaders who, like Strange, took major roles in the arbitration of disputes, were also generally corporation members and closely identified with either the McCarthy or the Parnellite wing of the IPP. The long drawn-out pig buyers' dispute which started in 1892, climaxed amid considerable violence and disorder during the winter of 1896–97 and was finally settled at great employment and organisational cost to the workers in July 1897, was an example of how this relationship functioned.

As the dispute moved into its most violent stage, Father Flynn was active in seeking a settlement. Taking a 'constant interest' in the dispute, he held private meetings with the Pig Buyers Association in its Ballybricken rooms and was present at a meeting between Denny and the pig buyers. He accompanied the mayor in a deputation which went to a meeting in Dublin to represent the pig buyers' interests.[150]

In court, Redmond successfully defended pig buyers accused of assault and disorder during the dispute.[151] He was kept updated on every significant move during its worse phase and was subsequently instrumental in bringing it to an end.[152] It was Redmond who acted as arbitrator and who drew up a programme to settle the dispute which was unanimously accepted by the Pig Buyers Association. He arranged interviews and discussions between Denny, representing the curers' interests, and association representatives who asked Redmond to be present. The curers' settlement proposals involved the loss of jobs and, although presenting a defiant front, association representatives asked Redmond to exert his influence, end the strike and recover lost jobs.

A fair assessment of the consequences of this dispute is that it strengthened working-class

146 Cronin, S. (1983), *Young Connolly*, Dublin, pp. 43, 47, 59–60.
147 O'Connor, 'Trades Councils in Waterford City' in Nolan and Power (eds.) (1992); O'Connor (1989), pp. 98–102.
148 Strange and Strange to Redmond, 29 July to 19 Aug. 1895 (Redmond Papers, 15,238 [11]), NLI.
149 Strange to Redmond, 18 Mar. 1896 (Redmond Papers, 15,238 [7]), NLI.
150 *Waterford News*, 31 Oct. and 28 Nov. 1896.
151 *Waterford News*, 13 Mar. 1897.
152 There is a bulky correspondence between Redmond, the Waterford curers and the Pig Buyers Association which leaves little doubt that Redmond was closely involved in attempts to settle the dispute. This account is based on: Maher to Redmond, 3, 6 and 15 Apr. and 8 May 1897; Farrell to Redmond, 1 July 1897 (Redmond Papers, 15,238 [8]), NLI.

conservatism by 'reinforcing the communal loyalty that bound the bacon trade, Redmondism
and Ballybricken'.[153] Also, not only were labour
institutions like the FTLU more social than radical
but public labour demonstrations were more communal and social events than genuine challenges
to the status quo. The fiery exhortations of men
such as Strange were no more than eccentricities.

The city's first Labour Day demonstration was
inaugurated in 1896 under the auspices of the
Trades Council. A procession, 1,500 strong and
accompanied by three city bands including the
John Street Fife and Drum Band, worked its way
from Trades Hall to the People's Park where
about 3,000 attended a public meeting. Patrick J.
Leo proclaimed that 'the cause of labour was
forcing itself in a very marked way because the
workers were beginning to consider the question
and to understand that no wealth could be produced without labour'. Charlie Strange called on
the workers to organise as they had done elsewhere in the world. The German people and
army were dominated by the idea of a labour
movement and 'the very Kaiser on his throne
[was] trembling at it'. He told the Waterford men

> until the labourers themselves recognised the
> nobility of labour it was impossible to do
> anything to raise their conditions, for the
> man who looked upon himself as being a
> minor factor in the community was a man who
> was a danger to his class. The man who looked
> to his employer as being something superior to
> him in the way of manhood was a man who
> was a danger to the labouring community.

Remarking on the fact that the mayor had
refused them the use of City Hall, Strange made
a threat which adumbrated the divisions of the
1899 municipal elections. The workers, he said,
would remember who was against them when
they got the franchise. Councillor James Power,
telling the gathering that they would soon have a

voice in local affairs, said it would be up to them
to vote for reforms. But he thought strikes, although sometimes inevitable, were a 'dreadful
resource' and war between rich and poor ended
in 'disaster for the poor man'. It was therefore
necessary for the Trades Council to step in and
negotiate.[154] A resolution was passed calling on
the central government to create employment
locally and on the corporation to build more
houses. It included a demand for the use of union
labour only and a protest against the excessive
use of boy labour.

The ITUC's fourth annual congress, hosted
by Waterford's Trade Council in June 1897, was
dominated by the skilled trades, notably the
printers, carpenters and tailors. It was yet
another occasion when the city's labour and civil
leadership demonstrated a common interest in
restraining a potentially radical, local labour
movement. The congress was opened with great
pomp and ceremony in City Hall and the mayor
entered in state. One of his entourage was of the
view there was nothing on the agenda that any
employer could object to.

Patrick J. Leo, a pork butcher and therefore
closely concerned with the Ballybricken pig buyers' dispute which destroyed the pork butchers
union, thought that as worker 'intelligence' grew,
and with it their ideas regarding relations
between employer and employee, 'the old time-
worn and barbarous method of strikes, will soon
become as obsolete as the hand-loom or the flint-
lock'. Stating that worker representatives were
'tolerant and broadminded', he thought their demands were just and reasonable. The purpose of
the congress was to 'cultivate better relations
between employer and employed ... mutual confidence and mutual self-respect [were essential
factors]'. And he noted that if the congress managed to bring together the FTLU and the Trades
Council which were so long apart 'to their own
detriment', then this would be a good thing.[155]

153 O'Connor (1989), p. 107.
154 *Waterford News*, 9 May 1896.
155 Clarkson (1970), pp. 190–95.

But the two organisations entered the local elections in opposition to each other.

Industrial unrest was frequently portrayed as McCarthyite agitation rather than the consequences of worker discontent. But the IPP split did create bitter antagonisms locally. Father Flynn's conduct in refusing to cooperate with the amnesty movement in 1893 because two of its secretaries were Parnellites was reported as being characteristic of 'Federationists'.[156] And during 1896 it was claimed that McCarthyites attempting to gain monetary benefits as well as political advantages, declared prominent Parnellites to be enemies of the church.[157] During the municipal elections three years later the McCarthyites were still being accused of having instituted a 'crusade' against 'every prominent Parnellite' in an attempt to destroy their businesses.[158]

These differences were not sufficiently traumatic to damage social homogeneity permanently. In 1898 at a meeting presided over by the mayor in City Hall, a fund was opened to help Father Flynn with his expenses in an action against him for bankruptcy. Despite a refusal to disclose his income and a claim that he was 'harassed and persecuted' by Charlie Strange,[159] the meeting was 'very largely attended' by men such as Henry Denny, and regardless of the IPP wing with which they sympathised.[160]

Labour and IPP factional politics were therefore enmeshed when Waterford entered the 1899 municipal elections. Following the Local Government Act, the 40 existing corporation members had to retire as a body and face the 'new electorate' at a time when the emphasis was on the need to improve social and economic conditions. The demand for home rule had fallen temporarily into the background.

A newly formed Ratepayers and Burgesses Association held its first meeting in December 1898 and put up over 20 candidates to contest the election. Described by one writer as a 'popular alternative to the merchants and gentry who had monopolized municipal politics for so long',[161] reports in the local newspapers encouraged the impression that it was a radical alternative to the existing corporation. However, claims that there was a 'new', pro-worker group of candidates contesting against the 'old' and corrupt corporation members was an illusion which confused real issues and distracted the newly enfranchised labouring class. Several association candidates were themselves members of the existing, or 'old', corporation.

The association was founded by Charlie Strange and a small group of men including W. G. D. Goff, who had 'been long and honourably identified with the commercial interests of the city'.[162] Strange abandoned his safe Centre Ward seat and stood with three other association candidates for Custom House Ward. Goff stood for West Ward, having been nominated by Banquo Redmond and John Strangman. Banquo Redmond did not stand for election himself as his business interests disqualified him under the Local Government Act.[163] George Nolan, builder and contractor, was one of five ratepayers' candidates in South Ward. And Robert Whalley, proprietor of the *Waterford Standard* and a councillor of 12 years' standing, stood as one of the six association candidates for Tower Ward.

Other conservative candidates included Dr George I. Mackesy who came from a family 'honoured in Waterford for nearly a century', and William R. Ward.[164] Banquo Redmond, George Mackesy, Harry Ward and other councillors such

156 *Waterford News*, 21 Jan. 1893.
157 *Waterford News*, 11 Jan. 1896.
158 *Waterford News*, 21 Jan. 1899.
159 *Waterford News*, 23 Apr. 1898.
160 *Waterford News*, 24 Sep. 1898
161 O'Connor (1989), pp. 107–09.
162 *Waterford News*, 28 Jan. 1899.
163 *Waterford News*, 7 Jan. 1899.
164 *Waterford News*, 21 Jan. 1899.

as Thomas Whittle, were all members of the Waterford Bicycle Club for which Goff had provided the track in the People's Park, and the *Waterford News* urged cyclists to support Goff in the election.[165] In defending itself against the accusation that it was an 'Orange and Blue Association', the Ratepayers Association declared its members were 'as good and true Nationalists as ever stood up for the old land'.

The election was fought primarily between different factions of the same interest group, both of which, with the few Conservative exceptions, were firmly locked into the same narrow nationalist sympathies. The split between 'old' and 'new' corporation factions was little more than a microcosm of the IPP split at national level. The association was Parnellite in composition and made up of seasoned Redmondite campaigners while the largest group in the 'old' corporation were McCarthyites. The groupings in the corporation were assessed as being 17 McCarthyites, 14 Parnellites, 7 Conservatives (along with 1 Parnellite all representing Tower Ward) and 2 neutrals. The McCarthyites were in the majority in Custom House and Centre Wards. Controlling the corporation as they did, the anti-Parnellites selected every municipal officer 'from the Mayor to the Street Scavenger'.

The two local labour organisations separated broadly along the lines of the IPP split and this made it impossible for either of them to present the kind of labour programme which would have benefited the unskilled worker. Whereas the FTLU had strong contacts with the 'old' corporation and nominated its own candidates for the election, the Trades Council with its enduring Charlie Strange connection and a synthetic flavour of labour radicalism, entered into an informal electoral alliance with the association. Five trade union candidates were nominated by the Trades Council with the backing of the Ratepayers Association.

However, because power was monopolised by a small group of people who all knew each other and because Waterford society was fundamentally cohesive, political groupings and loyalties were more fluid than this simple dichotomy suggests. W. G. D. Goff, a Protestant, unionist and association candidate, was also an honorary member of the FTLU who gave subscriptions when required.[166]. And in 1896 the pig buyers, the 'lifeguards of Parnellism', had affiliated with the FTLU. The overall impression is one of local dissension being due less to real and substantial divisions in political ideology or social outlook, than to parochial loyalties and personal differences.

But a genuine, if struggling, desire to challenge the status quo surfaced. The FTLU had resolved to form a Labour Electoral Association in November, chairman Stephen Farrell acknowledging that Waterford was far behind other towns and cities in not having such an association or any labour representatives on the public boards. Waterford, he commented, 'as a rule, is very hard to get forward in any movement'.

A member who claimed he was beaten in a previous election because of a lack of organisation and finance observed that the Local Government Act had been passed 'not for the grandees but for the men who have to earn their bread ... by the sweat of their brow'. Another speaker called on the city's workers, who had been 'too long quarrelling' to close their ranks. FTLU candidates would have the objectives of ensuring poor law contracts only went to those who employed bona fide workmen, stopping work going out of the city, reducing unemployment and ensuring skilled tradesmen were used as necessary and that they were paid current wage rates.[167]

But in the end it was what was good for John Redmond and the IPP which decided the election. Banquo Redmond's *Waterford News* echoed Redmond's call to walk 'the path of Toleration at

---

165 *Waterford News*, 28 Jan. 1899.
166 *Waterford News*, 12 Jan. 1900.
167 *Waterford News*, 17 Nov. 1899.

these elections'. An outgoing proportion of Conservative candidates should be returned as they were 'worthy of the support of all classes'.

Outside of the McCarthyite versus Parnellite framework, the campaign issues were bogus ones. An allegation that the corporation imposed an excessive tax provided the central issue for an election which was made acrimonious by personal attacks. The association pledged it would keep down rates and impose controls over official salaries and public spending. Anyone breaking the pledge would be required to resign. Election notices accused the 'old' corporation of having 'raised the rates; raised the salaries; misspent the public money'.[168] These issues had no direct relevance for the unskilled worker although high rates did generally mean high rents.

The corporation circulated a rebuttal of the 'terrible accusations' that rates were 9s 6d in the pound. Alderman W. J. Smith of Centre Ward was a wholesale and retail confectioner and a Cork man who upset Ballybricken residents by suggesting the removal of the bull-post, the historic focal point on Ballybricken Green.[169] He attacked the Ratepayers Association as a 'secret society' which made inaccurate statements. Any elected association member would have to consult a committee of 12 before registering his vote on any corporation issue. The association's policy of the non-levying of rates was also the direct antithesis of the principle and rights of the labourers because it would not be possible to build houses.

Another speaker accused the association's candidates of being 'high-fliers' put forward by a 'lot of schemers to serve their own purpose and bring down vengeance upon those they had a pick against'. Strange defended himself against the accusation that he only attended 6 out of 20 meetings in 12 months, of coming to the chamber only after work had been completed on the la-

bourers' dwellings and after 'giving up his luxurious yacht'—an interest he shared with W. G. D. Goff.

Three bands parading the principal city streets helped to fill City Hall, chiefly with the 'working classes', for an association meeting on 6 January. Strange read a telegram from W. G. D. Goff wishing the association every success. Another speaker called on the working men to put forward a strong representation through the association. John J. Breen, grocer and spirit merchant, hotel proprietor and farmer and one of the six association candidates for Centre Ward, having been defeated in the 1896 contest, called for the existing corporation members to be kicked out. Charlie Strange complained about the mayor ruling his name off the burgess roll two years previously and causing him considerable personal expense in fighting the case. He also used figures obtained from England to demonstrate that city officials were overpaying themselves.[170]

Strange and Breen were prominent in conducting the association's campaign. Accompanied by three of the city bands, 'vast' crowds carrying lighted torches gathered to hear them speak in Ballybricken Green and Barrack Street. When 'an organised gang led by two red-coated soldiers' created a disturbance as he got up to address the crowd, Charlie Strange deftly exploited the incident to achieve a propaganda advantage. He also denied the accusation that the association was a secret society, countering that the corporation excluded the press from its most important gatherings.[171]

The campaign was lively, effigies of W. J. Smith and John Harty, a candidate for South Ward, being burned in Ballybricken. 'Language, frequent and free' was used and a boy paraded outside of the O'Connell Street booth in Centre Ward with a sandwich board proclaiming 'Don't vote for Smith'.[172] W. J. Smith had replaced

168 *Waterford News*, 14 Jan. 1899.
169 CARA, *Ballybricken and Thereabouts*, pp. 30–32, 39–42.
170 *Waterford News*, 7 Jan. 1899.
171 *Waterford News*, 14 Jan. 1899.
172 *Waterford News*, 21 Jan. 1899.

bakers who had struck for shorter hours with non-union members and the bakers now picketed the Centre Ward poll booths. Councillors and colleagues when they were elected officials in the INL during the 1880s, attempts by the local press to make Smith and Strange now appear as ideological protagonists ring false. But it would no doubt have given Charlie Strange satisfaction to unseat Smith who had beaten him in a Centre Ward contest during 1896.[173]

The elections did result in candidates, whether 'old' or 'new', discovering a long, if seldom displayed, interest in the labourer's plight. One candidate, a city representative for over 40 years, declared in his election address: 'the improvement of the conditions of the working class is a matter in which I have taken, and always will take, a lively interest.' John Higgins, for 12 years a councillor, and standing for South Ward along with Harry Fisher of the *Munster Express* among others, declared his agreement with the 'labourer and artisan receiving full remuneration for their work in corporate contracts' in addition to houses. Harry L. Ward, four times returned as a councillor, appealed for the support of the newly enfranchised ladies in Tower Ward as well as that of the 'humbler classes' for whom he had worked in trying to provide healthier homes.

Over 60 candidates stood in the election. Polling day was on 16 January and of the 4,804 voters on the register, 74 per cent cast their vote. There was some surprise at how many females voted and generally they were considered to have 'displayed more intelligence and much quicker perception' than the men.[174] The association nominees took 20 of the 40 seats and Parnellites now formed the largest single group in the corporation. It comprised 20 Parnellites, 12 McCarthyites, 5 Conservatives and 3 neutrals. Charlie Strange, coming sixth, was one of the eight successful candidates for Custom House

Ward. The greatest advance was in Centre Ward where the McCarthyites had previously held five of the eight seats. On a 70 per cent turnout, 21 per cent of those voting being women, the Ratepayers Association now took seven of them. This may reflect the apparent absence of any significant clerical involvement in the election.

Generally illiterates and women polled strongly. In Centre Ward, when the presiding officer read the names of the candidates out to them and told them they need not decide their choice until the list was read a second time, 'the necessary discrimination was exercised' by them and there were only 12 spoiled papers. None of the Trade Council's candidates were elected. P. J. Leo, president of the council, came bottom of the poll in Centre Ward.

The only successful labour representatives were two FTLU nominees. Michael Cashin who had resigned as president of the Trades Council because it was a 'waste of time' was elected for Tower Ward and Michael Wyse for whom the illiterates voted 'almost to a man' at The Manor polling booth, Ballybricken, won a seat in South Ward. The Trades Council collapsed soon afterwards and the FTLU was restored to pre-eminence. Its membership rose to around 300 by 1900. In January of the same year at a meeting of its members, it was agreed to reform its electoral committee with the aim of increasing its representation on the corporation. But the reunification of the IPP secured the absolute dominance of Redmondite nationalism in Waterford's politics.

A deputation of the newly elected Catholic members asked Bishop Sheehan and his clergy to confirm their nomination of Charlie Strange as mayor. Strange, accused of being an atheist, denied he was a propagandist of any faith and the bishop chose to leave any decision to those 'who had more experience'.[175] None the less, Fathers Flynn, Furlong and O'Donnell were in City Hall

173 *Waterford News*, 24 Oct. and 14, 28 Nov. 1896.
174 *Waterford News*, 21 Jan. 1899.
175 *Waterford News*, 28 Jan. 1899.

to witness the contest between Strange and another nominee for mayor.

The councillor nominating Strange eulogised his nationalist background but mentioned nothing of any plans to improve the lot of the labourer. He told of how Strange's father, a rebel and supporter of the 1848 movement, had stood in the same chamber in 1853 and had been made mayor through the 'pluck' of conservative members. Goff seconded the nomination. Michael Cashin voted against him and Michael Wyse, prevented from speaking by hissing councillors, abstained. Strange was elected by a majority of two, with four absences and two abstentions. In his speech of acceptance, he claimed to have tried his 'level best' to secure a return of a larger number of labour councillors. It was therefore 'lamentable' that the two labour representatives elected were 'diametrically opposed' to him. At least the Kilkenny branch of the Typographical Association thought him a 'sterling Nationalist and consistent friend of labour'.[176] W. G. D. Goff, who had polled second out of 12 candidates in the election,[177] was then elected city high sheriff.[178]

Despite 'vile attempts to raise the religious cry', according to the *Waterford News* the city had demonstrated a 'spirit of tolerance' during the election and this 'may serve to open the eyes of our Saxon neighbours as to the wider possibilities which may exist under a Home Rule Bill'. But the city was 'needlessly vilified and her good name tarnished' when from elsewhere in the country there came accusations that Waterford was so conservative that it was the only main centre to have returned an increased number of unionists.[179]

Before long, familiar 'old' corporation names reappeared on the roll of city councillors but Strange continued to dabble in socialism. In 1899, as mayor, he presided at the first of a course of four fabian[180] educational lectures given at City Hall. Handbills, posters and syllabuses were supplied free by him and the price of a hall or gallery ticket was only 1d.[181]

There was a considerable distance between his views and those of the ISRP to which he had once belonged. Fabian tactics were to make thinking men socialists rather than to organise unthinking persons into socialist societies. Their strategy of 'permeation' was anti-union.[182] And Connolly was scathing about the fabians' lack of interest in the worker when they did not have the vote. Fabian 'gas and water schemes' were lost on them but 'Fabian missionaries' none the less arrived with the franchise. In Connolly's opinion,

> in order to prevent the Irish working class from breaking off entirely from the bourgeois parties and from developing a revolutionary tendency, the Fabians send their lecturers to Ireland, to induce the Irish working class ... [to] neglect ... the essential work of capturing the political power necessary for social reconstruction.[183]

The Redmondite nationalist hegemony buttressed the status quo by sapping local labour movements of any vigour, and it deprived the labourer of adequate political or industrial representation at national or local level.

---

176 *Waterford News*, 4 Feb. 1899.
177 *Waterford News*, 7 and 21 Jan. 1899.
178 *Waterford News*, 28 Jan. 1899.
179 *Waterford News*, 21 Jan. 1899.
180 The Fabian Society was founded in London in 1884, in the belief the 'competitive system assures the happiness and comfort of the few at the expense of the suffering of the many and that society must be reconstituted in such a manner as to secure the general welfare and happiness'. Bernard Shaw was one of its members. It developed as a non-Marxist socialist society, its primary object being to present the results of research into social and political questions, and to suggest practical recommendations on evolutionary socialist lines.
181 *Waterford News*, 10 Nov. 1899.
182 Adelman, P. (1986), *The Rise of the Labour Party, 1880–1945*, Harlow, pp. 6–10.
183 Greaves (1961), pp. 120–21; Allen, K. (1990), pp. 13–14.

VII

During the 1900 local elections Stephen Farrell, president of the FTLU, complained that in 1899 men had been elected on the pretext of being representatives of the working man but had done nothing much for him once voted onto the corporation. They were no longer to be trusted. The Dublin Trades Council had also identified 'feather-bedding' councillors as the major reason for being unable to maintain an 'independent, incorruptible' labour party[184] and James Connolly accused candidates of using the working class movement as a 'cover for the intrigues of a clique'.[185] Corporation members who were honorary members of the FTLU, including Charlie Strange now the Trades Council was defunct, had failed to support them in putting up candidates. This may account for Strange being 'beaten to blazes' in 1900 by Doctor Joseph T. White (the very popular 'Doctor Joe') for a vacant alderman's seat contest in Centre Ward.[186]

The FTLU failed to establish a Labour Election Association and Farrell therefore supported the nomination of John J. Rogers, a vintner and publican, as a candidate. In the absence of any genuine and willing labour candidate, this odd choice of 'worker representative' is a good illustration of Waterford's community approach to politics. Rogers met his own expenses and was a very old member of the FTLU. Farrell therefore recommended they should support him 'by every means in their power'.[187]

A few months later in a Centre Ward by-election, only 46 per cent of those registered voted. Stephen Farrell, a 'popular and capable representative of the artisan classes' came second. In a working-class ward, one newspaper found 'such apathy ... almost inexplicable ... the great majority of the new electors are content to allow matters municipal to wag along'.[188] The January 1914 municipal elections were also conducted without enthusiasm. In most cases the outgoing candidates were re-elected, including the ousted 1899 'old' corporation councillor, W. J. Smith who was returned as alderman for Centre Ward with 61 per cent of the vote.[189]

Greater interest was shown in February. The turnout was large but it was the issue of home rule which predominated. Richard Power, 25 years a councillor and elected mayor for the fourth time, declared that during his mayoralty he hoped to see 'our country free'. Home rule had been the 'height of [his] ambition' and he had been 'yearning' for it for years.[190] In Centre Ward a surgeon of Lady Lane and William Fitzgerald, a gentleman of Parnell Street and honorary secretary to the UIL, were elected to fill two councillor vacancies. Two labour candidates, a seaman and a hackney car owner who had been nominated by the Society of Jarveys and Trades Hall, were badly beaten.

In his victory speech William Fitzgerald referred to the labour challenge:

> I was never opposed to Labour not since I came to Waterford nor before I came ... . In fighting the capitalists they [the labour candidates] are fighting against their own interests ... they will injure themselves more than they will benefit themselves.[191]

Apathy extended to industrial organisation. In 1901, the Irish organising secretary of the Amalgamated Society of Railway Servants visited Waterford and was 'astonished' that worker organisation was at such a 'low ebb'. He found worker indifference 'difficult to understand' and thought it was due to 'want of thought rather

---

184   Clarkson (1970), p. 206, footnote 2.
185   Cronin (1983), p. 67.
186   *Waterford News*, 19 Jan. 1900.
187   *Waterford News*, 12 Jan. 1900.
188   *Waterford News*, 11 May 1900.
189   *Waterford Standard*, 17 Jan. 1914.
190   *Waterford Standard*, 25 Feb. 1914.
191   *Waterford Standard*, 11 Feb. 1914.

than the lack of opportunity'. At a well-attended meeting in Trades Hall, workers were called on to establish a Trades Council to replace the one which had collapsed in 1899, and to organise and expand union membership.[192]

But no council emerged for some years and the FTLU remained solidly conservative. By 1904, it claimed to be in association with 10 councillors but these were mainly business and professional men. A warrant officer and sergeant from the infantry barracks were made honorary members. It continued to function largely as a social club and its newly formed brass and reed band gave its first performance on Christmas Day, 1905.

The House of Commons' 'fair wages' resolution, agreed to by a Conservative government in 1891, is illustrative of the extent to which the FTLU and Waterford's workers were enfeebled. The resolution required that in awarding contracts efforts should be made to secure the payment of wages generally accepted as current in each trade for competent workmen.

In 1903 at a well attended meeting of tradesmen and labourers chaired by Patrick Flynn, president of the FTLU and city councillor, carpenters in particular were vociferous in calling on the corporation, the county council, the Board of Guardians and the governors of the lunatic asylum to adopt the resolution which had already been adopted 'by almost all' bodies in Ireland. A system whereby Waterford's employers searched for men who would accept a rate below the standard rate would 'not be tolerated in any other town in Ireland or England [and] it was nearly time for Waterford to look after its own interests'. Another speaker, noting the lapse of 12 years before the issue was raised thought that 'if the working

men of Waterford had half the energy and loyalty of the Cork working men, things would be very different in Waterford'.

Among the corporation officials on the platform was Alderman Thomas Whittle who thought the adoption of the resolution 'a simple act of justice'. But it was his experience that as soon as meetings were over people forgot their enthusiasm and the objective. If tradesmen and labourers

wished to make themselves felt and have their grievances heard they should unite [and] remain united ... it was the tradesmen, mechanics, and labourers who were ... the food, the up-keep of the merchants and shopkeepers.[193]

A tobacconist and cigar merchant with premises on the Quay who had been an honorary member of the FTLU for 22 years and who declared his personal support for the 'fair wages' resolution, was nominated as a 'Working Men and Labourers' Candidate' for a vacancy in Custom House Ward. He subsequently won a seat and opened a new 'Fancy Goods House' in time for King Edward's visit[194] but the 'fair wages' debate was still rumbling on in 1909. The local branch of the Irish Transport and General Workers Union (ITGWU)[195] asked the corporation not to accept a tender to supply coal from Murphy brothers because they were not yet paying fair wages and men who had gone on strike for more money had been sacked and replaced. Other public boards had disqualified them from submitting tenders. The Murphys were defended by one councillor who observed 'God knows the city is poor enough' and questioned whether a firm like theirs, which gave employment to large numbers, should be ruined. Their tender was accepted.[196]

---

192 *Waterford News*, 30 Aug. 1901.
193 *Waterford Mail*, 23 Feb. 1903; *Waterford News*, 27 Feb. 1903.
194 *Waterford Standard*, 4 May 1904.
195 The ITGWU was founded by James Larkin (1876–1947). Born in Liverpool of Irish parents and employed as a labourer and seaman, he organised a wave of strikes in Belfast during 1907 when he worked for the National Union of Dock Labourers, a New Union. Transferred to Dublin in 1908, he reformed the Irish branch of the Independent Labour Party and began to organise casual and unskilled workers. He broke with the National Union of Dock Labourers, and started the ITGWU in January 1909. The union affiliated to the ITUC in 1910 and by 1911 it had about 5,000 members. James Connolly became its Belfast organiser in 1911. Larkin backed James Connolly's call for an Irish Labour Party in 1912.
196 *Waterford News*, 12, 26 Mar., 9 Apr. and 14 May 1909.

In 1913, P. W. Kenny, told that the corporation was not legally bound by the resolution and that it was not certain the corporation always applied it, rejected the idea of a standard fair wage as producing distortions in the free market.[197]

However, skilled workers could sometimes demonstrate independence and defiance. In 1902 the bakers union sent out copies of a resolution to the city's master bakers in which the union's aim to ensure enforcement of the bread act was clearly stated. The act made it illegal for those in the baking trade to work on Sundays.[198] A new Trades Council was formed in 1904 but it managed to attract only 220 members and collapsed after a year. The major difficulties were in mobilising the unskilled workers and bringing skilled men to an acceptance of them.

Waterford did not escape the consequences of the second wave of New Unionism, more frequently described as syndicalism,[199] which arrived with Jim Larkin and the return of James Connolly. By 1908 Larkin had organised branches of the National Union of Dock Labourers in all major ports. He was welcomed in Waterford by bands and a torchlit procession. City Hall was packed for his reception and the city high sheriff presided. Corporation members and the president of the FTLU shared the platform and a small branch of the National Union of Dock Labourers was established.

In November the Cork dock workers, who had not received an increase in wages for 20 years, took successful industrial action but the Waterford branch of the union struggled to survive in the face of hostility from employers. However, a Trades Council, later restyled the United Trades and Labour Council (UTLC), was inaugurated in May 1909 and initiated a campaign to recruit non-union, unskilled labour. Larkin sent a telegram – 'Labour must rule' and the mayor told delegates not to fear being punished by their employers. Although not experiencing a typical Larkinite 'revolt of the unskilled', there was an acceptance of Larkinite values among local labour leaders.[200]

In 1911 the *Irish Homestead* reported 'labour has lost its old humility and its respectable finger touching its cap. It is one of the great powers of the world'.[201] And the Waterford UTLC endorsed a Dublin Trades Council resolution protesting against the IPP's attempt to exclude Ireland from the provisions of a bill proposing to pay MPs £400 annually. The councils saw the bill as the only chance of sending Irish worker representatives to parliament.[202]

Industrial unrest was widespread throughout the United Kingdom during 1911 and Waterford workers took sympathetic action. In August the ITGWU branch was reformed by P. T. Daly and during February 1912 James Connolly spoke at a UTLC meeting in City Hall. Daly, arrested and lodged in Waterford prison because of his activities during the Wexford strike, was released in April. Accompanied to Ballybricken Green by a torchlit procession led by the Trades Hall Brass and Reed Band, a resolution was passed congratulating him for his 'vindication of the cause of the toiling masses of Ireland' and he called on Waterford workers to unite. Three UTLC candidates were elected to the corporation and a political fund was established in 1912. The May

197   *Munster Express*, 11 Oct. 1913.
198   *Waterford Standard*, 5 July 1902.
199   Syndicalists rejected politics in favour of industrial action. They believed that trade union movements, as free associations of workers, should use the strike weapon as a means of seizing power. All control over the means of production would be transferred from the state to the trade unions. Syndicalist philosophy developed in France and the USA but the idea spread widely and it is frequently argued that labour unrest in the United Kingdom between 1911 and 1914 was a consequence of syndicalism. While in the USA James Connolly came into contact with syndicalist concepts and it inspired his idea of 'one big union'. James Larkin may well have anticipated Connolly in creating the ITGWU. However, both were pragmatic to varying degrees and never discounted political action. Pure syndicalist ideology was therefore modified by Irish and British trade unions.
200   O'Connor, 'Trades councils in Waterford city' in Nolan and Power (eds.) (1992).
201   Larkin (1989), p. 85.
202   *Waterford News*, 24 Feb. 1911.

Day parade later in the year was cinematographed by Theatre Royal Pictures.[203]

But the status quo was undisturbed by labour militancy. Although William Martin Murphy, in responding to the rise in labour militancy in Dublin, and more particularly to Larkin's ITGWU, had organised about 400 employers into an employers federation of which he was president, Waterford employers felt sufficiently secure in 1911 for the Chamber of Commerce to note that in view of the 'comparative immunity from labour troubles' there was no need to form an employers federation. The ITGWU suffered humiliating defeats in 1912 and employers dismissed some dockers for blacking. The leech-like Redmondite nationalist connection was still evident. A UTLC president was a member of the city's Irish Volunteer battalion committee and one of the UTLC workers elected to the council was chief ranger for the Irish National Foresters. The UTLC joined with the National Foresters in a commemorative parade for the Manchester martyrs.

The mobilisation of Waterford's unskilled workers was so limited as to be considered generally unsuccessful. Solidarity was not maintained. In August 1911 Larkin wrote,

life all around seems to stagnate; everything seems miserable and depressing. You want them [the workers] to realise there is great hope for the future—that there is something worth working for, if the workers will only arouse themselves. You plead with them to cast their eyes upwards to the stars, instead of grovelling in the slime of their own degradation; point out to them life's promised fulness and joy if they would only seek it. You appeal to their manhood, their love for their little ones, their race instinct, but all these appeals seem to fall on deaf ears; they turn away apparently utterly apathetic, and one tramps on to the next town or meeting, feeling it was hopeless to try and move them.[204]

With Larkin labelled the 'anti-Christ' by a priest,[205] Waterford Protestant and Catholic clergy warned trade unionists against associating with him and they offered no support for the Dublin lock-out.[206] The UTLC called for action in backing Dublin trade unionists, passed a lengthy resolution and arranged meetings for collections.[207] But the city and its quay labourers benefited as traffic was diverted from Dublin where Connolly had closed the ports. And in its review of 1913, the *Waterford Standard* observed, 'fortunately Waterford was not affected by the Dublin dispute'. Local labour did not take up a 'sympathetic attitude' and the editor wondered if the experience of 1911 had been enough for them.[208]

Responding to rumours that Larkin was going to visit the city, the *Munster Express* commented, 'it is doubtful the kind of reception he would receive if he came here'.[209] Pete Larkin, identified by the local press as Jim Larkin's brother, visited Waterford in September 1913 but the demonstration in Ballybricken Green was reported as poorly attended and lacking in enthusiasm. James

203 *Waterford News,* 5 Apr. 1912.
204 Larkin (1989), p. 86.
205 Curriculum Development Unit, *Dublin 1913,* p. 60.
206 Confrontation between Jim Larkin and the organised workers on the one hand and W. M. Murphy's employers federation on the other, culminated in the Dublin lock-out between September 1913 and February 1914. Employees who refused to submit a written undertaking that they would not join Larkin's or any other trade union were dismissed. Larkin called out workers from the Dublin Tram Company, of which Murphy was a director. In retaliation, the employers federation locked out 25,000 workers. Larkin and Connolly created the Irish Citizen Army to defend workers and Larkin was imprisoned. Keir Hardie was the only major British labour leader to support the Dublin workers whose resistance collapsed in consequence. Murphy subsequently supported recruitment into the British army and in November 1915 he convened a meeting of Irish employers at which a scheme to dismiss able-bodied men so as to force them to enlist was put forward. No cases of compulsion were reported, however (O'Flanagan (1985), p. 39).
207 *Munster Express,* 13 Sep. 1913.
208 *Waterford Standard,* 3 Jan. 1914.
209 *Munster Express,* 11 Oct. 1913.

Gleeson, a councillor and president of the UTLC, was supposed to be chairman but failed to turn up.

The weather was stormy and other speakers, including Richard Keane, labour councillor and founder member of the Amalgamated Society of Railway Servants and the UTLC, did not speak. Pete Larkin's speech was, with justification, described as 'vitriolic and abusive' but it was in tune with a popular and narrow nationalism. He denied there was any 'slimy Saxon blood' in him and called on the working class to resist 'William Martin Murphy, Isaac Butt, the Jew, and Jacob, the Quaker' in what was a class struggle. Waterford was the least resistant of the cities and he called on the workers to organise and not to buy the *Evening News* which was controlled by a 'clique or political gang'.[210]

But whereas by 1914 British politics had gone a 'great deal' of the way towards being class-based, Irish politics had not. One reason, it has been argued, was that Irish politicians constituted the only political parties not suffering from 'ideological bewilderment'.[211] As early as 1906 Keir Hardie had told Davitt excitedly that what was happening in Britain was 'revolutionary'. 'Everywhere there is a coming together of the labour forces and an awakening of consciousness amongst the workers.'[212]

Piecemeal industrial action by some Waterford workers brought limited success, however. In early 1913 the drapers' assistants won a living-out allowance after a 'hard and strenuous fight' with Hearne and Co.[213] The stonecutters and carpenters took industrial action for higher wages and during the May Day demonstrations there were calls for settlement of these disputes and for all of the city's workers to join a trade organisation.

Using the traditional method, Martin J. Murphy, Redmond's staunch supporter, mediated a settlement between employer and worker in the mayor's office.[214]

The masons and bricklayers struck in August, made a list of demands and picketed their employers. And casual labourers discharging timber on the quays stopped work and demanded an increase in pay.[215] Those employed by Graves and Co. were unaffected as, after 20 years without a rise in wages, they had now been given an increase of four shillings a week because, according to one councillor, working men were now asserting themselves.[216]

However, at its annual general meeting in February 1914, the Waterford branch of the Irish Drapers' Assistants Association offered an assessment which had general applicability. Given the number of employees in the city, the union should have had 75 per cent more membership. Working conditions were appalling. Waterford had 300 per cent more assistants on unemployment benefit than any other city. But assistants were 'so short sighted, so blind and so apathetic as not to make a serious effort to remedy that frightful evil and terrible sword which were constantly hanging over them'. Dismissals were more frequent in Waterford than elsewhere. They could be carried out with 'impunity' by Waterford's employers.[217]

But at least Bishop Sheehan and the Irish hierarchy now recognised the plight of urban workers. In their February 1914 pastoral the bishops urged the elimination of 'sweating' and 'wage-slavery', the introduction of a fairer wage system and the provision of improved housing and better education for labourers' children. The recommended methods of achieving these

210 *Munster Express*, 20 Sep. 1913. The images used by Larkin are odd. Butt had died in 1879 but it may be that Larkin called on people to resist his influence rather than him.
211 Turner (1992), pp. 36–37.
212 Hardie to Davitt, *c.* May 1906 (Davitt Papers, 9330), Trinity.
213 *Waterford Standard*, 25 Feb. 1914.
214 *Munster Express*, 10, 24 and 31 May 1913.
215 *Munster Express*, 4 Oct. 1913.
216 *Munster Express*, 11 Oct. 1913.
217 *Waterford Standard*, 25 Feb. 1914.

objectives were hardly radical: 'private enterprise, the provisions made by some employers, and the efforts of philanthropy need to be supplemented by municipal encouragement and State aid' as well as machinery for conciliation.

The unskilled labourer should be given a 'fair chance' and it should not be made 'too difficult for industry, ability, thrift and character to raise him to a position equal to his worth'. The bishops now asked for justice for the 'toilers who do the hardest and most necessary work of the community, sometimes in peril of their lives, living very much from hand to mouth off the earnings of employment that is not at all times available'.[218]

On the eve of the First World War, Irish labour was 'abnormally docile' compared with British labour. In Britain, the government was alarmed by the threatened strike by the 'Triple Alliance' of railway, miners and dockers unions which, combined with the possibility of war in Ulster, produced the 'greatest' danger to the country for centuries.[219] But the ITUC was ineffective. The ITGWU was on the brink of bankruptcy and at its height the militant trade union movement had caused minimal disturbance outside the major cities. What little had been achieved through industrial action had, by 1914, been lost and there was heavy unemployment.[220] The labour movement was 'exhausted'[221] and men such as James English, who lived perilously close to pauperism, were more susceptible to Redmond's and the recruiting sergeant's call to enlist. In October 1914 James Connolly observed that 'hunger and the fear of hunger have driven thousands of our class into the British army'.[222] Connolly had himself served in the King's Liverpool Regiment, a unit with strong Irish traditions.[223]

218 *Munster Express*, 28 Feb. 1914; *Catholic Directory*, 1915.
219 Turner (1992), pp. 17–18. Although pre-war British workers were industrially more active than the Irish, it has been argued that a wave of nationalist imperialism and racial hostility swept Britain and 'thrust the conflict of the classes into the background' (Hechter [1974], p. 255). This view is given some support by Turner (1992), p. 33.
220 Fitzpatrick, D. (1980), 'Strikes in Ireland, 1914–21', *Soathar*, **Part 6**, pp. 26–39.
221 Malone, A. E. (1918), 'Four years of Irish economics, 1914–1918: Irish labour in wartime', *Studies*, pp. 319–27.
222 Connolly, J. (1914), 'The hope of Ireland', *Irish Worker* (31 Oct.), reproduced in Connolly (1987), Vol. 1, pp. 453–55.
223 Greaves (1961), pp. 20–25.

CHAPTER 4

The Economic Factor

I

Three aspects of James English's economic condition help to explain his enlistment. Firstly, the nature, type and availability of pre-war employment and the level of wages were inadequate; and his housing and general living standards were substandard. Secondly, his economic hardship and his standard of living worsened in consequence of the war. And thirdly, enlistment into the army offered immediate financial relief and also the potential for economic and social improvement.

II

At the time of his enlistment, James English was employed as a general labourer by Michael O'Sullivan, who operated a mineral water manufacturing and bottling factory in the High Street. Equipped with the latest corking, filling and mineral water machinery, it opened for business in the 1890s. O'Sullivan also had a vintner's outlet in Broad Street and in 1898 he opened up a new grocery, wines and spirits establishment in Barronstrand Street.

In Waterford 11 such concerns were in competition with each other and, taken together, the bottlers probably employed some 200 people or more. John Garvey's in Johnstown had 12 horses and employed 30 men and John Kelly and Sons of Exchange Street had 14 horses and 40 employees. The Phoenix brewery stores in Waterside is likely to have employed many more. O'Sullivan's

delivered to places as far away as Kilmacow, Mullinavat, Dunmore and Tramore and James English's duties probably involved helping in the deliveries and in transporting the wooden barrels which arrived from Dublin by ship, from the Quay to the customs stores or to O'Sullivan's High Street premises for bottling. The work could be dangerous. In 1898 an employee descending into an empty but unflushed porter vat soon after the contents had been bottled, was overcome by poisonous gases and died.[1]

The mineral water and bottling industry was just one ancillary trade dependent on the breweries. The two Waterford breweries were important provincial concerns and crucial to the local economy. It has been estimated that over 50 per cent of Irish barley was used in the brewing industry in 1902 and that 60 per cent of malt used was from home-grown grain. The Davis, Strangman and Co. Ltd brewery in Mary Street with its six-storey high malt houses, cask washing sheds, industrial shops and stables was described in 1894 as standing at the 'head of Waterford industries'.

Many were employed in its collateral trades, including coopers, harness-makers and smith workers. The brewery provided the only secure employment for coopers since Graves and Co. started producing machine-made butter boxes as substitutes for traditional hand-coopered firkins. Although a major employer of skilled workers, automation limited the work available for labourers. Ale and porter produced by both breweries were held in 'high esteem' and exported to England and Wales.

1 *Waterford News*, 17 Sep. 1898.

Wages paid in Waterford varied, but James English's earnings while employed at Michael O'Sullivan's were probably between 12s and 14s. The average wage for a Waterford labourer in 1912 was officially given as 14s a week.[2] This figure was based on the building trade and in reality, a builder's labourer averaged much less over a year when time lost through broken weather was taken into account. One pre-war 1914 estimate put his average wage at 9s 6d per week, with 14s being the maximum earnings.[3] In March 1915, a councillor claimed that unskilled labourers in the city were earning between 10s and 12s a week only.[4] But carpenter and stonecutter labourers' wages were raised to 15s in May 1913[5] and corporation labourers were paid 16s to 17s a week in October of the same year.[6]

Workers in jobs where literacy was a stated requirement were better off. In March 1915 female attendants in the lunatic asylum received £17 per year rising by annual increments to £22. Allowances were valued at around £28. This meant a secure 17s weekly wage for the whole year and guaranteed increases in the future.[7] A male attendant in the workhouse hospital received £20 a year rising by annual increments to £30 with the usual allowances. He therefore received a guaranteed weekly wage of around 19s in the first year.[8]

Seventy-eight per cent of Irish workers received £1 or below in wages, compared with 40 per cent in England and 50 per cent in Scotland. There was some truth in James Connolly's accusation that 'middle class' municipal corporations, other public bodies and private employers were taking unjustifiable advantage of the crowded labour market to compel their employees to accept 'starvation wages'.[9]

In October 1913 the Waterford corporation debated whether or not to raise the wages of its labourers to £1. The proposer argued that the high rents and increased prices made it essential. It had recently been agreed to increase the salary of a corporation official and the labourers' case was no different. Moreover, the ratepayers would benefit as the labourers, not being keen savers, would generate business by spending their extra money in the local shops. One councillor rejected the proposal on the grounds it had originated in Liberty Hall (ITGWU headquarters), Dublin. Patrick W. Kenny did so because the idea of the corporation fixing a wage independently of the market was a 'revolutionary proposal'. Another claimed the workers were old men who could not live on their old age pension and did little work to earn their wages. The motion was rejected by 14 votes to 7.[10]

This debate, seen in the context of increased prosperity for some and of steadily rising prices, demonstrates the labourer's inability to obtain fair terms when the economy was bountiful. The year 1913 was a bumper one for the port. Good weather meant a quality and yield of oats well up on 1912. Although the rearing and killing of pigs had diminished and shipment of bacon from the port had fallen by 5,500 bales, high prices had been maintained. Traffic diverted to Waterford because of the Dublin lock-out ensured increased tonnage and dues from shipping, according to the Chamber of Commerce, had been 'substantial'. Consignments of livestock shipped to England had been 'very heavy'.[11] There was an 'air of prosperity' about the city and hopes that a

2 *Report of an Enquiry by the Board of Trade into Working Class Rents, Housing, Retail Prices and Standard Rate of Wages in the United Kingdom* (British Parliamentary Papers, 1913 [Cd. 6955] LXVI.393), p. 296.
3 *Waterford Standard*, 7 Feb. 1914.
4 *Munster Express*, 20 Mar. 1915.
5 *Munster Express*, 31 May 1913.
6 *Munster Express*, 11 Oct. 1913.
7 *Munster Express*, 27 Mar. 1915.
8 *Waterford Standard*, 7 July 1915.
9 Connolly, J. (1897), 'Patriotism and Labour', *Shan Van Vocht*, reproduced in Connolly (1987), Vol. 1, pp. 310–14.
10 *Munster Express*, 11 Oct. 1913.
11 *Waterford Standard*, 25 Feb. 1914.

reduction in American tariffs would mean even better trade in 1914.

Increased traffic was claimed to have created a 'great deal' of extra employment. The Clyde Shipping Company built an extension to its premises and the Harbour Board extended its Clyde jetty using direct labour. Overall, the building industry was in a satisfactory state. In addition to a number of corporation houses being constructed, a new Presbyterian church was built in Lady Lane and the foundation stone of a YMCA hostel laid in William Street. Further housing schemes were planned for 1914.

A new margarine factory, opened at the end of May, provided 'much additional local employment' and the prospect of further work was excellent. There had been an increased consumption of margarine in the United Kingdom and demand outstripped supply. The Tramore races had drawn record crowds and brought more business. According to the Chamber of Commerce, the labouring classes were finding 'plenty of work at a fair wage'. And the nagging 'bridge' problem had also been resolved. Old 'Timbertoes' was gone and the new bridge, named after John Redmond, was considered locally as 'one of the finest of its kind in the three kingdoms'.[12]

How far this prosperity had reduced the number of unemployed recorded in the 1911 census is uncertain but, despite the Chamber of Commerce's claim that labourers were now in a position to provide their families and themselves with better food and clothing, it is clear employers generally remained unresponsive to demands for higher wages. Expanded business probably resulted in some of the unemployed being provided with jobs and a number of the regularly employed men earning extra money by working longer hours. But the increase in wealth had no impact, for instance, when in early 1914, the question of improving the corporation labourer's wage again arose. Richard Keane was one of the UTLC's nominees elected to the corporation, and he calculated a labourer's living costs on the basis of a 16s wage:

Rent (based on the corporation minimum)	2s	6d
Coal (1 cwt)	1s	5d
Clothes (man and wife)	1s	0d
Oil (lighting)		3½d
Sticks		2½d
Matches		1d
National Insurance		3d
Mortality Insurance (man and wife)		3d
Food (3 meals a day for man and wife)		10s

The whole of a labourer's 16s was thus accounted for and Keane wanted to know if less than threepence was enough to buy a sufficiently substantial meal. This was a pertinent question. Ten years earlier Dooley's Hotel had charged 1s 6d for breakfast, 1s for lunch, 2s for dinner and 9d for tea.[13] Keane also asked what happened in the case of those married men who, like himself, had seven children. How were the children to be fed and clothed? But the motion was again rejected. Another councillor, highlighting the consequences of failure to implement the 'fair wages' resolution, described how 14 boys had been employed at wages of 8s on a building site he had visited. But the proposal that a guaranteed minimum labourer's wage should be required before accepting tenders from contractors was defeated on the grounds that the corporation's job was to secure the cheapest contracts and keep down the rates.[14]

A member of the Chamber of Commerce, recognising the inability of the poorer classes to exploit improvements in the economy, questioned the appropriateness of British economic and social legislation in Ireland. The traditional keeping of pigs had been outlawed by 'drastic and foolish' sanitary measures which had reduced the

12 *Waterford Standard*, 3 Jan. 1914.
13 Ward Lock & Co. (1904), hotel section.
14 *Waterford Standard*, 7 Feb. 1914.

number of pigs kept in England. The same effects had undermined the self-sufficiency and economic independence of the Waterford labourers who had traditionally kept pigs in their backyards. Now, if a rich person or rich corporation did not employ an individual, he must 'go to the wall'.[15]

In 1899 the same complaint had been raised by J. J. Breen, a Centre Ward councillor. Two or three pigs kept by struggling people could provide enough to maintain their homes. The removal of this 'little privilege' was 'tyranny'.[16] In 1913 poor people were unable to take advantage of a shortfall in the supply of pigs and of the high prices obtainable. P. W. Kenny, however, a member of the corporation's public health committee, assured council members that regulations were not rigidly enforced and the illicit keeping of pigs in the city was quite common.

At the time of his enlistment, James English was the only breadwinner in his family. He had five surviving children under the age of 15, two children having died at an early age. His wife, like 88 per cent of Waterford's women of working age, was a housewife. In 1901 only about 17 per cent of females of working age in Thomas's Avenue were employed. This had increased to around 59 per cent by 1911. In most households, women or girls found employment as domestic servants and brought in additional income. The work was heavy and the hours long. With an average wage of 4s a week, they represented the most poorly paid section of the community[17] but the extra money could make a very considerable difference.

Women sometimes generated extra income by selling fish, boiled cockles, periwinkles, dilisk (purple, dry seaweed) and sloughhakaun (sea cabbage). These might be brought in from Tramore or collected from the Quay and sold at St Peter's Street market or The Cross. Sometimes the fish was hawked in the streets or the women would call at houses. Such enterprise was not always appreciated, however. In 1887 fines were imposed on several fishwomen for obstruction,[18] and in 1904 a fishwoman selling fish from a car was summoned for obstruction and fined 5s with costs.[19]

Despite a 10 per cent increase in rents and a 19 per cent increase in coal and food prices between 1905 and 1912, the city's wage rates did not move from their 1905 level. Although Waterford still offered the cheapest rented accommodation in the United Kingdom, the increase in rents was greater than in any other Irish city and the third highest in the United Kingdom.

The rise in retail food prices was the highest in Ireland and the cost of some food items other than meat was more than in London. The price of coal rose by 25 per cent in Waterford and 25.8 per cent in Ireland as a whole. Bacon price increases ranged between 17.9 per cent and 40.2 per cent throughout the United Kingdom. This was due to a decline in imports from the United States and Canada and an increase in imports of the more expensive Danish bacon. Rising prices and a generally frozen level of wages meant the cost of feeding a couple and five children adequately was more than a labourer's family could afford. Some relevant local prices in 1912 were:[20]

Bread (a 4 lb loaf)	6¼d
Milk (quart)	2½d
Tea (1 lb)	1s 8d to 2s
Sugar (1 lb)	2s
Butter (1 lb)	1s 3d to 1s 4d
Potatoes (7 lbs)	4½d to 5d
Eggs (7 or 8)	1s
Bacon (1 lb)	9d to 10d
Meat (1 lb of beef, mutton or pork)	6d to 8d
Coal (1 cwt) –	1s 3d

15 *Waterford Standard*, 28 Feb. 1914.
16 *Waterford News*, 7 Jan. 1899.
17 Daly (1981), p. 105.
18 *Waterford News*, 1 July and 23 Sep. 1887.
19 *Waterford Standard*, 25 June 1904.
20 *Report on Working Class Rents, Retail Prices and Wages*, p. 297.

Assuming an income of 14s a week, the cost of these items represents 60 per cent of a family's income. But the list falls short of the weekly food requirement for seven people, the total cost of which therefore exceeded its income. In March 1915, providing for the average family of five persons in the Cork workhouse cost in excess of 13s 9d.[21]

In addition to rent, food and coal there were other outgoings. Shirts were advertised at between 2s 6d and 10s 6d in 1913 and 'Suir' boots were priced at 17s 6d a pair while the lowest tender for supplying workhouse inmates with boots was 9s a pair for boys and 8s 11½d for girls.[22] Fitzgerald of The Island passed down his discarded boots to employees. Although somewhat large (about a size 11), they were received with gratitude. Children going barefoot was commonplace.

Cost-cutting was part of the family's daily life and generally resulted in an inadequate diet. However, boiled Irish bacon and cabbage was a relatively cheap but nourishing meal. Sometimes, while the bacon cooked within, bread was baked on a pot's inverted lid.[23] In the 1880s some of the smaller city streets were still lit by paraffin lamps and in the dead of night residents 'borrowed' fuel from these public lamps. Catherine English used a 'sweet' gallon of sour milk, costing about 1d, to make bread. One hob fireplace served for cooking and heating. Coal slack, dampened with water, kept the house warm during cold winters. Oil lamps and candles were used for lighting.

Poverty and the corporation's reluctance to spend ratepayers' money also meant poor housing and generally poor living conditions for the labouring class in Waterford.

III

Ownership of land in the city centre was divided among a great many, but the largest landlords were the Holy Ghost Hospital Charity and the corporation. In 1884 the corporation received little in rents from the very few houses it had built but obtained an income of between £8,000 and £9,000 from reversionary leases. Large numbers of houses had been built privately on some of the leased land and rented out. Old tenements, grand houses located on corporation ground and abandoned by their 'well-to-do' tenants after the Act of Union, were rented out by leaseholding middlemen and slumowners. Located in Alexander Street, Little Michael Street, New Street, Kneeve's Lane, Smith's Lane, Patrick Street, Lady Lane, Brown's Lane, Stephen Street, Bakehouse Lane, Johnstown and Carrigeen Lane,[24] they made up 20 per cent of the 1,800 dwellings within the municipal boundaries. The middlemen, who included councillors, were alleged to have led 'almost luxurious lives' out of their income from the property. Although they were among the most unsanitary dwellings in the city, the corporation failed to exercise its legal powers and enforce sanitary regulations.[25] The corporation also owned prime industrial sites, such as those occupied by Denny's at Anne Street, Bridge Street and Penrose Lane.[26]

In 1871 it had been noted that among the lower-class Catholics there was 'great destitution' in the 'poor and over-crowded portions of the city'. Conditions were unsanitary. A visitor observed 'many nests of disease, a great deal of dirt, an imperfect supply of water in many places, and not a few tumble-down tenements that ought to be at once removed'.[27] Five years later, James Ryan, installed for the second time as mayor, considered the 'want of proper dwellings for the

21 MacSweeney (1915).
22 *Waterford Standard*, 4 Sep. 1915.
23 Davis-Goff (1990), pp. 32–33.
24 *Waterford Standard*, 17 Jan. 1914.
25 *Third Report into the Housing of the Working Classes*.
26 *Waterford News*, 5 Mar. 1915.
27 Anonymous (1871).

working classes ... [an issue] ... crying out for a remedy'.[28] He continued,

> I know from personal knowledge and sad experience the wretched conditions of the hovels at present inhabited ... for which dwellings they [the poor] are made to pay heavy rent—for mud walls falling away, with roofs through which the rain enters ... . They [the houses] would be a disgrace to the poorest village, and much more so to the important and prospering city of Waterford.

During his term in office, Ryan oversaw the building of 17 two-storeyed corporation houses in Green's Lane,[29] Waterford being among the first cities in Ireland to take advantage of The Labouring Classes Lodging Houses and Dwellings (Ireland) Act 1866. James English's parents were both residents of Green's Lane (see Map 2) when they married at Ballybricken Church in January 1858. They subsequently moved to John Street where James was born.

The 3s 6d rent charged by the corporation for the new houses was too expensive for labourers and tenancies went to artisans. This was a difficulty commonly encountered.[30] Because the people for whom they were intended could not afford the houses, the scheme was considered a failure. The corporation refused to levy the rates necessary to subsidise accommodation and the rents collected barely covered the interest on a £1,700 loan, the sinking fund and the cost of rent collection and repairs. The houses were 'wrecked very much' by the tenants[31] and it was argued that a private company should have been allowed to build and rent out the properties.[32]

The corporation abandoned house building, although the Dwelling Company and other private firms continued to build one-storeyed cottages for artisans. But there was sustained pressure on the corporation to provide accommodation for labourers and to improve health and sanitation conditions. The 1884 enquiry into working-class housing heard evidence that despite the 'very high' death rate caused by typhus, diarrhoea, virulent measles and other infectious diseases, the corporation had taken no action under public health legislation. The high number of deaths were due to the

> frightful conditions of the tenement houses ... and the general unsanitary conditions in which the people live; a great many ... are on the verge of pauperism and suffer from chronic starvation; they do not feel the pangs of hunger, but their bodies are insufficiently nourished.

The corporation's efforts to enforce health legislation were crippled by the shortage of housing. Families ejected from unsanitary dwellings were later allowed to return because they could not be rehoused. But it was 'peculiar ideas about taxation' which prevented some improvements being undertaken by the corporation. Just days before the enquiry, and having agreed that sewage works were 'absolutely necessary', the corporation refused to strike a rate and the work could not go ahead. One witness testified that 'the popular outcry is such that the corporation is almost afraid to levy a rate'.

The motion for a borough rate was reported to have collapsed under a tide of furious public opinion[33] but the *Waterford News* thought the accusation that the high death rate was due to an uncaring corporation was unfair. The risk to health, according to the editor, was not due to poor sewage but was the result of refuse and cesspools at the rear of poor dwellings. And the city had more charitable institutions for 'old worn-out people' than any city of its size in the

28   *Waterford News*, 8 Jan. 1876.
29   *Third Report into the Housing of the Working Classes*; *Waterford News*, 7 Jan. 1899.
30   Daly (1981), p. 102.
31   *Third Report into the Housing of the Working Classes*.
32   *Waterford News*, 8 Jan. 1876.
33   *Waterford News*, 8 May 1885.

three kingdoms. Without a mandate to strike a rate there was no income to pay for any improvements. No further money could be raised from the corporation's city properties which were already pledged to cover debts of £160,000. And other sources of income were just enough to cover paving and lighting costs. But by 1900 the more cynical were declaring that measures for improved sanitation were blocked by property owners and public boards because their own 'huge profits' would be reduced and because they feared their own property would be subject to orders later.[34]

The Summer Hill Terrace scheme, ready for occupation by 1890 according to a plaque fixed to one of the houses, signalled the corporation's re-entry into the housing market. Government loans were obtained, sites purchased and cottages erected under the various housing acts. When the corporation was unable to obtain further loans, it leased its own land to private builders who financed house construction in a joint public and private sector enterprise. Local builders George Nolan and Paddy Coston constructed the houses, as a contractual condition required the use of Irish labour, Irish materials and local builders. However, the lowest rent of 2s 6d still put the houses beyond the reach of the labourers whose housing needs remained in the hands of private landlords. It was suggested a private company could have built the homes, and rented them out, more cheaply.[35]

The city was still considered to be a long way from saving the 'really poor workers from the squalor, sickness and danger of moral contamination to which they are exposed by the tenanted house system'. And this at a time when a severe epidemic of scarlet fever required the disinfecting of homes. By 1896 it had become necessary to levy a rate of 2s 8d in the pound made up of an

8d borough rate, a 5d sanitary rate, a 1d free library rate and a 1s 6d water rate. In addition ratepayers had to pay 1s 11d towards the county railway and lunatic asylum charges,[36] a poor rate of 2s 8d, and a grand jury cess of 2s 8d.[37] This level of rates was defended on the grounds that Waterford remained the most lightly taxed city in the country.

The 1899 local election campaigns centred on the levying of rates and improved housing for the newly enfranchised labourer. The Ratepayers Association candidate John Breen, claimed he would not only keep down rates but the proper housing of the poor would also always have his best attention. There was, he insisted, little point in asking a labouring man for 2s 6d rent out of 12s wages. So he was going to ensure they had comfortable houses at a rent of 1s. The community would benefit because there would be less drunkenness and therefore less poverty and fewer people in the workhouse and prisons.[38] It was, he told a ratepayers' meeting, 'the landlord class' who made money out of local taxes. They passed on rate rises and obtained extra income by raising rents in excess of the rate increases. Moreover, the landlords, he claimed, were corporation members who exploited the shortage of housing by building below-standard houses.[39] Alderman W. J. Smith, the 'old' corporation member running in opposition to Breen, solicited first-time labouring-class voters. He promised to finance labourers' housing through the rates as 'it is impossible for a poor man with only 14s or 15s a week to give himself proper accommodation unless the governing body of the city stepped in and helped him'.

By early 1914, the city's water supply and drainage had been improved at a cost of £125,000, and £52,590 had also been spent on building 353 houses. The schemes were partly

---

34 *Waterford News*, 12 Jan. 1900.
35 *Waterford News*, 12 Jan. 1900.
36 *Waterford News*, 7 Jan. 1899.
37 *Waterford News*, 2 Nov. 1893.
38 *Waterford News*, 14 Jan. 1899.
39 *Waterford News*, 7 Jan. 1899.

financed by levying a rate of 11s 4d in the pound. It was planned to demolish most of the city's remaining 77 tenements (referred to as 'halls' locally). However, tuberculosis, known as the 'white scourge' or 'consumption', remained 'very prevalent' among the working classes, especially the residents of tenements. And there was still a desperate shortage of housing. In Alexander Street, where structurally dangerous premises had been torn down, people were sleeping in the open sites because they could not be rehoused.

The situation had been made worse by the Great Southern and Western Railway Company demolishing company houses in Ferrybank to make room for expansion. Some argued that the corporation had to provide low rental accommodation for the poor, even if this entailed a financial loss. Bishop Sheehan, pleased that the corporation had spent £190,000 on civic improvement in 1913, none the less wanted to see housing for letting at about 1s to those poorer than the artisans.[40] Further government housing loans were requested[41] and by 1916 over 400 corporation cottages had been built.

James English was more fortunate than many. Although occupying a non-corporation dwelling at 5 Thomas's Avenue, the rent of about 1s was reasonable and much cheaper than the lowest corporation rent of 2s 6d for two rooms. It had an outside flushed water closet and drinking water supplied by a tap in the yard. This accommodation was superior to many labourers' houses, some of which had a shared water supply, sometimes a community pump in the street, and frequently a waste pit instead of a water closet. Poverty did not extinguish pride so his home was comfortable. Catherine was scrupulously clean about the house. Concrete floors were scrubbed bright and knick-knacks adorned a polished sideboard.

However, the house, consisting of two rooms,[42] was grossly overcrowded. The living room was 7½ feet high and 10 feet by 9 feet. An upper bedroom, 6½ feet high and 11 feet by 9 feet, was used by James English, his wife and five children sleeping in two beds. Overcrowding worsened in Thomas's Avenue between 1901 and 1911.

As a member of the labouring class, James English was therefore particularly vulnerable to any adverse economic consequences resulting from war with Germany. A 1904 survey in Dublin showed that 57 per cent of a sample of 21 families, mainly of the unskilled labourer class, 'lacked the essentials for merely physical efficiency'.[43]

In the House of Commons on 3 August 1914 Keir Hardie, noting how under the threat of war a bill for the relief of the Stock Exchange and the business interests had been rushed through parliament with 'absolute unanimity', asked what was being done for the 'relief of the inevitable destitution which is bound to prevail among the poor.' He wanted to know how they would be protected against the 'unscrupulous gang who form the food ring [and who] will take advantage of the war crisis to rob the poor more than the market justifies'.[44] Hardie's concern was well-founded.

IV

By 1916 Ireland has been described as being 'relatively prosperous' with only some unemployment in industries which could not be adapted to the war effort.[45] And the country is said to have

---

40 *Munster Express*, 15 Feb. 1913.
41 *Waterford Standard*, 17 Jan. 1914.
42 Information provided by Dan Dowling of Waterford from official housing inspection records. In 1939 the rent for the cottage was 3s 6d and the rates were paid by the owner. Demolition was recommended at this time but did not take place until the 1960s.
43 O'Brien (1982), p. 167.
44 *Hansard* (Commons) 5th ser. LXV, 1839–41, 3 Aug. 1914.
45 Lyons (1973), p. 360; The generalisation was qualified in Lyons, F. S. L. (1979), *Culture and Anarchy in Ireland*, Oxford, p. 99, in which he acknowledged the different effects on urban and rural areas.

experienced a period of 'unprecedented prosperity' between 1914 and 1920.[46]

Available data support the impression of a general prosperity. The war resulted in a favourable Irish balance of trade for the first time since 1904 and Irish joint-stock bank deposits rose more than 220 per cent between 1910 and 1918.[47] Some industries did initially benefit from the war. In November 1914, for instance, all Irish woollen and hosiery mills were reported to be working at high pressure with orders that would keep them busy for months.[48] In Dublin the clothing, wool, tweeds and hosiery industries boomed. Boot, shoe and saddlery products were in high demand. Bottle-making plants worked to capacity, manufacturers of ironworks and tools were kept busy, and the shipyard was supplied with work throughout the period of war.[49] However, generalised assessments conceal the confused and uneven economic consequences of the war.

In February 1915 the Dublin correspondent of *The Times* extolled the prosperous condition of the Irish economy, reporting 'a new spirit of industry and enterprise is very noticeable in many parts of the country'. There was, he concluded 'very little distress' but added, 'except in the large cities'.[50] However, in September it was being argued that any 'impression' Irish manufacturers were 'reaping enhanced profits' was false except in a 'few instances' where they had derived 'satisfactory profits'.[51] And although admitting that there was still poverty in cities like Cork and Dublin, one writer wondered why amidst 'superabundant prosperity' the Easter Rising had occurred. The provisional government had made no reference to specific economic demands, reforms or grievances.[52] The Royal Commission which investigated the Easter Rising concluded that at the time Ireland was in a 'state of great prosperity' and discontent could not be attributed to economic causes, although poor housing conditions may have accounted for an 'underlying sense of dissatisfaction with existing authority'.[53] Alfie Byrne, the populist Dublin nationalist MP, however, considered bad housing conditions, unemployment and poor rates of pay to have been at the heart of dissatisfaction in Ireland at the time of the rising.[54]

In July 1916, Prime Minister Asquith declared Ireland to be in a satisfactory state because of its 'general prosperity'. Farmers he claimed were never so well off and industrially the country was 'not unsatisfactory'.[55] Chief Secretary Duke spoke of Dublin being a world apart from the misery being experienced in the rest of the world. 'Practically immune' from this misery, it was a city where there was 'prosperity in the great industries' of a kind not known in modern times.[56] In the same year Joseph Devlin asserted that agricultural prosperity had been exaggerated. He pointed up the paradox that while England was in a condition of 'boundless prosperity', in many Irish cities like Dublin and Cork 'there is practically no increased prosperity at all'. In parts of Dublin people were 'bordering on starvation'.[57]

Another contemporary wryly commented in 1918 that 'across the Irish sea the war is a money-making affair; here with us it is merely a device for accentuating our poverty, and plunging our

46 Johnson, D. (1989), *The Interwar Economy in Ireland*, Dublin, p. 5.
47 Ellis, P. B. (1985), *A History of the Irish Working Class*, London, p. 210.
48 *Cork Examiner*, 4 Nov. 1914.
49 O'Flanagan (1985), pp. 10–11.
50 *The Times*, 8 Feb. 1915.
51 Riordan, E. J. (1915), 'Chronicle: I—Irish industries—after twelve months of war', *Studies* pp. 463–70.
52 Fisher, J. R. (1916), 'The Irish enigma again—what is wrong in Ireland', *Nineteenth Century and After*, **LXXIX**, pp. 1184–89.
53 *Report of the Royal Commission on the Rebellion in Ireland* (British Parliamentary Papers, 1916 [Cd. 8311] XI.185).
54 *Hansard* (Commons) 5th ser. LXXXII, 1544, 17 May 1916; *Hansard* (Commons) 5th ser. XCV, 1268, 5 July 1917.
55 *Hansard* (Commons) 5th ser. LXXXIV, 2140–41, 31 July 1916.
56 *The Irish Times*, 24 Oct. 1917.
57 *Hansard* (Commons) 5th ser. XCIII, 944, 8 May 1917.

workers into greater depths of destitution'.[58] For sections of Dublin's working population, this was unquestionably true.

Generally the war brought prosperity to Waterford. It resulted in restored trade at higher prices after foot and mouth disease had practically closed Irish ports in the early part of 1914. By the end of the year the Chamber of Commerce reported that the livestock trade was at an 'unequalled stage of prosperity' and the port was 'booming' with no scarcity of employment on the quays. The Clyde Shipping Company ran extra ships to cope with the increased traffic. Bad weather had resulted in poor quality harvests but reduced quantities and war conditions, which disrupted world trade, produced shortages and this ensured abnormally high prices. An apple surplus was exported. The bacon trade was expected to maintain a high level of prices into the following year and people in the city suburbs were encouraged to go in for pig raising.[59]

The advice paid off for those who took it as bacon made a record price in 1915. High prices were maintained in the provisions trade generally during 1915 but there was a severe drop in port tonnage due to government requisition of shipping. Port revenues were consequently well down and the shortage of shipping contributed to the rising cost of freight. Much of the through coal traffic had been lost to Dublin because of the increased freight costs and less coal was handled at the port.[60]

It was therefore farmers, businessmen in the provisions trade and shopowners who were the beneficiaries of war. The extent to which the farmers benefited is disputed but even those who argued the 'allegations of profiteering ... are ridiculous' admitted farmers were doing far better than in pre-war days.[61] Some shops did so well their owners could expand. In February 1915 John Morgan opened a new victualling establishment in Broad Street[62] and Robertson, Ledlie and Ferguson Ltd spent months improving their shop premises on the Quay. When finished, the elaborate new shop front was expected to be 'one of the most modern and up-to-date of its kind in any city in Ireland'.[63]

Some enterprising individuals took advantage of the high bacon prices. Summonses against residents of Barrack Street, Convent Hill and Lower Yellow Road for keeping pigs within 30 feet of a dwelling were dismissed by magistrates who thought the bye-laws should not be 'so strictly enforced at present'.[64] But unskilled workers particularly suffered severe economic hardship. In Waterford the police identified a deepening antagonism against employers, shopkeepers and farmers who were believed to be profiteering from the war.[65]

Following the declaration of war there was a steep rise in prices throughout the United Kingdom. The general cost of living for the working class rose about 10 per cent in the last five months of 1914 and by about another 22 per cent in 1915. The Board of Trade's retail price index rose by 39 per cent between 1 August 1914 and 1 June 1915.[66] Price increases were not evenly spread and some staple items rose considerably in price. Bread increased by 25.8 per cent between July 1914 and March 1915.[67] Tea increased by 49 per cent and eggs by 45 per cent. But by November 1915, the price of margarine had dropped 12 per cent. In Dublin, there was a steep increase in food prices following the outbreak of

58 Malone (1918).
59 *Waterford Standard*, 10 Feb. 1915.
60 *Waterford Standard*, 9 Feb. 1916.
61 Lysaght, E. E. (1918), 'Four years of Irish economics 1914–1918: Irish agriculture', *Studies*, pp. 314–19.
62 *Waterford Standard*, 12 Feb. 1915.
63 *Waterford Standard*, 9 Feb. 1916.
64 *Waterford News*, 2 July 1915.
65 O'Connor (1989), pp. 128–29.
66 French, D. (1982), *British Economic and Strategic Planning 1905–1915*, London, p. 99.
67 Dearle, N. B. (1929), *The Economic Chronicle of the Great War for Great Britain and Ireland*, London, pp. 8, 22, 26, 29, 47 and 68.

war. Coal rose in price from 22s a ton in mid-1914 to 40s in early 1915.[68]

Within days of war being declared, it was reported that in Waterford, business was being 'keenly affected'. Sugar, meat, flour and coal prices were subject to an 'abnormal rise' as a result of panic buying. There was such a rush to the shops by country residents that city customers were unable to have their orders filled.

Readers of the *Munster Express* were assured the government was going to 'look after the markets and see that shopkeepers do not take advantage of the war to charge exorbitant prices'.[69] However, a demand for food control and the fixing of maximum prices was rejected by the government in February 1915. A pre-war government committee had concluded that attempts at price-fixing would discourage foreign exporters and result in shortages. Suppliers needed the stimulus of high prices and market mechanism would eventually result in lowered prices. Hunger and want were also used as a means of directing economic and human resources into the war effort. None the less, the government was prepared to intervene when it thought necessary. In August 1914, the Board of Trade was authorised to requisition any stocks of food speculators deliberately held from the public. By the end of March 1915, £12.5 million had been spent on buying and selling wheat, meat and sugar to ensure supplies to the public at reasonable prices. However, the extent to which food could be subsidised was limited as the Treasury found it expensive.[70]

Wartime governments which tried to control the food supply also entered a 'political minefield' and were cautious.[71] There was dissension within the cabinet on the degree of government intervention required and some ministers,

including Lloyd George and Winston Churchill, argued for greater intervention in order to put the economy on a war footing. In July 1915 the price of coal at the pit's mouth was limited through legislation, but attempts to restrict profiteering by controlling prices generally resulted in the rapid disappearance of designated goods from the shops.[72] Generally, price regulation in Britain had only a limited effect in curbing rent and price increases[73] and it was even less successful in Ireland.[74]

None the less in Waterford there was a growing demand for government controls. The government's failure to coordinate naval, military and civilian demands for shipping caused delays, congestion and shortages and this pushed up the price of freighted goods. However, in January 1915 the cabinet rejected a plan to take direct control of shipping. But the government was unable to secure even minimal voluntary cooperation from ship owners and it was forced to pay excessive rates for the use of refrigerated shipping.

In Waterford, between August 1914 and January 1915, the charge for freight on foodstuffs from the United States had gone up from 12s 6d to £3 7s 6d (537 per cent) a ton. Consequently, 1d was added to the price of a loaf. The *Waterford News* asked: 'what do we call the British shipowners who plunder the wives and children of the men who defend them?' The writer wondered if Irish working men should be expected to go abroad and fight when wives were paid a 'mean allowance [and] if on top of that one set of greedy pigs raise[s] her rent while another set of greedy pigs raise[s] the price of bread'.[75]

The UTLC passed a resolution calling on parliament to take over food supplies 'in order that the working classes may be protected against

68 O'Flanagan (1985), pp. 20–24.
69 *Munster Express*, 8 Aug. 1914.
70 French (1982), pp. 60–64, 89–90, 99, 101–02.
71 Turner (1992), pp. 59, 170–71.
72 Weller, K. (1985), *Don't be a Soldier—The Radical Anti-War Movement in North London 1914–1918*, London, pp. 33, 41–42.
73 Whiteside, N., 'The British population at war' in J. Turner (ed.) (1988), *Britain and the First World War*, London, pp. 85–98.
74 Johnson (1989), p. 4.
75 *Waterford News*, 22 Jan. 1915.

unjust and extortionate demands' and because of the 'high and rapidly advancing prices' of coal, bread, flour, meat and other necessities of daily life. These increases were pressing most heavily on those whose lives were already 'a struggle for bare existence'.

The Trades Council also called on the corporation to ensure bread was sold by weight. Although this demand was 'an old chestnut',[76] the war made finding a solution more urgent. Bread in Waterford was between 8d and 10d for a 4 lb loaf whereas the highest price in the rest of the United Kingdom was 7d or in some cases 6d.[77] The corporation was asked to investigate why the price of milk as well as bread had risen in Waterford but not in other Irish cities. In Dublin, for example, milk prices were pegged until the end of 1916.[78] And there was a complaint that vendors were buying milk at 7d a gallon and at least one of them proposed selling it to the consumer at 1s 4d contrary to a resolution passed unanimously by Waterford milk suppliers that the price would be fixed at 10d between 1 February and 1 May 1915.[79]

In March 1915, Mayor P. W. Kenny and a committee[80] reported back after meetings with a master bakers' deputation and confirmed the price was sometimes the same for loaves of varying weight. The price for loaves of the same weight also varied. One baker charged 6½d for a 4 lb loaf and another charged 9d. Councillor David MacDonald, the barm baker, defended the eightpenny 4 lb loaf as reasonable. The bread trade in Waterford was in a 'ruinous condition' through competition. However, it was recommended that the police be asked to en-force legislation requiring bread to be sold by weight.

Of the city's 17 master bakers 15 agreed to fix a standard weight.[81] But by May only one baker, O'Neill's of Michael Street, was selling by weight. Known popularly as the 'full weight baker' he sold 1 lb loaves at 2d and 2 lb loaves at 4d.[82] In June complaints that despite a drop in the price of wheat and flour the price of bread had not followed suit,[83] resulted in a number of city bakers being prosecuted for not selling bread by weight.[84]

By June 1915 the supply of coal was reduced because large numbers of British miners had joined the colours. This produced a scarcity which, combined with the increased wages for those still working, had driven up the price of coal in Waterford until it was almost 'prohibitive'. Further increases were expected and a local newspaper offered detailed instructions on how to cut and prepare turf for use as fuel.[85] In December increases in the cost of freight to Waterford from British and foreign ports were reported as being 300 per cent for coal and 785 per cent for goods shipped from the River Plate and other South American ports. The cost of freighting a shipment of timber to Graves and Co. was 571 per cent more that it had been just before the outbreak of war.[86]

There was undoubtedly an element of profiteering involved and dividends in some industries were well up. Coal profits in 1916 were treble those of the average of the last five pre-war years and shipping profits were up 33.33 per cent.[87] Freight increases, it was argued, were not justified as ship owners were well secured against

76 O'Connor (1989), p. 120.
77 *Munster Express*, 6 Feb. 1915.
78 O' Flanagan (1985), p. 24.
79 *Waterford News*, 5 Feb. 1915.
80 *Munster Express*, 13 Feb. 1915.
81 *Waterford News*, 5 Mar. 1915.
82 *Waterford News*, 21 May 1915.
83 *Waterford Standard*, 12 June 1915.
84 *Waterford News*, 2 July 1915.
85 *Munster Express*, 5 June 1915.
86 *Waterford News*, 17 Dec. 1915.
87 Marwick (1965), pp. 123–30.

loss and 80 per cent of the war risk had been taken over by the government at the outbreak of war. There were reports of 'fairy tale' profits while British as well as Irish working-class families found life extremely difficult. In London the increased freight costs from Durham raised the price of coal by 450 per cent.[88] Trade unionists were more aggrieved about profiteering than about shortages and high prices.

But wages in the United Kingdom rose only by about 11 per cent. To check inflation, the government refused to sanction large wage increases and they relied on the willingness of the working classes to 'submit to the necessary sacrifices' to bring prices down.[89] Real wages therefore declined markedly and a government statement in 1915 advised that the consequent rise in the cost of living was not sufficient reason for employers to increase the wages of their employees. Any price rise was regarded as a burden which had to be shared by all classes. It was a burden, however, which fell disproportionately on the poorly paid and unorganised, unskilled worker. Wage movements varied across industries and regions and in Waterford wages for unskilled workers generally remained pegged at 1914 levels up to 1916. A continued deterioration in their conditions provoked more urgent calls for price controls and for restrictions on food exports.

In December 1914 labourers employed by the corporation were again unsuccessful in their request for a pay rise. But during March 1915 Alderman P. Quinlan, who had opposed the December application on grounds that it had been pushed by 'Jim Larkin's union', moved for an increase in wages because prices had gone up 'in many cases [by] 20 per cent'. Others supporting the motion stressed the impossibility of expecting a man to live on 16s or 17s a week. An increase of labourers' wages to £1 was agreed by

resolution.[90] Within two weeks the finance and law committee asked for the resolution to be rescinded because of the additional rates it would be necessary to levy.

Councillor Richard Keane argued passionately for the need to increase wages in the 'sight of God and in the sight of man'. Moreover, bacon merchants as well as Graves and Co. had awarded wage increases, so the market was directing the route to be followed. Prices had increased 'to an exorbitant height' and poor men were unable to maintain their families. P. W. Kenny noted the difficulty of the lower paid in getting three meals a day, adequate clothing or 'covering during the winter nights'.

But other councillors thought that the already 'frightful, absolutely awful' city rates compounded the serious problem of creating new local industries and additional employment.[91] Echoing the government's policy, Councillor William Fitzgerald of Centre Ward considered the need to raise rates by 5d to meet any increase in wages a conclusive argument against the motion. Everybody, he contended, was suffering from the war and one class, the unskilled worker, should not be relieved to the disadvantage of another, the shopkeeper. It was decided not to award a rise but the finance and law committee was instructed to investigate the possibilities of giving workers some extra allowance 'during the war period, owing to the present high prices of provisions'.[92]

Waterford's treasury had more pressing priorities. Yet another epidemic of scarlet fever added to the number of those who died from tuberculosis and other respiratory diseases and Richard Keane asked the corporation to purchase a disinfecting machine and clean the streets to prevent the death of 'hundreds' of the city's children.[93]

However, some councillors suggested the wage

88 Pankhurst, E. S. (1987), *The Home Front*, London pp. 127–30.
89 French (1982), p. 109.
90 *Waterford News*, 5 Mar. 1915.
91 *Waterford Standard*, 20 Mar. 1915.
92 *Munster Express*, 20 Mar. 1915.
93 *Waterford Standard*, 20 Mar. 1915.

debate reflected the weak position of the unskilled worker rather than the corporation's concern for the ratepayer—a point made in previous years and one which is borne out. Two months later the Board of Guardians responded to a request by the workhouse schoolmistress for an additional weekly allowance of 5s because of the 'high price of provisions', by increasing the allowance to 8s 6d. Without debate, the guardians accepted the need for an increase, the only question being by how much.[94]

In November Councillor Keane brusquely dismissed a suggestion by the principal of the Technical Institute that he be allowed to help the war economy by running a week of lectures and demonstrations on suitable methods of cooking and growing food. Much more appropriate, Keane suggested, were lectures on how to obtain the food to cook. A pay rise would help. The institute would do better by offering their courses to those old ladies who were able to 'buy pounds of steak for their little dogs'.[95]

Pressure for wage adjustment mounted and in September 1915, the UTLC discussed the state of the city's trades. Shopworkers in general were 'most in need of thorough organisation'. There were cases of men being employed at 'sweated' rates and in poor conditions. The unorganised state of builders and general labourers was also a major concern but female workers received 'starvation wages with the added burden of long hours'.[96]

With the advantage of their industrial strength, British workers were militant in their determination to gain benefits from increased profits, and the threat of strikes forced the government to attempt some control of the rising cost of living. Irish workers had less muscle, but Waterford's shipping employers were vulnerable to industrial action. There was worker unrest in the Clyde Shipping Company in February 1915[97] and in early 1916 the Rosslare to Fishguard service was suspended because of strike action. Losses to the city's trade and commerce was considered to be 'very serious'[98] and the UTLC took the opportunity to press the corporation for the provision of proper bathing and swimming facilities.[99] But worker power remained limited. A seven-week strike by coal workers, which caused considerable hardship, was settled in December 1915 by a corporation committee proposed by Richard Keane and presided over by P. W. Kenny, the coal workers having reduced their original demand.[100]

In some areas the government was unable to resist calls for intervention in Ireland. It had taken control of the railways in Britain on 4 August 1914 and by February 1915 weekly war bonuses had been granted.[101] The Irish railway companies paid considerably less to their staff in war bonuses than was received by railwaymen in Britain doing the same job, and this was a major source of discontent. In March 1915 Waterford hosted a large meeting of railway employees but the company directors refused to meet National Union of Railwaymen representatives to discuss the war bonus issue.[102] Appeals were made for some form of state intervention and in December 1916 industrial action was threatened. The government took control of Ireland's railways and within days the men were awarded an all-round 7s per week increase to supplement the 14s or less that most of them earned.[103]

Conditions for the labouring class were bleak

94 *Waterford Standard*, 15 May 1915.
95 *Waterford Standard*, 6 Nov. 1915.
96 *Waterford News*, 1 Oct. 1915.
97 *Waterford News*, 26 Feb. 1915.
98 *Waterford Standard*, 9, 12 Feb. and 4 Mar. 1916.
99 *Waterford News*, 1 Oct. 1915.
100 *Waterford Standard*, 6, 17 Nov. and 8, 17 Dec. 1915; *Waterford News*, 5 Nov. and 17 Dec. 1915.
101 Dearle (1929), pp. 2, 26.
102 *Munster Express*, 3 Apr. 1915.
103 Pratt, E. A. (1921), *British Railways and the Great War*, Vol. 1, London, pp. 79–81.

but despite continuing unemployment the number of paupers in Ireland dropped by 3.4 per cent during the 12 months preceding 27 March 1915 and this United Kingdom-wide trend was reflected in Waterford, Cork and Limerick. In Britain too, the number of destitute generally declined and health standards and life expectancy rose. Fewer people claimed relief and fewer necessitous children required subsidised school meals.[104] However, Dublin, which experienced a rise in pauperism after a decline during 1914 to 1915, was an exception.[105] The limited number of new jobs created in Ireland cannot explain the reduced numbers of paupers. By the end of 1915, the war had created no significant additional work in Waterford and the problems of unemployment still dogged officials.

The drop in port tonnage during 1915 meant a reduction in men employed on the docks and in May 1915 those dockers with jobs were reported as working long 'arduous' hours. It was not uncommon for them to work 24 hours at a stretch.[106] In early 1915 County Waterford farmers complained of a 'great scarcity of male labour' and suggested a need to organise female workers.[107] But the urban Waterford Advisory Committee for Juvenile Employment reported the number of vacancies available in 1915 as being 13 per cent down on the previous year although applications for work remained at the same level. There was also a decline in jobs available to the adult workforce.[108]

Where new jobs were created, these merely soaked up some of the excess labour so wages and conditions remained static. The shortage of butter, for instance, resulted in an abnormal demand for substitutes and this ensured McDonnell's margarine factory worked to capacity. The company opened a new factory in 1917 but the 200 people employed worked 60 hours per week under poor conditions.

Irish emigration had dropped by about 50 per cent during 1915. It was stopped altogether following the Liverpool incident of November 1915, when about 650 young emigrants from west Ireland apparently fleeing the rumoured threat of conscription and on their way to America were humiliated by a Liverpool crowd. The shipping lines refused to carry them further. The incident was extensively reported in the Irish and English press, including the *Waterford News*.[109] Soon afterwards men of military age with a passport had to apply for a visa or, if applying for a passport, were required to give a satisfactory reason for going abroad.[110]

The war created three additional options for the unemployed and these help to explain the decrease in the number of paupers. They could enlist in the army, migrate to those parts of Ireland where war had stimulated the local economy or move to Britain where war work had created well-paid jobs.

In June 1915 the Waterford War Munitions Bureau, operating from City Hall, enrolled skilled tradesmen as volunteers to work on munition production for six months anywhere in the United Kingdom. Good wages, subsidies and travelling expenses were offered. Only employed men were taken on, the unemployed being instructed to apply through the labour exchange. Local employers were encouraged to release their workers and within four days 74 men were hired.[111] Local newspapers carried advertisements calling on navvies 'fully experienced in pick and shovel work' to apply for munitions work in Britain through the labour exchange.[112]

104 Whiteside, 'The British population at war' in Turner (ed.) (1988).
105 O'Flanagan (1985), pp. 28–29.
106 *Waterford News*, 21 May 1915.
107 *Waterford News*, 28 May 1915.
108 *Waterford News*, 11 Feb. 1916.
109 *Waterford News*, 12 Nov. 1915.
110 *The Times*, 10 and 15 Nov. 1915; *Cork Examiner*, 11 Dec. 1915.
111 *Munster Express*, 26 June 1915; *Waterford News*, 25 June 1915; *Waterford Standard*, 26 and 30 June 1915.
112 *Waterford News*, 24 Sep. and 31 Dec. 1915.

A total of 1,679 labourers were sent to work in Britain by the Lady Lane labour exchange during 1917 and 1918.[113]

Munitions work could be highly remunerative, some unskilled workers in Britain earning as much as £3 10s a week.[114] It became a major competitor for manpower, drawing men away from enlistment in the army or work on the land. John Redmond calculated that by the end of 1915, about 40,000 Irishmen were employed in munition work in Britain and Ireland.[115] In 1917 the minister of munitions reported that 35,000 people were employed in government and controlled establishments in Ireland. Others were employed in uncontrolled establishments.[116] And it has been estimated that more than 40,000 were employed in Britain alone.[117] The movement to Britain, therefore, was relatively large scale and it has been argued that this was one aspect of an increased mobility initiated by the war which helped expatriate Irishmen to broaden their outlook by forcing large numbers of Irishmen and Britons to test the 'abstract assumptions, attitudes and stereotypes' they had of each other.[118]

But the scale of local unemployment remained an absorbing concern in Waterford, as it did in other Irish cities. Efforts to create jobs locally by sharing war work with the British were persistently frustrated by what was often interpreted as hostility or a lack of government sympathy for, or an understanding of, the unique economic plight in Ireland. Indeed, government policy sometimes threatened established jobs. The experience sharpened suspicions of British government intentions in Ireland.

In 1914 the Waterford Chamber of Commerce had reported a noticeable depression in the building trade. But with a major building scheme approved by the Treasury, the construction of the new Munster and Leinster Bank branch underway and repairs to the tuberculosis dispensary necessary, it was hoped 'a much needed fillip will be given to this important trade on which so many artisans are dependent'.[119] A healthy, local building industry was also crucial for the employment of large numbers of unskilled workers. A Treasury loan of £23,138 in two instalments had been sanctioned for the housing scheme. The first instalment of £5,000 enabled the corporation to obtain and clear sites for the complete scheme and to commence construction.[120]

The housing act of 10 August 1914, extended to Ireland on 28 August, was intended to relieve unemployment. But in November 1914 there was a considerable drop in the initially high level of unemployment caused by the war and by the end of the year the Treasury was refusing to give funds for public works. The New Armies absorbed the unemployed during the winter and spring of 1914–15 and created a shortage of labour in Britain. By February 1915, therefore, lack of work was no longer a problem in Britain. The Treasury restricted the funds available and urged local authorities throughout the United Kingdom to stop all new public building works. The consequences in Ireland were devastating.

In Waterford during the same month, however, Councillor Keane was pushing for the immediate commencement of the agreed building work as there were a 'great many' men idle in the city. Although work was available in other parts of the country, the men did not wish to leave

---

113 O'Flanagan (1985), p. 47.
114 Winter, D. (1978), *Death's Men*, Harmondsworth, p. 167.
115 Gwynn (1932), pp. 435–37.
116 *Hansard* (Commons) 5th ser. XCII, 2606, 26 Apr. 1917.
117 Staunton (1986a), pp. 55–56.
118 Fitzpatrick, 'The overflow of the deluge' in MacDonagh and Mandle (eds.) (1986).
119 *Waterford Standard*, 10 Feb. 1915.
120 This account is based on the following correspondence: Murphy to Redmond, 6 Aug. 1915; Redmond to Sir Henry Robinson, 9 Aug. 1915; Sir Henry Robinson to Redmond, 10 Aug. 1915; Montague to Redmond, 11 Aug. 1915; Fitzgerald to Redmond, 27 Aug. 1915; Resolution of the Housing Committee of Waterford Corporation, 27 Aug. 1915; Redmond to Montague 2 Sep. 1915; Murphy to Redmond, 8 Sep. 1915; Montague to Redmond, 17 Sep. 1915; Redmond to the mayor of Waterford, 18 Sep. 1915 (Redmond Papers, 15, 261 [6] and [7]), NLI.

their homes.[121] After commencement of building was approved by the corporation,[122] the second loan instalment was withheld on Treasury advice. Martin J. Murphy, MP for East Waterford, urged Redmond to press for payment of the outstanding loan instalment. He reported unemployment as being 'rampant' in the city but the most important need was for 'decent homes'.

On taking the issue up, Redmond was told by the Local Government Board and the Treasury that builders would be ruined if held to old contracts because of the increase in the costs of building materials. But the applications for loans 'pouring in', all as urgent as Waterford's, could not be met mainly because of the prohibitive cost of the war. Redmond was urged to be 'patriotic' and be satisfied with the first instalment. The Waterford housing committee was unrepentant and passed a resolution calling on Redmond to continue pressing for the loan. If the building scheme did not continue, unemployment among tradesmen and labourers was expected to cause 'much poverty and distress'.

However, a failure to procure the outstanding loan had political implications for Redmond as leader of the IPP and as MP for Waterford city. In September he told the Treasury that if 'the promise publicly given is broken, there will be very serious trouble in the city of Waterford, and I personally, will be put into a position of extreme embarrassment'. The Treasury agreed to advance a further £4,000 and to review the situation 12 months later. A letter from the Local Government Board to this effect was read out to the housing committee.[123] Redmond asked the mayor not to make a 'public splash' about his part in securing the advance—an understandable request given that sorely needed housing schemes in Dublin and other cities were suspended.

In Dublin, where the construction industry employed around 17 per cent of the workforce, government contracts, worth £500,000 in 1914, had dried up by the middle of 1915. Public agitation and a resolution of no confidence in the Local Government Board passed by Dublin corporation, resulted in the release of £6,000 in funds. In the Dublin Trades Council it was remarked that the British government only believed in 'providing workhouses for the Irish'.[124]

Government policy on drinking represented a direct and serious threat to the livelihoods of men employed in the breweries and ancillary trades, as well as to farmers. Lloyd George's proposed liquor control measures in the April 1915 budget encountered immediate Irish opposition. He commented, 'the Irish Party was particularly angry in view of the big brewing and distilling interests in that country. One by one I was compelled to abandon ... these proposed taxes.'[125] Those with personal interests were undoubtedly concerned, but brewing was a major Irish industry and the consequences of liquor control would be generally far more serious in Ireland than in Britain.

There was some sympathy with the idea of control in areas where munitions were manufactured but outside of these they would create the 'utmost dissatisfaction, unemployment and dislocation of business'.[126] In response to rumours, city traders sent a petition to John Redmond pointing out that since the 1909 budget, 40 licences had lapsed in the city, there had been a 'curtailment' of labour in the two breweries and any reduction in the gravity of the Irish product would result in a loss of markets. But perhaps most telling was the observation that since munitions work in Ireland was almost non-existent, there was no need to protect war production.[127]

Waterford corporation passed a resolution

121 *Waterford News*, 5 Mar. 1915.
122 *Waterford Standard*, 27 Mar. 1915.
123 *Evening News*, 9 Oct. 1915.
124 O'Flanagan (1985), p. 16–19.
125 Lloyd George, D. (1938), *War Memoirs*, Vol. 1, London, p. 202.
126 *Munster Express*, 3 Apr. 1915.
127 *Waterford News*, 16 Apr. 1915.

strongly condemning the proposed taxes and called upon the IPP to 'strenuously oppose and vote against' them. The taxes would ruin the brewing, distilling and allied industries and would create 'distress' among the working classes employed in these industries, and barley-growing farmers in at least three counties would be ruined.

The proposals provoked accusations by councillors that the British government was following its traditional policy of destroying Irish industries. P. W. Kenny again raised the issue of over-taxation in Ireland and wondered why Ireland's parliamentary representatives had not been consulted before the budget was introduced. 'Ireland's connection with the Empire,' he declared, 'has been a series of disasters.' Waterford workers did not have much to thank the brewers for, as he believed they were the worst paid in the city, but if anything happened to the trade a great many would be thrown out of work and he concluded: 'God only knows [there are] enough men out of employment.'[128]

While the AOH delivered lectures on British intentions to destroy Irish industries to 'large and appreciative audiences' in Waterford and called on the need for a home government to impose tariffs,[129] the issue of taxation developed as a major cause of rift between Redmond and some corporation members. In July 1915 J. J. O'Shee, MP for West Waterford, told the UIL executive that the war would be an 'enormous cost and burden' on the people of Ireland which should be accepted in the interests of their country.[130] On a visit to Waterford in December, Redmond promised a free and prosperous Ireland but until that happened a 'crushing load of taxation was bound to fall' on the country. He asserted that 'every industry in Ireland was looking up. There seemed a future of economic and industrial welfare and happiness looming upon our country'.[131]

But fewer people believed this as the war dragged on. Alfie Byrne was one of several Irish MPs who persistently raised in the House of Commons the unfairness of wartime taxation in Ireland, the lack of munitions work and the destruction of employment-creating industries.[132] In February 1916 police reported the separatist Irish Volunteers as having decided on action to resist further taxation. The following month, P. W. Kenny convened a meeting in Waterford to discuss the question of over-taxation. The mayor, a Redmond supporter, was invited to preside but refused to attend.[133]

In a packed meeting called by the Irish financial relations committee and held in the Dublin Mansion House during the same month, Kenny proposed a resolution demanding the exemption of Ireland from war taxes which threatened the ruin and paralysis of the country's commerce and industry. He demanded complete 'fiscal independence' for Ireland, considering the provisions of the home rule act 'as dead as Queen Anne'.[134] The resolution was passed and copies sent to several public bodies. Redmond described the committee members as 'either avowedly pro-German or ... at least opposed to recruiting in Ireland and ... committed to the monstrous doctrine that Ireland should remain neutral in this war'. Claiming that public authorities had either rejected the resolution or adopted it with the reservation that the IPP was the only body that could deal with the question of over-taxation, Redmond asserted that the party was successful in ensuring Ireland's share of taxation was fair. 'The pretence that an agitation started and controlled by pro-Germans and Sinn Feiners is needed to whip the Irish party into doing their duty is a piece of colossal impudence,' he

---

128 *Waterford Standard*, 5 May 1915.
129 *Waterford News*, 11 Feb. 1916.
130 *Munster Express*, 24 July 1915.
131 *Waterford Standard*, 4 Dec. 1915.
132 *Hansard* (Commons) 5th ser. LXXXI, 1298 1530–1531, 10 Apr. 1916.
133 Mac Giolla Choille (1966), pp. xxxvi, 226.
134 *Waterford Standard*, 11 Mar. 1916.

declared. To raise the issue of taxation now was nothing short of a 'crime against the Irish cause'.[135]

Departing from its hitherto unquestioning support of Redmond, Waterford's *Evening News* defended committee members against accusations that they were 'Sinn Feiners' and 'Pro-Germans'.[136] And the extreme nationalist newspaper *Honesty*, in ridiculing Redmond and Dillon, reported the meeting as having been attended by the old, the young, MPs and business people.[137]

A conciliatory William O'Brien denied any intention of carrying out an obstruction campaign when he observed the 'future of our country [is] being fatally mortgaged by ... tremendous war liabilities' and called for a new enquiry on the lines of the 1896 Royal Commission. Chancellor of Exchequer McKenna's reply was to reassert the view that the 'great industry of Ireland is exceedingly prosperous' and the country therefore had no special claim for exemption from taxation.[138] Lawrence Ginnell MP considered taxation imposed on the Irish by the 1916 budget 'public plunder'. He described the Irish economy as stagnant and decaying while Britain's boomed. The idea of a prospering Ireland was invented for party purposes and was 'so devoid of foundation as to be ironical and offensive'.[139]

In May 1917, Tim Healy complained during the budget debate that to avoid ruin, Guinness was 'dismissing men by the hundreds every week' while English beer was still being imported into Ireland.[140] Beer output dropped by 54 per cent between 1914 and 1918, and in Dublin 1,500 workers, around 50 per cent of the workforce, were made redundant.[141] The consequence, he claimed, was 'intense' distress. It was clear, according to Healy, that no attention was paid to Ireland when framing the budget. The Treasury did not remember the country's existence.

Nor was the minimal wealth brought to Waterford by the war any compensation. At the same time as pressure mounted on the government to pay the second house-building instalment there were also calls for a greater use of the city's military facilities and for munitions work.

With the departure of British army recruits in April 1915 the barracks fell into disuse and by July, councillors were complaining of the buildings being left idle when there was unemployment in the city. They demanded some return for their contribution to the war effort. Patrick W. Kenny accused the councillors who now grumbled, of having driven the troops out of the city. In the early 1900s, they had been refused local hospital accommodation when there was sickness in the barracks. The War Office would not forget. 'What,' he asked, 'is the use of crying now?' However, it was unanimously agreed that the mayor and high sheriff should approach John Redmond and ask him to request the secretary of state for war to send more troops to the city for training.[142]

But by September the barracks hospital was closed and the accommodation shut up. Despite a promise that more soldiers would be quartered in the city when the 16th Division had finished training, it was rumoured that the site was to be used for storing hay compressed into bales by army service corps personnel. Councillors were alarmed at the potential loss of jobs and trade[143] and in November the mayor reported the prospect of getting more troops in the city was 'hopeless'.[144]

135 *Cork Weekly Examiner*, 1 Apr. 1916.
136 *Evening News*, 27 Mar. 1916.
137 *Honesty*, 1 Apr. 1916.
138 *Hansard* (Commons) 5th ser. LXXXI, 1293–95, 5 Apr. 1916.
139 *Hansard* (Commons) 5th ser. LXXXI, 2433–40, 19 Apr. 1916.
140 *Hansard* (Commons) 5th ser. XCIII, 563–64 567–68, 3 May 1917.
141 O'Flanagan (1985), p. 15.
142 *Waterford News*, 9 July 1915.
143 *Waterford Standard*, 29 Sep. 1915.
144 *Waterford Standard*, 6 Nov. 1915.

Corporation members were well aware of other employment opportunities created by the war. Following the decision to establish a Ministry of Munitions in May 1915 and the Munitions of War Act in June, national munition factories financed by the government and operated by boards of management were set up in Britain. An alternative cooperative scheme was also initiated. Under this scheme local munitions committees made an agreement with the government to deliver shell, fuses or cartridges and then contracted production work out to local manufacturers.[145]

The city had three or four foundries idle or working under capacity while, for the period to March 1918, just 0.22 per cent of expenditure by the Ministry of Munitions was in Ireland.[146] As well as completion of the housing project and greater use of local military facilities, Redmond was asked to press the government for more spending on munitions manufacture.[147] The Chamber of Commerce and the UTLC added their support to the corporation's drive for munitions work.[148] There were complaints that the War Office deliberately frustrated Irish munition manufacturers[149] and that Irish businesses could not secure significant munition contracts.[150] Against this background, two local firms took the initiative.

Frank Thompson of Thompson and Son who had taken over the Neptune Works from the defunct Waterford Steamship Company in 1912 to start manufacturing iron and steel structures,[151] and W. F. Peare, a motor engineer of Catherine Street, negotiated munition manufacturing arrangements with the Ministry of Muni-

tions in June 1915.[152] Both men travelled to Dublin where they met representatives of the local munitions committee and the Ministry of Munitions. After inspecting examples of shells, they returned to Waterford where a further meeting was held with the mayor and a local munitions committee was set up.[153] In August the Ministry of Munitions gave conditional approval to a Waterford scheme for producing 18-pounder shells.

The minister could not promise to provide machines, despite a pledge to Redmond from Captain N. E. Kelly of the ministry that he had been successful in 'earmarking' orders and machines for Ireland,[154] as they were 'extremely difficult' to procure in England. An initial firm order for a minimum of 6,000 shells and orders for shells subsequently produced at a rate of 250 a week was promised.[155]

Plans to form a company to produce the shells fell through and Thompson undertook the manufacture of them himself. Ireland was scoured for old machines, one of those taken into use dating from 1855. They were adapted so that shells were being produced at the rate of 500 a week by December 1915.[156] The War Office considered the contracts placed very important.[157]

Redmond also understood the importance of providing employment in Ireland and as early as October 1914 he had high hopes of fostering a rapidly developing munitions industry. In November 1915 he was reported as having told the House of Commons that thousands of enthusiastic Irish men and women throughout the country were engaged full-time in munitions work. It was, he thought, 'only the beginning'.

145 Revised memorandum on local organisation of shell production by Mr Tansley, 24 Sep. 1915 (MUN 5/142/1121/22), PRO.
146 Riordan (1920), pp. 196–214.
147 *Waterford News*, 9 July 1915.
148 *Waterford Standard*, 9 Feb. 1916.
149 *Irish Industrial Journal*, 19 June 1915.
150 Riordan, E. J. (1918), 'Four years of Irish economics 1914–1918: restraint of industry', *Studies* pp. 306–14.
151 *Waterford News*, 9 Feb. 1912.
152 *Waterford News*, 2 July 1915.
153 *Waterford Standard*, 28 Aug. 1915.
154 Kelly to Redmond, 9 Aug. 1915 (Redmond Papers, 15, 261 [6]), NLI.
155 Ministry of Munitions to W. F. Peare, 28 Aug. 1915 (Redmond Papers, 15, 261 [6]), NLI.
156 *Waterford Standard*, 4 Dec. 1915.
157 Ministry of Munitions Local Directory, 23 Dec. 1915 (MUN 5/11/200/13), PRO.

More work would be created in Ireland and he promised that, unlike in Britain, there would be no 'trouble and friction' from Irish workers.[158]

But there were demands for a fully-fledged munitions factory in Waterford and the Chamber of Commerce wrote directly to Asquith requesting this after unsuccessfully lobbying Redmond during 1915.[159] Redmond's promise of new machines for Thompson and Son, while on a visit to Waterford in December, did not dull these expectations. However, pledges to Redmond by the British government did not immediately materialise.[160]

By March 1916 he had lost the initiative. During a corporation meeting, P. W. Kenny was openly critical of his failure to establish Ireland's rightful claim to war work and to take the lead in attacking over-taxation. Another member suggested Redmond should be taken up on his December 1915 promise to ensure machines and more munitions work came to Waterford.[161] A flurry of questions in the House of Commons from various Irish MPs at the beginning of March 1916[162] made little difference and groups other than the IPP eventually forced through demands for war work.

A deputation from the all Ireland munitions and government supply committee, which included Frank Thompson and the city's mayor, saw Lloyd George to press its claim for a fair share of government contracts. By August 1916 a cartridge factory for the production of shell cases was established in the old Bilberry brick factory[163] although it was not yet giving output.[164] But there was still disgruntlement at the treatment of Irish manufacturers by the British gov-

ernment. A considerable amount of machinery including heavy plant was required for the Waterford factory and this had to be procured and maintained locally. And because of unreliable supplies of lathe tools from Britain, staff had to manufacture their own.

Nevertheless, by 1917 the factory was in production. It employed 519 people, 51 per cent of whom were males—a higher proportion by far than in any other Irish munitions factory. This may be an indication of the level of local unemployment. The factory produced cartridges to the value of £99,604—second only to Dublin.[165] In addition to munitions work, smaller but sometimes lucrative contracts were won by Waterford firms. Hearne and Co. won a contract for the production of ammunition boxes, for example.[166] But there were those who continued to argue that Ireland did not get its fair share of these contracts because of pressure from British firms. Nor was the additional work seen as an adequate compensation for over-taxation. In the view of one economist, 'our return for vastly increased taxation is a few small factories manned generally by Englishmen and Scotchmen, and always directed by a Briton'.[167]

As early as August 1915 others had demanded that sufficient munitions work be created in Ireland to allow men who had gone to England for employment, to return. No more people should be taken out of the country.[168] But in 1917 the combined floor space of the five munitions factories located in the Dublin and South of Ireland Munitions Area, and the total numbers employed in them, were dismissed as being far less that those of moderate sized munitions factories in

158 *The Times*, 3 Nov. 1915.
159 Cowman (1988), p. 52.
160 Gwynn, D. (1932), pp. 435–37.
161 *Waterford Standard*, 4 Mar. 1916.
162 *Hansard* (Commons) 5th ser. LXXX, 1055 1159–64, 1 Mar. 1916.
163 *Waterford News*, 8 Aug. 1919.
164 Speech on estimates – list of national munition factories (MUN 5/146/1122/5), PRO.
165 Riordan (1920), pp. 196–214.
166 O'Connor (1989), p. 135.
167 Malone (1918).
168 Burgess to O'Brien, 2 Aug. 1915 (Redmond Papers, 15, 261 [6]), NLI.

Britain.[169] Disenchantment was also evident in Cork where the threat of conscription, increased food prices, the question of over-taxation and the lack of war employment, especially in munitions, created tension.[170]

For James English the possibility of work in England and an increase in workers' bargaining power came too late to affect his decision to enlist, although very probably they were major influences on men after June 1915. After 1916 membership of the Trades Council increased to such an extent that it affiliated 3,000 members to Congress in 1919.[171] Early in 1915, however, Waterford labourers, with little protection, faced a grim future. There were considerable increases in prices but little movement in wages which were already inadequate. A high level of unemployment was made worse by threats to existing jobs. For a labourer who was the only breadwinner and who had a wife and five children, enlistment in the British army held compelling attractions.

V

In considering the extent to which men found army pay and allowances appealing, a distinction must be drawn between the skilled and the unskilled worker. A skilled tradesman could generally earn in excess of 30s a week when in employment in civilian life. Although certain skilled soldiers could get up to 6s a day in the army, the basic pay for ordinary soldiers such as James English was 1s. But the wages of most men were increased by the payment of at least one allowance. An extra 6d a day was paid to those with special shooting proficiency for instance. Very few men received just the basic 1s and 1s 9d was the more normal pay. This amounted to wages of approximately 12s 3d a week. In addi-

tion boots, clothing and rations were provided or allowances paid in lieu. Some men got a subsidy from their firm as well as army pay and allowances.

From his basic pay, including personal allowances, of about 12s 3d, James English would have made an allotment of 3s 6d, enabling his family to receive separation allowances totalling £1 7s. Compared with a family income of about 14s while working at Michael O'Sullivan's, therefore, James English and his family would have received an approximate income of £1 15s 7d. This amounts to an increase of 154 per cent in earnings. Other allowances may have added to this.

The family's situation would have been further improved because he was not consuming food or adding to expenses at home. Other important financial inducements to enlist, not available to those employed in munitions work, were the widow's pension and the disablement pension payable in the event of his injury while on service. As shown in Table 1, for an unskilled man these sums could be significant.

Personal circumstances had a fundamental bearing on the impact of these financial inducements. For married men whose wives were unemployed, or if employed worked long hours for little return, the financial advantages were considerable. And they increased with the number of children under working age. Female dependants of unmarried soldiers, including common-law wives, and their children also received separation allowances. If, on the other hand, a man was part of an extended family which formed one household and which pooled its income and expenses, or if he had a number of children of working age, then the financial advantages would have been much less enticing.

For some single men the financial magnet was as strong as for married men. Under certain

---

169 Riordan (1918). By 1917, apart from the cartridge factory in Waterford, there was a National Shell Factory and a National Fuse Factory in Dublin. Cork and Galway each had a National Shell Factory (List of land, buildings, factories and other properties taken over by or on behalf of the Ministry of Munitions and including properties in which the ministry has a present or reversionary lease, 30 June 1917 [MUN 5/146/1222/10], PRO, Kew).

170 Lucey (1972), p. 79.

171 O'Connor, 'Trades councils in Waterford city' in Nolan and Power (eds.) (1992).

1. Wife and Children

A. Separation allowance	Weekly rates		
	1914		1915
	Aug	Sep	March
Wife	11s 1d	12s 6d	12s 6d
Wife and 1 child	12s 10d	15s	17s 6d
Wife and 2 children	14s 7d	17s 6d	21s
Wife and 3 children	16s 4d	20s	23s
Wife and 4 children	17s 6d	22s	–

1. Plus 2s allowance for each additional child.
2. Allowances included a 3s 6d allotment from the soldier's pay. The allotment was compulsory for soldiers serving abroad.
3. In 1914 the allowances were payable for each girl under 16 years and for each boy under 14 years of age. In 1915 they were made payable for all children up to 16 years.

B. Widow's pension	Weekly rates		
	1914		1915
	Aug	Nov	March
Widow	5s	7s 6d	10s
Widow with 1 child	6s 6d	12s 6d	15s
Widow with 2 children	8s	15s	18s 6d
Widow with 3 children	9s 6d	17s 6d	21s
Widow with 4 children	11s	20s	–

1. Plus 2s allowance for each additional child.
2. In March 1915, 10s was payable to widows under the age of 35 years rising to 15s for those over 45 years. 5s was payable for the first child, 3s 6d for the second and 2s 6d for the third.
3. In the case of motherless children, 5s was paid for each of the first three children and 4s for each additional child.
4. Scales were subject to increase in cases of necessity and when recommended by the local Old Age Committee.
5. Allowances were payable for girls up to the age of 16 years and for boys up to the age of 14 years, or up to 16 years if attending a state school full time.

2. Disablement pension

For total disablement:	From 14s for an unmarried man and from 16s 6d for a married man up to 23s.
For partial disablement:	Between 3s 6d and 17s depending on the reduction in wage-earning capacity.
Note:	These pensions were awarded in addition to National Health Insurance payments

Table 1: A table showing separation allowances, widows' pensions and disablement pensions payable to soldiers and dependants, 1914 to March 1915

(Sources: Compiled from information contained in Allowances and Pensions *[British Parliamentary Papers 1914–16];* Munster Express, *20 Mar. 1915;* The Times History of the War, *Vol. 6 [London, 1916], pp. 287–96.)*

circumstances the parents, sister, or other close member of an unmarried soldier's family was entitled to a separation allowance proportionate to a voluntary allotment from his pay. The dependant received a higher rate if the soldier's children were in the dependant's care. A pension was also payable in the event of the soldier being killed.[172] Single men without responsibility for supporting close members of their families, however, may well have found army pay and conditions unappealing.

There is a consensus that pay and allowances were a major inducement for some men to enlist. Writers have recognised that they provided many working-class families with a regular income for the first time. And they were much more attractive in Ireland where the standard of living and rates of pay were lower. The position is neatly summed up by a Waterford man writing to the *Waterford News* from Drogheda in February 1915.

> Prices are going up all around, ordinary house coal is up to 35s a ton ... . Men are enlisting here not for love of England or fear of Germany, but for sheer want. It would surprise you the number of married men who enlisted here since the beginning of the war in order that their wives and families could have the separation allowance. It would be a good job if it were all over.[173]

This is a view endorsed by a writer who recollected that young men from the lanes of Mallow swore allegiance to the empire but joined the colours out of 'sheer grinding necessity'.[174] In Dublin conditions had been made worse by the lock-out. Many men enlisting were described by one nationalist officer in the 16th Division as being

real toughs ... Larkinites enticed to join the colours by the prospect of good food and pay, which was welcome to them after months of semi-starvation during the great strike of 1913 and 1914.[175]

No less alluring than allowances was the promised security of a widow's or disability pension. A 10s a week pension received by a widowed mother after the death of her soldier son was an enormous boon to the family and thought to be 'better than a crock of gold'.[176]

However, the impact of separation allowances and other financial inducements must also be considered in a time context. Men without strong home and family commitments usually enlisted first to be followed by men impelled by social and economic factors. Pay and allowances are more likely to have been decisive issues for men who enlisted in early 1915 when they were experiencing deteriorating economic conditions and when there were few opportunities for alternative work. And initially allowances were less of an inducement because of problems and delays in receiving them, but payment procedures were improved over time.

Rudyard Kipling had grounds for his confident statement that the 'younger men of the New Army do not worry about allowances',[177] but its applicability to older Irishmen who had family responsibilities and who experienced severe personal economic dislocation as a result of the war, should be viewed with some scepticism.

Social, economic and political conditions therefore shaped the world in which James English grew up and they moulded his attitudes in a way which made him responsive to the call for recruits. But there were other factors more immediately responsible for triggering his decision to enlist.

---

172 *Allowances and Pensions in Respect of Seamen, Marines, and Soldiers, and their Wives, Widows and Dependants* (British Parliamentary Papers, 1914–16 [Cd. 7662] XL.15); *Scheme for Allowances to Dependants of Deceased Sailors and Soldiers* (British Parliamentary papers, 1914–16 [Cd. 8131] XL.37).
173 *Waterford News*, 5 Feb. 1915.
174 Lankford (1980), p. 75.
175 De Montmorency, H. (1936), *Sword and Stirrup: Memories of an Adventurous Life*, London, p. 245.
176 McGinley, N. (1987), *Donegal, Ireland and the First World War*, Letterkenny, p. 136.
177 Kipling (1915), pp. 14–15.

CHAPTER 5

Enlistment

I

Fifty-four per cent of men enlisting in Ireland during the war were recruited between 4 August 1914 and August 1915. By the end of 1915 about 1,756 Waterford men, representing approximately 35 per cent of the male population of military age, had enlisted. About 366 soldiers born in Waterford city died while serving in the war.[1] This was approximately 57 per cent of all Waterford city- and county-born soldiers who died. As the county's population, 56,502 in 1911, was more than twice that of the city's 27,464 people, this confirms a very significant urban bias in recruiting.

How far the initially enthusiastic response was a direct result of Redmond's personal appeal for recruits or reaction to a general mood in favour of war is not clear. Redmond may simply have 'interpreted faithfully the instincts of the vast majority of Irishmen'[2] and this possibility was reluctantly conceded by many who did not sympathise with the war, the IPP or Redmond's policy. They accepted that he 'really represented the views of the majority of the Irish people'.[3] No doubt many Irish were touched to some extent by the 'pervasive anxiety' about British power in the world and nowhere in the United Kingdom was there any 'energetic public movement in favour of bringing the war to an end by negotiation rather than force of arms'.[4]

It has also been argued that several factors contributed to a universally held idea that war was a necessary and good thing. A popular preoccupation with 'manliness' was a constantly recurring theme of the period and was one aspect creating a pro-war mood in 1914.[5] Willie Redmond, however, thought the impulse to enlist was due firstly to a sympathy with the allies' cause and secondly to a belief that a 'new and a better and brighter chapter was about to open in the relations of Great Britain and Ireland'.[6]

But a contemporary remembered the potency of John Redmond's personal influence on ordinary Waterford men who were persuaded by his arguments to enlist. The wife of a local man who had joined the army kept a memorial card for Willie Redmond in her prayer book and in the 1960s old men still shouted 'Up Redmond! Up Redmond!'[7] However, the upsurge in local

1 Calculations are based on a list of Waterford-born soldiers who died in the war published in the *Munster Express* (Christmas supplement, Dec. 1991). From an anonymous contributor, the names on the list appear to have been culled from *Ireland's Memorial Records 1914–1918* (Dublin, 1923) and/or *Soldiers Died in the Great War* (London, 1924). The lists in these publications were compiled from official records. Although not precise, they provide a fairly complete overall picture (Perry, N. [1994] 'Nationality in the Irish infantry regiments in the First World War' in *War and Society*, 12, pp. 65–95). The soldiers identified in the *Munster Express* list were born in Waterford city and may have been living and recruited elsewhere but it seems safe to conclude most were Waterford residents. According to the list a total of 649 soldiers born in Waterford city and county died in the war. The list does not include officers who died as their names appear in different records.
2 Gwynn, D. (1932), p. 361.
3 Fitzpatrick (1977), pp. 107–08.
4 Turner (1992), pp. 48, 96.
5 Joll (1984), Chapter 8.
6 Redmond (1917), pp. 173–74.
7 Dunne (1991), p. 11.

military- and war-related civilian activities which flowed from John Redmond's decision to support the war, created its own momentum.

Mobilisation, feverish military preparations and general 'manifestations of the martial spirit'[8] were enough to inspire some men to enlist. The sight of uniforms, the pomp of military life and an infectious militarism touched the popular imagination and made a definite appeal.[9] As in Cork, where soldiers acquired a new respectability and attracted admiring glances, the lure of war's glamour 'pulled susceptible young Irishmen'.[10] In the heady early days, enlistment was sometimes an impulsively patriotic or spontaneous response to the 'rape of poor Belgium', or to the prospect of adventure in the belief the war would be a short one. For many of the working class it offered an opportunity to escape arduous, dead-end and depressing jobs. War as an exciting and adventurous opportunity could attract the Ballybricken labourer. As John Lucy recalled, he enlisted because he was tired of 'the soft accents and the slow movements of the small farmers who swarmed in the streets of our dull southern Irish town, the cattle, fowl, eggs, butter, bacon, politics filled us with loathing'.[11]

Naval preparations for war had been authorised by the cabinet on 29 July 1914. Mobilisation was ordered on 1 August. On Sunday 2 August Waterford's Custom House and Post Office staff had their leave cancelled and were recalled for duty, and on bank holiday Monday the Custom House was opened to process naval reservists. When a special train from Cork carrying reservists arrived at Waterford North Station, the crowd of spectators was so large the station gates had to be locked against them.

General mobilisation was ordered the next day and Waterford men belonging to the South Irish Horse, a special reserve regiment whose first commanding officer in 1902 was the Marquis of Waterford, were instructed to proceed to their headquarters in Limerick. On 5 August 'great excitement' was reported around the barracks, other mobilisation centres and in localities where reservists lived. The quays were bustling from early morning until the departure of late trains at 11 p.m. Irish Volunteers and their bands accompanied contingents of army reservists, some of whom were Volunteers and friends, to the station. They left the city amid scenes of 'wild enthusiasm' and to the sounds of exploding fog signals.

Police guarded the bridge and patrolled roads into the city. Entrenchments were dug overlooking the harbour and a masked fort and field gun emplaced. A number of firms had their horses and vehicles commandeered and the military took over St Patrick's Park as a centre for selecting mounts. By Thursday 6th, large drafts of horses acquired by the army were passing along the quays three and four deep.

Wireless stations at De la Salle College and at some schools were dismantled. Radios were also removed from shipping, and night-time sailings between Rosslare and Fishguard were suspended.[12] Throughout August Waterford North Station was very busy. Armed troops guarded the station through which requisitioned trains carrying ammunition, wagons, guns and stores passed continually.[13]

About 250 mainly English and Welsh recruits attached to the signalling corps of the Royal Engineers, were garrisoned in the local barracks, arriving in late 1914. They drilled, marched, learned to ride and listened to lectures from 7 a.m. to 8 p.m. Local men, 'idly parading the streets and participating in dances and other amusements', were accused of failing to rally to the call while young English and Welshmen were

8   *Munster Express*, 8 Aug. 1914.
9   Hannay (1915).
10 Lucey (1972), pp. 47–59.
11 Lucy (1992), p. 15.
12 *Munster Express*, 8 Aug. 1914.
13 *Waterford Standard*, 22 Aug. 1914.

preparing for war in the city.[14] And in early 1915 a section of cavalry arrived at the artillery/cavalry barracks.[15]

There was a constant flow of military traffic. During December 1914 men of the Royal Engineers, on their way to Kilworth, arrived at Adelphi Wharf on the SS *Waterford* and 'caused much attention'.[16] By early 1915 scarcely a train left without being heavily freighted with military equipment or personnel. For weeks troops constantly occupied the station, passing and repassing through the city. 'Heart-rending scenes and pathetic partings' were witnessed as relatives and friends saw soldiers off after Christmas leave.[17] In Cork, Lucy remembered how a recruit's mother had keened, torn her hair and filled the station with her lamentations when her son left for the front.[18] Other soldiers were returning home after being wounded or were in transit to join their units. Many had arrived wearing the newly issued goatskins and steel helmets. At least one Indian soldier in turban and red cloak aroused keen curiosity and the 'Death or Glory boys' of the 17th Lancers created interest when they paraded the city streets.[19]

In February 1915 the Royal Engineer recruits attracted large numbers of people when they had their first rifle practice on a range newly constructed at Tramore.[20] The troops were also fully engaged in Waterford's social life. It was reported that 'most cordial relations ... existed between civilians and military'.[21] Large numbers of soldiers were entertained by 'local ladies and gentlemen'.[22] One sapper recalled the friends, parties, concerts and the 'delightful evenings' he had in the Protestant Hall.[23]

Many of the men were talented musicians or singers and contributed to the entertainment. The engineers provided music in a packed Protestant Hall when there were singing and recitations at a YMCA reunion during March 1915.[24] And between 80 and 90 of them attended City Hall for the first of two 'popular patriotic concerts' held in aid of the Belgian relief fund.[25] The Lancers sergeants' mess organised an all-night dance in City Hall and the Large Room was decorated with flags, bunting, lances, swords, cuirasses, bayonets and a lance cap from each of the six Lancer regiments.[26]

At least one soldier was injured when the engineers helped to extinguish a fire which destroyed the Hearne and Co. building and the Granville Hotel in April 1915. Colours presented to the city's National Volunteer battalion by Redmond, and about 100 uniforms stored by Hearne and Co., were also burned. It was reported that the people of Waterford would 'ever feel grateful' for their help and the residents of the Quay, Barronstrand Street and George's Street wrote to them thanking them for their 'invaluable assistance'.[27] A lieutenant from the signallers and his commanding officer in their turn thanked the people of Waterford for their 'kindness and generosity'. Many people gathered to give the soldiers a 'hearty send-off' when, accompanied by the Barrack Street Band, they marched out of the city for the last time on 15 April 1915, and the occasion was seen as a

---

14 *Waterford Standard*, 21 Nov. 1914.
15 *Waterford Standard*, 27 Feb. 1915.
16 *Waterford Standard*, 23 Dec. 1914.
17 *Munster Express*, 9 Jan. 1915.
18 Lucy (1992), p. 321.
19 *Waterford Standard*, 20 Jan. 1915.
20 *Waterford News*, 22 Jan. 1915; *Waterford Standard*, 17 Feb. 1915; *Munster Express*, 20 Feb. 1915.
21 *Waterford Standard*, 17 Apr. 1915.
22 *Waterford Standard*, 21 Oct. 1914.
23 *Waterford Standard*, 3 Nov. 1915.
24 *Waterford Standard*, 20 Mar. 1915.
25 *Waterford Standard*, 14 Nov. 1914.
26 *Waterford Standard*, 1 Mar. 1916.
27 *Waterford News*, 16 Apr. 1915; *Munster Express*, 10 Apr. 1915.

'striking example of the changed attitude of the Irish people towards the army'.[28]

On the outbreak of war Redmond claimed that he and his colleagues faced the 'task of creating a new atmosphere in Ireland with regard to the British army' in order to appeal successfully for recruits. And the editor of the *Waterford News* thought the task fell to the editors of nationalist newspapers as well.[29] There is no doubt that in order to boost recruiting, a change in attitude among some sections of the Irish population would be necessary.

By 1913 Sinn Fein was circulating virulent anti-recruitment notices[30] and the Curragh incident occurred at a time when a battalion of the Leinster Regiment was the only Irish unit in the country, thus heightening the sense of the British army being one of occupation. It was consequently 'extremely unpopular' according to Stephen Gwynn.[31] And Lieutenant-General Sir Bryan Mahon, commander of the 10th (Irish) Division, noted in September 1914 that 'during the past few years in the south of Ireland a sort of prejudice has risen against joining the regular forces'.[32]

However, the extent to which a change in attitudes was necessary is far from certain. In February 1915 sets of dinner plates and gilt-edged postcards depicting soldiers of the various nationalities of the British Empire in their uniforms, issued in aid of the national relief fund, were in great demand.[33] And it was reported British recruits had brought much business to city shops.[34] In July Councillor Sir James A. Power, who when mayor in 1904 had been unexpectedly knighted by King Edward VII during his visit to Waterford, said 'Ireland had contributed largely in building up the success and glory of the British Empire'. Irishmen looked 'with pleasure on it, as many of their fellow-countrymen were associated with [its] success'. He looked forward to Irish deeds in the war being 'recorded in song and story as at Fontenoy and Waterloo'.[35] Although how far it was necessary to placate any local hostility towards the army is open to question, the backing given to recruitment by Redmond and the IPP undoubtedly lifted barriers and encouraged some men to enlist.

Apart from the presence of the army, Waterford men were exposed to a range of other conditions which helped to create the perception of a united community at war stimulated a sense of duty and encouraged a man to demonstrate his 'manliness' by enlisting. Wealthy citizens provided a fully equipped ambulance named 'The Waterford Car' for use at the front.[36] In April 1915 a 'magnificent response' to an appeal resulted in three motor ambulances being sent from Waterford, Tipperary and Kilkenny at a cost of £1,500. Subscribers included the Marchioness of Waterford, the Duke of Devonshire, Lady Goff, Sir W. Paul and Samuel Strangman. But members of the Fitzgerald family from The Island and staff from the lunatic asylum also contributed.[37]

The arrival of refugees and wounded soldiers stirred public sympathy. Appeals for clothing, magazines and other comforts were made on behalf of the recently arrived wounded from British regiments who were accommodated in the barracks hospital.[38] The master of the East Waterford hounds had a meet in The Mall for their

28 *Waterford Standard*, 17 Apr. 1915; *Munster Express*, 17 Apr. 1915.
29 *Waterford News*, 5 Nov. 1915.
30 Denman, T. (1991), 'The Catholic Irish soldier in the First World War: the racial environment', *Irish Historical Studies*, **XXVII**, pp. 352–65.
31 Gwynn, 'Irish Regiments' in Lavery (ed.) (1920).
32 Denman (1987).
33 *Waterford News*, 26 Feb. 1915.
34 *Waterford Standard*, 27 Feb. 1915.
35 *Munster Express*, 24 July 1915.
36 *Waterford Standard*, 2 Sep. 1914.
37 *Waterford Standard*, 17 Apr. 1915.
38 *Waterford Standard*, 28 Oct. 1914; *Munster Express*, 31 Oct. 1914.

benefit[39] and in February 1915 British army and navy uniforms dominated a fancy-dress ball held at City Hall under the auspices of the East Waterford hounds, the proceeds of which were donated for the comfort of the Irish wounded.[40] Local ladies and gentlemen assisted in dressing their wounds and the Marchioness of Waterford and other ladies gave them gifts of food and clothing, while Lady Paul took them for motor rides in the country and entertained them at Ballyglan.[41]

The funerals of soldiers dying at home also had a 'wonderful recruiting power' according to a Dublin contemporary. He recalled the burial of a slum inhabitant who was wounded in France and given a military funeral after dying at home. 'The widow's pride [was] ... nearly [as] open as her grief.' He claimed that nearly every able-bodied man in the area had enlisted within a fortnight. This account is probably exaggerated but military funerals with their 'intentional sadness and grandeur' were poignant and deeply moving affairs.[42] There can be little doubt that the sombre pomp and fanfare and the newly found status of the dead soldier impressed some men enough to encourage enlistment.[43]

When the body of a soldier was removed from his residence at Tanyard Arch, Waterford for interment at Ballynaneashagh Cemetery, the procession attracted large crowds. Preceded by the Erin's Hope Prize Band, six soldiers acted as pall-bearers for his coffin which was enshrouded with the union flag and bore the dead man's cap and belt.[44]

As part of the voluntary aid effort, the Irish war hospital supply network was an important aspect of Red Cross involvement across the whole of Ireland[45] and the Marchioness of Waterford consented to act as president of hospital depots to be set up in the city, Tramore and Portlaw.[46] Tramore school children collected 100 dozen eggs during the national egg collection scheme and when these were sent to military hospitals they received many letters of thanks from soldiers.[47] And there were appeals for clothes to be sent to men of the 72nd Battery Royal Field Artillery, who had been garrisoned in the city for two years,[48] as well as calls for money to buy wool and for knitted items to be distributed among men in Royal Navy patrol boats and minesweepers.[49]

A meeting to consider an appeal from Waterford soldiers who were prisoners of war was held on 22 March 1915.[50] Ballybricken men were among the prisoners, including the Barrack Street bandmaster's son.[51] Lady Goff was one of the ladies who unanimously decided to set up the committee for relief of prisoners of war in Germany and to send weekly parcels to the Waterford prisoners at Limburg. Collectors were appointed for different districts of the city including Ballybricken.[52] Subscriptions were soon being received from local firms as well as from ordinary men and women such as the County Infirmary nurses. The committee sent its first parcels, made up from gifts of cakes, clothing, various food items and cigarettes, on 24 March.[53] Within weeks more than 20 postcards were

39 *Waterford Standard*, 28 Nov. 1914.
40 *Waterford News*, 5 Feb. 1915.
41 *Waterford Standard*, 1 Nov. 1914.
42 Lucy (1992), p. 55.
43 Karsten (1983).
44 *Waterford Standard*, 6 Nov. 1915. The dead soldier was Private Martin Doheny of the Scots Guards.
45 Downes, M., 'The civilian voluntary aid effort' in Fitzpatrick (ed.) (1988), pp. 27–37.
46 *Waterford Standard*, 8 Dec. 1914.
47 *Waterford Standard*, 3 Mar. 1916.
48 *Waterford Standard*, 31 Oct. 1914.
49 *Waterford Standard*, 17 Apr. 1915.
50 *Waterford Standard*, 20 Mar. 1915.
51 *Waterford News*, 1 Jan. 1915.
52 *Waterford Standard*, 24 Mar. 1915 and *Munster Express*, 27 Mar. 1915.
53 *Waterford Standard*, 17 Apr. 1915.

received from prisoners in Limburg thanking the committee for its gifts, especially butter and milk,[54] or asking for items, tobacco and soap being particular favourites.[55] A flag day was held on 11 March 1916 for 80 Waterford men who were prisoners. A private soldier from Well Lane was one of a batch of prisoners exchanged in September 1915 and his claim that prisoners were living solely on the contents of parcels from home[56] is likely to have inflamed local anger.

The first Belgian refugees arrived from Dublin during February 1915 and were met by members of the local refugee committee, the Granville and Imperial Hotels providing temporary accommodation until houses in William Street were furnished.[57] The committee organised appeals and, as well as subscriptions, it received gifts of vegetables, apples and toys. A trip to Tramore was organised for the children who were also treated to tea and the cinema.[58]

There was concern about the safety of Waterford shipping and frequent reports of sinkings and submarine activity reinforced the impression that Ireland and Britain were under attack from a common enemy. Men could therefore be more easily convinced that it was their duty to enlist and defend their homes. In February 1915, it was rumoured the SS *Formby*, built for the Waterford cattle trade and launched on 5 April 1914, had been sunk. Cross-channel passengers were warned that enemy submarines had been sighted and livestock sailings were halted.[59] Soon afterwards, 50 sailors and firemen from the SS *Coninbeg* were paid off following a dispute over a war bonus.[60] But in early March 1915 it was reported

that all Waterford-bound vessels had so far arrived in port safely.[61]

Soon afterwards, however, the SS *Great Southern* on the Rosslare to Fishguard route, was enticed onto a 'pirate submarine' but avoided attack and escaped into the fog.[62] Within days the Clyde Shipping Company armed one of its steamers with a 12 pounder gun and announced its intention to mount weapons on its other vessels.[63] In May a submarine was rumoured to have been seen off Dunmore,[64] but it was not until December 1917 that Waterford lost its first steamers. The SS *Formby* was attacked and sunk by the German submarine U-62 on Saturday 15 December at about 8 p.m. and the armed SS *Coninbeg* was torpedoed by the same U-boat on 17 December at 11.45 p.m. Both ships, on the Waterford to Liverpool route, sank within minutes with all hands. A total of 83 lives were lost. Fifty-four of those who died were from Waterford city and altogether they left behind about 109 children and dependants.[65] The impact of this incident on the city's community would have been traumatic.

The excitement and activity which followed Redmond's pledge to support the war effort therefore boosted recruitment. But propaganda, disseminated through a variety of media, played a major role in triggering the decision to enlist.

II

The Central Council for the Organisation of Recruiting in Ireland, founded in April 1915,

54 *Waterford Standard*, 4 Mar. 1916. Letters were received from Privates P. Malone and Patrick Daniel, both in the Royal Irish Regiment.
55 *Waterford Standard*, 15 May 1915.
56 *Waterford News*, 17 Sep. 1915. The soldier was interviewed by staff from the newspaper and was identified as Private J. Casey of 6, Well Lane, an old soldier of 14 years' service. He confirmed German attempts to recruit an Irish Brigade at Limburg.
57 *Waterford Standard*, 20 Feb. 1915 and *Munster Express* 20 Feb. 1915.
58 *Waterford Standard*, 17 Apr. 1915.
59 *Waterford News*, 5 Feb. 1915.
60 *Waterford News*, 26 Feb. 1915.
61 *Waterford Standard*, 4 Mar. 1915.
62 *Waterford Standard*, 17 Mar. 1915.
63 *Munster Express*, 27 Mar. 1915.
64 *Waterford Standard*, 15 May 1915.
65 McElwee, R. (1992), *The Last Voyages of the Waterford Steamers*, Waterford, pp. 103–43.

distributed a variety of films for free showing to stimulate recruiting. And in July 1915 the Fermoy Cinema Theatre gave several showings of a film in which the 48th Brigade of the 16th (Irish) Division was paraded and inspected. Stephen Gwynn and Willie Redmond were prominent in the film.[66] But there was a ban on all filming, still photography and work by artists at the western front itself from August 1914. Two army photographers were assigned to the front but none of their photographs portraying realistic conditions of war were released. The maximum penalty for anyone else caught taking photographs was execution.[67] Kitchener resisted all calls to use film as a propaganda medium and it was not until 1916 that there was some easing of the severe restrictions.[68]

In February 1916 the films *Our Army* and *Our Navy*, described as a 'splendid film featuring our gallant tars at work', were the first in a series of films shown at Waterford's Coliseum cinema.[69] A film entitled *With the Irish at the Front* featured the Irish Guards at Loos with a flag emblazoned with an Irish harp. Shots included one of Major Willie Redmond leading his men from the front line to billets. Two other scenes were captioned 'Ruins of Wytschaete captured by North and South Irishmen fighting side by side' and 'Men of Ulster Division fight with their compatriots from other parts of Ireland'. German dead were shown and men of the Royal Dublin Fusiliers were filmed displaying captured trophies with much laughter and horseplay. And Cardinal Logue appeared with the Irish Canadians in Cork.[70]

Before 1916, however, men at home had four main sources of news about the war. Firstly, through contact with soldiers returning from the front, either personally or through their published letters, articles and books. Secondly, through soldiers' letters and news reports sent from the war zone and printed in newspapers. Thirdly, through public speakers and newspaper reports on their addresses. And fourthly, through published works written by propagandists who had sometimes visited the front. Illiterate men would have been dependent upon oral interpretations of written reports.

Soldiers returning from the front noted how the views of civilians were mainly taken from the newspapers. They frequently found the process of communicating the reality of the front difficult because those at home were susceptible to the 'attractive simplification' of the news medium. One officer noted how many civilians simply did not want to know the truth and he recounted the problems in trying to get the real picture of the war across.[71] And Robert Graves, in London on leave during September 1915, was surprised at the general indifference to, and ignorance about, the war.[72]

But home leave was not an easy experience. Returned soldiers frequently found there were barriers between themselves and civilians and John Lucy thought the 'division between the civilian and the man-at-arms was too sharp in thought and values'. The people at home found him 'very strange'. Nor could the warm sympathy of womenfolk 'alleviate a pain they had not shared'.[73] Soldiers wanted to forget everything to do with the war and most found language inadequate in conveying their experience and the facts

66 *Irish Times*, 29 July 1915.
67 Knightly, P. (1975), *The First Casualty*, London, Chapter 5.
68 Hiley, N.P. (1984), 'Making war: the British news media and government control 1914–1916' (Ph.D thesis), Open University, pp. 520–33.
69 *Waterford Standard*, 9 and 12 Feb. 1916.
70 The film is compiled from edited shots taken at different dates. Some of it appears to be genuine front line footage and some of the scenes appear to have been staged. It was originally released on 1 May 1916 but some of the edited film is dated from 1917. It can be seen at the Imperial War Museum Film Archives (IWM 212/1 and 212/2).
71 Hiley (1984), pp. 520–33.
72 Graves, R. (1960), *Goodbye to all that*, Harmondsworth, pp. 120–21.
73 Lucy (1992), pp. 318, 349.

of war. Few were interested in their bad news, so most remained silent.[74] Many soldiers also thought it only fair to the women to 'hush up the worse side of the war'. A consequence was that men at home saw the glory but not the 'sordid filth of trench life'.[75] When on leave in Cork, Lucy recorded how he 'spoke with caution of the fighting, and withheld most of the horrors. Anyway, I wanted to forget them'.[76] However, accounts of their experiences written by soldiers and published in newspapers generally demonstrated no such inhibition.

The press has been described as having had a 'potent impact'[77] in shaping a man's opinion and perceptions of the war and consequently it influenced any decision to enlist. James Connolly went so far as to claim enlistment resulted from 'newspaper-created ignorance' and from the false belief that Ireland had at last attained the status of a free nation.[78] His view that men from the slums were 'tricked and deluded' into joining the British army[79] is supported by another contemporary who thought 'our people were so simple, so unworldly, so idealistic that they never doubted the reports of Reuters' agency and the subsidised press'.[80]

These assessments oversimplify a complex phenomenon, but propaganda disseminated through a press subjected to government and military censorship, and owned or controlled by Redmond supporters or by people who supported the war, undoubtedly contributed to enticing men into the army. In addition to war reports, newspapers carried product advertisements which acted as oblique but constant reminders that a man's duty was at the front.

The information which newspapers could publish was restricted by the Defence of the Realm Act (DORA) of 1914 and its subsequent amendments, and by king's regulations. The Press Bureau, set up in August 1914, censored internal and external communications and instructed editors what to enlarge on or to suppress. In addition, the War Office and other government departments had their own censorship arrangements. But it is apparent that Waterford's local newspapers operated their own censorship when dealing with communications from soldiers. The lack of any significantly dissenting voice suggests only letters and reports which conformed with Redmond's policies were published.

Soldiers were forbidden to keep diaries while at the front but this did not deter many from doing so. A detailed account of a Ballybricken soldier's experiences in France compiled from notes kept during the Battle of Mons, the subsequent retreat and the battles of Aisne and Ypres, was published in the *Waterford News* on his return to Britain after being wounded. Although acknowledging the heavy losses and the severe hardships suffered by the Irish, the article was undoubtedly sanctioned for its propaganda value in publicising what the newspaper called 'the brilliant part played by the Irish troops'. References are made to a willingness to die on the battlefield 'with pride for my King and country' and to the Germans as an 'inhuman race' whom the Irish 'mowed ... down in the thousands'. Having described alleged German atrocities, the writer noted 'we are blood-thirsty for the Germans' and in one attack

> as we drew near the enemy they grounded their arms as a token of surrender; but I did not want prisoners: I wanted to see German blood, and I did see it. As I was driving the bayonet through I kept saying 'Take that and that, and one for old Ireland!'

There was exaltation in hardship and battle.

74   Fussell, P. (1975), *The Great War and Modern Memory*, Oxford, pp. 169–70.
75   Marwick (1965), pp. 135–36.
76   Lucy (1992), p. 318.
77   Callan (1984), Chapter 9.
78   Connolly, J. (1916), 'What is a free nation?', *Workers Republic*, reproduced in Connolly (1988), Vol. 2, pp. 141–46.
79   Connolly, J. (1916), 'The slums and the trenches', *Workers Republic*, reproduced in Connolly (1988), Vol. 2, pp. 147–51.
80   Bewley, C. (1988), *Memoirs of a Wild Goose*, Dublin, p. 41.

The writer found pride in witnessing his colleagues bearing their troubles 'like men'. Despite arduous marches, very little food and sore feet, he observed, 'yet I feel happy'. And of another charge to repel the enemy, he wrote, 'our regiment made a charge and did great work. More German blood! I thought I would die with excitement.' He described an attack by the Sikhs: 'They came back covered with blood, and each one had a German's head held by the hair. I had a good laugh ... . They laughed and raised the dead men's heads in the air.' He boasted:

> bravo, the Irish! I am proud to be Irish and in an Irish regiment. The Irish are great fighters—plenty of the devil in them. We stop at nothing. I wonder how the Germans would fight if they had the fighting blood like us! We have got the shamrock branded on us ... . We are in our glory when in battle. I have never seen an Irishman a coward ... . The Germans' losses must be very heavy compared to ours. It's good sport shooting and bayoneting them. I enjoyed it very much.[81]

This is probably one soldier's genuine account of his experiences but it is hyperbole which suited the propagandists and was selected for their purposes. The accusation that Patrick MacGill's books also reinforced the bias of civilian readers and failed to fully relay the realities of war[82] has some justification but they were published under the menace of censorship. And his *Amateur Army* invoked hostility because of its failure to 'regurgitate Hun-hating propaganda'.[83] However, some men *did* find excitement and fulfilment in war and they could adjust to the brutalities of the western front. A 20-year-old subaltern

with the 16th Division wrote to his mother after the battle for Wytschaete Ridge: 'I would not have missed this great battle for anything, although it was a terrible experience and there were some terrible sights, but looking at hundreds of mangled corpses does not worry me now.'[84]

Another Ballybricken soldier, returned to Waterford in an exchange of prisoners, was reported as describing how his battalion was 'very successful, and by heroic fighting, in which the bayonet played a great part, drove the enemy ... back'. When wounded and taken prisoner he claimed to have been beaten with rifle butts, given little food and operated on without chloroform. He said he saw men at Limburg tied to trees and kept there for six hours every day. One German asked him why he had joined the British army and not the Volunteers.[85]

Some Irish soldiers, however, had reservations about the war, although channels for the expression of their views were limited. An Irishman serving with a Scottish regiment who wrote to Bishop O'Donnell, thought it was a 'sin' that Irishmen were deceived and fought for 'their promised scrap of paper' when there would be home rule by name only after the amending bill took effect at the conclusion of the war.[86]

Soldiers at the front could only send home censored field service postcards, French postcards and letters. These were collected by platoon sergeants and censored by company officers who sealed and signed them. Sent to base, they were then forwarded to their destination after further scrutiny. After the Battle of Loos in 1915 Sir Arthur Paget, commander-in-chief of the army in Ireland, was moved to comment: 'the troops at the front are tongue-tied. They cannot

81 *Waterford News*, 1 Jan. 1915.
82 McGinley (1987), pp. 43–45.
83 Edwards, O.D. (1986), 'Patrick MacGill and the making of a historical source: with a handlist of his works', *Innes Review*, XXXVII, pp. 73–99.
84 Carrothers, J. S. (compiled by D. S. Carrothers) (*c.* 1992), *Memoirs of a Young Lieutenant* (privately published and distributed), Enniskillen, p. 57.
85 *Waterford News*, 17 Sep. 1915.
86 McGinley (1987), pp. 43–45. The third home rule bill was passed in May 1914. The House of Lords amended it to exclude nine northern counties permanently from its provisions. The act was placed on the statute book with the fate of this exclusion amendment left in suspension.

make known to, and in fact are bound to conceal, what they feel from those in authority over them'.[87] However, soldiers exercised a form of self-censorship which disguised the true nature of war. They tended to write home in a way which hid the 'discomfort of their lives, the unspeakable sights around them, and the risks'.[88] Generally, they offered assurances to those at home, complaining very little. Harold Macmillan, the future British prime minister, found reading the letters, written in a style of 'wonderful simplicity which is almost great literature', a 'humbling experience'.[89]

There was no independent reporting from the front. Kitchener allowed a limited number of war correspondents to accompany the British expeditionary force in August 1914, but this authority was soon withdrawn and correspondents who subsequently made their own way to the forbidden war zone were arrested, had their passports removed and were expelled.[90] In September an army officer was appointed to provide eyewitness accounts from the front. Reports that filtered into local papers could be trivial but the lifestyle depicted would appeal to men living in poverty and surviving on an inadequate diet. In 1914, for example, soldiers at Christmas dinner in the trenches were reported as having 'good things in super abundance'. The army had been flooded with parcels and soldiers had five or six puddings each.[91]

Published letters from soldiers were the only other source of information. In December 1914 the *Freeman's Journal* referred to 'terrible losses' reported in soldiers' letters, and wanted to know how Irish troops were faring. Events were hidden from people at home and the newspaper demanded that Irish war correspondents be permitted to report on Irish exploits at the front.[92] Action to enforce censorship at home was taken under DORA in the same month and private letters, which by 1915 had to be submitted to the Press Bureau for vetting before publication, declined as a source of news.

It was not until May 1915 that five representatives of the British press selected by the Newspaper Proprietors Association, and under strict military supervision, were allowed to send home censored despatches from the front.[93] However, as Sir Philip Gibbs admitted, there was little need for military censorship. 'We were,' he wrote, 'our own censors.'[94] Gibbs, an English journalist and novelist knighted in 1920, was special correspondent for the *Daily Chronicle* in France. He was one of the team from which five British correspondents were allowed to report from GHQ, France. According to one authority, the 'patriotic rubbish' printed was the invention of proprietors and editors rather than the government.[95] But in 1920, Gibbs wrote of the war being a 'monstrous massacre of human beings ... [who] had no hatred of one another except as it had been lighted and inflamed by their governors, their philosophers, and their newspapers'.[96]

Like many others, J. O. Hannay complained of censorship and of knowing nothing about how Irish soldiers named on the long casualty lists had fallen.[97] But his hunger was for information which could be used to counter reports having an adverse effect on public opinion and recruiting. In his view, stories of Irish gallantry in the field fired the imagination of men at home, especially

87 Memorandum, Nov. 1915 (Paget Papers, MS 51250), British Musuem.
88 Hiley (1984), p. 525.
89 Macmillan, H. (1966), *Winds of Change, 1914–1939*, London, p. 100.
90 Knightly (1975), p. 88.
91 *Munster Express*, 2 Jan. 1915.
92 Callan (1984), pp. 57–60.
93 Edmonds, Sir J. E. (1986), *The Official History of the Great War: Military Operations, France and Belgium Dec 1915–July 1916*, Woking, pp. 144–48; Hiley (1984), pp. 683–85.
94 Knightly (1975), p. 97.
95 Marwick (1965), p. 51; Knightly (1975), Chapter 5.
96 Hynes, D. (1990), *A War Imagined: The First World War and the English Culture*, London, pp. 286–87.
97 Hannay (1916).

in towns where the stories were more frequently read and passed more easily from mouth to mouth.[98] Descriptions like that appearing in the *Munster Express* served this purpose. A priest with the Irish regiments was reported as saying that

> the best fighting stuff in the whole world is supplied by the Irish regiments, supernaturally, as well as naturally, they are the best equipped men that I know to report themselves with effect to the enemy ... both on land and sea the Celtic race is serving the British Empire with a gallantry and dash and daring that falls nothing short of heroism. You would think that Paddy was born to fight and what is more, he knows how to prepare for the life-and-death struggle.[99]

In the opinion of some, public speaking was of little use in recruiting as there was a 'national toleration of oratory. We go to public meetings willingly and cheer whatever is said to us, but we do not enlist merely because we are told to do so in resounding periods'.[100] However, another contemporary observed that at the start of the war people were less sceptical and 'more easily carried away by high-sounding periods'.[101] But, according to Hannay, Asquith's and Redmond's recruiting speeches at the Dublin Mansion House on 26 September were 'almost entirely barren of visible results'. It is true there was no demonstrable upsurge in the numbers recruited in Waterford following speeches by Redmond, but public speakers were a major asset on occasion. Figure 1 illustrates the success of a three-week recruiting campaign in Waterford beginning 19 March 1915 in which public speaking played a significant role.

Because of their dampening effects on recruitment, Redmond did not acknowledge increasing doubts and misgivings in his public statements. An officer in the Royal Munster Fusiliers who took part in the Gallipoli peninsula landings in April 1915 was unable to write his memoirs because the 'pure butchery' was so 'sad and depressing'. He recalled how 'the dear men were just mown down in scores into a bleeding silence as they showed themselves at the *Clyde's* open hatches'.[102] None the less, a speech by Redmond in Waterford during August 1915 in which he proudly referred to the gallantry of the 10th (Irish) Division at the recent Suvla Bay landings[103] was well received. 'Already,' he told the gathering, 'we have seen in the casualty list the toll which has been paid by these gallant brothers of ours from the Curragh and from Dublin.'

But by September there was public condemnation of what was seen as gross military bungling. Redmond wrote to Kitchener pointing out how badly the Irish had been treated and attached a letter in which an officer complained bitterly about 'stupidity of a criminal character' which resulted in the Dardanelles debacle.[104] But it was the failure of government, the War Office and the British press to publicly acknowledge the part played by Irish troops in the 'V' beach and Suvla Bay landings which rankled. This omission sowed an enduring resentment. The Dublin woman who wrote that 'more than anything else the neglect and coldness towards the Irish regi-

---

98 Hannay (1915).
99 *Munster Express,* 1 Jan. 1916.
100 Hannay (1915).
101 Bewley (1989), p. 40.
102 Major Lane, late 1st Munsters, to Lieutenant-Colonel Holt, 4 Oct. 1969 (Holt papers, 7603–69–1), NAM. The 1st Munsters formed part of the 29th Division which landed on beaches on the toe of the peninsula on 25 April 1915, with the objective of forcing the Dardanelles and relieving Turkish pressure on the Russian army in the Caucasus. The *River Clyde*, a collier, disgorged troops at V beach through large openings cut in its side. The soldiers, attempting to reach shore using a bridge of lighters, fell in heaps before the defenders' guns. The attack was a failure and troops were soon bogged down in trench warfare.
103 Following a decision to reinforce the army in Gallipoli, the 10th (Irish) Division's 29th Brigade accompanied Australian and New Zealand units in a landing at Anzac Cove on 6 August 1915 where they were engaged in a great deal of fierce fighting. The division's remaining brigades landed at Suvla Bay on 6 and 7 August. The last of the British and dominion troops were withdrawn from the peninsula, without gain, in January 1916.
104 Redmond to Kitchener, 4 Sep. 1915 (Redmond Papers, 15,201 [1]), NLI.

Figure 1: A bar chart showing the approximate number of recruits raised daily in Waterford from 4 August 1914 to 5 May 1915

(Source: Chart compiled from raw data in PRO NATS 1/398)

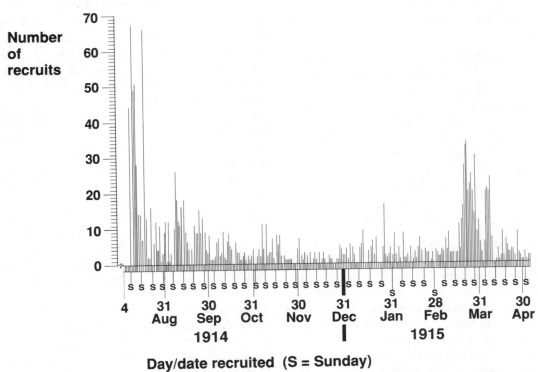

ments' heroism was one of the most potent deterrents to recruiting'[105] was far from being alone in her opinion. As early as February a Waterford soldier, wounded while serving with the Royal Irish Regiment and recuperating at home, complained that

> we are all Irish of course and mostly Catholic and yet our names scarcely appear in the war chart even in Waterford. We have lost roughly 1,600 men from our Regiment alone. Surely this fact speaks for itself.[106]

During November 1915, Redmond visited the Loos battlefield and confided in Stephen Gwynn that it was the 'most interesting, the most thrill-

ing, and the proudest week' of his life.[107] This view, expressed about a place where there was still ample and gruesome evidence of the recent battle in which the British and Irish suffered 22,504 men killed or missing and presumed killed, and 35,461 wounded, should be judged in the context of his belief that

> no people can be said to have rightly proved their nationhood and their power to maintain it until they have demonstrated their military prowess; and though Irish blood has red-dened the earth of every continent, never until now have we as a people set a national army in the field.[108]

105   Edwards and Pyle (eds.) (1968), pp. 202–09.
106   *Waterford News*, 12 Feb. 1915.
107   Gwynn, D. (1932), pp. 452–54; Gwynn, S. (1919), p. 201.
108   MacDonagh, M. (1916), *The Irish at the Front*, London, pp. 1–14; Gwynn (1919), pp. 195–98.

This concept of nationalism was shared by many throughout Europe at the time, and it complemented the notion of 'manliness'. Like Patrick Pearse,[109] Redmond's attitudes, as well as those of men such as James English, were coloured to some extent by the consequences of a post-1870 European literary obsession with the themes of 'carnage and bloodshed, of conspiracy and subterranean explosions, of the "breaking of nations" '. Redmond's thoughts echo those of Pearse who considered the slaughter of millions in war might be terrible but not evil. In Pearse's view, the first six months of the war were the most glorious in the history of Europe: 'homage was never offered to God as this, the homage of millions of lives given gladly for love of country.'[110]

On his return from the front, Redmond was 'inspired with a genuine enthusiasm for the cause of the allies and a real desire that Ireland should bear an honourable part in the struggle.'[111] In a speech about his visit, which was widely reported and considered by the king to be 'admirable', he spoke of how northern and southern Irish soldiers were like 'true comrades and brothers', spilling their blood together in the trenches. In a speech at a recruiting conference in Waterford during December, he described how the Irish troops felt they were fighting for 'the freedom and prosperity of Ireland'. His declaration that in respect of recruiting, Waterford had 'done its duty magnificently' drew applause.

In addition to public speaking, books and pamphlets espousing the allied cause were circulated. Redmond's speech in Waterford city during August 1915 was published as a pamphlet.[112] An account of his visit to the front was used to introduce a book about the Irish regiments. In it he recalled how he had met many of his Waterford constituents, one being shot and killed while he was there.[113] His experiences were included in a bilingual recruiting booklet entitled *Ireland's Cause* and sent to all Waterford householders by the Department of Recruiting in Ireland,[114] which replaced the Central Council for the Organisation of Recruiting in Ireland in October 1915. The speech describing his visit was circulated as a leaflet and had a print run of 240,000.[115] In his introduction to a book about the Irish at the front, he wrote:

> it is these soldiers of ours with their astonishing courage and their beautiful faith, with their natural military genius, with their tenderness as well as strength; carrying with them their green flags and their Irish war-pipes; advancing to the charge, their fearless officers at their head, and followed by their beloved chaplains as great-hearted as themselves; bringing with them a quality of their own to the sordid modern battlefield ... offering up their supreme sacrifice of life with a smile on their lips because it was given for Ireland ... . May Ireland, cherishing them in her bosom, know how to prove her love and pride and send their brothers leaping to keep full their battle-torn ranks.[116]

This introduction, claimed by some to be a work of 'real historical importance' which

109 Patrick Henry Pearse (1897–1916) was a republican writer whose study of old Irish history and literature convinced him that Irish nationalism could only be kindled through a revival of the language and culture. He founded a school in which these ideas were put into practice. Prominent in the Gaelic League, he supported Sinn Fein and was also a member of the Irish Republican Brotherhood. A founder member of the Irish Volunteers, he was a leader of the small band of Volunteers who refused to follow John Redmond when Redmond formed the National Volunteers after his Woodenbridge speech in September 1914. He also politicised the Gaelic League and was to observe: 'bloodshed is a cleansing and a sanctifying thing, and the nation which regards it as a final horror has lost its manhood.' He was executed for his part in the Easter Rising.
110 Lyons (1979), pp. 91–92.
111 Hannay (1916).
112 Redmond, J. E. (1915), *Speech delivered by J. E. Redmond at Waterford City and County Convention 23 August 1915*, London.
113 Kerr, S. P. (1916), *What the Irish Regiments have done—with a Diary of a Visit to the Front by John Redmond*, London, pp. 7–22.
114 *Waterford News*, 25 Feb. 1916.
115 Callan (1984) p. 289.
116 MacDonagh (1916), pp. 1–14.

demonstrated how a 'really United Kingdom met the Prussian Challenge',[117] was also issued as a pamphlet of 100,000 copies. Redmond sent out copies of *The Irish at the Front* and of the pamphlet describing his visit to the trenches to many people, including leading soldiers, the king and the Prince of Wales.

MacDonagh's book, written at Redmond's request, is a study in propaganda. At the Battle of Loos, he saw in the London Irish battalions, a

> stirring story of Irish gaiety and resolution ... . The battalions are also able to warm their hearts and fire their blood with the strains of the ancient war-pipes. This old barbaric music has magic in it. It transforms the Gael. It reawakens in the deeps of their being even in this twentieth century, impressions, moods, feelings, inherited from a wild, untamed ancestry for thousands of years, and thus gives them, more than strong wine, that strength of arm and that endurance of soul which makes them invincible.[118]

But Patrick MacGill, who fought with the London Irish, was left with a 'clear personal impression of man's ingenuity for destruction when my eyes looked on the German front line where our dead lay in peace with the fallen enemies'.[119]

Cardinal Bourne of Westminster, who 'rejoiced at the ringing words' of Redmond's introduction to *The Irish at the Front*,[120] had himself visited the war zone during January and February 1915. Born of an Irish mother and an English father who had converted to Catholicism, he claimed the union of Irish and English races was

necessary for the 'cause of God' and those who 'create, or foster, or perpetuate misunderstanding, are the enemies of Faith and Fatherland'.[121] At the front he exhorted Catholic troops to 'emulate the courage of those who had already given up their lives for King and Country'.[122] The *Waterford News* described the cardinal's address to the wounded as 'touching', his words 'bringing tears to the eyes of many of his hearers'.[123] After a further visit to the front in 1917, he published a pamphlet in which he claimed that for those soldiers with conviction, the war had strengthened their religion and their hold on the 'truths of revelation'. They did their duty because it was a duty 'given to them to perform by Almighty God'.[124]

A war-hardened and cynical soldier with the London Irish who had never heard of a 'curate's regiment', considered any talk of a holy war to be nonsense. However, he thought curates would probably make 'damned good bomb-throwers'.[125] But in Ireland, despite a contemporary view that on the whole religious conviction had little to do with forming opinions about the war,[126] religion figured prominently in the propaganda campaign. The *Waterford News*, declaring that there were still mysteries 'despite the scoffing of a sceptical age', published a letter from a soldier in the 47th Brigade in which he described to his mother a miraculous escape from death. His equipment was torn from him, his water bottle was shattered and he was buried under debris but he escaped injury from an exploding shell when a piece of shrapnel struck him at the place he wore the Sacred Heart. He asked his mother to write to the *Messenger* 'thanking the Sacred Heart of Jesus for our miraculous preservation'.[127]

117 *Cork Weekly Examiner*, 19 Feb. 1916.
118 MacDonagh (1916), pp. 110–127.
119 MacGill, P. (1984), *The Great Push: An Episode of the Great War*, Kerry, pp. 85–86.
120 Oldmeadow (1940), Vol. 2, pp. 108, 176.
121 Higgins, G. (1912), *Cardinal Bourne—A Record of the Sayings and Doings of His Eminence Francis 4th Archbishop of Westminster*, London, pp. 11, 55–56.
122 *Cork Constitution*, 8 Feb. 1915.
123 *Waterford News*, 5 Feb. 1915.
124 Anonymous (1918), 'A British cardinal's visit to the western front', *The Universe*, London.
125 MacGill (1984b), pp. 179–80.
126 Hannay (1915).
127 *Waterford News*, 28 Apr. 1916.

In Hannay's opinion stories of the shelling of cathedrals by Germans and stories of their mistreatment of nuns and priests 'produced some, but not very much effect on Irish opinion'.[128] But the press generally represented the Catholic Church as a supporter of the war. In urging Irishmen to enlist and protect 'our nuns and priests' the *Waterford News*, under the heading 'Massacre of Priests', described how more than 50 Belgian priests had been put to death by the Germans without the 'least excuse'.[129] The enemy was reported as callously singling out the church at Albert for destruction by their artillery but it survived as a 'manifestation of Divine interposition'.[130] Cardinal Bourne said mass before the 'miraculous statue' on his 1917 visit to the front.[131] The staid, conservative *Waterford Standard* thought the evidence 'would convince many who are at present sceptical that undoubtedly visions were seen at the great Battle of Mons ... the story of the angels of Mons is not fiction'.[132] Other stories published at home included that of a soldier who saw the figure of Christ, surrounded by a luminous halo, detach Himself from a damaged cross, put the fallen parts back into place and then resume His position.[133]

God was clearly on the side of the allies in their war against a Germany whose rulers wanted to 'utterly annihilate freedom' and whose teachers and philosophers wanted to 'abolish Christ and set up a new religion of their own'. Irishmen were urged 'fix your mind on these: freedom and religion, and ask yourself are there, could there be any more glorious ... institutions for our country to fight for?'.[134]

Public speakers, books, articles and pamphlets,

and the local media, therefore, taking a pro-Redmond stance and subject to government and self-imposed censorship, promulgated propaganda which added to the pressures on men to enlist. However, Redmond's policy meant the National Volunteers had to find a new role *vis-à-vis* the British army and this presented problems.

III

James English appears to have been a National Volunteer. In March 1915 tickets were drawn by the mayor for 16 uniforms at the Volunteers' headquarters. One of the names drawn was J. English of 'D' Company.[135] Volunteers would have been under considerable peer pressure to carry out Redmond's policies. As well as being a paramilitary unit, the city battalion, which consisted of nine companies and up to 100 women in a nurses corps established in March 1915,[136] operated much like a social club with strong local support and financial backing. The list of subscribers included nearly all of the city's business people. Gerald P. Fitzgerald of The Island and Councillor Dr Joe White each subscribed £5 but many other people gave as little as 1s, collections being carried out in all the electoral wards.[137]

Officers were elected. In February 1915 John Kearney, a bootmaker of Patrick Street was elected as a second lieutenant and delegates were elected to go to the Dublin convention on Easter Monday.[138] In April 1915 William J. Smith, alderman for Centre Ward and Charlie Strange's 'old corporation' adversary in 1899, was elected as lieutenant-colonel of the battalion[139] and acted

128 Hannay (1915).
129 *Waterford News*, 15 Oct. 1915.
130 *Cork Weekly Examiner*, 19 Feb. 1916.
131 Anonymous (1918).
132 *Waterford Standard*, 12 Feb. 1916.
133 MacGill (1984b), p. 216.
134 *Cork Weekly Examiner*, 26 Feb. 1916.
135 *Munster Express*, 20 Mar. 1915.
136 *Munster Express*, 20 Mar. 1915.
137 *Waterford News*, 15 Jan. 1915.
138 *Waterford News*, 26 Feb. 1915; *Thom's Directory*.
139 *Waterford Standard*, 15 May 1915; *Waterford News*, 16 Apr. 1915.

as chairman of the battalion committee. Strongly Redmondite and the local UIL secretary, he was also contractor to the army for all bread and flour supplied to the troops in Waterford and district. The old fenian sympathiser and mayor, Richard Power, was honorary colonel and four city councillors sat on the 18 man battalion committee. It also included three solicitors and the president of the UTLC.

There were Irish Volunteer (and, following the split, National Volunteer) connections with the clergy as well as with City Hall. Priests were in attendance at every function and in an 'indescribable solemn ... touching and effective' ceremony, the administrator of the cathedral blessed the city battalion's colours before they were presented by John Redmond in October 1914.[140]

The Volunteers undertook regular training and manoeuvres. These included arms drill, lectures, officer and NCO classes and practice in the headquarters' miniature rifle range.[141] When a Volunteer was killed in a shooting accident, he was buried with military honours. Preceded by a firing squad with reversed arms, the coffin was draped with a green flag and the deceased's accoutrements. The Erin's Hope Fife and Drum Band followed behind and the mourners included Canon Tom Furlong, now parish priest of Ballybricken, Father W. B. O'Donnell and other priests.[142]

The centrepiece of the replica flags decorating the interior walls of the Hennessy's Road headquarters was a 'splendid portrait' of John Redmond, surrounded on each side with two large stars formed of bayonets. Men were provided with games facilities while others took their turn on the miniature rifle range. At Christmas the room was decorated with bunting, evergreen and Chinese lanterns and all-night dances were planned for St Patrick's night. In 1915 about 60 couples turned up.[143] For men such as James English, with limited economic means and restricted leisure and social outlets, membership of the Volunteers would have consolidated group identity and personal loyalty to Redmond. They were more vulnerable to local Redmondite propaganda and to the heightened mood of wartime militarism. The *Munster Express* reported that the Volunteers felt 'bound to show ... their loyalty and fealty to their trusted leader ... personally ... as the inspiring spirit of their great organisation'.[144]

It was not at first clear what Redmond's policy was in respect of the Volunteers *vis-à-vis* the British army, and the initial response to his 3 August speech was for men to enrol in nationalist paramilitary organisations rather than join the British army. In Waterford large numbers, among them many Protestants, were recruited into the city's Volunteers battalion. Gerald Purcell Fitzgerald of The Island was one prominent Catholic who wrote to the city's Volunteer commander 'expressing his delight at Mr Redmond's offer' and asking to be enrolled. A similar response was recorded in neighbouring counties. In Carrick-on-Suir 200 new Volunteer recruits doubled the local corps strength and a large number of boys flocked to *Na Fianna Eireann*. In Piltown 200 recruits formed a new Volunteer corps and members continued to enrol daily. It was reported that the 'stirring and history-making events of the past few days have ... throughout Ireland given a great impetus' to the Volunteer movement.[145]

But Redmond rejected the advice of Colonel Maurice Moore, the Volunteer inspector-general, not to allow the mobilisation of military reservists who were also Volunteers until home rule had been implemented. Over 7,500 Volunteers, constituting nearly 44 per cent of the reservists mobilised in Ireland, were called to the colours

---

140 *Munster Express*, 17 Oct. 1914.
141 *Waterford News*, 5 Feb. 1915. Training programmes were regularly advertised.
142 *Munster Express*, 6 Feb. 1915. The deceased was William Hartery, a widower aged 61 years and employed as the clerk of St Patrick's Church at the time of his death. He had been previously employed as the caretaker of Temperance Hall.
143 *Waterford News*, 1 Jan. 1915; *Munster Express*, 20 Mar. 1915.
144 *Munster Express*, 17 Oct. 1914; *Freeman's Journal*, 12 Oct. 1914.
145 *Munster Express*, 8 Aug. 1914.

on the outbreak of war. According to Maurice Moore these men had 'formed the backbone' of the Volunteer organisation, 'being everywhere the drill instructors and officers and NCOs of the various companies. It was impossible to replace them'.[146]

Redmond adopted a dual policy, Daniel Sheehan recalling that he and his friends 'were neither one thing nor the other ... publicly asking the National Volunteers to stay at home and [also making] half-hearted speeches in favour of recruiting'.[147] Redmond wanted the Volunteers to be transformed into an officially recognised home defence force, trained and armed by the War Office. Simultaneously the IPP would create in Ireland 'an atmosphere ... and sentiment ... favourable to recruiting [into the British Army]'.[148] The consequences were bizarre. On 9 August 1914, when a contingent of city Volunteers planned a nationalist recruiting march to Geneva Barracks,[149] the first large batch of Waterford men enlisted in the British army. Over the next few days even greater numbers were to enlist, as shown in Figure 1.

Initially, the emphasis was on an effective Volunteer force. P. W. Kenny, Father W. B. O'Donnell, Martin J. Murphy, Willie Redmond and Joseph Devlin were among the large number of guests present on Sunday 11 October 1914, when Redmond, after presenting the Waterford city battalion with new colours at a review in the sports field, promised an estimated 5,000 Volunteers from Waterford, Kilkenny, Wexford and Tipperary, a reorganised headquarters, firearms and ammunition, uniforms, a weekly newspaper, training facilities and an Irish parliament within months. 'We mean business,' he told them. 'We have taken hold of this thing, and we are going

to organise this force, closely, all over the country.' And he explained that Colonel Moore proposed to start a camp to train officers 'of Irish birth, of Irish feeling, with Irish hearts and Irish sympathies'.

Maurice Moore had implemented a scheme for creating a small corps from within the Volunteer ranks. The force would have its own officers and was intended to be used for the defence of Ireland against foreign invaders and to 'perfect the military efficiency' of the National Volunteers. The first step in a plan for several officer and instructor training centres throughout the country was the establishment of a camp in Limerick.[150] By 7 October the camp commandant had reported a full programme of training was underway and that the men were anxious for coast defence work.[151] Three-week, seven-day and, exceptionally, weekend instruction courses were being offered.[152]

But the Irish were charged with 'funking' the war and Redmond proclaimed that 'when an Irish Brigade has been formed composed entirely of Irishmen, bearing the name of Ireland and officered entirely by Irishmen' recruitment into the British army, already good, would improve. In October Lieutenant-General Sir Lawrence W. Parsons, who formally took command of the 16th (Irish) Division on 23 September 1914, was instructed to clear a brigade and fill it with National Volunteers and others that Redmond 'induces to enlist'. Within days Parsons told Maurice Moore that the 47th Brigade was ready to take about 4,300 men.[153] Waterford's *Evening News* quickly announced under the headline 'Everything made in Ireland', that the 16th Division was manned in Ireland by Irishmen and commanded by Irishmen. It claimed Irishmen

146 Staunton (1986a), p. 181 (footnotes 763 and 764).
147 Sheehan (1921), p. 285.
148 Gwynn, D. (1932), pp. 451–52.
149 *Munster Express*, 8 Aug. 1914.
150 *Freeman's Journal*, 12 Oct. 1914.
151 Captain J. J. Holland to Moore, 7 Oct. 1914 (Maurice Moore Papers, 10561), NLI.
152 Publicity leaflet and application form (Maurice Moore Papers, 10561), NLI.
153 Parsons, diary entries, 17, 23 and 30 Oct. 1914 (Parsons Papers, 1914–16, MD 1111) Royal Artillery Institution Library, Woolwich (hereafter Woolwich); Parsons to Moore, 29 Oct. 1914 (Maurice Moore Papers, 10561), NLI; Denman (1987/1988).

could join it from anywhere in the United Kingdom and be transferred to Ireland at War Office expense.[154]

Despite Redmond's efforts, the War Office failed officially to recognise the National Volunteers or to make use of them. And his argument that official recognition of the National Volunteers as a home defence force would stimulate recruiting into the British army was just one inconsistency which made Redmond's policy increasingly less convincing. His view was that once the Volunteers were trained and accustomed to barracks and camp life, 'the certain and inevitable result would be that large numbers of these men would volunteer for service abroad'.[155] To some extent Redmond's actions can be explained. He saw veterans of the 16th Division and a trained and armed home defence force fusing together to form an Irish national army. There were several practical difficulties in this idea, however, and Redmond does not seem to have clarified his thinking on how the two military forces would relate to each other or how the 'fusion' would be achieved. The home rule act prohibited any Irish government from passing laws affecting the military.

In time, Redmond's commitment to recruiting for the 16th Division deepened. In February 1915, he wrote that he was 'ready and willing to assist in any method calculated to promote more rapid recruiting' of the younger men and 'we have done a good deal already in this direction'.[156] Membership of both the National Volunteers and the UIL was already in decline and by August 1915, it was reported that in encouraging enlistment the IPP had faced 'great difficulties and ... charges of inconsistency not easily borne'.

By now, according to Hannay, the 'general tone of Nationalist opinion' was 'very far from enthusiastic for the cause of the allies ... . Ordinary working' nationalists were 'even more un-

comfortable than Northern Orangemen' about Redmond's stand. Noting that a dislike of British imperialism and sympathy for Britain's enemies were 'important and necessary parts of Irish Nationalism', he recorded that there was a 'great deal of anti-English feeling, smouldering, lacking public expression, but strong'. Although nationalists were prepared to support Redmond and pass 'any resolution sent down to them from Headquarters' at local government meetings, there was a greater apathy towards the war effort in Ireland than in England because of a 'vague feeling that to fight for the British Empire was a form of disloyalty to Ireland'.[157]

How much of a strain the need to choose between the British army and the Volunteers placed on men is not clear. It would have varied between groups and individuals, much depending upon their attitude to, and experience of, the British army. Some men no doubt found it relatively simple to follow Redmond's instructions while others experienced uneasiness. Lieutenant-Colonel L. Grattan Esmonde, National Volunteer inspecting officer for the south-east district, reviewed the Waterford battalion at their Hennessy's Road headquarters in January 1915. But within days he had accepted command of a battalion of the Tyneside Irish and subsequently went with them to the front.[158]

He was succeeded by his brother Sir Thomas H. Grattan Esmonde MP who had appointed Charlie Strange as county sub-sheriff and was himself removed as County Waterford's sheriff in 1887. In March 1915 the *Munster Express* reported how a Cork Volunteer who had obtained a commission in the 'Celto-British' army and was 'proud' to be under the leadership of John Redmond, was feted by the Waterford Volunteers who, together with the Erin's Hope Prize Band, escorted him to the station. But in the same edition, the newspaper complained about

154 *Evening News*, 29 Oct. 1914.
155 Redmond, J., memorandum, *c*. Sep. 1915 (Redmond Papers, 15,261 [7]), NLI.
156 Gwynn, D. (1932), p. 413.
157 Hannay (1915).
158 *Munster Express*, 9 Jan. 1915; *Waterford News*, 22 Jan. 1915.

the lack of Volunteer recruits. 'Come on boys, fall in, and swell the patriot ranks of Waterford', it urged. 'You are proud of Waterford's martial and immortal Meagher—why not ... imitate his example and become a soldier of Ireland and a soldier for Ireland?'[159]

On 21 March, two days before James English enlisted, Sir Thomas Esmonde inspected the city battalion and expressed disappointment at the low turnout of between 400 and 500. But he praised the patriotism of those who did parade, declaring that the working classes from whom Volunteers were mainly drawn, were the 'backbone' of the movement.[160] A month later the *Waterford News* reported that the 'comparatively small' numbers of Volunteers turning out for a march to Tramore could not be wholly explained by enlistments in the army.

Reminding its readers that home rule was not yet in place and that the Ulster Volunteer Force remained intact, the newspaper reiterated the need for a strong Volunteer force. It asked if the young men of Waterford were too 'ashamed or afraid to stand in defence of their freedom'.[161] But Redmond's failure to fulfil his promises of November 1914 was dispiriting. By February 1915 there were complaints about a shortage of uniforms and equipment. It was feared that the Waterford contingent going to the Phoenix Park review in April would parade in caps and bandoliers only, as it was found 'next to impossible to procure arms owing to the demands of the European conflict'.[162]

By June, when Maurice Moore inspected the battalion, 450 National Volunteers had enlisted in the army. By the end of 1915, Volunteers made up between 35 and 50 per cent of Waterford men recruited. But only about 13 per cent of their total strength volunteered. One hundred and fifty had also been called up as reservists. Moore was concerned by the drop in strength, and called for additional Volunteer recruits, telling those on parade of the need to prepare for war after the European conflict was over in defence of the rights they had won. However, his own son, Second Lieutenant Ulick Moore, was wounded in 1916 while serving with the Connaught Rangers.[163] Father W. B. O'Donnell, who was present at the parade, reinforced Moore's plea for Volunteer recruits.[164]

But at the party convention held in the city during August Redmond restated his commitment to a dual policy. Referring to Waterford's army recruiting figures, he described Ireland's contribution as 'magnificent' and called on young men to enlist and fill manpower gaps in the Irish divisions. Ireland must 'gallantly continue to fulfil her duty in this war'. Simultaneously, he made an urgent appeal for Irishmen to maintain the strength of the party's 'civil political organisation' and of its 'armed military organisation'.[165]

If men such as James English had any difficulty in deciding whether to join the British army or remain a Volunteer, their minds may well have been made up by more immediate personal and communal pressures.

IV

Propagandists targeted women in their recruiting campaigns. At a recruiting meeting in City Hall, Stephen Gwynn claimed that 'women could do more than men' in urging Irishmen to go to the front. Many had been held back by 'mothers or sisters or sweethearts or wives' but this made things worse in the long run. In April 1916 when recruiting was at a low ebb, the *Waterford Standard* declared that 'the women of Ireland have decided to appeal to the men of Ireland ... . Irishwomen seem to appreciate even more fully

159 *Munster Express*, 20 Mar. 1915.
160 *Munster Express*, 27 Mar. 1915.
161 *Waterford News*, 30 Apr. 1915.
162 *Waterford News*, 26 Feb. 1915; *Munster Express*, 13 Feb. 1915.
163 Staunton, M. G. (1986), 'Ginchy: nationalist Ireland's forgotten battle of the Somme', *An Cosantóir*, XLVI, pp. 24–26.
164 *Waterford Standard*, 12 June 1915.
165 *Munster Express*, 28 Aug. 1915.

than men do the realities of the world crisis and its bearing on Ireland'.[166]

Doubting that Irish working men were 'belaboured' into the army with the broomstick of their wives, one contemporary none the less thought it was true that Irishwomen, with the separation allowances tempting them, did nothing to prevent their husbands enlisting.[167] In some cases the allowance could be decisive. For six months a quay labourer from Glass House Lane had given his wife only 2s 6d each week to support herself and four children in a house with no furniture. The woman's father gave her the 3s 6d he received weekly from a son fighting at the front.[168] Summoned for neglect, the court of petty sessions withdrew the charges against her husband when he joined the army and she began receiving 25s a week in allowances.[169]

Although an incentive, the allowances sometimes created rather than solved problems. Bishop Sheehan, speaking in Ballybricken Church, referred to the 'considerable number of women, wives or dependents of soldiers at the front' and accused the women of not learning 'thrift and care' and of abusing the allowances, often spending the money on drink.[170] In one instance a woman receiving a separation allowance was fined five shillings with costs for drunkenness and disorderly conduct. The magistrate thought it a 'disgrace' for women to use public money to buy drink and instructed that the War Office should be requested to give allowances to the local Catholic clergy who would keep it in trust.[171]

Soon after the outbreak of war men were faced with the threat of conscription and this was a factor which sometimes compelled them to volunteer. Those who complained about able-bodied men who 'hang about the quays and corners of the city ... [and] ... prefer living on the charity of others' demanded conscription.[172] People were uncertain of government intentions. The *Munster Express* hoped that the advocates of conscription who 'fancied they were within sight of their cherished goal' would be disappointed[173] but in March 1915 it was admitted there was a diversity of opinion.[174] The *Waterford Standard* suggested that conscription was probable because voluntary recruiting was no longer considered to be effective.[175] The issue was eventually to transcend all others in 'driving a wedge between government and people' and the threat of it 'produced significant reactions' in Ireland.[176]

Men were also responsive to the mood and pressures of their small and close district and street communities. The communal climate favoured enlistment. Not only was Ballybricken a Redmondite stronghold but many Ballybricken men had joined the pre-war British army. A boy aged 14 from Thomas's Avenue, for instance, was recruited into the Royal Irish Regiment in July 1914 and was the youngest soldier to be killed in the First World War.[177] His death and that of other soldiers killed, would have been a keen

---

166 *Waterford Standard*, 19 Apr. 1916.
167 Hannay (1915).
168 *Waterford News*, 16 Apr. 1915.
169 *Waterford Standard*, 12 June 1915.
170 *Waterford Standard*, 15 May 1915.
171 *Waterford Standard*, 20 Nov. 1915.
172 *Waterford Standard*, 2 Sep. 1914.
173 *Munster Express*, 6 Mar. 1915.
174 *Waterford News*, 19 Mar. 1915.
175 *Waterford Standard*, 31 Mar. 1915.
176 Townshend (1983), pp. 280–81.
177 The soldier, 6322 Private John Condon, was killed in action on 24 May 1915 at Ypres. According to CARA, *Ballybricken and Thereabouts*, p. 133, Condon lived in Teapot Lane, off Ballybricken. However, an article by Kevin Myers in the *Irish Times*, 23 May 1986, reports him as being the son of John and Mary Condon from Wheelbarrow Lane (Thomas's Avenue). This latter piece of information is confirmed by *Thom's Directory* which records a John Condon as being resident at 15 Thomas's Avenue in 1909. The 1911 census return submitted by John Condon senior, shows that he had three sons and two daughters living with him in Thomas's Avenue. One son, aged 12 years and attending school, would have been 14 or 15 years old in 1914. John Condon and both his working sons were employed as general labourers.

topic of conversation among the residents of Thomas's Avenue. The local press constantly carried reports of enlistments and accounts of Waterford soldiers which fed local gossip and heightened a man's awareness of his 'unmanly behaviour' in letting others do his fighting for him.

During February 1915 the *Munster Express* reported that 200 men from Tramore, with a total population of 1,700, had enlisted and that Redmond's brother, Willie, had obtained a commission in the 6th Royal Irish Regiment.[178] On the same day the *Waterford Standard* carried a report of how Second Lieutenant Fitzgerald had been mentioned in despatches for bravery. The son of the Bank of Ireland agent from The Quay, he had joined the Royal Irish Regiment and was sent home wounded after four days in the firing line.[179] And Lieutenant George Carew, the son of a Waterford grain importer, was reported as receiving a decoration for gallantry after having his arm and leg shattered. Captain H. L. Meagher's embarkation for the front in April was also given coverage. A nephew of T. F. Meagher, he had joined the Royal Field Artillery in 1910.[180] In its account of the death of Captain Frank Robertson, the brother of Messrs Robertson Brothers of The Quay, from wounds received in the Dardanelles, the *Waterford News* described how he was buried near the grave of Pasha Sheehan in Alexandria. Sheehan was a pre-1914 soldier and son of a Waterford merchant from Newtown.[181]

Men from a variety of backgrounds were recruited and James English was almost certainly acquainted with some of them. At least 27 members of the YMCA joined the colours.[182] The son

of a saddler from Patrick Street was killed while serving with the Irish Guards soon after he had notified the death of another Waterford man who was in the Guards.[183] The Waterford Boat Club did not hold a regatta in 1915 out of respect for 16 of its members who were on active service and defending 'their country, their hearths and homes and keeping the horror of war from our shores'.[184] Nearly 40 members of the Erin's Hope Band enlisted.[185] The bandmaster of the Barrack Street Band, as well as having a son held as a prisoner of war, had another serving in the Royal Engineers and a third was in the Royal Navy.[186]

In a probably unique instance of a Waterford firm commemorating employees who served in the forces, Graves and Co. had a scroll of honour mounted on its office wall and this provides evidence of the extent to which Waterford's community was affected by the war. The plaque shows that of the 45 men enlisting, 17 per cent were killed or missing in action, 9 per cent were wounded and 7 per cent were taken as prisoners. It is likely there is some truth in the claim that southern Irish unionists provided a proportionately greater number of recruits than other sections of the community.[187] Of the 93 names appearing on a scroll of honour displayed in Waterford's Protestant cathedral, 14 per cent were killed in action.

Although Kitchener's New Armies, acquiring social acceptability and an improved status, attracted 'decent self-respecting, industrious working men',[188] many Waterford recruits, especially Protestants and those of the upper or middle classes, chose to join British regiments rather than the 16th Division. Around 35 per

---

178 *Munster Express*, 20 Feb. 1915.
179 *Waterford Standard*, 20 Feb. 1915.
180 *Waterford News*, 16 Apr. 1915.
181 *Waterford News*, 15 Oct. 1915.
182 *Waterford Standard*, 29 Sep. 1915.
183 *Waterford Standard*, 6 Nov. 1915.
184 *Waterford Standard*, 4 Mar. 1916.
185 *Cork Examiner*, 14 June 1916. The newspaper report included photographs of 30 members of the band. Two had been killed in action, two had been wounded in action and five taken as prisoners of war.
186 *Waterford News*, 1 Jan. 1915.
187 Hannay (1915).
188 Beckett, 'The Nation in Arms' in Beckett and Simpson (eds.) (1985).

cent of Waterford-born soldiers who died in the war served in British or general units. Of the 44 Graves and Co. employees enlisting, and whose regiments are identified, 46 per cent joined the Royal Irish Regiment, 27 per cent joined other Irish regiments and 27 per cent joined British regiments or general army units. Members of the Redmondite nationalist Erin's Hope Prize Band who enlisted conform with this general pattern. Of the 29 identified members recruited, 66 per cent were in the Royal Irish Regiment, 7 per cent were in other Irish regiments and 27 per cent joined British regiments. Higher percentages joined the Royal Irish Regiment because Waterford was located within the regiment's recruiting district. It was also Willie Redmond's local regiment and was the one in which he served. Redmondite nationalists, therefore, probably felt a stronger loyalty to the regiment. In February 1915 Herbert Goff left for England to join a Motor Transport Corps in which he had been gazetted captain.[189] The son of a city wine merchant joined the Black Watch.[190] A staff member of the *Waterford News* was commissioned and served with the 12th Welsh Regiment[191] and of the five grandsons of Colonel E. Roberts killed in action, only one served with an Irish regiment.[192]

The 'unashamedly elitist' Sportsmen's Battalions of the Royal Fusiliers[193] were particularly popular. Men initially joining the regiment acted as a magnet to others, either encouraging their friends to join, or reports of their joining creating a communal interest. In February, a member of

Denny's clerical staff who joined the unit was seen off by a large gathering.[194] And the son of a brewer employed by Davis, Strangman and Co. also joined.[195] By April a large number of men were reported to have enlisted in one of the battalions. Several of them were on holiday in the city over Easter and two of the Clyde Shipping Company's clerical staff subsequently enlisted in the regiment.[196]

When recruiting in Waterford during March, 1915, Stephen Gwynn attempted to entice men of the middle class, described as the 'better educated young men', into the 16th Division. He promised commissions would become available as 'close on 800 officers were knocked out in two or three days fighting'. And any man who joined the division's officer cadet company, a special unit of the 7th Battalion Leinster Regiment in which men were trained for the specific purpose of taking commissions in the division, would be in 'precisely the same sort of society as he would meet if he entered the national universities in Dublin, Cork or Galway'.[197]

In July, Lieutenant Lynch, a Waterford man, offered this class of recruit their own 'pals' platoon or company.[198] These were 'allegedly superior' units for 'upper and middle-class men'[199] and were also a way of tapping the sentiments of loyalty felt by men to their town, county or community. The Commercial Company of the 5th Dublin Fusiliers, regarded as a 'splendid lot', and the Clerical Battalion (10th Dublin Fusiliers) were successful attempts to create 'pals' units. Their existence probably accounts to some extent

189 *Waterford News*, 5 Feb. 1915.
190 *Waterford Standard*, 20 Feb. 1915.
191 *Waterford News*, 8 Oct. 1915.
192 Three serving in British regiments were killed in action in France in 1915, 1916 and 1917. One was killed in action while serving with a British regiment in Gallipoli in 1915 and one was killed in action with the Royal Munster Fusiliers in France in 1918. This information was obtained from a memorial and the scroll of honour on display in the Protestant cathedral, Waterford.
193 Simkins (1988), p. 92.
194 *Waterford News*, 5 Feb. 1915.
195 *Waterford Standard*, 20 Feb. 1915.
196 *Waterford News*, 16 Apr. 1915.
197 *Munster Express*, 27 Mar. 1915; *Waterford Standard*, 27 Mar. 1915.
198 *Munster Express*, 24 July 1915.
199 Beckett, 'The Nation in Arms, 1914–18' in Beckett and Simpson (eds.) (1985).

for the 'great wave of recruits' among urban clerks and shop-assistants in November 1915.[200]

However, whatever unit they decided to join, the activities of local pro-Redmond lay and clerical leaders exerted pressure on men to enlist.

V

Waterford corporation, like many other boroughs, promptly carried a resolution supporting Redmond's pledge of 3 August 1914. And despite hints of a weakening consensus by the end of 1915, the city's leaders provided solid support for Redmond and the IPP throughout 1914 and 1915. In response to a speech by Redmond on 15 September 1914 and Asquith's promise of home rule, Hearne and Co., a supplier to the Volunteers and employing over 240 people in 1907, offered to keep open the jobs of those who enlisted in the British army and to make up any difference in pay.[201] In March 1915 the firm provided a four-course banquet in the Granville Hotel for all of its staff as a sendoff for those employees who had enlisted. Over 20 of them were National Volunteers and had been recruited into the 16th Division's officer cadet company.

In October 1914 councillors, noting that an assistant clerk employed in the surveyor's office who enlisted deserved 'a lot of credit for his pluck', concurred with his requests for half pay and for his job to be kept open.[202] And during February, the district lunatic asylum also agreed to give half pay to men enlisting and to reinstate them when they returned from the front.[203] The Clyde Shipping Company decided to keep open the jobs of those who enlisted and to pay any difference between wages and army pay and allowances.[204] Graves and Co. was another firm which promised to make up a man's wages and keep his job open while he was in the army.[205]

When Sergeant Michael O'Leary VC visited the city on a recruiting drive in July 1915 in what was described as 'one of the largest and most enthusiastic demonstrations witnessed in living memory', High Sheriff Edward Walsh, the proprietor of the *Munster Express* who had been so voluble in his denunciation of the British connection at the time of the Howth incident, led a huge procession with O'Leary. Both were later photographed together. Declaring he had 'never felt prouder of his native city', Walsh urged more young men to enlist.[206]

In August 1915 among the approximately 51 city delegates giving Redmond a 'tremendous ovation' when he entered the party convention was Michael O'Sullivan, James English's employer. The delegates were drawn from all the city's organisations, six of them representing the UTLC. In its address, the corporation placed on record its 'full, absolute, and entire confidence in [Redmond] as our valued, cherished, and esteemed representative and as the skilful, able, and wise leader of the Irish people'. In the terrible crisis of war, Redmond was told he had

> spoken words of wisdom and acted with great courage and calmness, and we earnestly and emphatically endorse and approve all your words, acts, and deeds, your valiant conduct and the prudent course pursued by you ... we believe we represent the feelings and sentiments of all classes and creeds in the *Urbs Intacta*.

Even the recalcitrant and irrepressible Patrick W. Kenny, critical of British legislation and over-taxation in Ireland and holding the view that

---

200 Colonel Hammond to Parsons, 26 Nov. 1915 (Parsons Papers, MD 1111), Woolwich.
201 *Evening News*, 16 Sep. 1914.
202 *Waterford Standard*, 17 Oct. 1914.
203 *Waterford Standard*, 10 Feb. 1915.
204 *Waterford News*, 16 Apr. 1915.
205 Information obtained during an interview with Clive MacCarthy in August 1990. His father was the W. E. MacCarthy recorded on the Graves & Co. memorial plaque as joining the Royal Fusiliers.
206 *Munster Express*, 24 July 1915.

Ireland owed nothing to the British Empire, none the less called on

> every Irishman [to] become a soldier and fight for the Empire to safeguard his own assets and our own assets that we have invested there and for which we want to get something back now or at some future time.[207]

A material stake in their own country, let alone elsewhere in the empire, was beyond men such as James English but Kenny no doubt had personal as well as corporation and national assets to protect.

When the Central Council for the Organisation of Recruiting in Ireland was formed, Kenny and George Nolan, the builder, were two of the city representatives on the county recruiting committee.[208] Gerald Purcell Fitzgerald of The Island held recruiting meetings like the 'largely attended' one during July 1915 in Ballygunner after 11 o'clock mass.[209] And Lady Goff, Mrs Fitzgerald of The Island, JPs, corporation members, local employers and other prominent local citizens loaned their cars during recruiting campaigns. In May 1915 the corporation passed a vote of sympathy with the victims of 'German barbarity' after the *Lusitania* sinking.[210] This may have acted as a spur to recruiting.[211]

But Kenny could not avoid trouble with his more sycophantic colleagues. When William Fitzgerald, a councillor for Centre Ward in which James English was a resident, gushed with fulsome praise of Redmond, Kenny accused him of going too far in expecting 'no criticism whatsoever' of Redmond. He complained that for years it had been expected that people should accept 'cut and dried' the opinion formed by an inner

circle or the leaders of the IPP and 'swallow it wholesale without questioning ... . I absolutely refuse to suborn my opinion and, as it were, to disenfranchise myself in that way'. Kenny thought acceptance of the amending bill had been a 'cardinal error' as it threatened the 'dismemberment of Ireland'. He concluded that the IPP had 'gambled with high stakes. The game is played out now ... . They lost'.

In the angry debate which followed, Kenny was isolated and variously accused of 'ridiculing' Redmond, of 'posing' as a nationalist and of sour grapes because his nomination for IPP candidature years previously had failed.[212] His experience epitomised the view that the IPP's helplessness after the Easter Rising resulted from the constitutionalists' belief that the party and its leaders 'could do no wrong' and that any critic of their policies was a 'factionist', 'wrecker' or 'traitor'.[213] In Daniel Sheehan's opinion, the majority of IPP members were 'automatons' who meekly submitted to directions from a 'secret cabinet' and were responsible for the 'catastrophies and failures' that overtook the party in later years.[214]

Two months later, at the party convention in August, High Sheriff Edward Walsh, in telling Redmond the country was behind him, repudiated the 'carping cavillers, croakers, and prophets of evil'. And Councillor David MacDonald, referring to P. W. Kenny as being the sole representative of opposition to Redmond's policy, considered this 'fairly represented the state of things in the city'. As far as he was concerned, Redmond represented the views of nine-tenths of the Irish people.[215]

In March, at a meeting of the West Waterford UIL, Father W. B. O'Donnell called on the

207 *Waterford Standard*, 5 May 1915.
208 *Waterford Standard*, 7 July 1915.
209 *Munster Express*, 17 July 1915.
210 *Waterford Standard*, 19 May 1915.
211 W. E. MacCarthy, the son of the Graves and Co. manager, was moved to enlist after the sinking. This information provided by his son Clive MacCarthy during an interview in August 1990.
212 *Munster Express*, 5 June 1915.
213 Miller (1973), p. 343.
214 Sheehan (1921), pp. 143, 146, 151–54.
215 *Munster Express*, 28 Aug. 1915.

organisation to be made 'stronger and better' to meet any contingencies after the war. He proposed a resolution declaring 'confidence in their great and noble Leader ... their indomitable Leader always so sure and unerring in his judgement' and concluded, 'as Nationalists we fully recognise the generous support which has been so steadfastly given to the Home Rule cause by the democracy of the British Empire'. Echoing Redmond's belief, he thought Ireland would come out of the war with 'redoubled life and prosperity'.[216] And in July, during Sergeant Michael O'Leary's visit to the city, Father O'Donnell read out a letter of support from Willie Redmond at a recruiting meeting. In the priest's opinion O'Leary's 'conduct was a shining light and an inspiration to the youth of Ireland.'[217]

Bishop Sheehan, whose call in July for priests from his diocese to enlist had brought responses from four clergymen including the chaplain from the city's Ursuline convent,[218] sent a letter of support to Redmond at the city convention and Canon Tom Furlong was present to pay a 'tribute of deep respect' to Redmond as well as offer a strong expression of support. He thought Waterford people were always able to 'give strong proof ... of their love of fatherland and of gratitude to the leaders of their cause' and in an apparent reference to P. W. Kenny, he considered unfair criticism by some 'so-called Nationalists' as being 'lamentable ... contemptible and intolerable'.

There was, therefore, considerable clerical and lay pressure on men to enlist. But there were counteracting influences. In November 1915, the *Waterford Standard* complained of having 'shirkers and slackers' among the business class which had responded poorly to the call for recruits. In one unidentified business house employing large numbers of young men, there was 'an utter disinclination to volunteer [and] a suspicion of anti-

Britishness about their talk and language that would surprise many people'. As in Dublin, where a 'few young ladies' distributed white feathers to men of military age wearing civilian clothes,[219] a number of Waterford men had been sent white feathers through the post. In an age and culture conscious of the need to demonstrate 'manliness', the receipt of white feathers could shame some men into enlisting. And although 'the working classes have done exceedingly well ... [it was thought] they could do better'.[220]

VI

In November 1914, the *Waterford Standard* reported that newspapers which seditiously reported on behalf of the 'anti-British, anti-recruiting and pro-German campaigns' in Ireland had small circulations and little influence. But some of them were distributed free and reinforced by leaflets and 'that personal propaganda which counts for so much in Nationalist Ireland'. Conceding that they had a 'pernicious effect on enlistment' in their efforts to 'vilify the British Army, poison Irish sentiment against England, and destroy Mr Redmond's position', the *Standard* accused the government of delay and irresolution and called for the suppression of identified newspapers.[221] But despite a number of papers being outlawed, by 1915, according to the Royal Commission on the Rebellion in Ireland, sedition had become so widespread that juries and magistrates could not be trusted to give decisions in accordance with the evidence.

An example of such reports is that of a speech by James Connolly appearing in the *Irish Worker*. He denounced Redmond's action in pledging the Irish people to war without consultation. Rather, the opportunity should have been taken to 'start

216 *Munster Express*, 3 Apr. 1915.
217 *Munster Express*, 24 July 1915.
218 *Munster Express*, 17 and 24 July 1915.
219 Bewley (1989), p. 45.
220 *Waterford Standard*, 6 Nov. 1915.
221 *Waterford Standard*, 28 Nov. 1914.

our own Parliament' as it was 'better to fight for our own country than for the robber empire. If ever you shoulder a rifle, let it be for Ireland'.[222]

In Waterford during March 1915 a local cattle driver was charged under DORA after using subversive language to a soldier in a Barrack Street pub.[223] A Post Office official arrested for tearing down recruiting posters during a recruiting campaign was released with a caution by the officer in charge of the recruiting campaign because of Waterford's 'splendid reception' of him and after intervention by Martin J. Murphy, MP for East Waterford. And a traveller refused to take a hackney cab because of the 'Remember Belgium' poster displayed on it.[224]

By November 1915 the *Waterford News* was reporting separatist Irish Volunteer activity. A large audience attended a Manchester martyrs' concert organised under the auspices of the Waterford Irish Volunteers at City Hall. But it was a tentative flirtation with extremism. A visiting speaker proclaimed that the 'fenian spirit ... has set Irishmen on fire within the past few months' and it had 'made Ireland more nationalist today than it ever was before', but, he assured his audience, he refused to set up a party in opposition to John Redmond. He would back Redmond although it was the fenian movement which had preserved nationality and had done more for Ireland in five years than a century of constitutionalism.

A priest claimed that it was the blood of the Manchester martyrs which had brought about reform by bringing the Irish question before the 'fair-minded and honest-minded English people'.[225] In February 1916, under the auspices of the Gaelic League and with a priest presiding, Patrick Pearse gave a lecture on nationality in

City Hall. Patrick W. Kenny, the mayor and several other 'prominent citizens, clerical and lay' attended. A man who shouted 'this is not Ireland's war!', during a recruiting speech by Fitzgerald of The Island in March 1916, was charged with making a statement likely to prejudice recruiting.[226]

When five soldiers formerly employed by the corporation asked for half pay after enlisting in November 1915, one councillor objected on the grounds that ratepayers should not be 'mulcted' by people who got help from the state in the form of separation allowances. The case was referred to a committee after another councillor pointed out the men might be single and not entitled to allowances,[227] but the mood was very different from that of twelve months earlier. By the end of 1915, in an apparent reference to the Central Council for the Organisation of Recruiting in Ireland, Hannay commented, 'the recruiting committee has received very small help hitherto from the IPP' and the 'great bulk of the party has stood aloof'. He also concluded from the few signs of 'dilution', when semi-skilled, unskilled, and female labour was used for jobs previously reserved for skilled men, that the Irish employer was not as patriotic as his equivalent in England.[228]

An explanation for the change in mood may be found in that catch-all phrase 'war-weariness'. The war involved hardships and was costing money, lives and energy with no obvious prospect of it coming to an end. Home rule was as far away as ever and, as early as May 1915 when the coalition was formed, there were those who thought it was 'dead and buried'.[229] In the view of one historian, this was a turning point and criticism of the IPP began to surface.[230] But

222 Connolly, J. (1914), 'Connolly's speech on war's outbreak', *Irish Worker*, reproduced in Connolly (1988), Vol. 2 Dublin, pp. 48–49.
223 *Munster Express*, 6 Mar. 1915.
224 *Munster Express*, 27 Mar. 1915; *Waterford Standard*, 24 Mar. 1915.
225 *Waterford News*, 26 Nov. 1915.
226 *Waterford Standard*, 25 Mar. 1916.
227 *Waterford Standard*, 6 Nov. 1915.
228 Hannay (1916).
229 Gwynn, D. (1932), p. 431
230 Fitzpatrick (1977), p. 112.

Waterford Corporation passed a resolution endorsing Redmond's actions at the time of the coalition crisis and declared its confidence in him and the IPP.[231] Bishop Sheehan and his priests remained loyal.

But events had magnified the belief that treatment of Irish nationalists by the British was unjust, insensitive and lacked empathy or understanding. An intensifying disgruntlement with government economic policy in relation to Ireland and especially in respect of taxation and munitions and other war production, reflected a resurgent mistrust. Suspicion of the amending bill and a fear that the government intended to 'diddle' the Irish on finance turned a tentative Catholic clerical support for the war in 1914 to apathy, and in some cases to open hostility, by late 1915.[232] In Redmond's opinion the recruiting campaign in Ireland had also been 'greatly mismanaged' and he disliked the Central Council for the Organisation of Recruiting in Ireland. According to Lloyd George, Kitchener was hostile to the 16th Division and attempted to 'damp the ardour of the Redmonds'.[233]

By the end of 1915 Redmond was of the view that the failure of Kitchener and the War Office to train and arm the Volunteers for home defence had been a 'very serious mistake'[234] and that Parsons had 'dampened down all enthusiasm for the 16th Division and it is essential he should be replaced at once'.[235] Redmond catalogued his grievances during a speech in the House of Commons in November 1915. He included, as matters 'gravely affecting recruiting', what he saw as a bungled Dardanelles campaign and the absence of official recognition of deeds by Irish regiments.[236]

He complained of not being allowed to exercise any real power or influence. Government did not provide him with any information about the state of Ireland and he was not allowed access to official or confidential reports. His opinions were disregarded and his suggestions rejected. The cumulative effect was to undermine Redmond's credibility and authority. None the less, in March 1916 staff of the *Waterford Standard* could still write unrealistically of a 'vast tide of sons of Ireland' flooding into the 'Irish Army' from all over the empire. Ireland, it declared, was not a subject nation but Britain's gallant ally.

> The number of people who are still dissatisfied with their countrymen's firm resolve to give practical help to the Allies has dwindled away, whilst the ungenerous people who would slander or pour scorn on our Irish soldiers are contemptible. But in any case they are so few in numbers that they have long since ceased to be reckoned.[237]

Although DORA was used extensively in Britain to detain and deport dissenters, its enforcement in Ireland fomented nationalist anger. Corporation members led by Patrick W. Kenny adopted a resolution protesting against the imprisonment of separatist Irish Volunteer members without trial and against the banishment of Irishmen. Incorrectly believing that the IPP supported the British policy of arrests and deportations, Councillor William Fitzgerald attempted to have the resolution rescinded. Kenny, prosecuted for declaring 'to hell with England and this war', was accused of being 'hostile to Britain' and of wanting 'total separation from England'. 'Anti-Britishness' was claimed by Fitzgerald's supporters to be a 'prevailing characteristic with many people' although Irishmen were fighting at the front. 'Germanism and German money' was alleged to be behind the resolution.

Councillor Hacket, describing himself as a

231 *Munster Express*, 5 June 1915.
232 Miller (1973), pp. 308–25.
233 Lloyd George (1938), Vol. 1, pp. 417, 452–53.
234 'Notes for Statement', apparently written by John Redmond, *c.* Oct. 1915 (Redmond Papers, 15,259), NLI.
235 John Redmond, memorandum, *c.* Oct. 1915 (Redmond Papers, 15,261[7]), NLI.
236 *The Times*, 3 Nov. 1915.
237 *Waterford Standard*, 25 Mar. 1916.

sworn member of the Fenian Brotherhood, now urged the corporation to back Redmond and constitutionalism: 'I will follow Redmond until I die, and whatever doctrine he proposes I am bound to follow.' The move to rescind the resolution was defeated by eleven votes to seven. Most councillors considered the issue was about the imprisonment of Irishmen without trial by the British, not disloyalty to Redmond. A number of them saw the principle as being no different to that of 1848 when 'leading citizens [were] whipped up here and crammed into quad without any charge against them but mere suspicion'. In his November speech to the House of Commons, Redmond condemned the imprisonment and banishment of Irishmen and made reference to the resolutions of protest passed by the Dublin, Limerick and Waterford corporations.[238]

But at a recruiting conference held in Waterford during December 1915, destined, according to Edward Walsh, 'to seal the union of hearts between Great Britain and Ireland', the lord lieutenant noted how employers in 'patriotic' Waterford had encouraged recruiting. He expressed the view that those who 'doubted that this was Ireland's war ... were few and dwindling'. He thought 'Ireland was sound on the necessity of supporting the gallant army'. Redmond urged on the audience the necessity of keeping up the 16th Division and thought there was 'no city in the United Kingdom less likely [than Waterford] to leave her brave boys in the lurch'.

Referring to his visit to the front, he said Germany's power 'was rapidly on the wane'. He was convinced the war 'would come to an end sooner than the majority of people believed and the sacrifices asked of Ireland would not be as great as if the war continued one year more'.[239] And in February 1916, when the 16th Division was at the front, he called for recruits to fill the division's reserve battalions. Men in the division

'appeal to-day through me from the trenches to the farmers, labourers, artisans, and every class of people, not to desert them'. He told Irishmen:

we have to-day a huge Irish Army in the field. Its achievements have covered Ireland with glory ... and have thrilled our hearts with pride. North and South have vied with each other in springing to arms, and, please God, the sacrifice they have made side by side on the field of battle will form the surest bond of a united Irish nation in the future. We have kept our word. We have fulfilled our trust. We have definitely accepted the position ... of a self-governed unit amongst the nations which make up the Empire.[240]

However, James English enlisted at a time when opposition to the war was still minimal.

VII

The unskilled labouring class was potentially the single largest source for army recruits. The bulk of men making up the category 'persons not producing' were unemployed, unskilled workers. In total, therefore, approximately a third of Waterford's male population of enlistment age was in this class.

The unskilled working class provided the bulk of recruits, the total also being proportionately greater than that of any other section of the Catholic community. This had implications for labourers remaining at home. For instance, the number of Waterford quay workers recruited into the army so reduced and weakened the local ITGWU branch membership that it dispensed with its full-time official. Nationally, by 1916, the ITGWU had as many members in the trenches as in Ireland.

James English almost certainly enlisted on 23

238 *Waterford Standard*, 6 Nov. 1915; *Waterford News*, 5 Nov. 1915.
239 *Munster Express*, 4 Dec. 1915.
240 *Cork Weekly Examiner*, 26 Feb. 1916.

March 1915[241] and it is likely he was one of a group of Ballybricken men who enlisted together. A cluster of Waterford men in the Royal Munster Fusiliers, all from Ballybricken, were recruited around this date.[242] Possibly they were friends or at least knew each other. In this case the need to retain respect of social equals or to emulate the actions of relatives may have been a factor in any decision to enlist.

They enlisted at a time when Waterford was the target of an intensive, highly professional recruiting campaign commencing on 19 March 1915 and lasting approximately three weeks. The campaign was managed by Hedley Le Bas who employed slick and sophisticated marketing techniques. The *Munster Express* recorded the extensive use of posters and pictures illustrating the consequences to Ireland should the Germans succeed in their 'wholesale slaughter, murder, burnings, and outrages'.[243] A series of newspaper advertisements consolidated the themes developed during the campaign. The *Freeman's Journal* reported 'recruiting "fever" was in the air; practically, it was the only subject discussed during the week'.[244] Figure 1 demonstrates how successful the campaign was.

The first contingent of recruits enlisting since the campaign started left Waterford North Station for Clonmel on 23 March. Enough interest was generated to pack the Large Room, City Hall to overflowing when a recruiting meeting was held there during the same evening. It is probable James English was one of those present at the meeting, enlisting after it closed at 10.30 p.m. On the platform were speakers whose names were familiar to Ballybricken men and whose views and words undoubtedly influenced their decision to enlist. According to the *Munster Express*, recruits were 'pouring [in,] in batches' for days after the meeting and Stephen Gwynn, who spoke at the gathering, recorded that 'there was no mistaking the temper of Redmond's constituency; we got men there in hundreds, including a score or so of cadets—young men of education'.[245]

A telegram from Redmond declaring how glad he was to know Waterford 'has done and will continue to do its duty' was read out. High Sheriff Edward Walsh endorsed Redmond's policy and justified recruitment on the grounds men were prepared to make sacrifices 'buoyed up by the ... thought that they now had a country worth fighting for'. The British expeditionary force was necessary for 'self-preservation'. But for it and the 'gallant and plucky deeds of the Irish troops ... they would have ... the invader on their shores and [would be] experiencing all the dreadful horrors of war'. Walsh would not himself be going to the front but it did not prevent him telling his audience that

> if blood has to be shed they would see it shall not be shed on defenceless women and children. It shall be the blood of brave men going where they most effectively could strike a blow to stem the tide of war.

H. Forde JP whose only son had enlisted, appealed to every young man to do 'his duty to his God, his duty to his family and his duty to his country' and enlist. He appealed to his listeners'

---

241 His regimental number, 4414, is next to that of Patrick Duggan who, according to the information at Appendix N, enlisted on this date and served with him in the 9th Royal Munster Fusiliers. The system of regimental numbers was confusing and it does not necessarily follow that both enlisted on the same date. It is, however, more than probable, given that the Duggan referred to appears to have been from Ballybricken. *Thom's Directory* records a Patrick Duggan, labourer, residing at 5 Pump Lane off Barrack Street, Ballybricken. The PRO records show him as being discharged with wounds on 31 March 1917.
242 This information was provided by M. Staunton. Working with *Soldiers who Died in the Great War*, he identified a cluster of men from Waterford serving in the Royal Munster Fusiliers whose regimental numbers indicate they were recruited around the same period as James English. All residents of Ballybricken, they were 4388, Patrick Cuddihy, 8th Munsters, killed in action; 4394, William McGuire, 2nd Munsters, killed in action; 4398, James Walsh, 8th Munsters, killed in action; 4399, John Walsh, 8th Munsters, died of wounds; 4412, Patrick Dower, 2nd Munsters, died of wounds.
243 *Munster Express,* 20 Mar. 1915.
244 Callan (1984), pp. 278–80.
245 Gwynn, S. (1919), p. 187.

ambitions and imaginations: 'think of the opportunity of having your name passed down in history and the chance of rising from the ranks, like
the Chief of Staff Sir William Robertson.' And
M. J. Murphy MP described how Tramore as
well as Waterford had done its duty. In Tramore
22 out of 24 golf caddies had enlisted despite
'earning a fair amount in summer' and two of
them had been killed.

In Bishop Sheehan's opinion the objective of
the meeting 'appeals powerfully to every man in
the land'. A letter in which he stated the war was
'an Irish war to save our country and our people
from ruin and misery' was read out. According
to Gwynn, Bishop Sheehan was 'strong for the
war' and represented a force which was not often
'active on our side'.[246] Father W. B. O'Donnell
spoke with emotion about the outrages carried
out by the Germans against 'old men and women
and helpless children' and he condemned the
'savagery' inflicted on the convents. He proudly
proclaimed that there was 'hardly a poor house
in his parish of St Patrick's' without someone at
the front. He appealed to young men to take up
guns 'in defence of principle and to help maintain
the poor ... and the fallen in Belgium' and called
on every young man who could handle a gun to
walk up to the platform and enlist in the 'cause
of freedom and right'.

Another priest, urging the country to 'rise to
do honour to Mr Redmond', accused those who
tried to prevent men from enlisting of being
'unmanly and cowardly' and not themselves having the 'manhood' to join the army. He did not
care what class of man joined the army, whether
he came from the 'corners or slums or lanes, such
a man must have a fearlessness within him that
won all respect'. He was in London when
Redmond made his speech on 3 August 1914 and
was so moved that the 'tears ran down his eyes
and made mud of the dust at his feet'.

Stephen Gwynn wore khaki when he appeared
on the platform. In calling for recruits he evoked
the memories of T. F. Meagher and his links
with Ballybricken. And John Redmond, 'leader
of the Irish race', had sent his only son to war
and his brother had also gone because the cause
was a worthwhile one. Noting that the 'really
poor of Ireland ... the labouring man' had done
'magnificently', he accused the 'middle class, the
people who send their sons to the Irish universities, or send their sons into the priesthood or
make clerks of them, or in some cases make shop
assistants of them' of not sending its 'fair proportion to the war'. He called on them to join the
ranks[247] offering his first squad commander, Mr
Lynch, 'a brilliant young Waterford man', as an
example to be followed.

Lieutenant Lynch subsequently spoke at a
recruiting meeting in the city during Sergeant
Michael O'Leary's visit in July 1915. Referring
to Germany as an 'unmanly nation', he urged
men to enlist. If they didn't 'their wives and
sisters and their homes would be threatened with
the barbarous hordes of Eastern Europe'. He also
declared, 'if any class in Waterford has not played
up it is the middle class, the class to which a lot
of you and I belong'.[248]

James O'Meara, a Ballybricken man, told the
audience that he had given up a £1-a-week job
to join the army and avenge his brother Michael
of Peter's Lane, Ballybricken, who 'had done his
duty like a man' and had saved the life of an
officer, Lieutenant Fitzgerald from the Quay,
before he was himself killed in October 1914.
Employed as a plasterer before his enlistment, it
is family tradition that he used to like 'the drink'
and while in drink declared his intention to get
the 'Bastard' who killed his brother. By this time
about 54 Waterford-born soldiers had died in the
war and no doubt several men who enlisted were
responding to emotions similar to those experienced by the speaker. O'Meara, a rifleman in the
7th Battalion Royal Irish Rifles, the same

246 Gwynn, S. (1919), p. 187.
247 *Munster Express*, 27 Mar. 1915; *Waterford Standard*, 27 Mar. 1915.
248 *Munster Express*, 24 July 1915.

regiment in which his brother had served, died of wounds on 17 April 1916.[249]

James English may well have found the rhetoric and excitement of the meeting overwhelming. But other more practical concerns are likely to have clinched his decision. As Table 1 shows, separation allowances were revised during March 1915 and Le Bas's use of this information during his propaganda campaign was considered to be a 'great inducement'. And Gwynn appealed to the Irishman's need to do his manly duty. The 16th Division was still thousands below strength. He told the audience that 'the honour of Ireland is bound up with the filling up of this Irish Division', observing 'wouldn't it be a poor thing' if it were filled up with English, Scots and Welsh.[250] He warned that if the war dragged on there would be conscription. Threats of conscription clearly had an impact on some men. James English told his wife that as he had volunteered to join the army he would not have to be 'dragged out from under the bed' by the government. He had done no more than his 'manly' duty.

He was among one of the batches of new recruits leaving Waterford North Station between 24 March and 1 April 1915. Seen off by large numbers of friends, many of the recruits belonged to the National Volunteers and were escorted to the station by the Erin's Hope Band.[251] As shown in Figure 2, the only battalion of the Royal Irish Regiment in the 16th Division was attached to the 47th Brigade. The battalions in this brigade were over strength but some battalions in the 48th Brigade and all battalions in the 49th Brigade were under strength.[252] This probably accounts for James English being posted to the 9th Munsters which was already in training at Ballyvonare camp.

Willie Redmond also left Waterford North Station for Mallow on 1 April when about 50 new recruits, including 20 cadets for the 7th Leinsters, were given an 'enthusiastic send-off'. Trains pulling out of the station were visible from Katey English's home in Thomas's Avenue on the hill, and after the war she frequently reminisced on how they had carried away the people she most loved.

249 *Waterford Standard*, 24 Mar. 1915. The personal family information was obtained in August 1990 from Mr William O'Meara, James and Michael O'Meara's nephew. Officially confirmed details were contained in a letter to him dated 20 January 1987 from Ypres Branch of the British Legion. At the time of this interview William O'Meara was secretary of the Waterford branch of the British Legion.

250 *Waterford Standard*, 27 Mar. 1915.

251 *Munster Express*, 3 Apr. 1915.

252 John Redmond, memorandum on recruiting, 16 June 1915 (Redmond Papers, 15,259), NLI.

Figure 2: A chart outlining the organisational structure of the 16th Division in relation to the First Army and with special reference to the 9th Battalion Royal Munster Fusiliers, as at 16 March 1916

(Source: Compiled from several sources, but the chart is built around the First Army's 'Order of Battle', 2 Mar. 1916 [PRO, WO 95/5467])

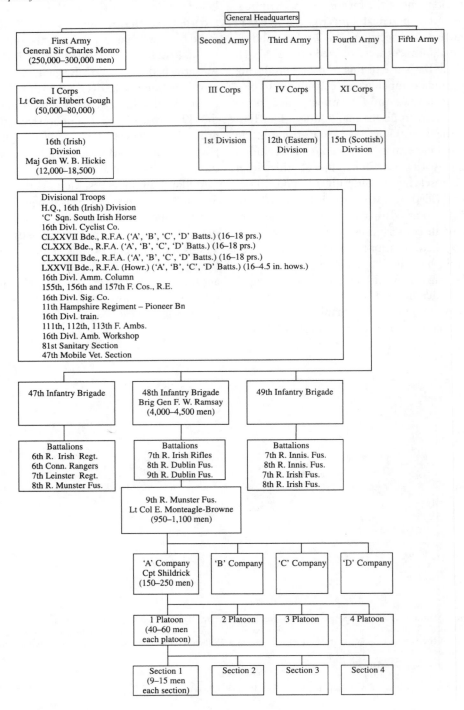

Plate 5

Army recruiting poster (August 1915), using the image of John E. Redmond,
leader of the Irish Parliamentary Party and MP for Waterford city
(National Library of Ireland)

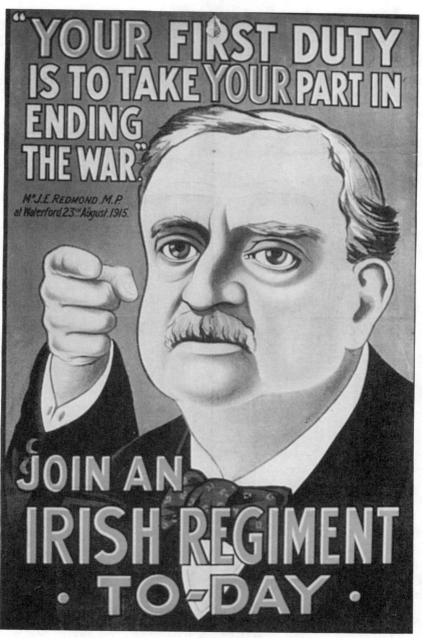

Plate 6

An army recruiting poster designed for use in Ireland (Imperial War Museum, London)

Plate 7

Examples of army recruiting advertisements appearing in the local Waterford press during 1915 (those from the *Waterford Standard* are reproduced by permission of the British Library)

YOUNG MAN

Is anyone proud of you?

Is your <u>mother</u> proud of you?

Is your <u>sister</u> proud of you?

Is your <u>sweetheart</u> proud of you?

Is your <u>employer</u> proud of you?

Is <u>IRELAND</u> proud of you?

If you are not making munitions, <u>get into khaki</u> at once.

Join an Irish Regiment
TO-DAY

and they will all be proud of you.

Waterford Standard
4 Sep. 1915

To the Young Women of Ireland.

Is your "Best Boy" wearing Khaki? If not, don't <u>you think</u> he should be?

If he does not think that you and your country are worth fighting for—do you think he is <u>worthy</u> of you?

Don't pity the girl who is alone —her young man is probably a soldier—fighting for her and her country—and for <u>you.</u>

If your young man neglects his duty to Ireland, the time may come when he will <u>neglect you.</u>

Think it over—then ask your young man to

JOIN AN IRISH REGIMENT TO-DAY.

Ireland will appreciate your help.

Waterford Standard
3 Mar. 1915

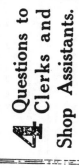

Questions to Clerks and Shop Assistants.

1. If *you* are between 19 and 38 years of age, are you really satisfied with what you are doing to-day?

2. Do you feel happy as you walk along the streets and see brave Irishmen in khaki who are going to *fight* for Ireland while you stay at home in comfort?

3. Do you *realise* that gallant Irish soldiers are risking everything on the Continent to save you, your children, and your womenfolk?

4. Will you tell your employer *to-day* that you are going to join an Irish Regiment?

Ask him to keep your position open for you—tell him that you are going to fight for Ireland. He'll do the right thing by you—all patriotic employers are helping their men to join.

TELL HIM <u>NOW</u> AND

JOIN AN IRISH REGIMENT TO-DAY.

Waterford News
5 Mar. 1915

Plate 8

Examples of product advertisements appearing in local Waterford newspapers during 1915, showing how military themes were used to heighten awareness of the war

Waterford News, 7 May, 1915

Waterford News, 15 Oct. 1915

Waterford News, 6 Aug. 1915

CHAPTER 6

In Training

I

Nationalists of all shades shared Roger Casement's fear that the British army 'anglicised' Irishmen and they saw this as explaining why men such as James English remained loyal to the 16th Division and to the British and allied cause. The loyalty of Irish soldiers to the 16th Division and the process by which it developed, however, is not adequately accounted for by the ill-defined concept of 'anglicisation'.

II

The practical consequences of the 16th Division being a British army unit and under the command of British or unionist officers could not be escaped. Only the infantry brigades of the division were predominantly Irish Catholic. The divisional troops which, as Figure 2 shows, formed a substantial part of the division, were overwhelmingly British. Other than three or four officers there were hardly any Irish in the division's field artillery, for example.[1] Moreover, the army was notoriously conservative, and as an institution it was not noticeably any different in 1921 from what it had been in 1912.[2] Irishmen were bound to the monarch by an oath and, like his British counterpart, the Irish soldier was required by military procedures to routinely demonstrate his loyalty to the crown. When in

church, for instance, soldiers of the 16th Division were required to stand to attention while singing the national anthem.[3]

Any political manifestations of an Irish nationalist identity could have been nothing more than symbolic. Redmond's vaguely articulated ambition that the division should constitute an Irish army owing allegiance to him and a future Irish home rule government was unrealistic within the existing institutional and legal framework. Therefore, in so far as they belonged to a British institution, Irish soldiers can be said to have been 'anglicised'.

But in a cultural sense, the degree to which the army corrupted a man's Irishness is far from obvious. Firstly, despite the rise of the Irish-Ireland movement, isolating significant differences in British and Irish cultural heritage outside of the traditional Irish-speaking areas is difficult, especially in the case of a Waterford-born man. Secondly, where cultural differences can be identified, for instance in respect of an Irishman's Catholicism and his nationalism, there is no evidence that these were deliberately or crucially undermined by the army. The 16th Division's infantry brigades retained their strongly Catholic, and to some extent their nationalist, character. Culturally, therefore, the charge that Irish soldiers were 'anglicised' is inconclusive.

The greatest potential danger to an Irish soldier's nationalist sentiment was on a more basic

---

1 De Montmorency (1936), p. 248.
2 Beckett, I., 'The British army, 1914–18: the illusion of change' in J. Turner (ed.) (1988), *Britain and the First World War*, London, pp. 96–116.
3 *Standing Orders—9th (Service) Battalion the Royal Munster Fusiliers* (Aldershot, 1914), p. 36. The copy to which reference is made in this book was issued to Lieutenant Francis Moran and is currently in the possession of Martin Staunton.

human level. The British army captured and institutionalised loyalty by a process which crossed national differences and bound soldiers to their unit and the other men in it.

In April 1916 around 85 per cent of men in the 16th Division's infantry battalions were Irish, with Britons making up the remainder. The loyalties and friendships which sprang up between individual soldiers and between units reinforced corporate rather than national loyalties. Englishmen in Irish regiments brawled with Englishmen in English regiments in 'defence of the honour of their chosen corps'. Although swearing an oath to serve a British monarch 'with some national qualms of conscience' in 1912, by 1914 John Lucy found, after the severe trial of war, that two of his 'best chums were Belfast Orangemen, and we all shared and suffered together and made merry too. We had nothing tangible to hold on to except each other' and they 'preserved and passed on the diluted *esprit de corps*'. There was also a mix in the commissioned ranks, although senior positions were generally held by Irish and English Protestants. But English officers could be 'genuinely fond' of Irish soldiers who, in their turn, 'well liked' the officers.

Irish and British soldiers shared experiences which set them apart from other men. Lucy observed how he and his comrades

> drew closer to each other than ever before in our lives, and we got to know and love each other as men never do in peace-time ... . My mind embraced my comrades, and my spirit bound them, and swept out protectingly over them in prayer, while my body pulsed to their marching.[4]

An intense training period as part of a virtually closed community was the beginning of a process which forged this powerful *esprit de corps*.

In the view of one officer 'the spirit of comradeship, and devotion to duty ... fostered at home never left the battalion, even in the hardest trials'.[5] And the rapport built up between soldiers and local residents in Ireland and England consolidated the process. An English recruit of Limerick parentage recorded how he had 'grown to love these Irish people' while training in Cork, even though the Irish recruits laughed at his accent.[6] Kipling, biased though he may have been, was none the less fair when he observed of men in training: 'there is a gulf opening between those who have joined and those who have not.'[7]

But the process did not entirely kill off political consciousness. A leader of the Connaught Rangers' mutiny in India in 1920 observed that when he joined the army in 1914 he had been told he was going to fight for the liberation of small nations, but found on his return to Ireland that 'as far as one small nation was concerned, my own, these were just words'.[8] And in 1922 the assassins of General Sir Henry Wilson, known in Ireland as the 'Orange Terror', were both ex-British soldiers. Private Reginald Dunne served with the Irish Guards on the western front and was medically discharged with an unblemished military record after being wounded. Lance Corporal Joseph O'Sullivan, permanently crippled as the result of a war wound, served in the Royal Munster Fusiliers and was medically discharged with a 'very good' military record. In a written statement submitted on behalf of both men at their trial, Dunne explained,

> we both joined [the army] voluntarily for the purpose of taking human life, in order that the principles for which this country stood should be upheld and preserved. Those principles we were told, were self-determination and Freedom for small Nations ... We came back from France to find that Self-Determination had been given to some nations we

4 Lucy (1992), pp. 191, 201, 294.
5 Walker, G. A. C. (1920), *The Book of the 7th (Service) Battalion Royal Inniskilling Fusiliers*, Dublin, p. 20.
6 Roworth, J. W., 'Experiences of "E. Casey" ', (unpublished MS) (Roworth Papers, 80/40/1), IWM.
7 Kipling (1915), p. 15.
8 Staunton (1986a), p. 10 (footnote).

have never heard of but that it had been denied to Ireland.

From the dock he said, 'I feel … proudly conscious that I am an Irishman … . I take a particular pride in … being a member of the Irish race.'[9]

However, Redmond acknowledged the potential potency of the socialisation processes in overcoming conflicting loyalties when declaring his belief that the war was an opportunity for north and south to bridge their differences. But this ideal foundered on the ingrained habits of separatism. Although Ireland formed a single army command, in composition and character the 16th (Irish) and the 36th (Ulster) Divisions conformed to traditional sectarian and political patterns.

The Ulster division was one of the most closely knit of Kitchener's formations. Its infantry battalions, wholly raised in Ulster, were largely comprised of Ulster Volunteers. They were exclusively Protestant and unionist. Only 14 Catholics joined the division and they were required to sign the Ulster covenant.[10] Ulster Catholics generally joined the 16th Division. When an arrangement for him to inspect the 36th Division was cancelled, General Sir Lawrence Parsons was 'very glad not to go'.[11] When he visited a northern Irish unit, Parsons was not saluted by a single officer—an apparent 'lesson for being a renegade, commanding Papists'. And men of the 36th Division daubed the musketry butts in Aldershot with slogans such as 'to hell with the Pope and the 16th Division' which had to be cleaned off before the 16th Division could use them.[12]

The concept of separateness was so fixed that there was panic when it was thought Protestant northerners joining the 16th Division were being mixed with Catholic southerners. Parsons had to reassure the under-secretary for war that the

Royal Inniskilling Fusiliers battalion concerned was made up of Ulstermen who were Catholics and largely nationalist Volunteers.[13] However, the rapid expansion of the army in 1914 threw men together from all social classes and backgrounds and recruits had to come to terms with each other as well as adjusting to army life, and this was part of the process which bound a man to his unit and comrades.

III

The 9th Munsters was overwhelmingly urban and Cork in composition and included members of the Royal Irish Constabulary as well as factory and brewery workers. However, social cohesion was largely achieved through the arduous training programme which wrought such a physical transformation in recruits that their appearance could encourage other men to enlist. But some of those who enlisted were physically ill-suited to army life.

Despite rejection rates estimated at over 48 per cent for Irish recruits generally and 58 per cent for Waterford city, with dental deficiencies as the primary cause, physically or mentally defective men were still recruited. Doctors were paid between 1s and 2s 6d for each man medically examined and nothing for those rejected. Examinations therefore tended to be fast and cursory and as the demand for recruits grew, standards were officially relaxed. Easily detectable disabilities were missed or deliberately overlooked. In one instance a sergeant invalided out of the 1st Munsters with a pension before the war, re-enlisted under a false name when war was declared and was soon a sergeant again.[14]

Of the men recruited into the 9th Munsters,

9 Taylor, R. (1961), *Assassination: The Death of Sir Henry Wilson and the Tragedy of Ireland*, London, pp. 106–10, 160–71. O'Sullivan joined the army in January 1915 and Dunne in June 1916.
10 Denman (1992b), p. 27.
11 Parsons, diary entry, 7 May 1915 (Parsons papers, MD 1111), Woolwich.
12 Robertson (1960), p. 129. She identified the unit as being the 16th Division's 49th Brigade. However, the brigade was mainly filled with Ulster Catholics and she is probably referring to a visit by Parsons to the 36th (Ulster) Division.
13 Tennant to Parsons, 26 Feb. 1915 and Parsons to Tennant, 27 Feb. 1915 (Parsons Papers, MD 1111), Woolwich.
14 Holt, H. B., untitled and undated MS (Holt Papers, 7603–69–1), NAM.

at least five can be identified as having been discharged with various illnesses within two or three months. One soldier who enlisted on 2 September 1915 was discharged unfit on 24 February 1916. He suffered 'from chronic asthma and never did a day's work since he joined: he has never been on parade; he has an attack of dyspnoea about twice a week and in the intervals has symptoms of bronchitis. Not due to military service'.[15]

However, the army provided those unskilled men who did manage the strict regime, with a standard of living better than that in civilian life. Food was generally superior to that ordinarily available to the lower working classes, one discriminating recruit in the 16th Division regarding it as 'excellent'. And there was plenty of it. Battalion orderly officers were required to certify that the meat and bread rations issued were of 'good quality and in proper quantity'.[16]

Recruits in training at Fermoy had more bread and tea than they needed. A pail of 'hot sweet tea' at 6 a.m. was followed two hours later by a breakfast of bowls of steaming tea, piles of fresh bread, a chunk of golden butter and tins of sardines or a plate of cheese or tinned salmon or a lump of brawn. Dinner at 1 p.m. could consist of soup, stewed beef and baked potatoes. The last meal of the day was tea at 4.30 p.m.[17] but men then had access to the wet and dry canteens. By December 1915 most camps had two trained cooks for each 100 men.[18] Kipling's assessment was that the men were 'extremely well looked after'.[19] And soldiers were encouraged to enter for technical instruction, qualify in a trade or take

up skilled army employment which would qualify them for 'good employment in civil life'.[20]

The army also offered advancement, the names of private soldiers likely to make good NCOs being called for periodically. However, those selected had to be 'smart, clean, well-educated men, and good shots'. But once a man was promoted to NCO rank, 'all intercourse and familiarity with his former comrades ... must be broken off',[21] and Lucy, who served in the rank, thought a 'newly made lance-corporal can be the unhappiest man in the army'.[22]

By late March 1915 the battalion had already been in training for about five months and had moved to Ballyvonare, near Buttevant, in January 1915. The training programme, calculated to break down a man's individuality, then to rebuild him 'in his new army role as a servant, pliant and totally subservient' has invoked criticism and anger in some war memoirs. Lucy recalled the 'repressive system of training which robbed us of our independence'.[23] But Robert Graves was of the view that the corporate spirit inculcated by the training methods won battles and this justified the loss of individual initiative.[24] Some men in the 16th Division found the experience 'very interesting'.[25] Training started with squad drill and recruits gradually progressed through platoon, company, battalion and brigade training to divisional exercises.

The section, the smallest unit within the army's hierarchical structure (see Figure 2), is a small, intimate unit commanded by a corporal and is considered by one authority to have been the 'strongest single sustaining force in the war'.

15 Lists of War Badges and Certificates issued to men discharged with wounds or through illness, 1914 to 1918 (WO 329/3006–09) PRO. The case cited is that of Private Charles McMahon.
16 'Report of orderly officer for the day', 7th Battalion Leinster Regiment, 27 June 1915 (Staniforth Papers), IWM.
17 Staniforth, letters, 18 and 24 Oct. 1914 (Staniforth Papers), IWM.
18 Printed War Office circular letters 103/General no./1280/A.G.2B dated 2 Sep. 1914 and 103/General no./1278/A.G.1 dated 9 Oct. 1914, (WO 162/3), PRO; *The Times*, 28 Dec. 1915.
19 Kipling (1915), p. 7.
20 1915 edition of 'The Small Book' issued to Corporal J. A. Smith, 3rd Battalion Royal Munster Fusiliers, pp. 23–25 (6404–96–8), NAM.
21 *Standing Orders—9th Munsters*, p. 14.
22 Lucy (1992), p. 63.
23 Ibid., p. 43.
24 Graves (1960), pp. 156–57.
25 Staniforth, letter, 18 Oct. 1914 (Staniforth Papers), IWM.

Soldiers were on first name terms and friend- ships could be close. Platoons were also small enough to foster intimate friendships and forge bonds between officers and men. New Army subalterns spent eight hours a day with their platoons and generally identified themselves with the men's interests on and off parade. The army considered the company a crucial unit. Officers and NCOs were instructed that the company

> should be complete within itself, ready for detached duty, and to act independently whenever required to do so. The Officers, Non-Commissioned Officers and Privates should be intimately acquainted with one another, animated by a common feeling and spirit, and should endeavour, under all cir- cumstances, to make their company the best in the battalion.[26]

The battalion tended to give a man his prestige and the divisional unit fostered pride and a close identity. Despite its size, most men in a division could know each other by sight. The army thus created a sense of belonging and place. For the first time, deprived and frequently under-valued men with a low social status were provided with a clear and valued purpose to their lives.

In Paul Fussell's opinion, Ian Hay's 'cheerful half-fictionalised account' of the 'wholesome fun to be had at the training camp' closely resembled the real army being trained in 1914.[27] Ian Hay, whose real name was John Hay Beith, was a journalist and prolific writer who served with the the Argyll and Sutherland Highlanders during the war. He described how training and sociali- sation processes could take a recalcitrant recruit from thinking of himself as one of an 'awkward, shy, self-conscious mob' complaining of being treated as a 'nobody' degraded by 'meaningless and humiliating gestures [saluting]' to the point

of observing that 'fresh air, hard training and clean living began to weave their spell'. He soon decided things could be done in the army 'with- out losing one's self-respect'.

The 'relentless schooling, under make-believe conditions'[28] was tough and tested the resolution and stamina of all ranks. Almost immediately on arrival at camp men were subjected to strict order and discipline with eight to ten hours a day, including Sundays, of squad drill, physical in- struction, running, marching, night-work and entrenching.[29] There was particular concern that a soldier's feet should be properly cared for. Detailed instructions on how to prevent sore feet was provided, and Parsons issued orders on how boots and socks should be properly fitted. Pla- toon commanders were instructed to ensure their men's feet were kept clean and to inspect them carefully after a long march or a long day's train- ing.[30] In camp or on the line of march, company officers were required to have a daily foot inspec- tion and an NCO trained in chiropody and with medical supplies was required to march at the rear of the battalion.[31]

Preliminary recruit training, in squads of be- tween 12 and 20 men or as individuals, lasted 'all day and every day' for about two months. Typi- cally, the day began at 6 a.m. with a run round the barrack square or parade ground which could make 'old fat men ... hideously stressed'. After pay night this would last for 20 minutes to sweat the drink out. Leap-frogging exercises followed. Then there was a 200 yards obstacle course until 8 a.m. when the men breakfasted and cleaned their quarters. Between 9 a.m. and 12.30 p.m. squad drill and physical training made up the heaviest work of the day when recruits were 'gathered up, flung out, shuffled and re-dealt on the parade ground'.

After dinner they would relax, shave and clean

26 *Standing Orders—9th Munsters*, p. 35.
27 Fussell (1975), pp. 28–29.
28 Hay (1915), p. 166 and Chapter 3.
29 Germains, V. W. (1930), *The Kitchener Armies.*, London, pp. 111–28.
30 Printed divisional circular letter from Lieutenant-General L. W. Parsons, 'Company training—16th Division', 15 Feb 1915 (Parsons Papers, MD 1111), Woolwich.
31 *Standing Orders—9th Munsters*, pp. 27, 42–43.

their rifles and kit. The 2 p.m. parade could be a short route march or further squad and physical drill with lectures on musketry and signalling until tea at 4.30 p.m. At 6 p.m. there would be lectures or a night outpost scheme. Alternatively, an evening pass might allow a visit to the shops or a pub in town. The gaslight was switched off at 10 p.m.

Preliminary training was completed when platoon drill was judged satisfactory. Company drill and field training, which followed, involved a completely different and more complicated set of manoeuvres. Trench digging was perfected and route marches were extended from about 6 to 30 miles. Rifle practice on the full range replaced that on the miniature range. In these activities there was 'great personal competition in the various platoons' and companies vied with each other to achieve the highest aggregate score. Battalion drill followed. When paraded for the first time at full strength, fully equipped and with its band, a battalion could be an 'imposing sight'.[32]

Tactical exercises involved simulated skirmishing in the Galtee mountains with men in full marching order including picks, shovels and rifles as well as the 'usual hardware shop'. During February 1915, when it rained or snowed nearly every day and the men had soaked and frozen feet and were drenched regularly, Staniforth observed of the Galtees, 'I never dreamed that God had made any spot like this'. The troops were 'curse[d], threaten[ed], and encourage[d] ... forward, leaping ditches, brushing through hedges, splashing into bog holes'. Brigade training, carried out by columns of fully equipped troops manoeuvring though the woods and mountains, was for Staniforth 'packed with interest and not a dull moment'.[33] Patrick MacGill also thought

brigade tactical training was more exciting than divisional exercises even though he found the latter 'on the whole an intensely interesting and novel experience'.[34]

During June the 9th Munsters moved to 'the renowned'[35] tented camp at Ballyhooly for about two months of field training. Soldiers were 'herded' 12 to a tent and the rain poured in. An officer in the Royal Dublin Fusiliers commented, 'the men are to be pitied'. The roads through the camps were badly cut up and deep in mud. Boots failed to keep out the wet and even the horses were 'wet and miserable'. By the end of July the camp was 'very unhealthy' and in one company 19 men were infected with lice. But pay night brought some relief. The men made an 'awful row' partying and singing, the language being 'quite indescribable'.

The 48th Brigade route marched and manoeuvred through torrents of rain. Entrenching practice from 8 a.m. until 11.30 p.m. was frequent and 'everyone [became] very tired and a bit fed up'. There were practices in manning and relieving trenches, lectures, rifle inspections by the brigadier, battalion ceremonial parades and kit cleaning when the rain was too heavy for outside work. Brigade and divisional schemes involved mock attacks by cavalry, and by infantry across precipitous mountains covered with heather and loose rocks, through the woods and on troops defending the bridge. The brigade returned to Ballyvonare camp on 10 August.[36]

On 18 August the 47th and 48th Brigades were inspected at Doneraile. General inspections involved 'much labour in the way of preparation'[37] but Parsons thought the turnout was 'very good' and Lord Lieutenant Wimborne wrote to Kitchener telling him of his own pleasure.[38] On 27 August, the *Waterford News* reported rumours

---

32 Staniforth, letters, 24 Oct. and 19 Dec. 1914, 3 Feb. and 23 May 1915 (Staniforth Papers), IWM; Simkins (1988), pp. 296, 304–09; Walker (1920), pp. 3–8.
33 Staniforth, letters, 14 Feb. and 27 June 1915 (Staniforth Papers), IWM.
34 MacGill (1915), pp. 45–46, 90.
35 Staniforth, letter, 18 Oct. 1914 (Staniforth Papers), IWM.
36 Beater, O. L., diary entries, 22 June to 20 Aug. 1915 (Beater Papers, 86/65/1), IWM.
37 MacGill (1915), p. 99.
38 Parsons, diary entries, 18 and 19 Aug. 1915 (Parsons Papers, MD 1111), Woolwich.

that the men from Hearne and Co. who joined the cadet company during Le Bas's campaign would be commissioned.[39] Four second lieutenants who were commissioned the following day joined the 9th Munsters.

Because opportunities to socialise with civilians were restricted, the sense of belonging to a close and self-reliant community was enhanced and this was bound to strengthen the corporate identity. Local pubs were compelled to close early and there was no leave for at least 10 to 15 weeks. Entertainment in camp was in the form of nightly variety turns. There was, for example, a 'highly successful' concert at a 'splendid new recreation hall' recently opened by the YMCA at Aghada camp[40] and concerts and lectures were provided at Fermoy barracks.[41]

Ballyvonare camp was located on land leased to the War Office by the Harold-Barry family. On the outbreak of war more land was acquired and hutments constructed.[42] The subaltern commanding a party of troops helping to set up a camp, found the 'Barry tribe ... most hospitable'.[43] And Sir Francis Vane, a major in the 9th Munsters, also became friendly with the family when contractors were commissioned to build hutments.[44] The standard hutted camp housed one battalion at war strength and the Ballyvonare camp was one of 260, accommodating 850,000 men and 150,000 horses, erected in the United Kingdom by July 1915.[45] Hutting costs were approximately £22,578,000 by August 1916,[46]

only about £750,000 (three per cent) of this being spent in Ireland.[47]

In the camps, wooden huts generally accommodated 30 men, although the *Waterford News* reported them as housing up to 100 personnel.[48] Huts were heated by stoves and recruits slept on hay palliasses. Each camp, accommodating about 1,150 men and 36 officers with their horses, was self-contained. Typically, they included sleeping huts, guardroom, cookhouse and wash up, regimental institute, and dry and wet canteens. There were separate messes for officers, sergeants and instructors. Other accommodation and facilities included a hospital, shower baths and ablution block, latrines, drying room, quartermaster stores, stables, harness room, forage store, dung pit, vehicle shed, electricity plant, coal yard, destruction shed, disinfector shed, rifle range (sometimes a miniature range), a revolver range and a parade ground.

With about 30 feet between huts there was no lack of space, but shortage of camp accommodation meant some troops had to be billeted with civilians. Kilworth had facilities for the setting up of several tented camps,[49] although commanders were instructed to provide hutments as sleeping accommodation in severe weather[50] and it was reported War Office regulations did not provide for sleeping under canvas after 1 October.[51] In the early stages of the war, however, a severe shortage of accommodation made this an impractical policy.

---

39 *Waterford News*, 27 Aug. 1915.
40 *Cork Constitution*, 14 Sep. 1915.
41 *Cork Constitution*, 24 Nov. 1914.
42 This information is extrapolated from an ordnance map of the locality containing information superimposed by the War Office on 25 Aug. 1916 (WO 78/4728), PRO.
43 Lyon, W. A., typescript memoirs, Vol 1, pp. 56–57 (Lyon Papers, 80/25/1), IWM.
44 Vane (1929), p. 249.
45 Dearle (1929), p. 48; Simkins (1988), p. 237.
46 *Approximate cost of the hutting provided, or being provided, for the accommodation of troops (including hospital patients) and horses in the United Kingdom in the years 1914 to 1916* (Aug. 1916 [Cd. 8193] XVII.559), British Parliamentary Papers.
47 O'Flanagan (1985), p. 16.
48 *Waterford Standard*, 11 Nov. 1914.
49 This account is extrapolated from: map of Kilworth camp, drawn up on 14 Apr. 1919 and corrected to 30 June 1921 (WO 78/3021), PRO; plans, Crosshaven hutted camp (WO 78/2540), PRO; Aghada, no. 1 east camp and west camp (WO 78/3425), PRO; site plan—proposed hutment at Belmont (WO 78/4706), PRO; Staniforth, letter, 4 May 1915 (Staniforth Papers), IWM.
50 Handwritten War Office memorandum, apparently written by Kitchener, *c.* Sep./Oct. 1914 (WO 162/20), PRO.
51 *Waterford Standard*, 7 Oct. 1914.

Although largely self-reliant, men in the camps were not isolated from local communities. Evening and weekend passes were possible and towns could be filled with soldiers who sought entertainment and female company, one pioneer officer noting that Fermoy and its environs was the 'sort of place where one needs to know where to go, or you'd be most unutterably bored'.[52] Soldiers attended races at Fermoy[53] and visited locally, sometimes making girlfriends.[54] An officer went to Cork reckoning it was 'worth spending money to get out of Kilworth for a few hours'. In Cork he slept in a real bed and lazed about in the sunshine. Civilisation after Kilworth, 'just a wind-swept collection of huts up among the hills', meant 'electric trams and cafes and plateglass windows and theatres'.[55]

The relationship between soldier and civilian was good, the 47th and 48th Brigades being made up of men considered to be 'manly, honourable and self-respecting'. They 'fraternised in the kindest way with the people' and made many friends.[56] Irishmen were thus encouraged in their British army role. The division conducted a butchery and bakery business. Soldiers were hired out to farmers for hay harvesting at 3s a day plus food and an army driver, wagon and pair of horses could be hired for 15s. In July the Central Council for the Organisation of Recruiting in Ireland resolved to publicise fully the availability of certain battalions for harvesting operations and to inform each rural district council that under certain conditions, horses and vehicles would also be available. The division's pioneer battalion (the 11th Hampshires) worked on repairs with the Great Southern and Western Railway Company and in return for the use of extensive camping grounds, they built roads for landowners.[57]

The War Office was at pains to avoid friction with landowners and farmers. Good prices were paid for horses[58] and stringent instructions regarding the acquisition of rights over land, compensation, and the use of land, were issued. Trenches constructed during training, for example, had to be reinstated.[59] Sir Francis Vane was sent a variety of gifts, including a blackthorn stick, eggs and a chicken, by local farmers. And a hotelier refused to take his money when he stayed the night.[60] Parsons told Redmond with some satisfaction that 'everywhere the farmers are obliging and the people receive the troops enthusiastically'.

The division was incomplete when it left for a period of final intensive training at Blackdown Camp in England. Parsons addressed the 48th Brigade before they went. The men were all well turned out, although he considered the 7th Royal Irish Rifles the best battalion on parade.[61] He saw the 11th Hampshires and the 47th Brigade off on 4 and 6 September. They were, he recorded, 'all sober and quiet and smart'.[62] Fermoy's townspeople gave them a 'hearty send-off', many scaling the railway station's walls to cheer the departing troops as regulations did not allow them onto the platform. A local newspaper commented that the troops were 'justly popular' and their conduct 'exemplary'. In the opinion of one local councillor, they were

in general, a different class to the ordinary

52   Sulman, P. L., letter (Sulman Papers, 82/29/1), IWM.
53   *Irish Times*, 17 Oct. 1917.
54   Roworth, J. W., 'Experiences of "E. Casey"' (unpublished MS) (Roworth Papers, 80/40/1), IWM.
55   Staniforth, letters, 3 Feb., 25 Mar., Sep. 1915 (Staniforth Papers), IWM.
56   *Cork Weekly Examiner*, 25 Sep. 1915.
57   Parsons to Redmond, 20 June 1915 (Redmond Papers, 1526 [14]), NLI; Sulman, letters (Sulman Papers, 82/29/1), IWM; *Daily Express* (Dublin), 8 July 1915.
58   *Cork Constitution*, 6 Aug. 1914.
59   Printed War Office circular letters, General no. 16/2976 (MT2), 25 Aug. 1914 and General no. 5/415 (MT2), 2 Oct. 1914 (WO 162/3), PRO; Simkins (1988), p. 237.
60   Vane (1929), p. 256.
61   Parsons, diary entry, 3 Sep. 1915 (Parsons Papers, MD 1111), Woolwich.
62   Parsons, diary entries, 4 and 6 Sep. 1915 (Parsons Papers, MD 1111), Woolwich.

soldier. They had no previous experience of military life, and their coming forward to join the brigade was a token of the good feeling which had recently grown up between the English and Irish people.

Another councillor thought they would do 'their duty faithfully to their King and country, and reflect credit on their own dear isle'. The conduct of the British units in the division was also considered to be good and a 'warm friendship existing between the Irish and English units was a very pleasing factor'.[63] A representative from Kilworth Rural District Council addressed the 11th Hampshires while they were drawn up on the parade ground at Moore Park and told them of his 'deep sense of regret' at their departure. The battalion's last march through Kilworth was accompanied by 'much cheering and handshaking'.[64]

There was also 'great cheering' as the 48th Brigade marched through Buttevant and entrained for Dublin's North Wall Quay on 8 September on what may well have been James English's first trip to the city. Within hours of their arrival in Dublin the troops were issued with rations and embarked on a boat trip of just over three hours during which guards equipped with a thousand rounds of ammunition watched out for submarines. A train journey of over nine hours to Frimley through Banbury, Oxford and Reading and with a stop for breakfast at Birmingham, followed disembarkation at Holyhead. They then marched the four and a half miles to their hutments in Blackdown Camp.[65] If this was James English's first visit to England, he had little time to explore it or savour any sense of adventure, as the 16th Division was promptly put to work.

The men were also brought closer to the war than they had been in the Irish camps. In Waterford, the suggestion by police that a flag should be flown on the workhouse building as a warning of aerial or other invasion prompted Alderman Hacket to ask jokingly if an attack was expected from the Fanning House charity men.[66] But on the same day as the 48th Brigade left for England, London was bombed by zeppelins. Twenty-two people were killed and 87 wounded. By the time the 16th Division left for France at the end of 1915, zeppelin raids had killed 127 people, wounded 352 others and caused damage to the value of about £713,000.[67]

Although shaded lighting had routinely been permitted, by the end of October Camberley's streets were in total darkness. A government order prohibited the use of outside lights in homes and business premises, and public lamps were only allowed by the police where necessary for public safety.[68] People prosecuted for driving cars with bright lights were fined between 10s and 21s.[69]

IV

On the day following their arrival at Blackdown, men of the 48th Brigade were cleaning up and whitewashing the camp, and unloading or loading transport at Farnborough Station. Three months of more training followed. There were kit inspections, route marches in 'incredibly dusty' conditions, company training and digging.[70] By late November it was snowing, but trenches continued to be dug and occupied for 48 hours. Socks received in a parcel from home were 'absolutely priceless'[71] and Father William Doyle

63 *Cork Constitution*, 9 Sep. 1915.
64 *Cork Constitution*, 10 Sep. 1915.
65 Beater, diary entries, 8 and 9 Sep. 1915 (Beater Papers, 86/65/1), IWM.
66 *Munster Express*, 3 Apr. 1915.
67 Young, P. (ed.) (1984), *World War 1 (1915–16)*, Vol. 4, New York, p. 1036; *Southern Daily Echo*, 9 Sep. 1915.
68 *Camberley News*, 30 Oct. 1915.
69 *Camberley News*, 11 and 18 Dec. 1915.
70 Beater, diary entries, 10 Sep. to 19 Dec. 1915 (Beater Papers, 86/65/1), IWM.
71 Staniforth, letters, 10 and 28 Nov. 1915 (Staniforth Papers), IWM.

was moved to remark that camp life was 'in many respects repellent … my eyes have been opened still more to the awful godlessness of the world'. A battalion marching out at 5 a.m. in torrents of rain 'for exercise' would return in the evening and 'dry their wet underclothing by sleeping in them'![72]

It took nearly two months for the whole division to complete its course on the Pirbright rifle ranges, working daily from 8 a.m. until 4.30 p.m. with a 15-minute sandwich break.[73] Rumours that the division, which contained a 'great many Waterfordmen' who joined during the special recruiting campaign in March and April, was going to the Dardanelles were circulating in Waterford by the end of September[74] but were wildly inaccurate.

The process of building an *esprit de corps* and bridges to the local community continued. In camp, bands entertained the men and with beer at 2d a pint there was lots of singing. The troops fraternised with the local community which included a small Irish colony. They played football together and the soldiers flocked in their 'thousands' to Camberley in search of entertainment. Father Twomey, a local Irish priest, and members of his congregation established the Catholic Schools Club for men of the division. Open Saturdays and Sundays between 3 and 9 p.m., an average of a thousand men used its tea rooms during weekends. Increasingly popular with all ranks, and with only enough tables to accommodate 30 customers at a time, men were admitted on a 15-minute ticket. A green flag hung over the entrance and the club offered Irish newspapers, writing materials, games and Irish songs, dance and music. Among the soldiers were several 'excellent' singers and entertainers who performed while local residents accompanied them with musical instruments.

Lady and General Sir Lawrence Parsons visited the club in October. He thanked Father Twomey and his local helpers for their kindness to the division and told the men of complimentary remarks made about them by the people of Camberley. Soldiers sang and danced for the Parsons and Father Twomey told the men,

> we are deeply … grateful for all you are doing to defend us who are living here in safety and security; from our hearts we are deeply grateful to all the soldiers and sailors of the British Army and Navy.

Telling them they had a reputation to maintain, he concluded, 'we will take a deeper interest in your welfare as our own division'. And in October, Major-General Dalrymple read out a letter from the officer commanding the 5th Connaught Rangers, which had fought in the Dardanelles, to 300 soldiers in the club. They listened with 'rapt attention' as the letter described how bravely and gallantly the Rangers had performed.

A squadron of the South Irish Horse was included in the divisional troops, and 170 members of the unit who arrived in November were billeted in the Camberley Drill Hall. Some of them participated in choir concerts at the local Wesleyan chapel. The minister also organised Saturday evening concerts to which soldiers were admitted free. Recreation, games and billiards were also available. One Camberley resident, concerned that the various denominational clubs were so overcrowded that troops were left to wander the streets, called on the town's population to invite soldiers into their homes. Sacks, it was advised, could be used to protect carpets.[75] Races at the camp were organised under the auspices of county clubs. In October company teams ran a course between Blackdown and Pirbright and prizes were distributed.[76]

---

72 O'Rahilly, A. (1925), *Father William Doyle, S.J.*, London, p. 395.
73 Staniforth, letter, 10 Nov. 1915 (Staniforth Papers), IWM; Beater, diary entry, 19 Dec. 1915 (Beater Papers, 86/85/1), IWM; Walker (1920), pp. 12–13.
74 *Waterford News*, 1 Oct. 1915.
75 *Camberley News*, 9, 23 Oct., 13 Nov., 18 Dec. 1915 and 8 Jan. 1916.
76 *Camberley News*, 30 Oct. 1915.

The local community also showed their interest in the Irish troops in other ways. A committee for the despatch of parcels to the 600 soldiers of the Royal Munster Fusiliers who were prisoners in Germany was organised at Farnborough. That only 200 of the prisoners were unwounded should, it was urged, 'secure the sympathy of everyone. The valour and the fine fighting qualities of the Irish are known ... there is not one who has not a warm corner of his or her heart for the Irish'.[77] And the local press reported the effect of John Redmond's visit to the Arklow munitions factory as being to encourage workers who are already 'straining their efforts to the utmost'.[78]

Locals were also impressed with the division's Catholicism. In what was regarded as a 'unique' occasion at Aldershot, Cardinal Bourne took a parade of the 47th and 48th Brigades. 'The reverence with which the whole assembly sank to their knees as he pronounced the benediction made the spectacle one that will not be easily forgotten.' Accompanied by Parsons, Cardinal Bourne addressed the men, telling them it had been 'their own sense of duty, their own conscience ... which had impelled them to take up arms in defence of their country, of the Empire and of their King'. Their enemies had thought there would be dissension at home,

> but the historical declaration of the leader of the Irish Party at the outset of the war ... swept away at once the hopes of their enemies. The 16th Division was the living embodiment of the wish and the declaration of that illustrious leader.

The cardinal cautioned them, 'there will be many who in the chance of war will never see Ireland again. Be prepared, if God asks [you], to make the supreme sacrifice of [your] own lives.

Be prepared to pass into the Divine presence.' He was reassured to know they were ready to 'do their duty as good children of Ireland, as good sons of the King, as good sons of the Catholic Church'. Led by its own fife and drums band each battalion then marched off to continue its preparations for war while Bourne and Parsons lunched together.[79]

It was customary for the king to inspect army divisions before they left for the front. Because he had been injured, however, the queen took the review of the 16th Division on a 'cold, bleak' Thursday afternoon on 2 December. She was reportedly the 'recipient of a splendidly loyal demonstration', during which the Irish troops gave a 'hearty cheer'. The effect of the monarch on Irish troops during a ceremonial parade was probably similar to that on Scottish soldiers as described by Ian Hay. Observing there was little rapport between the working-class soldier and the monarch, the soldier none the less responded to an infectious emotion and found himself cheering lustily.[80] The queen gave the king's message to General Parsons and this was later communicated to the troops:

> Your loyal response to the call to arms and the keen, cheerful spirit which I am told you evinced during a long and arduous period of training are most gratifying to me, and convince me that on the field of battle you will not only maintain but add to the glorious tradition of my Irish regiments.[81]

On 10 December 1915 the division was notified that embarkation for overseas would begin on the 17th. This, according to MacGill, was a time when the 'heart of every man thrilled with excitement'.[82] The 47th and 48th Brigades began preparing for their departure to the front. The 49th Brigade, still undermanned, left during

77 *Aldershot News*, 19 Nov. 1915.
78 *Southern Daily Echo*, 2 Sep. 1915.
79 *Aldershot News*, 19 Nov. 1915.
80 Hay (1915), pp. 19–24.
81 Parsons, diary entry, 2 Dec. 1915 (Parsons Papers, MD 1111), Woolwich; *Camberley News*, 4 and 11 Dec. 1915; *Cork Weekly Examiner*, 22 Jan. 1916; Walker (1920), pp. 14–15.
82 MacGill (1915), p. 106.

February 1916. Furlough was granted to troops before embarkation overseas and James English almost certainly spent his final 48 hours leave at home. During the week following the queen's review a number of Waterford men, including those Hearne and Co. employees who had joined the cadet company, were reported to have finished their training at Blackdown and to be on short leave in Waterford.[83] The final four days before embarkation were spent packing kit, receiving vaccinations and being inoculated.

A farewell concert was given for the infantry brigades and the South Irish Horse at Father Twomey's Catholic Schools Club and was reported by the local English press in a way which emphasised the Irish-English connection. 'Never again,' it was declared, 'will there be in these schools such fun, frolic and light-hearted laughter.' A 'genuine Irish welcome' had been given to 'the boys' and in return for this hospitality they had made the time 'merry, bright and cheerful' for themselves and for their entertainers. 'Merry peals of laughter' had filled the rooms.

Private Walsh of the cadet company proposed a toast of thanks to the 'English people of the whole district' as well as to Father Twomey's congregation. A spokesman from the South Irish Horse said 'the Irish soldier had never before, in any other place, been so well received as in Camberley district'. All the Protestants of the cavalry unit were said to have a 'great regard for Father Twomey ... the fearless bravery of the Catholic chaplains at the front made a deep impression on the non-Catholic soldier'. Father Twomey told the men his work for the division had been 'a labour of love. They all would follow with deep interest the history of this division and they all felt sure that the "Irish Brigade" would uphold the fighting qualities of the Irish soldier'. The term 'Irish Brigade', as in this instance, was gen-erally used to describe the 16th Division but was also frequently used to describe the 47th Brigade which had been cleared and filled by National Volunteers.

The 47th Brigade left for France on 17 December. Major-General William B. Hickie, now in command of the 16th Division, was at the station to see it off. He wrote to Redmond to tell him that there were no 'malefactors' and only one man out of 4,200 was drunk.[84] Parsons, also present to see the brigades off, noted the men were 'very sober and quiet' with the one drunken exception being left behind.[85] The 48th Brigade marched out of Blackdown Camp for the last time on Sunday 19 December 1915. An officer of the 9th Dublin Fusiliers probably summed up the feelings of most men when he wrote,

after ... fifteen months of solid strenuous training, in hail, rain, heat and snow, we were off! How often during the past year had the wail gone up from anxious and impatient subalterns, 'Will we ever get out?' ... [Now it was the] beginning of a new chapter in the great adventure.

But it had apparently been worth it. When soldiers filed out to form up on the parade ground, he reflected on how

we feel proud and happy as we look along the ranks ... how different they looked a year ago, and what months and months of unremitting toil, and love, and patience have gone to make them what they are.

As the officer glanced back over the rifle range on that 'bright December afternoon' he knew that some men would 'never see it again'.[86] One young officer recalled how his morale was so high when he left for France that he thought the enemy's only option was to 'pack in'. He was soon to record how he was 'sadly disillusioned'.[87]

83 *Waterford News*, 10 Dec. 1915.
84 Hickie to Redmond, 17 Dec. 1915 (Redmond Papers, 15 261 [10]), NLI.
85 Parsons, diary entries, 17 and 19 Dec. 1915 (Parsons Papers, MD 1111), Woolwich.
86 Beater, diary entry, 19 Dec. 1915 (Beater Papers, 86/65/1), IWM.
87 Lyon, typescript memoirs, Vol. 1, p. 57 (Lyon Papers, 80/25/1), IWM.

Between 17 and 19 December the 16th Division, short of the 49th Brigade and some divisional troops, left Farnborough with 396 officers, 11,447 other ranks, and its horses and equipment, in 27 trains.[88] Battalions were played out of barracks by their own bands, the men marching in full kit of around 65 lbs deadweight. They carried a rifle and bayonet, 120 rounds, entrenching tool, filled water bottle, mess tin, mug and plate, their pack containing shirts, socks and underclothing, and a holdall. A service blanket and waterproof sheet were strapped to the outside of their pack.[89] The 9th Munsters, comprising 30 officers, 999 other ranks and 72 horses, entrained for Southampton in two parties at 9.35 a.m. and 10.50 a.m. at Farnborough Station for a journey of about one hour and 40 minutes.

Embarkation followed within about an hour of their arrival at Southampton and they crossed to Le Havre in three steamers, two carrying troops and the third carrying their transportation. Pipers played the ships out of port. The passage was of about four to seven hours duration and two circling warships acted as escort. The 9th Munsters arrived in Le Havre at 1 a.m. on Monday 20 December and marched the two miles to a rest camp where they breakfasted and awaited the arrival of their transportation. From the rest camp, the battalion marched to the railway station where the men drew rations and they and their transport were loaded into trains about three times longer than the normal British passenger train. Officers had a carriage of their own, while other ranks wearing full marching packs were crowded into closed cattle trucks with straw on the floor and marked '40 *Hommes 8 Chevaux*'. For some, the journey appeared to be the beginning of a great adventure 'full of thrill and excitement' as they stood on the 'threshold of momentous events'.[90]

The men did not know where they were going, how long it would take to get there or what the eating arrangements were. Sleep was impossible and the soldiers suffered 'many, many hours of discomfort'. However, the train moved so slowly they could exercise by walking alongside it. The battalion arrived at Noeux les Mines at midnight on Tuesday 21 December. Stephen Gwynn recalled that 'as we shook ourselves together for the march to strange billets' his first impression 'was the sound of guns'.[91] It was a sound Patrick MacGill found 'ominous and threatening'.[92]

88 War Diary, 16th Division, entries 17 to 19 Dec. 1915 and appendix (WO 95/1955), PRO.
89 Beater, diary entry, 20 Oct. 1915 (Beater Papers, 86/65/1), IWM.
90 MacGill, P. (1984), *The Red Horizon*, Kerry, pp. 25–26.
91 Gwynn, S. (1919), p. 213.
92 MacGill (1984), p. 29.

CHAPTER 7

At the Front

I

The process of bonding, developed during the period of training in Ireland and England, was intensified when men entered the war zone and shared the dangers and experiences of a world little understood by those outside of it. There was no evidence of Irish and British soldiers dividing along national lines and after living in the trenches with the Irish, Scottish soldiers expressed 'a great admiration' for them.[1] Within the 16th Division, Irishman, Briton, Protestant and Catholic closed ranks as they struggled to survive in a troglodyte world of sustained tension and sudden death.

A London-born soldier in a predominantly British divisional unit recalled his deepening regard for the Irishmen in his unit and how 'very attached we became' to men of the 16th Division while in France.[2] And an Englishman, for two years an officer in an Irish regiment, when visiting Ireland for the first time in the autumn of 1916, was struck by the difference between Irishmen at home and the Irishmen he knew at war.[3] English troops serving in Irish regiments grew to identify strongly with them and with the 16th and 36th Divisions.[4] Tom Kettle, although writing 'I am calm but desperately anxious to live',

none the less turned down opportunities to get out of action because 'I have chosen to stay with my comrades'.[5] And he caught the sense of a greater ideal surmounting the divisions of nationality when he wrote:

> I have mixed [too] much with Englishmen and with Protestant Ulstermen to know that there is no real or abiding reason for the gulfs, saltier than the sea, that now dismember the natural alliance of both of them with us Irish nationalists. It needs only a *fiat lux*, of a kind very easily compassed, to replace the unnatural with the natural.[6]

A pre-war extreme nationalist who knew some of the executed insurgents personally, considered deserting the army and taking up the 'cause' after the Easter Rising. He decided against it because he thought desertion was wrong in principle but also as part of the Royal Inniskilling Fusiliers he had a sense of being a 'unit in the Great War, doing and suffering, admiring great endeavour and condemning great dishonour'. He reconciled this stand with his Irish nationalism: 'is not every honour won by Irishmen on the battlefields of the world Ireland's honour, and does it [not] tend to the glory and delight of her posterity?'[7] Long after the war had ended Irishmen who survived,

1 *Waterford Standard*, 1 Mar. 1916. A letter written by a Scottish soldier expressing the views of men in his Scottish unit. Originally published in the *Glasgow Herald*, it was reproduced in the *Waterford Standard*.
2 Newman, R. H. (*c.* 1974), 'Guns, guts and gunners' (unpublished MS), p. 46 (Newman Papers, MD 1169), Woolwich. Newman was a bombardier, later promoted to sergeant, with the 177th (Fulham) Brigade, Royal Field Artillery. The brigade was a divisional unit with the 16th Division (see Figure 2).
3 Colyer, W. T., 'War diary' (Colyer Papers, 76/51/1), IWM.
4 Perry (1994).
5 Denman (1992b), p. 97.
6 Gwynn, D. (1932), p. 525.
7 Karsten (1983).

like their British comrades, had a sense of pride in belonging to the First World War army.

Service at the front drew men of the 16th and 36th Divisions closer together. Lucy remarked on how Orangemen and nationalists 'buried the hatchet of bigotry' during the war, Ulstermen and southerners cheering when John Redmond inspected them.[8] In December 1916, the Commander of V Corps noted that the 16th and 36th Divisions were 'the best of friends. ... What a pity it is that the Irish are not made to enlist. They would like it and it might help a lot to make the two parties agree'.[9] And the commander of IX Corps, in which both divisions served and fought together, had no doubts that the friendship would last and 'be of great value later on in more troublesome times that may be in store'.[10]

Lieutenant-General Sir Hubert Gough of Curragh 'mutiny' fame, underwent a change of opinion as a result of his war experiences. Initially suspicious of the 16th Division, he asked for it to be placed under his command. But nationalist officers won his 'esteem and affection' and he used men described as 'Sinn Feinners and Fenians' as his bodyguard.[11] Both the 16th and 36th Divisions served under Gough and in his opinion they got on 'admirably together in the most friendly way and full of good companionship'. His subsequent view was that the 'North and South could get on very happily together if they were wisely handled'. The 'wise handling' should include 'some form of Home Rule for Ireland, within the Empire'.[12] Willie Redmond also spoke of Irishmen from north and south coming together as friends and a priest, ironically seeing the European war as a vehicle for reconciliation in Ireland, commented 'would to God

that the whole of Ireland were in Flanders today! Then there would be peace'.[13]

Collective experience of trench life in the struggle against a commonly identified enemy was a powerful dissolvent of political and national differences. In one view, 'ethnic hostilities engendered in peacetime seemed feeble and irrelevant compared with shared hatred of the Hun'.[14] Emotions functioned at a more basic level, intensifying the common bonds and mutual interests among men who lived according to a unique set of values and standards.

However, politicians who did not share their experiences saw things differently. When amalgamation was suggested as one way of overcoming recruiting difficulties in the 16th and 36th Divisions, John Redmond and Edward Carson objected. Officers of the 36th Division thought the loss of the title 'Ulster' would be 'deeply felt', but their reaction was just as likely to be a consequence of divisional pride as of political prejudice. Loyalty to their regiments, friends and comrades has been assessed as having isolated Irish troops from divisive attitudes at home and kept them going.[15] Some knowledge of a soldier's daily routines is necessary for an understanding of how this loyalty could burgeon and how he could become divorced from events at home.

II

Noeux les Mines, in which the 9th Munsters had been billeted on their arrival, was a 'one horse place' about five miles behind the firing line.[16] Christmas Day was 'wet, blowing and altogether cheerless' but relatively quiet. In Waterford there

8 Lucy (1992), p. 345.
9 General Fanshawe to Parsons, 17 Dec. 1916 (Parson Papers 1914–1916), King's College, London, Liddell Hart Centre for Military Archives (hereafter King's College).
10 Alex Hamilton Gordon to Parsons, 7 Dec. 1916 (Parsons Papers, MD 1111), Woolwich.
11 Denman (1992b), pp. 68, 142.
12 Gough (1954), p. 182.
13 Redmond (1917), p. 27.
14 Fitzpatrick, 'The overflow of the deluge' in MacDonagh and Mandle (eds.) (1986).
15 Perry (1994).
16 Marks, T. P. (1979), *The Laughter Goes from Life*, London, pp. 79–84.

was a marked absence of drunkenness,[17] a condition no doubt due to the large number of men away with the army. But there was 'plenty of good cheer' reported among the men in the waterlogged environment of the front.[18] One soldier thought the dinner was 'quite good'. There were no fowls but it 'rose to the dignity of a fine plum pudding'.[19] In the trenches, however, the weather was so cold that frozen army-issue Christmas cakes (probably a reference to plum puddings) could be struck against the side of the trench with no effect.[20] For one soldier

> the only thing that broke the monotony of an otherwise dark, dreary Christmas was the mail. It came in early and nearly everybody had something in the way of a parcel, and everybody had letters with Christmas cards and good wishes from home. We spent almost an hour chatting and talking of home and other Christmases after dinner until the whistle went for parade when all was forgotten in the usual run of duty, and from then on Christmas, as far as we were concerned, was at an end. We went to bed that night quite early and quite sober. It was the most dreary and commonplace Christmas I ever had.[21]

The division was assigned to the Loos salient until August 1916 (see Map 3). It was, according to one journalist, 'hideous territory'.[22] Between 4 and 10 January 1916 the 9th Munsters had their first experience of the war when the battalion's companies were attached to veteran Scottish units for initial instruction in the trenches. It was a moment when the heart of a young soldier was stirred with the 'romance of a mission'.[23]

Soldiers of the 9th Munsters joined thousands of men occupying the trenches in front of Philosophe. But there was 'not a sign of human life above ground'. The terrain was

> flat and chalky. Every trench showed up clearly as a ragged white line scratched on the surface of mother earth. The stiffness of the soil permitted trenches to be dug of great depth and with perpendicular sides.[24]

If the Irishmen did not see the enemy, they heard him. Two soldiers from 'B' Company reported the German lines as being 'quite close' as they could hear enemy soldiers talking.[25]

An unidentified journalist's despatch appearing in an Irish newspaper during March 1916 described this sector of the front as a 'squalid slum of war, filthy and disgusting'. It was a

> foul stretch of country in which all the obscenity of war lies naked ... . There is a look of death over all the ground, white and leprous as though the earth had gone bad under the blight of war, and everywhere it is scarred by trenches and shell craters.

The writer was 'fascinated and frightened by the desolation'. Many of the trenches abandoned by the Germans during the Battle of Loos in September and October 1915 were disintegrating. The relics of German occupation, tools, weapons and top-boots, protruded from the soil. The smell of gas lingered as did a 'sense of spectral things'. The fierce fighting had

> left behind ... an exaltation of horror, not

---

17 *Waterford News*, 31 Dec. 1915.
18 *Cork Examiner*, 27 Dec. 1915. Letter from a soldier at the front.
19 *Cork Weekly Examiner*, 15 Jan. 1916. Letter from Lance-Corporal M. J. Duffy of Kerry, a soldier of the 16th Division, to his father, an ex-RIC sergeant.
20 Staunton (1986a), p. 223.
21 *Waterford Standard*, 9 Feb. 1916. Letter from H. P. Barron, with a field ambulance unit attached to the 16th Division, to a local business man.
22 Gibbs, Sir Philip, 'Prelude to Loos tragedy' in J. A. Hammerton (ed.) (c.1930), *The Great War, I was there*, Vol. 1, London, pp. 459–64.
23 MacGill (1984a), p. 300.
24 Jervis, H. S. (1922), *The 2nd Munsters in France*, Aldershot, pp. 21–24.
25 *Cork Weekly Examiner*, 26 Feb. 1916. Letter from Privates John Walsh and Martin Malville, both of 'B' Company, 9th Munsters.

Map 3 A map of the Loos salient, March 1916, showing some of the trench system. See also Plate 15
(Sources: Adapted from HMSO trench maps 36b NE4; 36b SE2; 36c NW3; 36c SW1)

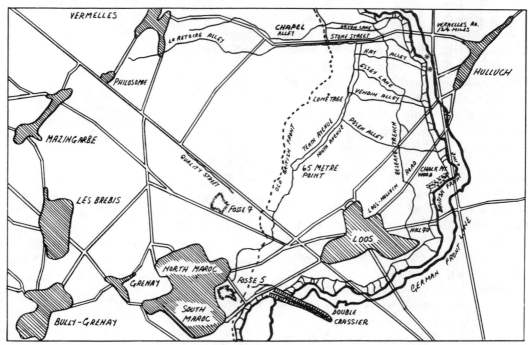

* Sites where German mines exploded 26 March 1916

supernatural, but creeping actually about ... from the litter of destruction, where many mangled bodies lie half-buried beneath bricks and dust and many graves are scattered among the rubbish heaps, and scraps of cloth, bits of soldiers' letters, blood-stained rags are stirred by the wind.

Guns were busy in the sector before dusk and despite bursting shells and the ground being mined beneath them, the soldiers carried on.

No single figure stirred in all this grey solitude of chalk fields which holds great armies ... . I wondered at the valour of the men who dwell in these ditches ... . It is a bad, sad place, haunted by the spectre of a murderous war, and nothing of good is there, between

Loos and Hulluch, except the coming and going of men who face all its horror with grave, steady eyes, and a fine patient faith in things that are better than this.[26]

In something of an understatement, a soldier in the 11th Hampshires thought the battlefield 'interesting but rather grim'.[27] Another officer found the front line 'a world so unreal that it was like being on another planet'.[28] Before long debris belonging to dead Irishmen also littered the battlefield. Photographs belonging to Joseph Twohig of the 9th Munsters who was killed in April, were found in a dug-out.[29]

German shelling of the sector and British retaliation occurred every day and night during the battalion's first period in the trenches. Bom-

26 *Cork Weekly Examiner*, 1 Apr. 1916.
27 Sulman, letter, 19 Jan. 1916 (Sulman Papers, 82/29/1), IWM.
28 Staunton (1986a), pp. 330–31.
29 *Cork Weekly Examiner*, 24 June 1916.

bardments varied in intensity but shells fell on Chapel Alley, Devon Lane, Hay Alley, Essex Lane, Vendin Alley, Posen Alley, Chalk Pit Wood, 9th and 10th Avenues, Fosse 7, the old British line, Quality Street, 65 Metre Point and the Loos–Hulluch Road. Mazingarbe, Grenay, Maroc, Loos and their trench systems were also shelled, sometimes heavily. Bombardments of a location could be intermittent or lasted an hour or more with rounds fired at the rate of one a minute. Some days were considered 'comparatively quiet'.[30]

Patrick MacGill wrote of there being 'no escape from their [the shells'] frightful vitality, they crushed, burrowed, exterminated; obstacles were broken, and men's lives were flicked out like flies off a window pane'. He recorded the 'terrible anxiety' of men who waited passively for their arrival,[31] and Tom Kettle thought the use of artillery was 'an outrage ... against simple men'.[32] Soldiers either harboured in a dugout and hoped for something other than a direct hit or made themselves as small as possible in a funk hole. A mortar bomb killed a man standing next to Staniforth and another soldier was decapitated by an exploding shell.[33] After his first experience of the trenches, Willie Redmond wrote the 'shelling was terrific' and added, 'the destruction, havoc and suffering I have encountered ... is truly appalling'.[34] Death in the trenches was, according to Tom Kettle, 'random, illogical, devoid of principle'.[35]

In a letter home, however, one soldier wrote that the trenches were 'not altogether so dangerous as some of the returned chaps would have you believe, and if you keep well under cover, and not get curious as to what is in your imme-

diate front, you are all right'. Considering the amount of 'metal flying around' casualties were few. At night, however, the scene was an 'eerie one' with shells screaming overhead and star shells bursting. And snipers 'are everywhere'. He firmly believed that they could 'take your little finger off if you put it over the parapet'.[36] The experience provoked a London Irishman into accusing the newspapers at home, with their false pictures of war, as being 'great liars'.[37] According to another, enemy gunfire on 10th Avenue, the old German front line, was seldom accurate and the trench's greatest drawback was the 'abundance' of rats infesting it.[38] Rats, ceaseless noise and the fear of shelling and snipers were just some of the discomforts suffered by soldiers of the Irish division.

For Staniforth life in the trenches was 'just squalor and sordid beastliness past all describing'. Water in the fire trench was ankle deep and in some places thigh deep. Mud covered men head to foot and chalk stuck to their boots. Within a week he sought to dissuade people at home of any romanticised notions. In order to get a correct picture of the front line, he told them to

imagine a garbage heap covered with all the refuse of six months—rags, tins, bottles, bits of paper, all sifted over with the indescribable greyish ashen squalor of filthy humanity. It is peopled with gaunt, hollow-eyed tattered creatures who crawl and swarm about upon it, and eye you suspiciously as you pass—men whose nerves are absolutely gone: unshaven, half-human things moving about in a stench of corruption.[39]

30 War Diary, 9th Munsters, entries, 4 to 10 Jan. 1916 (WO 95/1975), PRO; War Diary, First Army, entries, 4 to 10 Jan. 1916 (WO 95/160), PRO; Reports on Operations of the IVth Corps, 31 Dec. 1915 to 7 Jan. 1916 and 7 to 14 Jan. 1916 (WO 95/161), PRO; War Diary, IV Corps, entries, 4 to 10 Jan. 1916 (WO 95/713), PRO.
31 MacGill (1984b) p. 34.
32 Denman (1992b), p. 145.
33 Staniforth, letter, 29 Dec. 1915 (Staniforth Papers), IWM.
34 Cork Weekly Examiner, 19 Feb. 1916.
35 Denman (1992b), p. 64.
36 Cork Weekly Examiner, 15 Jan. 1916. Letter from Lance-Corporal M. J. Duffy.
37 MacGill (1984a), p. 103.
38 Walker (1920), p. 32.
39 Staniforth, letter, 29 Dec. 1915 (Staniforth Papers), IWM.

He noted the 'boredom and weariness, utter and absolute' of these first days in the trenches. There was 'nothing to see but mud walls, nowhere to sit but on a wet muddy ledge; no shelter of any kind against the weather ... no exercise to take in order to warm yourself '.[40] An unforgettable experience of the trenches was the sense of 'enclosure and constraint' and of being 'unorientated and lost'.[41] Letters from home, reading papers and the prospect of leave were the only things to distract minds from the dullness and monotony.[42] News from home was, therefore, an important morale booster. An officer observed how, when mail was given out, he had seen 'hardened men turn away broken hearted because they hadn't a letter'.[43]

Newspapers, including advertisements, were read through more than once. They provided the front line soldier with information on how the war was going; they helped him to pass the time and they provided topics of conversation.[44] A despairing soldier wrote home 'we are in a bad way as regards news, as we rarely see a paper'.[45] However, a private in the 1st Royal Irish Regiment told how the *Waterford News* was greatly welcomed by the 'lads from the old city' at the front. It was read and passed on every week.[46] Illiterate soldiers like James English were therefore thrown more completely onto the support of comrades.

Soldiers at the front were told nothing of the war and became concerned only with the immediate job in hand.[47] A veteran recalled how 'very often we hardly knew where we were or why we were there until we found ourselves in some unpleasant situation'.[48] They lived a day-to-day existence until things happened.[49] Ordinary soldiers, told they were 'only to obey', often did not know when a battle was taking place.[50] Only in headquarters did the war make any sense.

In the trenches, the absence of information and lack of sleep produced mental depression and physical sluggishness. Troops were soon worn out by the unrelieved tension and the fear produced by vigilant inaction and confinement below the surface. There was a constant drain on men in the trenches and the prospect of death or mutilation weighed heavily on their minds.[51] Before long the 'see-saw of death and disease' made a 'strong unit ... weak'.[52] Too fearful to move during the day because of enemy snipers, soldiers longed for darkness when they could ease their cramp. An officer of the 11th Hampshires reported: 'we have turned into human moles and live underground all day ... only coming out after dark'.[53] Night, however, brought isolation and fear.

But war in the trenches had its routines and habits which helped men hang on to their sanity. Each soldier was allocated his post, worked a certain number of hours and slept at stated times. He 'stood-to' half an hour before dawn at which time he had breakfast. Spare hours would then be spent cleaning rifles, burning lice from the seams of his clothing and playing nap. There was free franking on two letters a week, so time would

40   Lloyd (1976), Chapter 1.
41   Fussell (1975), p. 51.
42   Walker (1920), 43.
43   Carrothers (*c.* 1992), p. 41.
44   Hay (1915), pp. 284–85.
45   *Cork Weekly Examiner*, 15 Jan. 1916. Letter from Lance-Corporal M. J. Duffy.
46   *Waterford News*, 15 Oct. 1915.
47   Nelson (1973–74).
48   Warner, P. (1976), *Battle of Loos*, London, p. 149.
49   Brown, M. (1978), *Tommy Goes to War*, London, p. 30.
50   Moynihan, E. (ed.) (1973), *People at War 1914–1918*, Newton Abbot, p. 219.
51   Terraine, J. (1992), 'Understanding', *Stand To*, 34, pp. 7–12.
52   A comment by Tom Kettle, quoted in Denman (1992b), p. 64.
53   Sulman, letter, 19 Jan. 1916 (Sulman Papers, 82/29/1), IWM.

be spent writing home. Letters were posted in boxes fitted in the parados walls with the hours of collection written on them.

Men washed and shaved as best they could but clothes and boots were not removed. Officers inspected the trenches and the platoon sergeant detailed jobs. Sentries, spaced out at 25 yards, had to be relieved; a party was sent back for rations and the mail which included letters, parcels and newspapers. And the heavy, seemingly unending fatigues had to be completed. The contents of parcels would be shared among mates, adding a touch of the unexpected. Dinner was at noon and tea at 4 p.m. And work was routinely carried out under the protection of darkness.

Rations as a prime comfort became important. The rum ration issued at the dawn stand-down could turn 'sullen and cursing men into a whistling, buzzing group in a minute'.[54] One officer in the 8th Inniskillings recorded that the spirit was of extra strength and his men were 'very fond of it ... . Half a glass would make an ordinary man drunk'.[55] In addition, the film *With the Irish at the Front* shows Irish soldiers being issued with stout rations.

Propagandists claimed troops were better fed than they were at home, and there was some truth in this. One man with the 16th Division found army food 'very good, the cost must be stupendous'. Rations included tea, sugar, tinned milk, jam, bread or biscuit, tinned or fresh milk, tinned butter, rice, dried figs or dates. An Irish officer thought the rations 'splendid. We use the tinned milk in its purity and it is far better than cream ... . There is no scarcity of sugar or anything else out here like at home'. Officers' food was generally better than that eaten by other ranks, however. Everyone was given 4 ounces of tobacco or cigarettes and matches every week, and candles were also issued as an extra.[56] Dry rations included bully beef, maconochie stew and bread. Stew and porridge was brought up to the front with the mail by the rations party. Denis Winter has concluded that 'many working-class men had seldom eaten better than during the war', in or out of the trenches.[57]

When the 9th Munsters left the trenches three men had been killed and ten wounded. One of those killed had been an employee of Beamish and Crawfords in Cork and one of the wounded was a Welsh miner who had been hit by shrapnel. The battalion was sent into back billets about 15 miles behind the lines for 12 full days' rest. They went to mass, bathed, were deloused, had a change of clothes, bought tobacco and wrote letters. Consolidating friendships, together they ate eggs and fresh bread, drank beer in *estaminets*, gambled, and may have used the semi-institutionalised brothels. There was also the opportunity to 'lorry-hop' to other nearby towns.

But free time was strictly limited. Reveille was at 6 a.m. and there were inspections, drills, training sessions and fatigues which could include repairing wire entanglements and forming burial parties. In between drills and parades or in the evening there were cricket and football matches, band and battalion concerts, gymkhanas, swimming galas and athletics.

Between 26 January and 9 February, some units from the battalion were held in reserve in Loos and Maroc. Other units provided working parties or occupied support and fire trenches near the villages. Men in reserve were billeted in South Maroc as Loos was 'merely a heap of broken bricks, rubble and mud' around which lay a 'world of trenches, secret streets, sepulchral towns'.[58] Maroc, before the Battle of Loos a 'pretty mining village of brick terraced houses, with nice gardens front and rear' and water pumps in the streets, was now a heap of rubble.[59]

54 Winter (1978), pp. 102–03.
55 Carrothers (*c*. 1992), p. 47.
56 Sulman, letter, 3 Feb. 1916 (Sulman Papers, 82/29/1), IWM; Carrothers (*c*. 1992), pp. 46–47.
57 Winter (1978), p. 147.
58 MacGill (1984b), pp. 103, 121, 125.
59 Moynihan (1973), pp. 110–14.

Troops were unable to light fires in their billets in case they brought down enemy fire, and the men had to dig communication trenches between the cellars of the houses in which they were billeted.

South Maroc, Loos and their fire and support trench systems were continuously and heavily shelled throughout the period. Patrols were sent out and bombing parties retaliated against hostile rifle-grenade fire. Gas shells fell on North and South Maroc and an aeroplane dropped four bombs. When the battalion was withdrawn to back billets, nine men had been wounded.

While in rest, the men were initially billeted in accommodation which was 'very compact, clean and comfortable'. Later they stayed in barns, commonly used as accommodation for troops. Mincing machines were taken into use for the first time and scraps of meat, bacon and biscuits were used in rissoles 'making a nice change'. The battalion's sergeant-shoemaker and his four assistants repaired boots at the rate of 25 pairs a day and the tailor also provided a 'service of comfort to the men'. The band with pipers played at retreat every night.

Training included route marching; assault practice; drill; gas mask drill; signalling, sniper, rifle, machine-gun and grenade practice and physical exercises with rifles to 'strengthen the arms for bayonet fighting'. Inspections by General Hickie, the brigadier and General Gough elicited high praise for improvements shown and a smart turnout. There were lectures on a range of topics. The medical officer instructed officers and NCOs on the danger of venereal disease. Some officers and other ranks attended courses while just under three per cent of the unit reported sick, mainly with colds and rheumatism. By 3 March, training grounds were under water after heavy rain and snow falls. Confined to their billets, men cleaned equipment, ammunition and clothing.

On 25 March the battalion prepared to evacuate the billets for duty in the trenches. An advance party, Lewis gun and trench mortar detachments, and the machine-gun squadron left for the front. The combined bands of the 9th Munsters and the 8th Dublin Fusiliers played at the last retreat before the remainder of the unit moved into the front line the following day.

III

The 9th Munsters arrived by train at Noeux les Mines at 9.15 a.m. on Sunday 26 March and marched to Mazingarbe where the men ate dinner. Guides met them at Philosophe and led the way into Le Retoire Alley and up to the front line where the battalion relieved a Scottish unit. The weather was 'vile'. It was cold with squalls and clothes were soon damp through and rifles rusty. Men in the trenches were 'fed up' with the snow, sleet, rain and fog.[60] The relief was complete at 6.15 p.m. Two companies took over the fire trench on an 800 yards' frontage between Stone Street and Hay Alley. Men therefore occupied it at intervals of approximately nine feet. One company was in support, about 100 yards behind the front trench, and the fourth company was in the reserve trench. The German lines were about 200 yards away.

At 6.31 p.m. the enemy exploded two mines (see Map 3). An officer recalled how mines 'put the wind up most of us'.[61] On ignition of a mine the ground trembled like a 'miniature earthquake' and soldiers 'cringed like animals'.[62] They felt the vibrations rushing towards them and through the soles of their feet then a great pressure on their chest. 'It was the impression of vast power, greater than any shell, combined with the lack of warning which men could not accept'.[63] Hundreds of tons of soil and rocks were hurled 300 feet or more into the air then fell back to

60   Redmond (1917), p. 151.
61   Carrothers (c. 1992), p. 62.
62   Coppard, G. (1986), *With a Machine Gun to Cambrai*, London, pp. 34–35.
63   Winter (1978), pp. 126–27.

earth, obliterating trenches and the men in them. Resulting craters could be over 100 feet across and 30 feet deep. Father Doyle witnessed such a mine explosion.

> A mighty roar in the bowels of the earth, the ground trembled and rocked and quivered, and then a huge column of clay and stones was shot hundreds of feet in the air. As the earth opened, dense clouds of smoke and flames burst out, an awful and never to be forgotten sight. God help the poor fellows ... who were caught in that inferno and buried alive or blown to bits.[64]

One of the detonated mines destroyed about 70 yards of fire trench and left a crater 50 yards in diameter. The second obliterated 50 yards of fire trench and the crater was about 30 yards in diameter. A number of NCOs and men were buried in the debris but most were dug out. Five other ranks were killed and 17 unaccounted for. A veteran recalled that one of those killed 'looked as if nothing was wrong with him' and that the casualties were mainly among 'A' Company and the battalion's grenadiers.[65]

On 30 March the battalion was relieved. After four days in the trenches its casualties were 7 other ranks killed, 17 missing believed killed and 32 wounded. James English was among the missing and was most likely one of the bomb-throwers (grenadiers) or among the 'A' Company personnel who perished in the mine explosions.

Although the comradeship fostered by shared isolation and dangers, and personal experiences, routines and the daily minutiae of war drew Briton, Ulsterman and southern Irishman closer together, this by itself does not account for James English's and the division's sustained loyalty. Two other factors helped to create the cohesion necessary to maintain it. These were firstly, the authority exercised by the infantry brigades' Catholic priests and secondly, the deference men showed to their officers.

IV

The 16th Division's priests, tacitly or otherwise, endorsed Redmond's war policy. For Catholic Irishmen joining the pre-war army, the War Office's neglect of their religious needs does not appear to have been an obstacle to their enlistment. In the 1890s the colours of predominantly Catholic Irish battalions were consecrated by Protestant clergy and Lord Roberts's suggestion that Catholic priests should conduct the ceremony was dropped when it was resisted by the largely Protestant officer corps.[66] But for men joining the New Armies, an adequate recognition of, and provision for, their faith was demanded.

As early as September 1914 there was evidence the lack of priests was creating discontent among Irish Catholic soldiers at the front.[67] In October Cardinal Logue complained of Irish Catholic soldiers falling on the battlefield 'without having priests to give them absolution'.[68] A published letter claimed the issue was of 'pre-eminent importance to Irish Catholics'. It voiced a frequently expressed concern about the 'deplorable want of Chaplains for the Catholic soldiers at the front'. Some soldiers have

> never heard Mass or even so much as seen a priest. ... Our Irish people cling to their priests in life for Mass and for sacraments. In their dying hour there is nothing they crave so much as the presence of a priest. ... Dying Irishmen ... were denied a chaplain by the country for which they were giving up their lives.

64 O'Rahilly (1925), pp. 430–31.
65 This information was provided by Martin Staunton, who interviewed the veteran. He was 5552 Private Michael Donoghue of 'A' company, who enlisted in Cork. He died in 1985; Staunton (1986a), pp. 223, 227.
66 Muenger (1981), p. 267.
67 Anonymous (1917), 'Catholic army chaplains: a diary', *Catholic Bulletin*, **VII**, pp. 250–57.
68 *Irish Catholic Directory* (1915), pp. 543–46, 549–50.

Demands were made for priests to be provided for each Irish battalion and in prisoner of war camps, rest camps, trenches and battlefields. In its editorial, the newspaper considered the War Office failure to meet these complaints a major obstacle to Irish recruiting.[69]

Although J. O. Hannay thought the complaint a mistaken one, he agreed the Irish Catholic soldier 'attaches enormous importance to the ministrations of his priest when death is near' and that not enough was being done to dispel any misunderstanding.[70] A letter to Redmond from the under-secretary of state for war, explaining the steps taken to satisfy the religious needs of Irish soldiers, was published in local newspapers.[71] But although the British expeditionary force had in fact been accompanied by a number of Catholic priests proportionately greater than that allowed to any other denomination, Logue's criticisms of War Office policy continued into 1915.[72] However, in November 1915 Cardinal Bourne assured the men of the 16th Division that they now had their chaplains. He had spoken to the prime minister and the army would not create any problems if there was a need for more.[73]

When the 16th Division crossed to France, Fathers Maurice O'Connell, S. T. Wrafter and C. T. Brown were attached to the 47th Brigade. Father Jim Cotter was one of those attached to the 48th Brigade and Father William Doyle went with the 49th Brigade. Each held a commissioned rank and had a batman and cycle but sometimes travelled on horseback. Ideally the priest at the front was between 30 and 40 years of age, 'not afraid of some rough and tumble with ... an adventurous vein ... and with plenty of zeal and sympathy'.[74]

As the military chaplain at Fermoy, Maurice O'Connell had been associated with the 47th Brigade since it was first raised in Ireland. In November 1914, having reassured the troops that he was pleased with their good conduct and their attendance at mass, he told them that he would be going with them wherever they went – even to danger.[75] When O'Connell left with the brigade for Blackdown in September 1915 he was seen off by a local band. The chairman of the Fermoy Urban Council remarked that he was a good priest and they were all sorry to lose him but 'proud that he was gone in such good company'.[76] Wrafter, 'a universal favourite with all',[77] and Doyle were both awarded the Military Cross, with Doyle being recommended for the Victoria Cross.

Priests were central characters in Irish units and anecdotes and stories about them abounded. A veteran recalled how Father Jim Cotter, chaplain to the 9th Munsters and later to the 1st Munsters, was disturbed by noise when celebrating mass. He left the altar rolling his sleeves up and returned after silencing the miscreant by pulling him out by the hair. A Gaelic footballer on the Fermoy diocesan college team, Cotter was one of the toughest players one officer had ever met. He insisted on being saluted and was also reputed to have knocked a senior officer unconscious.[78] And Hickie remarked of Father Doyle: 'I think he was the most wonderful character that I have ever known'.[79]

They played a crucial role in holding men in the 16th Division to the course set for them by John Redmond. Despite the propaganda intent behind such claims, and the problems of gauging the depth and sincerity of religious and spiritual

69 Cork Examiner, 4 Nov. 1914.
70 Hannay (1916).
71 Cork Constitution, 25 Nov. 1914.
72 Leonard, J., 'The Catholic Chaplaincy' in Fitzpatrick (ed.) (1988), pp. 1–14.
73 Aldershot News, 19 Nov. 1915.
74 MacDonagh (1916), pp. 105–06.
75 Cork Constitution, 24 Nov. 1914.
76 Cork Constitution, 9 Sep. 1915.
77 Denman (1991).
78 O'Shea to 'Bertie' (presumed to be Lieutenant-Colonel Holt), 20 Mar. 1969 (Holt Papers, 7603–81), NAM.
79 O'Rahilly (1925), p. 555.

commitments, there is none the less truth in the assertion that the average Irish soldier in the 16th Division was by temperament and training 'profoundly religious at all times'. When confronted by sudden death he was under a 'constant and reverent sense of the nearness of the unseen power [and there was an] eagerness to have sin washed away by confession and the absolving words of a priest'.[80] Willie Redmond, reporting how Irish troops prepared for battle by reciting the rosary with their chaplain, wrote that

> these men, so gay and light-hearted, are filled with the deepest and purest feelings of religion ... even those who cannot agree with the doctrines [of Catholicism] never fail to admire the devotion and steadfastness with which the Irishmen adhere to their faith under all circumstances.[81]

Redmond further described how the priest remains 'Father' 'and as they [Irish Catholic soldiers] address him as such there is the ring of the old faith in their voices'. Rosary beads were treasured and unlike many other things seldom got lost. If a man was killed in the line, his rosary was placed around his neck before burial. In Redmond's view 'the fortitude the men seem to draw from their faith is great and marked'. Officers were often heard to declare their pleasure at the devotion of the men to their religion.[82] One soldier remarked his rosary was 'like having someone strong and brave and comforting by you'.[83] It was claimed that there were few men who did not carry rosaries or Catholic medals around their necks, regardless of denomination.[84] Patrick MacGill remembered finding a dead Munster Fusilier with a rosary around his neck and carrying a letter in which his girlfriend promised to pray to the Holy Mother to keep him safe. She and her mother made the rounds of the cross for him.[85]

And there was astonishment in a British regiment on the part of those who heard a corporal 'invariably coarse of speech' singing a hymn to the Virgin in Latin.[86] Observing that hardly one soldier in a hundred was inspired by religious feelings of 'even the crudest kind', Robert Graves noted that the attitude of Catholics was different.[87] Father Gleeson of the 2nd Munsters thought his battalion 'as Catholic and devoted a body of Irishmen as an Irish priest need wish to meet or minister to',[88] while Father Doyle considered his men 'wild and reckless, and at the same time so full of faith and love of God and His Blessed Mother'.[89] And a Scottish soldier at Gallipoli considered it 'most charming and edifying to see these fine chaps [the Irish troops] with their beads and the way in which they prayed to God'.[90]

A Waterford chaplain recalled the 'intense piety' on the faces of about 400 men of all ranks who received absolution during mass and communion having come 'straight out of the trenches, mud from head to foot, uniform stained and torn, unshaved and unwashed'.[91] An officer from Cork described how he always prepared for an emergency by going to confession and communion before an attack. In one instance, among about 30 men who heard mass and received a general absolution and communion in a corner of the trenches with shells 'whizzing overhead', was a soldier who was mortally wounded an hour or

80 MacDonagh (1916), pp. 103–04.
81 *Cork Weekly Examiner*, 30 Sep. 1916; also reproduced posthumously in Redmond (1917), p. 89.
82 Redmond (1917), pp. 111–13.
83 Denman (1991).
84 O'Rahilly (1925), p. 497.
85 MacGill (1984a), pp. 146–47.
86 Winter (1978), p. 172.
87 Graves (1960), pp. 157–58, 183.
88 Staunton (1986a), p. 213.
89 O'Rahilly (1925), p. 397.
90 MacDonagh (1916), p. 1.
91 *Waterford News*, 10 Sep. 1915.

two later. But 'he was lucky' because he had been anointed beforehand. 'It shows how ready one must always be.'[92] It was also important for relatives to know that a soldier had attended to his religious duties and received holy communion before being killed in the trenches.[93]

A soldier in the 8th Munsters wrote home claiming troops had mass regularly and could go to confession any time. 'This enables us to face the German shells without fear ... this is a place where a man must put himself in the hands of God and trust Him to do what he knows best'.[94] After their first spell in the trenches, Willie Redmond told a bishop that 'our men are very attentive to their Chaplain and flock into the churches in the little French villages'.[95] However, mass would be said anywhere. Father Doyle converted a support line dug-out into a church where he said mass and heard confessions. Of the Catholic chaplains he noted: 'we share the hardships and dangers with our men'. Soldiers attributed the dug-out with a protective power, and non-combatants squeezed in whenever there was heavy firing.[96] In another case an altar of biscuit boxes and bully beef cases made up inside a barn, shook from the concussion of bursting shells.[97]

The devotion of Irish Catholic soldiers might appear naive to outsiders. Amidst the destruction and death which caused others to question or abandon their faith, men of the Royal Munster Fusiliers warned an officer against taking stained glass from a church as a souvenir as to do so was sacrilegious and would bring bad luck.[98] While on sentry duty in the trenches, men of the London Irish Regiment claimed to have often heard the organ being played in a destroyed church in which the ghosts of dead monks prayed nightly at the shattered altar.[99] And soldiers of the 8th Munsters were reported to 'love' with 'pride and devotion' a banner of the Sacred Heart financed from penny subscriptions, made by nuns and presented to them by friends and well-wishers from Limerick. It had been sent in the 'hopes that it would bring that blessing on the regiment which Our Divine Lord promised Blessed Margaret Mary would be the special portion of those families in which a picture of the Sacred Heart was exposed and venerated'. On the other side of the banner was O'Neill's war cry *Ave Maria*. The battalion suffered fewer casualties than other units in the Battle of the Somme and Father Doyle attributed this fact to the banner.[100]

There were those who claimed that because of his faith, the Irish Catholic soldier was a superior warrior. Father Doyle thought him 'the bravest and best man in a fight, but few know that he draws that courage from the strong faith with which he is filled and the help, which comes from the exercise of his religion'. Strong faith imbued him with a degree of fatalism and he saw the hand of God in everything, even his own death.[101]

A soldier joining the Irish Guards in England recorded how he 'used to envy [his] Catholic comrades their sure faith, which, [he was] certain was a great support to their courage in battle'.[102] In the view of another contemporary the Irish Catholic soldier was a fine fighting man because the 'two characteristics, religious fervour and fearlessness of danger have always been very closely allied'.[103] And a young Presbyterian

92   *Evening Echo* (Cork), 15 Apr. 1916.
93   Letter, Second Lieutenant A. W. Henchy to Mr Forde, father of Frank Forde from Dungarvan, County Waterford, a soldier in the 10th Royal Dublin Fusiliers, who was killed in the Loos salient, 23 Sep. 1916 (copy held by M. Staunton).
94   Staunton (1986a), p. 226.
95   *Cork Weekly Examiner*, 19 Feb. 1916.
96   O'Rahilly (1925), pp. 412–13, 426, 434.
97   *Waterford News*, 10 Sep. 1915.
98   Graves (1960), p. 100.
99   MacGill (1984a) pp. 80–81.
100   *Cork Weekly Examiner*, 24 June 1916; Staunton (1986a), p. 231; O'Rahilly (1925), p. 440.
101   O'Rahilly (1925), pp. 437–39.
102   Nelson (1973–74).
103   MacDonagh (1916), p. 104.

officer with the 8th Inniskillings thought Methodists 'harmless soldiers' but his own Catholic battalion was a 'fighting battalion' and he claimed Irish troops did best of all at Wytschaete Ridge.[104]

Catholic chaplains therefore carried an authority which could decisively shape the attitudes of men with such beliefs. According to the view of one officer, the influence of the priest 'on all ranks was immense', whether Catholic or Protestant.[105] Father Gleeson, for example, taking charge of Royal Munster Fusilier survivors, held the line when their officers were killed or wounded. In another action, Glasgow Catholic soldiers, allegedly prepared to follow a priest where they would not follow an officer, were led to safety by the Catholic chaplain.[106] And Father Gwynn was killed as he advanced with the Irish Guards at the Battle of Loos. Priests enhanced their authority by echoing the spiritual-nationalist motif and the cult of blood-sacrifice despite the attempts at monopoly by separatists such as Patrick Pearse.

Father William Doyle, reported as having a 'burning love of Ireland', was convinced that 'one day God would give me the grace of martyrdom … I am not afraid of sacrifice. He has given me an intense love of suffering and humiliation'. For Doyle it was the Irish cause at the front which gave him 'a glorious chance of making the "auld body" bear something for Christ's dear sake'. Of the Irish dead he wrote: 'they have nobly given their lives for God and country'. In his last sermon to Irish soldiers before he was killed, he told them they were fighting for what they believed was Ireland's cause as well as Belgium's. He thought that

> in spite of all the misery and suffering caused this war will turn out to have been the biggest act of God's love, saving the souls of scores of poor fellows … . It is a consolation

to know what a comfort the mere presence of a priest is to both officers and men alike. They are one and all going to face their duty with the joy of heart which comes from a clean conscience.[107]

The British army had traditionally adopted an 'instrumentalist view' of religion, and priests of Father Doyle's calibre were an asset. This explains the War Office's concessions, however reluctantly given, to the demand for Catholic chaplains in the 16th Division. Priests contributed to the maintenance of morale and good order. Church parades reinforced military systems and chaplains performed necessary functions. They comforted the sick and wounded, buried the dead, wrote letters for the illiterate and generally kept other ranks under 'watchful surveillance'. For this reason they were expected to be practical men.[108]

An important duty was the notification of relatives when a soldier was killed and Father Doyle was kept busy writing home and answering letters from the relatives of soldiers. The way in which this task was performed could tacitly justify, and sustain support for, the war. Of her soldier son killed in action, a priest wrote to a mother that he had borne his suffering willingly.

> God and his Blessed Mother were helping him a lot … you could see the happiness in his features when Our Blessed Lord came to him again to give him new strength and grace to bear up … . I know … you have long since put your son in God's holy hands, leaving him entirely to God … . Your poor Paddy passed away to the God whom he loved so much.[109]

The simple fact of their presence and the carrying out of their routine duties legitimised involvement in the war and endorsed the respect-

104 Carrothers (c. 1992), p. 57.
105 Nelson (1973–74).
106 Graves (1960), pp. 158–59, 183.
107 O'Rahilly (1925), pp. 132–35, 392–93, 396–98, 503, 522.
108 Hanham, 'Religion and nationality in the mid-Victorian army' in Foot (ed.) (1973).
109 MacDonagh (1916), p. 118.

ability of the army. A soldier at the front wrote of a priest being so brave 'he only laughs at the bullets'. He celebrated mass with the shells flying around him and heard confessions anywhere. 'It is easier to get prepared for death than at home ... . The priest encourages them all the time ... . Such encouragement would keep up the heart of any soldier.'[110]

A comradeship which crossed national boundaries and the role played by priests therefore cemented the loyalty of Irish units. But the extent to which soldiers were able legitimately to express their political and cultural identity was also an important factor.

V

Redmond thought of himself as the national leader of a country which would soon have its own parliament. His vision of the 16th Division was of it forming part of an Irish army which would identify with his leadership and with the parliament and Irish government which would emerge after home rule. A clash between Redmond and Sir Lawrence Parsons was therefore inevitable.

The rift between Parsons and Redmond was a serious one. A series of disagreements reflected differences in personalities, background, perceptions, priorities and interests. Redmond was attuned to the political implications and subtleties of raising and fielding Irish troops and he was determined to play a decisive role in the 16th Division's formation. Parsons, however, was a

traditionalist and a professional soldier with a distaste for what he saw as political interference. At a time when politics permeated every aspect of Irish life, his attitude towards Redmond and the 16th Division was politically inept. In Stephen Gwynn's view he had an 'unhappy lack of comprehension' despite 'sympathetic acquaintances with Irish troops of the old army'.[111]

Parsons had been in retirement and on the reserve officer list for two years when he was recalled to the colours on the outbreak of war.[112] Appointed by Kitchener to raise the 16th Division, in October 1914 he published an appeal in the newspapers for women to make and present colours to 'my battalions as an advertisement that the 16th is an Irish Division'.[113] Telling Redmond he had been given command of the division because he was an Irishman and understood his countrymen, he asked Redmond to acknowledge the division as the 'Irish Brigade' for which Redmond had been pushing.

> We are both working in the same cause. ... I am one of the Birr, King's County family of Parsons, was born there and, I think, may call myself an Irishman and descendant of one of the strongest opponents of the Union, and an equally strong supporter of Catholic emancipation and endowment of the Catholic church.[114]

But Parsons had signed the Ulster covenant[115] and was unlikely to see things the same way as Redmond did. Convinced that John Redmond had him removed from command of the division in November 1915, by December 1916 he was

110 *Waterford News,* 18 June 1915. Letter home from a soldier at the front and reported in the newspaper. The priest referred to was Father Gill from Dublin.
111 Gwynn, S. (1919), p. 173.
112 Parsons, L. W., 'Notes by Sir Lawrence W. Parsons on the First World War and his part in it, 1917' (Nora Robertson Papers, Call no. P7476), NLI.
113 Parsons, diary entry, 15 Oct. 1915 (Parsons Papers, MD 1111), Woolwich.
114 Gwynn, D. (1932), p. 397. Lieutenant-General Sir Lawrence Worthington Parsons (1850–1923) of Parsonstown, King's County was a descendant of Sir William Parsons who settled in Ireland in 1590 and as commissioner of plantations, obtained considerable grants of land from the crown. As MP for Dublin University, 1789 to 1790, Lawrence Parsons, 2nd Earl of Rosse, recognised the need for a limited admission of Catholics to the franchise and was considered 'an eloquent speaker against the union'. Wolfe Tone thought him 'one of the very very few honest men in the Irish House of Commons' (*Dictionary of National Biography* [1917], Vol. XV, Oxford).
115 Denman (1987/1988).

referring to him as an 'ass'.[116] According to his daughter, for men like Parsons, loyalty

> combined King, country, religion, one's personal safety, one's family property and, above all, one's class. ... The sense of loyal superiority was recognised and cherished down to the Protestant charwoman, copying her betters, whose scorn of her R.C. opposite would be uninhibited.

A dozen or so 'loyal' Catholic families like the Kenmares with whom Parsons would stay after a shoot, qualified for admission into this society.[117] Not surprisingly, therefore, Lord Kenmare's was one of at least five Catholic estates on which the 'plan of campaign' had operated. They were no more popular than Protestant land owners. Lord and Lady Kenmare discussed his plans for battalion colours with Parsons and they made 'most wise suggestions'.[118]

But the war made for strange bedfellows. Parsons commissioned nationalist officers and made friends with nationalist MPs such as Devlin, Dillon and O'Connor.[119] And when Willie Redmond reciprocated an invitation to tea, Parsons found himself among 'ex-fenians and now MPs'.[120] None the less, he built up a close relationship with several nationalist officers, and recorded that Willie Redmond was 'weeping' on receipt of the news that he had lost command of the division. Despite being 'terrified' for his men because of Willie Redmond's 'eminently unwarlike habit of mind', Parsons had given him a commission. Lady Parsons, a home ruler, was politically sympathetic to Willie Redmond and influenced her husband's opinions and actions.

Willie Redmond wrote frequently to them from the front and thanked Parsons for the 'kindness and consideration which alone enabled me to fill a position so unfamiliar to me. Believe me, I am grateful and so are my friends in whom you kindly took an interest'. And in 1917 he wrote to Lady Parsons, 'you and the General can understand how unhappy we are about the Irish question—alas! Poor old Ireland! One thing—your husband's division saved the situation. How glad I am he gave me my commission'.[121] He told Parsons, 'your division did wonders' at Guillemont and Ginchy.[122] Willie Redmond's death was a personal sorrow for Lady Parsons.

It was also Parsons who opened the division to nationalist subaltern entrants. The officer cadet company was intended to give him control over junior officer appointments and to provide an incentive for nationalist Irish recruits. Between November 1914 and December 1915, 161 men were commissioned from the cadet company.[123] And a Sandhurst-trained Protestant subaltern of mixed Scottish and Ulster descent received a 'cold reception' when he was posted to the Leinsters.[124]

The cadets were 'by no means all Catholics' but they were 'broadly speaking ... Nationalist by opinion and by tradition'. Generally, however, officers in the division tended to be Irish Protestants or British. But because of the lack of politics, this caused minimal discord among soldiers. Nobody wanted to change the colonel of Gwynn's battalion for example, and claims that Catholics and nationalists were relegated to inferior positions of authority were denied.[125] However, the infusion of junior officers commissioned

---

116 Parsons, diary entry, 20 Dec. 1916 (Parsons Papers, MD 1111), Woolwich.
117 Robertson (1960), pp. 1–36.
118 Parsons, diary entries, 18 and 19 Oct. 1914 (Parsons Papers, MD 1111), Woolwich.
119 Esmonde Robertson, 'John Redmond and General Parsons' (unpublished MS produced using edited diary and papers), (Parsons Papers, 1914–16), King's College.
120 Parsons, diary entries, 18 and 25 Sep. 1915 (Parsons Papers, MD 1111), Woolwich.
121 Parsons, diary entry, 27 Nov. 1915; W. H. Redmond to Parsons, 28 Nov. 1915; W. H. Redmond to Lady Parsons, 16 Mar. 1917 (Parsons Papers, MD 1111), Woolwich.
122 W. H. Redmond to Parsons, 14 Sep. 1916, (Parsons Papers, MD 1111), Woolwich.
123 List of names of men commissioned through the cadet company (Parsons Papers, MD 1111), Woolwich.
124 Lyon, typescript memoirs, Vol. 1, pp. 57–58 (80/25/1). IWM.
125 Gwynn, S. (1919), pp. 187–89; Gwynn, D. (1932), p. 447.

from the cadet company met, to some extent, John Redmond's demand for a division with a more Catholic and nationalist character. About 38.5 per cent of officers in the 9th Munsters were Catholic and this was undoubtedly increased by men joining from the cadet company.

Promotion of officers from within the battalion meant there were few changes in commissioned personnel. The command structure was therefore relatively stable and this would have reinforced the closed and corporate nature of the unit. And although officers were from a variety of backgrounds, generally their education, class and professional status provided common ground. When in the 6th Connaughts, for example, John Staniforth thought it was full of 'indescribable villains' but the officers were 'mostly English and very nice'. He subsequently obtained a commission through the cadet company.[126]

Friction among officers from such diverse political and religious backgrounds could not be entirely avoided, especially during the period of the division's formation and before the bonding influence of training and service at the front could take full effect. In February 1915, when Redmond and his supporters were pushing for their concept of an 'Irish Brigade', one officer, noting the arrival of Tom Kettle and Willie Redmond, observed 'there is altogether too much politics in this Irish Brigade business'. Even his batman referred to the nationalists forming a clique.[127] Sir Francis Vane, a retired captain, home ruler and founder of the World Order of Socialism in 1913, joined the 9th Munsters with the temporary rank of major, but was soon reprimanded by Parsons for his politically tainted public recruiting appeals. He was subsequently removed from the division.[128]

Daniel D. Sheehan, appointed as a lieutenant in the 9th Munsters and later promoted to captain, thought the British subalterns first drafted into the division a 'horde of English cockneys who never understood Irishmen, or how to treat them decently'. Sheehan, whose father had been evicted from his home because of his fenian activities, and who resigned his parliamentary seat and called for support of Sinn Fein when the British failed to grant home rule after the war,[129] was of the opinion that some of the British officers were 'blatantly antagonistic' towards the nationalist cause. When a group of officer cadets were posted to the battalion, its adjutant, F. Harrison, 'a mere insurance clerk in London before the war', told him 'four more bloody Irishmen' were coming.[130]

In perspective, however, such incidents were relatively incidental. Lieutenant-Colonel E. Monteagle-Browne, commander of the 9th Munsters, was an old soldier, who had served in the Irish Fusiliers and the Northumberland Fusiliers. When he was removed from the command of another battalion on disciplinary grounds, Sheehan, speaking in the House of Commons, called for his reinstatement. 'I took a certain pride in the battalion [the 9th Munsters]', Sheehan told the house. 'Colonel Monteagle-Browne came along to control the battalion at the front, he brought them to a peak of efficiency and as a result they became the top battalion of the division.' An old soldier of the battalion wrote to Monteagle-Browne assuring him of the sympathy of 'all the boys who remain' from the 9th Munsters and hoping the injustice he was suffering would soon be righted.[131]

In the absence of any political ethos, although Irish soldiers serving in other divisions frequently perceived both the 16th and 36th Divisions as being 'political' units,[132] an officer's religion or national background did not determine a soldier's opinion of him. One ranker

126 Staniforth, letters, 12 to 18 Oct. 1914 (Staniforth Papers), IWM.
127 Staniforth, letter, 27 Feb. 1915 (Staniforth Papers), IWM.
128 Vane (1929), pp. 253–56.
129 *Irish Law Times*, 4 Dec. 1948 (an obituary).
130 Denman (1987/1988).
131 Staunton (1986a), pp. 175–77.
132 Perry (1994).

thought Major Shildrick, James English's company commander, was a 'genuine' man and 'not a bad fellow'. Dublin-born, Shildrick was a Cambridge graduate[133] who achieved rapid promotion in the battalion. He, with several other officers and men, was commended by General Hickie and presented with divisional parchment certificates for distinguished conduct following the mine explosion on 26 March 1916. His promotion to major on the same day probably resulted from the actions for which he was commended.

The same ranker, however, thought Lieutenant P. J. Lyne, commissioned from the cadet company, was a 'right bastard'. D. J. Baily, the son of a county councillor from Tralee, was very popular among the men, the most humble of whom he treated with respect.[134] Lieutenant Baily, later killed in action and whose Requiem Mass in Tralee was 'thronged',[135] was among those commended for his work on the night of 26 March. Lieutenant Francis Moran, the eldest son of a Methodist minister from County Down, was killed in action. A corporal who served under him thought he had 'fine, manly qualities [and he] ... endeared himself to all ... . He was one of the best' and had a 'kindly smile and cheerful word, which is the soldier's dearest friend'. Another soldier reported Moran as being 'dearly loved and respected ... a perfect gentleman and a God-fearing man'.[136] And Lieutenant J. R. Colfer, killed in action in 1917, was leader of the Mitchelstown National Volunteers and a well-known and respected footballer at the time of his enlistment.

Parsons was sufficiently sensitive to the religious character of his division to maintain cordial relations with the Catholic clergy. He was thanked by Willie Redmond for entertaining Cardinal Bourne and for inviting the officers to meet him. And Cardinal Logue only declined an invitation from Parsons to visit the troops in England on the grounds it would not be politic. It might be seen as an ecclesiastical intrusion now they were no longer in Ireland.

As well as the nationalist officers, Parsons would sometimes have the division's chaplains to tea. They had been appointed in consultation with Dr Browne, Bishop of Cloyne, from whom he received numerous letters of appreciation. An 'outstanding respect' was shown to Browne by officers and men of the 16th Division.[137] In a probable reference to the incident in which Father Cotter was alleged to have knocked a senior officer unconscious, Bishop Browne wrote of his concern about a report that Father Jim Cotter had been subjected to 'some kind of punishment' at Blackdown after an altercation with an officer who was supposed to have insulted him. Reassured about Parsons's intentions, the bishop wrote to him expressing the certainty that men of the division 'will prove themselves to be brave soldiers in the field of war, true to the spirit of their race'.[138]

On 24 November 1915, when Parsons heard that he was to be replaced, he promptly informed Bishop Browne who sympathised with his reluctance to hand over a division he had 'so splendidly trained; and the men on their side will also bitterly feel the parting'. The bishop assured Parsons that he would be welcome in his diocese where his 'consideration for all interests is highly appreciated'. He concluded, 'we shall all follow with greatest interest their [men of the 16th Division's] conduct at the front as we are in high hopes that they will not only sustain but add to the fame of the Irish regiments for discipline and valour'. Old suspicions soon soured good feelings about the British however. In January 1916 the Gaelic League organised a monster meeting in protest against the withdrawal of education grants in Ireland and Bishop Browne was one of

133 The information regarding Major Shildrick and Major Kelly (see p. 195) was supplied by M. Staunton.
134 Information provided by M. Staunton from his interview with Michael Donoghue.
135 *Cork Examiner*, 28 Feb. 1917.
136 *Irish Times*, 29 Aug. and 28 Sep. 1916.
137 Robertson (1960), p. 125.
138 Parsons, diary entries, 3 Oct. 1915, 13 and 14 Nov. 1915; Willie Redmond to Lady Parsons, undated; Robert Browne to Parsons, 22 Nov. 1915; Browne to Parsons, 29 Nov. 1915 (Parsons Papers, MD 1111), Woolwich.

those who 'vigorously' protested against government policy.[139]

Parsons made his final speeches to men of the 47th and 48th Brigades and described all the farewells as 'very tearful'. He was presented with a cup by his old Mallow staff.[140] There was regret locally that Parsons would not be going with the division to France. He was described as the 'private soldier's genuine friend' and in his farewell address he was reported as expressing his sorrow at parting from his 'dear Boys' but was consoled at the thought of handing them over to 'another Irishman, a younger, more brilliant and more efficient officer than himself'.[141]

Hickie, when he replaced Parsons, was described by fellow officers as 'always either violently condemning or extremely eulogistic, he seems to see only in extremes'[142] and as a 'very clever fellow, and ... really a good sort, though a great talker and a bit of a "gas-bag" '.[143] He was, like Parsons, also a professional soldier but he was a Catholic and Parsons later claimed that he had been told he was 'put out of command to make way for an RC'.[144] But Hickie's family was of the view that Hickie advanced no further than the rank of major-general because as an Irish Catholic, Field-Marshal Sir Henry Wilson thought he had gone far enough.

However, Hickie had crossed the religious divide and married the daughter of J.O. Hannay. Although a firm advocate of home rule[145] and politically conscious, he was a career soldier. When he recommended the rationalisation of troop dispositions in Ireland, for example, he noted that 'political reasons must be considered' in deciding the mobilisation scheme for the Connaught Rangers and Leinster Regiment. 'Political and civil considerations (including the misuse of troops as police)' were taken into account by him in drawing up his plan, although its essential purpose was economic.[146] Hickie's political acumen easily won him a senator's seat in the Free State.

Hickie and Parsons socialised, sometimes playing bridge together, and Hickie maintained a professional regard for Parsons. The division became no more nationalist under Hickie's command than it was under Parsons. Hickie designed the LP monogram used as the divisional sign on vehicles as a tribute to Parsons and told him it was a way of ensuring that the 'division which loved you ... will always remember you'. In letters to Parsons, Hickie laboriously sketched in the monogram at the top of the notepaper and told him the divisional mark was well known from north to south.[147] And in September 1916, Willie Redmond sent Parsons an 18 pounder brass shell inscribed with the LP monogram to remind him that he was not forgotten by the division.

In his determination to emphasise the division's Irish identity, Hickie demonstrated an extraordinary concern for detail. He adopted the practice of awarding divisional commendations. These took the form of parchment certificates which he drew up in his own hand, sketching in a shamrock and the words 'The Irish Brigade' in Celtic lettering.[148] In February 1916 he told paraded troops that the parchments 'specially prepared in Dublin' would be awarded for meri-

139   *Cork Weekly Examiner*, 15 Jan. 1916.
140   Parsons, diary entries, 1 and 4 Dec. 1915, and 23 Jan. 1916; Browne to Parsons, 29 Nov. 1915 (Parsons Papers, MD 1111), Woolwich.
141   *Camberley News*, 18 Dec. 1915.
142   Captain W. Rennie to Parsons, 15 Jan. 1916 (Parsons Papers, MD 1111), Woolwich.
143   Hammond to Parsons, 26 Nov. 1915 (Parsons Papers, MD 1111), Woolwich.
144   Parsons, diary entry, 7 Mar. 1916 (Parsons Papers, MD 1111), Woolwich.
145   Information kindly supplied by W. B. Hickie's nephew, J. F. Hickie (letter to author dated 29 Sep. 1988); unidentified newspaper cuttings (papers relating to General Hickie and the 16th Division, 50904–116), NAM.
146   Hickie, Colonel W. B. (*c.* 1912), 'A suggestion for the better distribution of regular infantry battalions in the Irish Command' (Hickie Papers, 8095), NLI.
147   Hickie to Parsons, 6 Dec. 1915 and 17 Sep. 1916 (Parsons Papers, MD 1111), Woolwich.
148   Commendation to Lieutenant-Colonel Bellingham, Royal Dublin Fusiliers, 10 Sep. 1916 (Parsons Papers, MD 1111), Woolwich.

tous deeds so that 'the heritage worth preserving might be passed on to future generations to the glory of the Irish Brigade'.

The band played *The Wearing of the Green* and Hickie was reported to have 'held his audience' as he told them of his pride in the division. He cautioned the soldiers to think of the future and not fritter away their pay and he warned 'wasters' who failed to appreciate that the 'honour of old Ireland was in his personal keeping' would be sent home labelled 'not wanted'.[149]

Parsons and Hickie were both members of an institution in which there was a profound regard for tradition. Regiments were the primary units with which regular soldiers identified, and loyalty to the regiment frequently overrode all other loyalties. Regimental pride, with its roots in tradition and great deeds, was inculcated into men through lectures, but it also flowed from the heightened corporate identity they shared. When men from deprived social backgrounds joined their regiment, squalor, poverty and rejection were replaced by cleanliness, security and acceptance. The readiness of men to die for the regiment was a real facet of army life. Robert Graves thought regimental pride was the 'strongest moral force' which kept a battalion going as an effective fighting unit. It was more powerful than religion, while patriotism was 'too remote a sentiment'.[150]

Battalions were independent units forming part of a regiment. They each had their own band, colours, officers and men. Soldiers felt an attachment to them within a greater loyalty to the regiment. Any number of battalions could be grafted onto an existing regiment, so there was no requirement to create new regiments which lacked traditions and *esprit de corps*. During the Le Bas recruiting campaign in Waterford, Stephen Gwynn, in the officer cadet company at the time, told the audience in City Hall on 23 March that the regiment in which he was serving was 'able to stand comparison with other inheritors of famous names'. The Irish regiments bore names made 'illustrious' and men joining the ranks would have the 'memory of the great deeds that were done by these regiments to inspire them'.[151] For James English, the regiment's history may have been of some significance.

The Royal Munster Fusiliers had its eighteenth-century origins in the East India Company's 1st and 2nd Bengal European Regiments which had been largely composed of Irishmen. Lieutenant-Colonel F. Williams, commanding the 9th Munsters until relieved by Lieutenant-Colonel Monteagle-Browne on 12 February 1916, had been commissioned in the 104th Bengal Fusiliers (forerunner of the 2nd Munsters) as a second lieutenant in 1879. He retired as a major in 1907, being brought out of retirement and given the temporary rank of lieutenant-colonel when war was declared in 1914. And the battalion's second in command, Major V. J. Kelly, educated at the Jesuit-run Beaumont School, was also an old soldier. He enlisted in the army in 1888 and joined the reserve of officers when he went to work for the Guinness brewery.

The regiment's colours carried many battle honours and the Munsters acquired the nickname 'Dirty Shirts' after the regiment fought a fierce action in its shirt sleeves in Delhi in 1857. The nickname was popularly known and a source of pride. Katey English often boasted of her husband having been a 'Dirty Shirt'. Described as a regiment whose bones come from Bengal but whose blood and sinews were Irish, its rich history was symbolised by the tiger on its cap badge.

The most serious disagreement between Parsons and Redmond was over the general's refusal to allow the 16th Division its own special and distinctive badge. He told Redmond:

> I want my soldiers to feel that they belong to time-honoured regiments, in the glory of whose past history they are entitled to share.

149 *Cork Weekly Examiner*, 26 Feb. 1916.
150 Graves (1960), pp. 156–59.
151 *Munster Express*, 27 Mar. 1915.

I have lectures given to the men on wet days on the history of their regiments, selecting especially glorious actions of the regiment; the origins and history of the regiment is explained to them, why they have a sphinx on their badge, a tiger, or an elephant etc. This instils *esprit de corps*.

He thought a newly invented badge would militate against these advantages and concluded, 'all the old officers and NCOs of the regiments who have rejoined ... are opposed to any addition to or alteration in the badge they have worn all their lives'.[152]

But the comments demonstrate a failure to understand the nature of Kitchener's New Armies and the war they had to fight. In one view, most new recruits were essentially civilians in uniform. The 'creed of regiment was hardly more than a fiction'.[153] Regimental badges may have been 'a source of unit pride and morale' but they were rarely seen at the front. In an attempt to conceal unit identification, regimental insignia were replaced by battle patches worn on uniforms. In addition there were divisional signs used on vehicles. The 16th Division did not have a scheme of battle patches but had two divisional signs. One was the LP monogram for use on transport and for generally identifying the division, and the other was a green drab shamrock worn by men on their uniforms. Much of the loyalty formerly invested in the regiment was transferred to the division and its insignia were worn and displayed with pride. Although these emblems had no history earlier than 1915, they soon 'meant more to the men who wore them than many of the ancient and honourable devices on their traditional badges'.[154]

The bonding power of the battalion, and of the division with its new battle insignia symbolising its corporate identity, was expressed by Stephen Gwynn. When commissioned from the cadet company, he joined the 6th Connaught Rangers. No more than six of the subalterns would have described themselves as nationalists and there were few Catholics or nationalists above the rank of subaltern. But there was 'very little political discussion' and every man in the battalion, even though practically all of them were Catholic and nationalist, 'desired the success of the division ... absolutely with a whole heart'.[155] For most, the division was the 'real' unit of the Great War. Divisional pride and *esprit de corps* was at least as important as regimental traditions.[156]

Various observers have noted that the relationship between officers and Irish troops was different to that between officers and British soldiers. A fair assessment of this consensus is that Irish soldiers could be led and not driven. Discipline and relationships were easier and the bonds closer, so that a 'strong, personal, sympathetic leadership' was essential in handling Irish soldiers.[157] And Parsons made a point of weeding out those men enlisting in the cadet company because they thought it 'beneath their dignity to enlist as common soldiers to be herded as "riff raff" '.[158] However, these assessments are expressed from the perspective of officers.

Although he was not above inviting private soldiers to tea,[159] Parsons was out of touch with the ordinary ranker. Failing to recognise the urban character of his own division, he rejected Irish recruits from Britain because it

would mean filling us with Liverpool, and Glasgow, and Cardiff Irish, who are slum-birds that we don't want. I want to see the

152 Gwynn, D. (1932), pp. 404–09.
153 Fuller, J. G. (1990), *Troop Morale and Popular Culture in the British and Dominion Armies 1914–1918*, Oxford, p. 45.
154 Chappell, M. (1986), *British Battle Insignia (1): 1914–18*, London, pp. 3–5.
155 Gwynn, S. (1919), p. 189.
156 Perry (1994).
157 Denman (1991).
158 Parsons to the secretary, War Office, 9 Nov. 1914 (Parsons Papers, MD 1111), Woolwich.
159 Parsons, diary entry, 12 Sep. 1916 (Parsons Papers, MD 1111), Woolwich.

clean, fine, strong, temperate, hurley-playing country fellows such as we used to get.

He could display the patronising arrogance of his class. Explaining to John Redmond the need for discrimination when selecting officers, he said, 'you know as well as I do how Irish peasants can judge of a man whether he is a gentleman or not'. Of the 16th Division, he wrote:

> the devotion of those rough Irishmen to myself and their [commanding officers], all of us Unionists and Protestants, shows what can be done with the Irish peasantry if properly handled with firmness and sympathy.[160]

In July 1914 he dismissed Irish Volunteers he had seen on parade as 'a poor undrilled collection of men with not a man of position among them' and he noted of Maurice Moore, 'he is no use'.[161] Parsons's frequent references to the 'wise handling' required in turning Irish peasants into 'Irish Tommies' and the opinion of Captain Beater, from Trinity College's Officers' Training Corps, that 'the Irish Tommy is such a careless individual' because of his dirty habits in camp,[162] may just as easily be interpreted as a thoroughly condescending paternalism.

Sir Francis Vane, arriving in Buttevant on his way to join the 9th Munsters recalled being greeted with cheers and the 'good humoured chaff of the Irish peasant'. Noting that it was 'grand to see these fine Irish peasants developing into first class soldiers', he thought the Irish had to be treated differently from the British 'if the best is to be obtained from them'. In his opinion 'a kindly familiarity which might injure discipline in a British regiment, will never be presumed on by the Irish'.[163] At least one historian agrees with

an officer's conclusion that 'typical' Irish soldiers were pliant and 'easily handled'.[164] Irish regiments cannot be compared with black colonial units. British soldiers, for example, regularly served in Irish regiments but would never be found in the ranks of a black regiment. And, unlike Irishmen, blacks would not be found in the officer ranks. However, the attitude of the regular British army officer class towards the Irish soldier was still a colonial one.

However, the character of the New Armies remoulded class attitudes to some extent, and there may not have been such a wide gulf between the attitudes of some officers in British regiments and those in Irish units. Trench life could break down the rigid social stratification of the class system. Ian Hay recalled the 'outstanding feature of the relationship between officers and men' was their being brought together by a process which produced a 'real life regiment, with a morale and soul of its own'.[165] There is substance in the view that the experience of the trenches initiated a 'process of discovery' which fuelled a transformation of middle-class attitudes towards the lower classes.[166] Harold Macmillan is one veteran who recorded such a transformation. He learned

> for the first time how to understand, talk with, and feel at home with a whole class of men with whom we could not have come into contact in any other way. Thus we learn to admire their steadfastness, enjoy their humour, and be touched by their sentiment.[167]

Even so, any argument that the war brought officers and men together should not be overstated. Social and class differences still existed.[168]

160 Gwynn, D. (1932), pp. 398, 400, 458.
161 Esmonde Robertson, 'John Redmond and General Parsons' (unpublished MS produced from edited papers); Parsons, diary entry, 8 Nov. 1914 (Parsons Papers, 1914–16), Kings College.
162 Beater, diary entry, 20 Oct. 1915 (Beater Papers, 86/65/1), IWM.
163 Vane (1929), pp. 247, 249.
164 Karsten (1983).
165 Hay (1915), pp. 179–80.
166 Keegan (1978), pp. 219–29.
167 Macmillan (1966), p. 100.
168 Beckett, 'The British army, 1914–18' in Turner (ed.) (1988).

Differences in class and traditions also separated officers from other ranks in Irish regiments. But it is no doubt true that for men coming from the type of tight, traditional and homogeneous Irish society such as that existing in Waterford, the 'process of discovery', if necessary, was less traumatic or startling. John Lucy had a preference for Irish officers because they were 'more friendly than the English, and ... more democratic, or at any rate less feudal'. But Irish soldiers 'gave a great deal of affection and loyalty' to all officers in his company.[169]

For James English, having a man such as Daniel Sheehan serving as an officer in the battalion was very probably a significant factor in cementing his loyalties. Sheehan, seven years old when his family was evicted from its farm in 1880, was a fervent nationalist and all his relatives were fenians. His 'love of motherland' has been described as 'passionate and intense'. In 1921 he denounced the British for their past and present 'savage repressions and ruthless oppressions', and their over-taxation of Ireland since the Act of Union. But he believed the solution to Ireland's difficulties lay through conciliation rather than confrontation and he opposed any form of partition. His convictions drew him into conflict with the IPP.

He was general secretary of the All for Ireland League, formed in 1910 when William O'Brien, who was also completely opposed to the third home rule bill and partition, broke with the UIL. Including prominent unionists among its membership, the organisation's motto, 'Conference, Conciliation, Consent' was unacceptable to John Redmond and the majority of IPP members. Sheehan was hounded out of the IPP in its 'foul attempt to exterminate Mr. O'Brien's friends' and he stood for his mid-Cork constituency as an independent nationalist in the general election of

January 1910. Against the odds, and claiming that 95 per cent of illiterates voted for him despite opposition from the priests, Sheehan beat the IPP candidate, taking 59 per cent of the votes cast.

However, his main interests lay in the need to 'lead the labourers out of the bondage and misery ... [resulting from] their own sad legacy of generations of servitude and subjection'. A founder member of labour organisations which led to the formation of the Irish Land and Labour Association[170] in 1894, Sheehan entered the IPP in 1901 'for one purpose, and one alone, of pushing the labourers' claims upon the notice of the leaders and of ventilating their grievances in the House of Commons'. He recalled how, as a boy, he saw other children without shoes who 'shivered in insufficient rags and whose gaunt bodies never knew any nourishment' other than 'Indian meal stirabout'. Poverty was a shared condition which bound labourer and small farmers into a community with few class distinctions. It was a period, however, when 'otherwise good and honest men ... thought the labourers had no citizen rights and that it was the height of conscious daring for anybody to lift either hand or voice on their behalf'.[171]

The rural labour movement brought Sheehan into contact with James J. O'Shee, the young Carrick-on-Suir solicitor who was secretary of the Irish Land and Labour Association and MP for West Waterford. Sheehan considered him a man of advanced views with an 'intense sympathy' for the labourer's plight. Although Sheehan complained that the rural labour movement received little support or assistance from urban labour organisations, in 1895 Charlie Strange and a delegation from Waterford's FTLU attended a meeting near Ring for the purpose of setting up a County Waterford branch of the association.[172]

---

169   Lucy (1992), pp. 68, 353–55.
170   The Irish Land and Labour Association sought to organise agricultural labourers and small tenant farmers. It demanded 'houses for the people, land for the people, work and wages for the people, education for the people, state pensions for old people and that all local rates should be paid by the ground landlords'. The ILLA broke up after the formation of the Irish Labour Party and Trade Union Congress in 1912 and its members were mainly absorbed into the new labour movement.
171   Sheehan (1921), pp. 1–2, 35, 53–56, 74, 147, 170–71, 174–78, 180, 198, 201, 222–32, 276–78.
172   *Waterford News*, 23 Mar. 1895.

Sheehan joined the 16th Division in November 1914 because he had his own 'strong and earnest conviction about the war and the justice and righteousness of the Allied cause' and because he wanted to advance the 'cause of Irish freedom'. It was his view that Irishmen should fight abroad where the 'issue between right and wrong' would be decided under battle conditions. Throwing himself enthusiastically into the recruiting campaign and using a range of selection tests, he claimed to have recruited nearly every soldier in the 9th Munsters. Under the slogan 'Fight for Right and Duty, Home and Motherland', he conducted extensive tours throughout the regimental district, which included Cork. The battalion was largely made up of Corkmen and Sheehan probably exerted a personal influence in his constituency. Three of his sons enlisted. Martin Joseph joined the cadet company and was given a commission in the 9th Munsters at 16 years of age. He was wounded in May 1916 and was one of two of Sheehan's sons later killed in action. Daniel Sheehan later wrote:

> I served and I suffered, and I sacrificed, and if the results were not all that we intended let this credit at least be given to those of us who joined up then, that we enlisted for worthy and honourable motives and we sought, and sought alone, the ultimate good of Ireland in doing so.

In his opinion, Willie Redmond also 'offered his life as surely for Ireland as any man who ever died for Irish liberty'.[173] Willie Redmond evoked affection among British and Irish alike. A sergeant of the 8th Inniskillings, witnessing his fatal wounding in 1917, remarked, 'It's a sorry day for Ireland'.[174] Parsons thought John Redmond's son was a 'perfectly poisonous bounder'[175] and one British officer, recalling the difficulty in restraining himself from striking Redmond's son, was

none the less 'destined to remember with the profoundest admiration and respect' Willie Redmond.[176]

Stephen Gwynn recalled him as being 'quiet, reserved, and rather shy' and feeling 'strange' among a society in which they were 'almost the only Nationalists'. In his view Willie Redmond was 'made for the simple life of disciplined obedience and utter loyalty which is the soldier's ideal'. On 16 March 1916, Willie Redmond told the House of Commons:

> I am happy to say that I am going back to the front almost immediately .... Nothing in the world can depress the spirits of the men that I have seen at the front. I do not believe there were ever enough Germans born into the world to depress them.

And he never applied for leave at Easter because he could not bring himself to leave his post with his company. In a telling symbolic gesture, Willie Redmond would not ride but marched with his men. Of the practice whereby officers rode, a British veteran wrote:

> as if to remind us of the inferiority of our station, the colonel and company [commanding officers], looking soldierly and unfatigued, rode well-groomed horses. Looking at it today it seems a display of class privilege, but fifty years ago the Tommy accepted it as the natural order of things, for the changes enjoyed by the masses were not even thought of.[177]

A traditional explanation of why men in British regiments at the front accepted their lot and were 'cheerful and stoical rather than outraged and introspective' was their poverty-stricken antecedents. It has been estimated that a third of those in the British lines were from urban slums

173 Sheehan (1921), pp. 287–88.
174 Carrothers (c. 1992), p. 58.
175 Parsons, diary entry, 24 Feb. 1915 (Parsons Papers, MD 1111), Woolwich.
176 Colyer, 'War Diary' (Colyer Papers, 76/51/1), IWM.
177 Coppard (1986), p. 17.

and were better off in the trenches than at home. Moreover, the poverty

> produced a vast number of men with a stunted response to novelty [and] the relatively static class divisions ... put a premium on social deference and correctness [and there was a] low level of cultural interchange through passive schools and stunted media.[178]

'Tommy' was also too busy staying alive to plot revolution. Patrick MacGill explained, 'we had one job to do and that job took up our whole attention' so 'few of us knew of the importance of the events in which we took part, and cared as little'. But by 1917 there were signs of questioning, discontent and indiscipline.[179] Poverty and its consequences, poor education and the deference of Edwardian working classes as explanations of the generally stoic, unquestioning loyalty of soldiers at the front, apply to Irishmen as well as to Britons, despite feelings like those of John Lucy who thought his family 'could not easily sacrifice for a cause not directly connected with Ireland'.[180] Moreover, soldiers, irrespective of nationality, may have shared a more profound, although illusive, conviction which sustained them in battle. Unlike people at home, it has been argued, they continued to believe in the ideals for which they enlisted.[181]

But the nationalist sentiment shared by many Irishmen in the division distinguished them from their British counterparts. In a sealed message opened after his death at the front, Willie Redmond wrote, 'if I should die ... I shall die a true Catholic ... in joining the Irish Brigade and going to France, I sincerely believed, as all Irish soldiers do, that I was doing my best for the welfare of Ireland in every way'.[182] James English, raised in a community in which so many expressed personal loyalty to John Redmond and

the IPP, was likely to have been swayed by such sentiments.

Although banning political party songs and institutionally emasculating nationalism, the British army did not suppress its constitutional manifestation. When Augustine Roche, the former IPP member for Cork city who lost his seat to an independent nationalist in December 1910, died in 1915, Corkmen in the 9th Munsters wrote to his friends and relatives offering their sympathy. According to the battalion's band members Roche had 'great generosity towards the poor'. Another letter from 'the boys of the 9th Munsters' referred to him as being 'honest, straight forward, generous and kindly'. They knew him well, admired him and would 'revere' his memory. Declaring their pride in following a man with such 'good and manly Nationalist principles', they concluded 'when we come back victorious after we do our little bit [we will] "fall in" again under the old banner and with the old Party'.

Nationalist MPs such as Joe Devlin were permitted visits to the infantry battalions while they were in training and at the front. They reinforced the message that the division was fighting for a good cause.[183] When an Irish journalist was allowed to visit troops in February 1916, he was accompanied by Colonel Jamieson-Davis of the National Volunteers' Vinegar Hill battalion. Jamieson-Davis, in full Volunteer uniform, met some of his own Volunteers in the trenches and had 'interesting chats with them'.[184]

The infantry brigades of the 16th Division asserted their cultural autonomy and distinct Irishness in a number of ways. For men raised in a 'band culture', music was an important element in their identity. In October 1914, the War Office notified all army units that drums and fifes would

178 Winter (1978), p. 230.
179 Englander, D. and Osborne, J. (1978), 'Jack, Tommy and Henry Dubb: the armed forces and the working class', *The Historical Journal*, 21, pp. 593–621; MacGill (1984b), pp. 131, 134.
180 Lucy (1992), p. 318.
181 Hynes (1990), p. 119.
182 Keating, J., 'Major Willie Redmond' in Lavery (ed.) (1920), pp. 81–90.
183 *Cork Constitution*, 22 Jan. 1915.
184 *Cork Weekly Examiner*, 26 Feb. 1916.

not be issued. On a visit to training camps Kipling noted the absence of music and despite the need to save money, he thought it 'surely could do no harm to cheer the men with a few bands'.[185] At the Battle of Loos a soldier identified the importance of battalion bands. Met by pipers at Le Brebis, the music 'put new life into us, and gave us just that little extra strength to get to our destination'.[186] From money provided by a benefactor, John Redmond supplied the brigades with fife and drum equipment.

The War Office order was rescinded in December and band instruments were issued but musicians, selected from men with previous experience in their instruments, were trained as soldiers and their band duties were additional.[187] Men of the 9th Munsters, however, wanted Irish bagpipes and these were initially hired for them. Staniforth recorded that when his battalion marched out of camp in February 1915 'we made a great impression coming up through the glens, with those fierce little Irish war-pipes they have screeching and echoing among the hills'.[188] And in July 1915, John Redmond sent sets of Irish pipes to the 2nd Munsters at the front. Redmond also provided each of the 16th Division's infantry brigades with an Irish wolfhound as a mascot. Referred to as 'great boarhounds' by the local English press, these animals, each led by a drummer boy, took part in the queen's parade at Aldershot in December 1915.[189]

For St Patrick's Day 1916 each Irish battalion at the western front received large hampers of shamrock from Redmond. As far as possible, shamrock was also sent to Irish soldiers in British regiments at the front and in Britain.[190] Right up to the front line, the Irish battalions celebrated the feast-day in 'good old Irish style'. Led by Irish war-pipes and drums and gaily decorated with a 'lavish display of shamrock and green ribbon', they marched to meet their chaplains to celebrate mass in the open.

Brigade sports took place in the afternoon. There were races, an officers' race, a wheelbarrow race and other events of a 'comical nature'. Bonfires were lit after special prayers with concerts and dancing until the late hours.[191] In the 48th Brigade sports the 9th Munsters won the individual and battalion grenadier event, the machine-gun competition, the tug-of-war, and the dancing and the mule racing competitions. It came second in wiring.[192] The battalion's band probably played the tunes traditionally played by the Royal Munster Fusiliers on St Patrick's Day. These included *The Wearing of the Green*, *The Harp that Once Hung in Tara's Hall*, and *The Battle March of Munster*. During the playing of *Brian Boru* there was a pause for cheering.[193] These leisure activities reinforced *esprit de corps* and boosted morale.[194] On 30 May 1916, however, the 9th Munsters was broken up and ceased to exist.

It may therefore be concluded that while Irish battalions in the 16th Division formed part of a British institution and were largely integrated with British soldiers and units, they none the less retained a distinctly Irish identity in several respects. And the belief of many men who made up the battalions was that they fought in Ireland's cause.

185 Kipling (1915), p. 4.
186 Dolden, A. S. (1980), *Cannon Fodder*, Poole, p. 35.
187 Printed War Office circular letters Ref. 114/infantry/1412 (A.G.1), 20 Oct. and 11 Dec. 1914 (WO 162/3), PRO.
188 Staniforth, letter, 5 Feb. 1915 (Staniforth Papers), IWM.
189 *Camberley News*, 11 Dec. 1915.
190 *Waterford Standard*, 15 Mar. 1916.
191 *Cork Weekly Examiner*, 1 Apr. 1915.
192 War Diary, 9th Munsters, entry 17 Mar. 1916.
193 Holt, notes (Holt Papers, 7603–69–1), NAM.
194 Fuller (1990), Chap. 8.

Plate 9

Officers of the 9th Battalion Royal Munster Fusiliers, *c.* April 1916 (*Irish Life*, Vol. 18 [July–Oct. 1916], p. 12, National Library of Ireland)

A photograph taken in France of the 9th Batt. of the Royal Munster Fusiliers, who have so gallantly upheld the traditional fighting spirit of the regiment. The officers sitting are Major Sheldrick, Major Keely, Col. Monteagle Brown, Capt. and Adjutant Harrison, and Capt. Fletcher.

Plate 10

Band of the 9th Battalion Royal Munster Fusiliers, *c.* April 1916 (*Cork Weekly Examiner*, 22 Apr. 1916, by permission of Cork Examiner Publications)

BAND OF A FAMOUS IRISH BATTALION.

The drums and pipes of the 9th Batt. of Royal Munster Fusiliers. Several members of the band are from the city of Cork.

(Layette).

Plate 11

A standard, combining the union flag and an Irish harp, flown by the 2nd Battalion Royal Munster Fusiliers over their headquarters on the western front (Courtesy of the Director, National Army Museum, London)

Plate 12

Ruins of Loos, October 1915 after the Battle of Loos (Imperial War Museum, London)

Plate 13

The main street of Maroc, November 1915 after the Battle of Loos (Imperial War Museum, London)

Plate 14

British attack on Hohenzollern Redoubt, near Hulluch, during the Battle of Loos, September 1915. Note the flat terrain and the lines of chalk thrown up when trenches were dug
(Imperial War Museum, London)

Plate 15

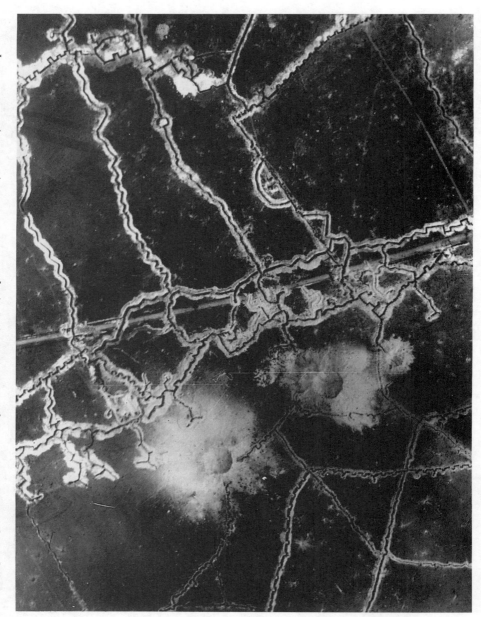

Aerial photograph (taken 28 March 1916) of German mine craters in front of Hulluch. The explosions, occurring during the evening of 26 March, destroyed part of the trench system, on the left of the picture, occupied by the 9th Battalion Royal Munster Fusiliers (Imperial War Museum, London). See also Map 3

Plate 16

A headstone located in the graveyard of Trinity (Ballybricken) Catholic Church
commemorating the death in action of a Ballybricken woman's soldier
son and of her grandson, a passenger on the SS *Coninbeg*.
Note the incorrect date of the sinking

Plate 17

A memorial plaque erected by Graves and Co., Waterford city, to commemorate
members of their staff who served in the war

Plate 18

The grave of an 'Old contemptible', Ballynaneashagh Cemetery, Waterford

CONCLUSION

James English's body was never found. Presumed dead, he was one of 236,573 soldiers in the British army reported missing in action in France. At the grave of an 'unknown' soldier whose exposed head was covered in 'almost golden hair', Father Willie Doyle reflected on the 'sorrowing mother, far away, thinking of her boy who was "missing" and hoping against hope that he might one day come back'.[1] This reaction was similar to that of many wives. Despite official notification of her husband's death, Katey English refused to accept it. For years afterwards she sought out and questioned returned Waterford soldiers about James's whereabouts and joked about him having abandoned her for a French woman.

Other traces of James English have also vanished. Apart from the parish records and his death certificate, which presumes his death in France and incorrectly records his age as being 25, no written record of his life remains. Thomas's Avenue has been demolished. The contents of his cottage and of a trunk in which Katey kept his Sunday best suit, the documents notifying her of his death and a 'war plate', a probable reference by his daughter Margaret to an engraved bronze plaque sent on behalf of the king to the next-of-kin of all those soldiers who died in the war, have gone. And during the Second World War his official military records were destroyed in enemy air raids.

However, James English has been rescued from complete anonymity. His name, along with those of 20,692 other soldiers from Ireland and Britain, is inscribed on a memorial in Dud Corner military cemetery. The cemetery over-looks Loos and the chalk-scarred meadows which sweep on to Hulluch. The memorial bears the names of officers and men who died in the trenches in the Loos salient but to whom 'the fortune of war denied the known and honoured burial given to their comrades in death'.[2]

But the memorial says nothing of why men such as James English went to war. Despite the trappings of democracy, he lived in a society in which his mental and social development and his personal and political freedoms were stunted by social and economic deprivation. It was a society in which his opportunities were limited and which, short of emigration, thwarted his aspirations and debased the value of his contribution. Nor was the 'freedom' promised by nationalists, of whatever colour, likely to radically alter the status quo.

In war, however, the government needed the services of men from the labouring class. It spent huge amounts of money accommodating, equipping and training recruits who would otherwise have remained unskilled and uneducated. Labourers acquired greater value and status. The army rewarded them for their willingness to serve it and for their loyalty. It fed and clothed them and provided for their families. Enlistment meant a job which offered escape from drudgery. It promised excitement, the potential for advancement and a future. The army gave their lives purpose and importance.

Nor does the memorial's inscription take cognisance of the thoughts and feelings of men such as the Connaught Ranger who expressed the view of many of his British and Irish comrades who survived the war, when he observed that the

---

1 O'Rahilly (1925), p. 411.
2 Commonwealth War Graves Commission, *Their Names Liveth*, Vol. v (1961).

government had 'thrown those of us now demo-
bilised aside as of no further use'.[3] The bulk of
recruits in the Irish regiments were from the
urban labouring class. But before and after the
war they were considered by some of those in
positions of power and authority, to be outside
the mainstream.

This study is an attempt to present James
English, a representative of the Irish urban
labouring class, as a 'sentient, reflecting being'[4]
and to rescue him from what has been described
as the 'enormous condescension of posterity'.[5]
However, for any understanding of why he was
motivated to enlist and what then kept him loyal
and obedient, the historian is thrown back on
oblique evidence.

The relevant general backdrop against which
he acted out his life, and as far as possible his
personal routines and the tight community in
which he lived, have therefore been recreated in
some detail. Economic theory, political strategy
and military tactics did not preoccupy him. But
the availability of work, the opinions of his parish
priests, political leaders and neighbours, the exciting blend of band music and politics on his
city's streets, the daily trench routines shared
with other men and the number and quality of
meals, were all of significance to him. The detail
helps to explain, to some extent, his mental set,
and his case also supports a number of generalisations.

Men in Ireland joined the pre-war regular
British army in a context and under conditions
different from those prevailing after war was declared and when the New Armies were being
raised. Conclusions in respect of Roger Casement's claim that recruits in the First World War
army were not Irishmen but English soldiers
therefore need to be modified according to
whether they refer to pre-war army regulars or
New Army recruits. The circumstances affecting
a man's decision to enlist also differed between

individuals and localities. But generally the
soldier's perspective of Irishness differed from
that of Casement's in four major respects.

Firstly, Casement, a knighted member of the
consular service, belonged to a class which was
privileged and remote from the world to which
the bulk of men joining the ranks of the Irish
regiments belonged. He thought the prisoners at
Limburg a 'poor lot' and the 'scum of Ireland'.[6]
In this sense labourers such as James English had
far more in common with many British soldiers
than they had with Irishmen of Casement's class.
Mainly unskilled urban workers, many of whom
were illiterate, they played a subordinate role in
Irish society. Their wages were low and their
living standards were generally substandard.

Government intervention in the local economy
was negligible and the unskilled labouring class
grew up depending on rate- and taxpayers. A
small group of entrepreneurs were responsible
for creating work and wealthy citizens provided
charity in time of need. They lived in poverty
and under the constant threat of unemployment
and pauperism. Liberal social legislation provided some relief and the promise of a change for
the better, but their conditions worsened considerably as a result of the war. The army offered
financial improvement and security for many,
especially married family men, as well as improved status and enhanced future prospects.

Secondly, although there were contradictions
which complicate the general picture, Waterford
city society was homogeneous. Its Catholicism,
traditional class structure, nationalist culture,
Redmondite hegemony and social matrix made
the Ballybricken community a close one. And this
created a range of communal pressures on men
to enlist when John Redmond committed IPP
support to the British government's war policy.

An anti-German mood among city leaders
resentful of German competition and protection-
ism already existed when war was declared.

3 Fitzpatrick, 'The overflow of the deluge' in MacDonagh and Mandle (eds.) (1986).
4 Tosh (1984), p. 86.
5 Thompson, E. P. (1980), *The Making of the English Working Class*, Harmondsworth, p. 12.
6 Parmiter (1936), pp. 186, 206.

There was also a general sense that war was good and part of the human condition. And mobilisation brought feverish military activity to the city. An enthusiasm for the war which crossed class and religious lines fuelled militarism and stimulated enlistment. Military funerals at home, stories circulated by returned soldiers, the death of hundreds of Waterford soldiers, the arrival of refugees, wounded soldiers and exchanged prisoners of war, all contributed to drawing the Ballybricken community together to face a common enemy and to making men more susceptible to the call to arms.

Thirdly, Casement considered the British link and imperialism reprehensible. His work on the violation of human rights in Africa and South America reinforced a distrust of European empires and made him cynical about the alleged rape of 'little Belgium' by the Germans. Like James Connolly, he also expressed the view that in declaring war it was Asquith's and the British government's intentions to 'glut the greedy jealousy of the British commercial mind. Germany's sin has been her efficiency'.[7] But many Irishmen with nationalist sentiments could still identify with Britain and British imperialism. The consequences were sometimes strikingly paradoxical. Using extreme rhetoric, leading Waterford nationalists denounced 'shoneenism' but played cricket with the British garrison team although the game was outlawed by the GAA.

This duality in attitude created an ambivalence towards the army and men could hold, or be exposed to, conflicting loyalties. Father Crotty, one of two priests appointed to Limburg through the German embassy at the Vatican, told the prisoners to 'keep the oath you have taken to be loyal to your King',[8] while Father Nicholas who travelled to Limburg from the United States, spread pro-German propaganda.[9]

However, the British army was an institution which inspired an overarching loyalty. Although preserving distinctly different Irish, Scottish, Welsh and English regiments with their own local and national culture and traditions, it generally defused national antagonisms and drained national differences of their political potency. There were exceptions, but generally men were drawn together in a frequently close comradeship by a system of training and by commonly shared daily routine, danger and exceptional experiences which set them apart from the civilian population, whatever its nationality. Soldiers were primarily loyal to their comrades and their battalion, regiment or division.

Political sensitivities in the 16th (Irish) Division were further assuaged by diluting the traditionally Protestant and unionist officer corps. Catholics and nationalists were commissioned as subalterns through the officer cadet company and a Catholic commander was appointed.

And fourthly, while Casement was a committed physical force separatist, the pre-war Irish soldier was frequently apolitical. However, this was much less true of men joining the New Armies. But those who were politically conscious were generally home rulers and Casement was of the opinion that the constitutionalists spouted treason but did nothing practical for Irish freedom.

Some leading IPP members who had advocated a boycott of the British army at the turn of the century, now enthusiastically campaigned for recruits. Although a constitutionalist such as John Dillon did not share the vision of Ireland being part of a great British empire and thought Germany had been pushed into war by British and French foreign policy, he nevertheless urged Irishmen to enlist, considering it necessary to cooperate with the British in order to achieve home rule.

Differences between the two nationalist traditions partly explain why the bulk of army recruits were unskilled urban workers while the urban

7 Parmiter (1936), p. 168.
8 Taken from an unidentified and undated newspaper cutting. The report was printed in *The Times* and originated with Mr F. Sefton Delmer, an Australian professor who had recently returned from Germany (Papers relating to Father Crotty, 13,100), INL.
9 Parmiter (1936), pp. 192–93, 215.

middle class and farmers and their families remained aloof. Key explanations for Waterford men enlisting were the local supremacy of Redmond's home rule hegemony and the subordinate place of unskilled workers in local society.

The city's clerical and lay leaders in all spheres of public life, in business, the professions and the skilled trades, were Redmond supporters and politically active. Civic institutions were under their control and nationalist and non-political organisations were infiltrated and aligned with the constitutionalist cause. This produced contradictions. Casement was a member of the Gaelic League but Redmond supporters also managed an active local branch of the league. And the local contingent of *Na Fianna Eireann* participated in Redmondite demonstrations.

Redmondite nationalist politics therefore profoundly influenced the outlook and lives of Waterford labourers. Although possessing a local and parliamentary franchise, in practice their freedom to exercise it was restricted. They were poorly educated and deferred to the authority of a small group of clerical and upper- and middle-class lay leaders who monopolised political and economic power and who were also generally Redmond supporters and actively encouraged enlistment.

Allegiance to Redmond reinforced the traditional class homogeneity. Redmondism, in pulling together conservative and nationalist strands of the ruling group and consolidating their common interests, was a major factor in reconciling religious, class and political differences. And it undermined any potential challenge from a generally deferential, economically weak and unorganised labouring class. Redmond and Redmondites usurped the role of labour leaders at parliamentary and local levels. Unskilled workers were largely unresponsive to militant New Unionism and on the whole the Irish working class was docile when the United Kingdom entered the war.

Pro-war propaganda was disseminated through the local Redmondite newspapers and through films, books, public addresses and or-

ganised recruiting campaigns. It appealed to the need to demonstrate 'manliness' and was used to exploit Irish military traditions, the promise of home rule, Catholic religious sympathies and loyalty to Redmond. And it marketed the financial and practical advantages of joining the army.

By the end of 1915, however, the Redmondite consensus had been fatally weakened. Redmond's commitment to recruitment for both the British army and the National Volunteers resulted in inconsistencies which became increasingly difficult to rationalise after the government spurned the offer of the National Volunteers for home defence, and as the war wore on. Membership of the Volunteers and the UIL rapidly declined. Redmond's authority was undermined by the British in their inept handling of recruitment and the conscription issue. Doubts about their use, and the inadequacy of information and praise in respect of the achievements of Irish troops, fuelled dissent. The situation was made worse by a series of disputes with the Anglo-Irish commander of the 16th Division.

Redmond's support thinned with the inclusion of Edward Carson in a coalition government. More people also now considered home rule in a united Ireland unlikely. The government's insensitive application of war policies in Ireland and its failure to recognise Redmond's role as Irish leader accelerated a decline in his influence. Of particular harm to him were the perceptions that he had failed to resist job-destroying policies, or to secure a fair share of munitions work, other war work or extra employment and that he had been unable to stave off harmful and unjustifiable taxation. This aggravated a traditional distrust of British economic intentions in Ireland.

There were significant differences between them in background and in class and political attitudes, but it may be concluded that soldiers who fought with the British army were just as Irish as Casement. Although belonging to a British institution and sometimes confused about their national identity, they, as well as Casement, were the products of peculiarly Irish conditions and their mental outlook was shaped by an Irish world, despite historical British influences and connections which left their mark on all things Irish. But Casement failed to comprehend the gulf which separated the labouring class from his own and his judgement that men such as James English were more English soldiers than Irishmen was based on nothing more than the fact that they were either apolitical or held a political view different from his own.

Finally, James English's case gives substance to the view that the war 'as an agent of social, economic, administrative, political and mental revolution', dwarfed other factors.[10] It has been remarked that 1914 marked the 'beginning of processes of which 1916 was rather the symptom than the cause'.[11] The question of how far the Easter Rising, its aftermath, and post-war events in Ireland were the consequences of the First World War is an enticing one.

10 Fitzpatrick, 'The overflow of the deluge' in MacDonagh and Mandle (eds.) (1986).
11 Townshend (1983), p. 278.

APPENDICES

Appendix A

A table showing the distribution and religion of Waterford city's population, 1881 to 1911

City wards	Population			Percentage change in population 1881–1911		Density in 1911 (Sq. ft per person)	Religion of population (percentage in 1881)		
	1881	*1901*	*1911*	*Increase (+)*	*Decrease (–)*		*R.C.*	*Protestant*	*Other*
Centre	1,992	3,509	3,781	89.8	–	70.4	90.5	9.0	0.5
Custom House	3,279	3,244	3,092	–	5.7	103.3	90.2	9.5	0.3
South	9,086	9,485	9,947	9.5	–	167.9	95.3	4.4	0.3
Tower	4,462	6,439	6,802	52.4	–	362.2	78.3	18.0	3.7
West	3,638	4,092	3,842	5.6		583.3	92.1	7.0	0.9
TOTALS	22,457	26,769	27,464	22.3	–	–	–	–	–

(Source: Calculations based on census statistics 1881, 1901 and 1911)

Appendix B

A table showing changes in Waterford city's population between 1901 and 1911 as compared with other Irish cities

City	Population	Percentage increase 1901–1911
Belfast	386,947	10.82
Dublin	304,802	4.87
Cork	76,673	0.72
Londonderry	40,780	2.23
Limerick	38,518	0.96
Waterford	27,464	2.60

(Source: Calculations based on census statistics 1901 and 1911)

Appendix C

A table showing changes in the categories of employment and the percentage increase in jobs in Waterford city between 1881 and 1911

Employment category	Numbers employed			Percentage change 1881–1911	
	1881	1901	1911	Increase (+)	Decrease (–)
Chemicals and compounds	19	35	53	178.9	–
Commercial occupations	271	402	489	80.4	–
Tobacco and pipes	20	16	34	70.0	–
General or unspecified commodities	1,523	2,162	2,338	53.5	–
Books, prints and maps	83	145	127	53.0	–
Agriculture	165	121	244	47.9	–
Professional occupations	832	850	1,110	33.4	–
Textile fabrics	287	406	359	25.0	–
About animals	253	222	313	23.7	–
General or local government	240	308	293	22.1	–
Machines and implements	78	92	87	11.5	–
Houses, furniture and decorations	548	582	590	7.7	–
Conveyance of people, goods and messages	1,185	1,133	1,258	6.2	–
Mineral substances	332	292	304	–	8.4
Carriages and harness	83	80	73	–	12.0
Defence	224	212	186	–	17.0
Vegetable substances	213	161	170	–	20.2
Food and lodgings	1,202	1,014	899	–	25.2
Domestic offices or services	2,346	2,098	1,582	–	32.5
Dress	1,165	883	772	–	33.7
Ships and boats	42	27	26	–	38.1
Animal substances	50	9	8	–	84.0
Refuse matters	57	6	9	–	84.2
TOTALS	11,218	11,256	11,324	0.9	–

(Source: Calculations based on census statistics 1881, 1901 and 1911)

Appendix D

A table showing changes in the total working population, and in the composition of the 'non-producing population' (15–65 years) of Waterford city between 1881 and 1911

Year	Population (totals)	15–65 year olds in population						Non-producing population (15–65 year olds)					
		Numbers	Composition by gender (Numbers and %)		Percentage of total population			Numbers	Composition by gender (Numbers and %)		Percentage of 15–65 year old population		
			Males	Females	Total	Males	Females		Males	Females	Total	Males	Females
1881	22,457	14,377	6,513 (45%)	7,864 (55%)	64.0	29.0	35.0	3,945	297 (7%)	3,648 (93%)	27.5	2.1	25.4
1901	26,769	17,131	7,882 (46%)	9,249 (54%)	64.0	29.4	34.6	6,491	889 (14%)	5,602 (86%)	37.9	5.2	32.7
1911	27,464	17,279	8,432 (49%)	8,847 (51%)	62.9	30.7	32.2	6,713	808 (12%)	5,905 (88%)	38.9	4.7	34.2

(Source: Calculations based on census statistics 1881, 1901 and 1911)

Appendix E

A bar chart showing the percentage of population employed in the various categories of work in Waterford city in 1911

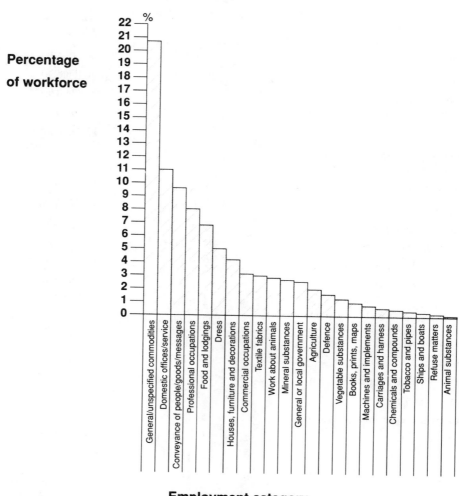

(Source: Calculations based on census statistics 1911)

Appendix F

A table showing the two employment categories, 'general/unspecified commodities' and 'domestic offices/service', broken down into their sub-classifications

Employment category	Numbers employed and percentage of total according to gender		Total
	Males	Females	
General labourer	1,909 (99.8%)	3 (0.2%)	1,912
Domestic indoor servant	39 (3.2%)	1,186 (96.8%)	1,225
General shopkeeper, dealer	57 (25.2%)	169 (74.8%)	226
Inn, hotel servant	31 (30.4%)	71 (69.6%)	102
Hospital and institution service (excluding nurses)	45 (57.0%)	34 (43.0%)	79
Engine driver, stoker, fireman (not railway, marine, nor agric.)	55 (100%)	–	55
Bathing and washing service	1 (2.0%)	48 (98.0%)	49
Factory labourer	11 (27.5%)	29 (72.5%)	40
Charwoman	–	37 (100%)	37
Domestic—coachman, groom	34 (100%)	–	34
Costermonger, huckster, street seller	17 (60.7%)	11 (39.3%)	28
Machinist, machine worker	8 (30.8%)	18 (69.2%)	26
Domestic gardener	22 (95.7%)	1 (4.3%)	23
Pawnbroker	22 (100%)	–	22
Miscellaneous service work	17 (85.0%)	3 (15.0%)	20
Artisan, mechanic	14 (100%)	–	14
Manufacturer, manager, superintendent	10 (76.9%)	3 (23.1%)	13
College, club—service	6 (100%)	–	6
Lodge, gate, park-keeper (not government)	5 (100%)	–	5
Cook (not domestic)	1 (50.0%)	1 (50.0%)	2
Contractor	1 (100%)	–	1
Apprentice, assistant	1 (100%)	–	1
TOTALS	2,306	1,614	3,920

(Source: Calculations based on census statistics 1911)

Appendix G

Bar charts showing changes in the employment of residents of Thomas's Avenue (Wheelbarrow Lane) between 1901 and 1911

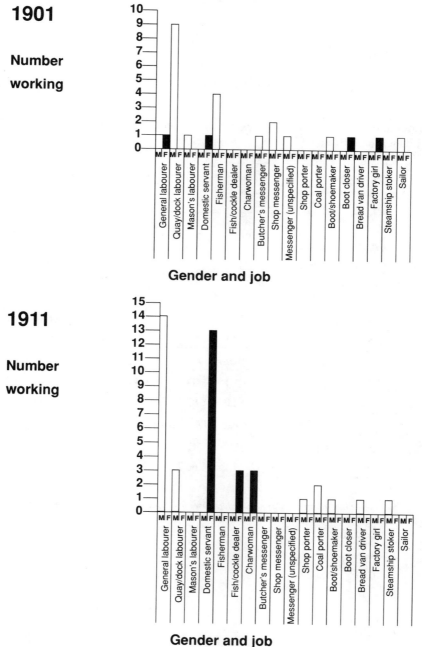

(Source: Calculations based on census statistics 1901 and 1911)

Appendix H

A table showing comparative literacy figures for all Ireland, Waterford city and Thomas's Avenue (Wheelbarrow Lane) for 1901 and 1911

| Year | Whole population (15 yrs and over) (%) | | | Population by gender (%) | | Literacy standards by gender (%) | | | | | |
| | | | | Male | Female | Male | | | Female | | |
	Read and write	Read only	Neither read nor write			Read and write	Read only	Neither read nor write	Read and write	Read only	Neither read nor write
All Ireland											
1901	80.9	5.8	13.3	48.7	51.3	82.4	4.8	12.8	79.4	6.8	13.8
1911	86.2	3.5	10.3	49.6	50.4	87.1	2.8	10.1	85.3	4.1	10.6
Waterford city											
1901	78.5	6.4	15.1	45.9	54.1	83.4	5.3	11.3	74.3	7.5	18.2
1911	83.8	3.6	12.6	48.0	52.0	87.4	2.9	9.7	80.4	4.3	15.3
Thomas's Avenue (Wheelbarrow Lane)											
1901	27.3	4.5	68.2	47.7	52.3	47.6	–	52.4	8.7	8.7	82.6
1911	55.4	3.5	41.1	42.9	57.1	66.7	4.2	29.1	46.9	3.1	50.0

(Source: Calculations based on census statistics, including raw data contained in returns submitted by residents of Thomas's Avenue 1901 and 1911 [National Archives, Four Courts])

Appendix I

A table showing the number and employment status of Thomas's Avenue (Wheelbarrow Lane) residents according to gender and working age (taken as any age over 15 years) in 1901 and 1911. (Note: this table should be read in conjunction with Appendix G, which shows changes in the categories of employment)

Year	Totals	Under 15 yrs (by gender)		15–65 yrs (by gender)		Over 65 yrs (by gender)		Numbers in employment (by gender) 15 yrs and over		Percentage of over 15-year-olds in employment	Non-producers (over 15 yrs) (by gender)	
		M	F	M	F	M	F	M	F		M	F
1901	82	18	20	18	22	3	1	21	4	56.8	–	19
1911	97	20	21	24	30	–	2	23	19	75.0	1	13

(Source: Compiled from raw data contained in census returns 1901 and 1911)

Appendix J

A table and bar chart showing the number of residents in Thomas's Avenue (Wheelbarrow Lane) and their place of birth, the number of bilingual speakers and the number of persons occupying accommodation in 1901 and 1911

Table showing the number of residents, their places of birth, language spoken, the number of families and the number of houses occupied. **Note:** All accommodations occupied consisted of two rooms only

Year	Total number of residents	Place of birth				Bilingual English and Irish speakers	Total number of families	Number of houses occupied	Number of two-room accommodations occupied
		Waterford city	Waterford county	Wexford county	England				
1901	82	79 (96.3%)	1	1	1	3 (3.7%)	22	16	22
1911	97	94 (96.9%)	3	–	–	4 (4.1%)	22	16	22

Bar chart showing the number of persons in each of the 22 families occupying accommodation.

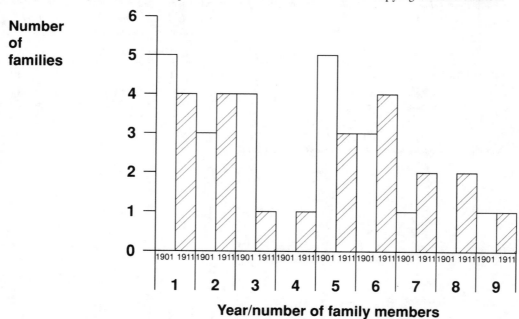

(Source: Compiled from raw data contained in census returns 1901 and 1911)

Appendix K

Southern Irish regiments and their recruiting districts in 1914

Southern Irish Infantry Regiments in the First World War

Army reforms initiated in 1868 and finalised in 1881 established regimental districts throughout the United Kingdom. Each district, which comprised a number of counties, was identified with a particular regiment. The regiment's depot was located in the district and drew on local manpower for recruits, thereby establishing a local identity and cultivating strong county links.

Until 1914 regiments comprised two battalions, identified as the 1st and 2nd battalions, which were filled with regular soldiers. These regular battalions were supported by local militia and volunteer units which generally made up a 3rd battalion. When Kitchener began raising the New Armies in 1914, extra battalions (the 'Service' battalions) were grafted on to regiments, thus increasing the number of battalions to ten or more.

There were five southern Irish regiments. These were:

Royal Irish Regiment
Regimental District (R.D.) no 18 (Tipperary, Kilkenny, Waterford). Depot at Clonmel.

Connaught Rangers
R.D. no. 88 (Galway, Clare, Roscommon). Depot at Galway.

Leinster Regiment
R.D. no. 100 (Longford, Meath, West Meath, King's County, Queen's Country). Depot at Birr.

Royal Munster Fusiliers
R.D. no. 101 (Tralee, Kerry, Cork). Depot at Tralee.

Royal Dublin Fusiliers
R.D. no. 102 (Naas, Kildare, Wicklow, Carlow). Depot at Naas.

The Royal Irish Fusiliers, the Royal Irish Rifles and the Royal Inniskilling Fusiliers were northern Irish regiments.

The Irish Guards were raised in April 1900 and had no specific regimental district. The regiment was made up of men drawn from the north and south of Ireland.

Appendix L

A table showing the approximate percentages of Waterford men available as recruits according to their employment category

Category of employment	Percentage of total population
Unskilled labour	31.6
Commerce	23.0
Skilled worker (artisans)	18.2
Clerical/professional	14.6
Persons not producing (including unemployed)	4.8
Farming/commercial gardens/dealing with animals	4.4
Manufacture	3.4
TOTAL	100.0

(Source: Percentages calculated using figures for the age range 20–45 in the census 1911)

Appendix M

A detailed breakdown of the employment categories of potential army recruits in Waterford, 1915

Unskilled labour		
General labourer	1,172	
Domestic service (coachman/groom/lodge keeper/hospital and institution service)	113	
Non-government messenger/porter/watchman	89	
Coalheaver	48	
Civil service messenger	40	
Agricultural labourer/cottager	35	
Road labourer/railway labourer/factory labourer/navvy	12	
Scavenger	1	
Toll collector	1	
		1,511
Commerce		
Provisions (creamery worker/dairyman/provision curer/dealer/butcher/ fishmonger/baker/corn miller/corn dealer/grocer/mineral water maker, dealer)	303	
Commercial clerks	141	
Draper/linen draper/mercer	129	
Tailor/milliner	123	
Merchant/bank worker/accountant/salesman/insurance	116	
Publisher/printer/newspaper agent	56	
Timber, wood merchant/sawyer/cooper/bark cutter, maker	42	
Publican/hotel keeper/lodging house keeper	36	
Blacksmith/whitesmith	35	
General shopkeeper/dealer	32	
Brewer/distiller/wine, spirit merchant	23	
Ironmonger/hardware dealer	18	
Pawnbroker	12	
Tobacconist	10	
Omnibus, coach, cab owner/livery stable keeper	9	
Costermonger/street seller/huckster	7	
Silversmith/jeweller	5	
Coal dealer	3	
Glass dealer	2	
Stationer	1	
		1,103

Skilled worker

Building trade (carpenter/plumber/bricklayer/woodcarver/gilder, etc.)	317
Carman/carrier/carter/drayman/motor car driver/chauffeur	99
Ship steward, cook/boatman on seas/harbour, dock, wharf service	79
Horse keeper, breaker/groom	53
Railway worker, stoker, guard	52
Furniture and fittings (locksmith/cabinet maker/upholsterer/french polisher, etc.)	51
Engine, machine maker/fitter and turner	40
Engine driver, stoker, fireman (not railway, marine nor agricultural)	37
Quarries/stone cutter, etc.	33
Cabman/coachman/flyman	18
Watch, clock maker/electrical apparatus maker	17
Gasworks service	16
Cellerman	11
Shipwright/ship carpenter	10
Inland navigation/barge, lighter, waterman	7
Artisan/mechanic	7
Machine worker	6
Gasfitter	5
Meter weigher	4
Chimney sweep	4
Musical instrument maker, dealer	3
Non-government telegraph, telephone service	2
Hay/straw cutter, dealer	1
	872

Clerical/professional

Student (undefined)	199
Railway official/servant	145
Police	63
Civil service officer and clerk	43
Teacher (schoolmaster/lecturer/professor)	41
Chemist/druggist	34
Artist (painter/theatre/photographer, etc.)	26
Legal (barrister/solicitor/law clerk/student)	26
Clergy (all denominations)	22
Monk	21
Local government officer	20
Medical (physician/surgeon/dentist, etc.)	19
Engineer and apprentice	11

Literary (journalist/author, etc.)	9
Performer/sportsman	7
Manager/supervisor/undefined manufacturer	7
Prison officer	4
Theological student	3
	700

Persons not producing

No specified occupation (mainly unemployed)	231	
		231

Farming/commercial gardens/dealing with animals

Pig dealer, salesman	104	
Farmer/grazier	47	
Farm bailiff/woodman/nurseryman/seedsman/florist/gardener/other	21	
Horse breeder, dealer	17	
Farrier/drover	15	
Farmer's son, grandson, brother, nephew	5	
Fisherman	1	
		210

Manufacture

Shoe, boot maker and dealer	74	
Coachmaker/motor car body maker/railway carriage, wagon maker/wheelwright/bicycle maker, etc.	31	
Iron, steel goods, tinplate manufacturer/manufacturer in other metals	19	
Saddle, harness, whip, etc. maker	11	
Hemp, jute manufacturer/rope, twine maker/bag, sack maker	7	
Paper bag maker	6	
Furrier/skinner/leather goods maker	5	
Tobacco, pipe, snuff box maker	4	
Ship, boat, barge maker/sail maker	2	
Basket maker/brush broom maker	2	
Paint manufacturer	1	
		162
	Total:	**4,789**

(Source: Census 1911)

Appendix N

Men identified as being posted to the 9th Battalion Royal Munster Fusiliers and subsequently discharged from the army with wounds or through illness

Serial no.		Rank and name		Date enlisted	
801	Pte	Michael Redmond	31	Aug	1914
777	Pte	John A. Jones	7	Sep	1914
780	Pte	James Jones	7	Sep	1914
786	Pte	Timothy Mahoney	14	Sep	1914
1201	Pte	Paul O'Connell	26	Sep	1914
1420	L/Cpl	Percy Rockley	23	Sep	1914
1850	Pte	James Dutton	11	Sep	1914
3361	Pte	John Creed	8	Sep	1914
3364		Thomas Kirk	3	Sep	1914
4126	Pte	William F. Davis	12	Sep	1914
5971	Pte	Edward Sheehan	7	Sep	1914
1327	Pte	Robert Cassidy	2	Oct	1914
1340	Cpl	Christopher Donohue	16	Oct	1914
1442	Pte	John H. Woods	1	Oct	1914
1489	Pte	William McMahon	19	Oct	1914
1521	Pte	Daniel Driscoll	24	Oct	1914
1080	Pte	Peter Stuart	16	Nov	1914
1461	Cpl	Michael Griffin	2	Nov	1914
1586	Pte	Arthur J. Heathfield	9	Nov	1914
1627	L/Cpl	James Vose	9	Nov	1914
1710	Pte	Herbert Hickson	9	Nov	1914
3750	Pte	Frederick O. Hodgins	2	Feb	1915
3877	Pte	James Mullany	13	Feb	1915
3915	Pte	Michael Long	15	Feb	1915
4345	Pte	Jeremiah Sheehan	18	Mar	1915
4406	Sgt	Michael Cleary	22	Mar	1915
4409	Pte	Cornelius Collins	16	Mar	1915
4413	Pte	Patrick Duggan	23	Mar	1915
4450		Michael Slattery	23	Mar	1915
4609	Pte	Martin Duggan	28	Mar	1915
4645	L/Cpl	David Egan	31	Mar	1915
4649	Pte	Augustine Kelly	30	Mar	1915
4582	Pte	Thomas Frawley	3	Apr	1915
4735	Pte	John Lister	20	Apr	1915

Serial no.		Rank and name	Date enlisted		
155	Pte	Ernest E. Hayes	26	May	1915
4782	Pte	Edward Lacy	6	May	1915
4787	Pte	Thomas Murphy	6	May	1915
4816	Pte	Daniel Leonard	15	May	1915
4819	Pte	Thomas O'Connor	13	May	1915
4901	Pte	Jeremiah Buckley	29	May	1915
4957	Pte	Maurice O'Callaghan	22	May	1915
4960	Pte	Michael Roche	20	May	1915
4961	Pte	Maurice Flynn	25	May	1915
4974	Pte	Frederick Allen	27	May	1915
4988	Pte	William J. Willis	26	May	1915
4993		Thomas William	26	May	1915
4968	Pte	Michael Mulcahy	1	Jun	1915
5202	Pte	Daniel Hegarty	10	Jun	1915
5209	Pte	Jeremiah Martin	2	Jun	1915
5385	Pte	James Smith	4	Jun	1915
5421	L/Cpl	Patrick Graham	10	Jun	1915
5428	Pte	John Joy	15	Jun	1915
5477	Pte	Michael Buckley	23	Jun	1915
5481	Pte	James Barrett	25	Jun	1915
5491	Pte	Frank Long	30	Jun	1915
5497	Pte	Frank Coghlan	28	Jun	1915
5583	Pte	Jeremiah Crowley	16	Jun	1915
5585	Pte	James White	14	Jun	1915
5519	Pte	William Hallissey	5	Jul	1915
5542	Pte	Patrick Driscoll	5	Jul	1915
5543	Pte	Frank McEvoy	7	Jul	1915
5551	Pte	Richard Walsh	8	Jul	1915
5644	Pte	James Cronin	19	Jul	1915
5672	Pte	Robert Roche	27	Jul	1915
5727	Pte	William Duggan	8	Aug	1915
834	Pte	Thomas W. Booker	27	Aug	1915
5860	Pte	James O'Brien	23	Aug	1915
5889	Pte	Charles McMahon	2	Sep	1915

(Source: PRO, WO 329/3006–3009)

Appendix O

List of men killed while serving with the 9th Battalion Royal Munster Fusiliers
* Died at home
** Reported missing in *The Times* on 24 Apr 1916

Date of death		Rank, number and name			Home town
May 1915					
16/4/15	Pte	1536	John Cusack		Ballingarry, Limerick
Sep 1915					
20/9/15	Pte	4585	John Hickey*		–
22/9/15	A/Cpl	3353	Patrick McLoughlin		Cloghan, King's County
Jan 1916					
8/1/16	Pte	393	William O'Donnell		Ardpatrick, Limerick
8/1/16	L/Cpl	727	Michael Punch		St Finbarr's, Cork
9/1/16	Pte	10388	Michael Hayes		Killarney, Kerry
Feb 1916					
27/2/16	Pte	5905	John Callaghan		St Ann's Cork
Mar 1916					
18/3/16	Pte	1534	Patrick Cusack		Glin, Limerick
26/3/16	Pte	4921	Thomas Dempsey**		Skibbereen, Cork
26/3/16	Pte	4425	John Hopkins**		French Park, Roscommon
26/3/16	L/Cpl	568	Jeremiah O'Connell**		Swansea, Glamorgan
27/3/16	Pte	5677	Michael Callaghan**		Donoughmore, Cork
27/3/16	Pte	311	Denis Breen		Millstreet, Cork
27/3/16	Pte	4157	Jacob Delmage		St Finbarr's, Cork
27/3/16	Pte	4414	James English**		Waterford
27/3/16	A/CSM	3423	Frank Fitzpatrick**		Dublin
27/3/16	Pte	601	Patrick Haughey**		Portadown, Amagh
27/3/16	Pte	3350	William Higgins**		St Mary's, Cahir
27/3/16	Pte	5433	Michael Joyce		St Ann's, Cork
27/3/16	Cpl	3978	Michael Lyons**		St Ann's, Cork
27/3/16	Pte	1497	Charles McCarthy		St Ann's, Cork
27/3/16	Pte	4825	Cornelius O'Connell**		St Ann's, Cork
27/3/16	Pte	5674	William O'Connell**		Pallas Grean, Limerick
27/3/16	Pte	5429	Timothy O'Grady**		Upton, Cork
27/3/16	Pte	4907	Cornelius Sugrue**		Kilmacomogue, Cork
28/3/16	Pte	3440	Peter Farley		–
28/3/16	Pte	1532	David Hegarty		St Nicholas', Cork
30/3/16	Pte	3938	John Whelton		Clonakilty, Cork

Date of Death		Rank, number and name			Home town
Apr 1916					
2/4/16	Pte	5521	Charles Lynch		St Finbarr's, Cork
3/4/16	Pte	4729	Timothy Ahern		Newcastle West, Limerick
4/4/16	Pte	3435	Cornelius Doherty		Milltown Malbay, Clare
20/4/16	Pte	5443	Michael Cooney		Ballincollig, Cork
22/4/16	Pte	1325	James Allen		Murntown, Wexford
27/4/16	Pte	4502	Thomas Dwane		Castletown, Cork
27/4/16	L/Cpl	4129	James Fitzgerald		St Finbarr's, Cork
27/4/16	Pte	4970	Edward Fitzpatrick		Dublin
27/4/16	Pte	4959	Denis O'Leary		St Finbarr's, Cork
27/4/16	L/Cpl	1688	Mark Rigley		Ilikeaton, Derbyshire
27/4/16	Pte	5827	James Rogan		St Comgalls, Down
27/4/16	Pte	213	Michael Sullivan		Sneem, Kerry
27/4/16	Cpl	1440	Joseph Twohig		Blarney, Cork
28/4/16	Pte	4584	George Gardiner		St. John's, Limerick
28/4/16	Pte	4435	Patrick McGee		Killaloe, Clare
28/4/16	L/Cpl	5578	Patrick Nevin		Kilkee, Clare
29/4/16	Sgt	1435	William Smith		St Ann's, Birkenhead
May 1916					
1/5/16	Pte	3464	Patrick Pender*		Waterford
8/5/16	Pte	1097	Edward Twohig		SS Peter and Pauls', Cork
8/5/16	Pte	1697	William Hickson		Pendleton, Lancashire
13/5/16	Pte	1624	John Atherton		Wigan, Lancashire
13/5/16	Pte	1148	Edward Connell		Ballydehob, Cork
15/5/16	Pte	4625	James McMahon		–
17/5/16	Pte	4922	Timothy Scully		Dromgafiff, Cork
22/5/16	Pte	3704	John Maloney		Ballynoe, Cork
25/5/16	Pte	5549	Maurice Callaghan		St Finbarr's, Cork
25/5/16	Pte	1616	William A. Molyneux		Stenton, Cumberland
28/5/16	Sgt	3347	Peter Casey		Milltown Malbay, Clare
Jun 1916					
3/6/16	Pte	4565	Joseph O'Donnell		St Ann's, Cork
16/6/16	Pte	3940	Daniel McGillicuddy		Tralee, Kerry
22/6/16	Sgt	5370	James Murphy		Fedamore, Limerick
Jan 1919					
5/1/19	Pte	5859	Timothy Forde**		–

(Sources: McCance, S. (1927), History of the Royal Munster Fusiliers, 1861–1922, Vol 2, Aldershot, pp. 284–85; Ireland's Memorial Records 1914–1918, Dublin, 1923)

Appendix P

A table showing the number of Waterford-born soldiers who died at home, 1914–18

	1914	1915	1916	1917	1918
January				1	
February		2			
March					
April					1
May		2	1		
June					
July					
August		1			
September			1		
October		1		1	1
November		1			
December		1	2		
Total	nil	8	4	2	2

(Source: Compiled from a list of Waterford-born soldiers who died in the war appearing in the Munster Express *[Christmas supplement, Dec. 1991])*

Appendix Q

A bar chart showing the yearly totals of deaths of Waterford-born soldiers during the war

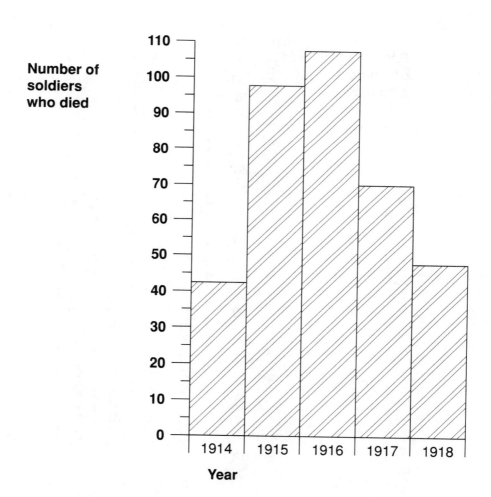

(Source: Compiled from a list of Waterford-born soldiers who died in the Great War in the Munster Express *[Christmas supplement, Dec. 1991])*

Appendix R

A bar chart showing the proportions of Waterford-born soldiers who died during the war while serving in the Royal Irish Regiment, other Irish infantry regiments, British infantry regiments and general units of the British army

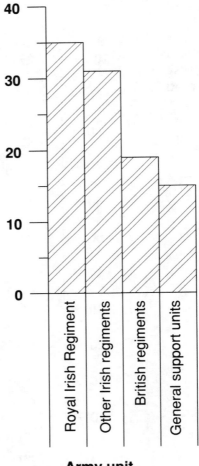

(Source: Compiled from a list of Waterford-born soldiers who died in the Great War in the Munster Express [Christmas supplement, Dec. 1991])

Appendix S

A graph showing the month and year in which Waterford-born soldiers died during the war

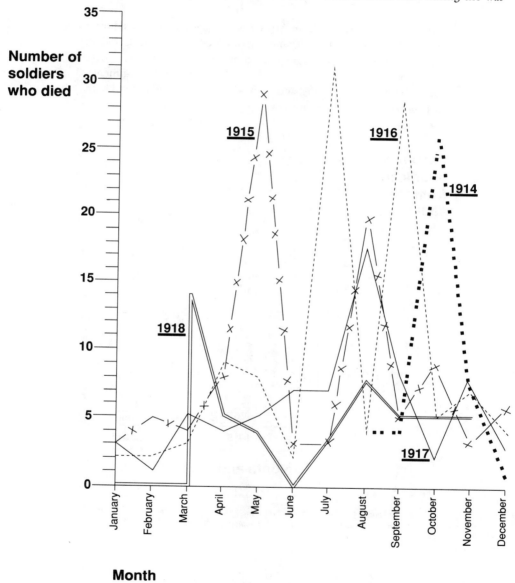

Number of soldiers who died

1915

1916

1914

1918

1917

Month

(Source: Constructed from a list of Waterford-born soldiers who died in the Great War in the Munster Express *[Christmas supplement, Dec. 1991])*

Appendix T

A bar chart, constructed from Army Lists for selected months during 1915 to 1916, showing the proportion of officers in the 9th Battalion Royal Munster Fusiliers who were commissioned from the officer cadet company ('C' Company, 7th Battalion Leinster Regiment). Note: the battalion was disbanded in May 1916 but officer strength was shown in the July Army List

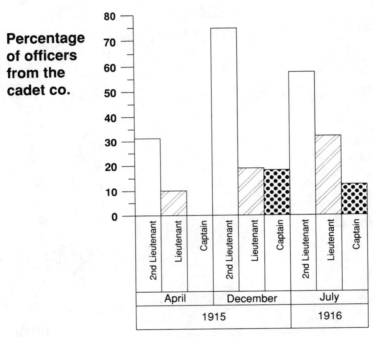

Month and year/rank

(*Sources: Compiled from the Army Lists for Apr. 1915, Dec. 1915 and July 1916; list of names of men commissioned through the cadet company [Woolwich, Parsons Papers, MO 1111])*

Appendix U

Lists of officers serving in the 9th Battalion Royal Munster Fusiliers in April and December 1915 and recorded as being on the battalion's strength in July 1916
** Officers commissioned from the Cadet Company ('C' Company, 7th Leinster Regiment)
(-) Dates shown are dates of attaining rank

April 1915	December 1915	July 1916
In Command	**In Command**	**In Command**
Lt Col H. F. Williams (6 Sep 1914)	Lt Col Williams	Lt Col E. Monteagle-Browne
2nd in Command	**2nd in Command**	**2nd in Command**
None	Maj V. J. Kelly (1 Sep 1915)	Maj V. J. Kelly
Majors	**Majors**	**Majors**
Fletcher-Vane, Sir F. P. (8 Sep 1914)	None	Shildrick, L. R. (26 Mar 1916)
Kelly, V. J. (12 Dec 1914)		
Earl of Kenmare (15 Dec 1914)		
Captains	**Captains**	**Captains**
Bateman, H. V. (4 Dec 1914)	Bateman, H. V.	Bateman, H. V.
de Andrade, F. J. (7 Nov 1914)	Fletcher, M. (19 Oct 1915)**	Fletcher, M.**
	Harrison, F. *Adjutant* (4 May 1915)	Frizell, R. A. (14 Dec 1915)
	Quare, H. A. B. (19 Oct 1915)	Harding, J. P. (14 Dec 1915)
	Sheehan, D. D. (1 Jul 1915)	Harrison, F. *Adjutant*
	Shildrick, L. R. (21 Sep 1915)	Quare, H. A. B.
		Sheehan, D. D.
		Watts-Russell, J. C. (14 Dec 1915)
Lieutenants	**Lieutenants**	**Lieutenants**
Bainbridge-Bell, L. H. (25 Sep 1914)	Bainbridge-Bell, L. H.	Bainbridge-Bell, L. H.
Fletcher, M. (30 Dec 1914)**	Collins E. F. (19 Oct 1915)	Casey, M. F. (8 Mar 1916)
Frizell, R. A. (1 Feb 1915)	Cregan, M. D. (27 Jul 1915)	Colfer, J. R.**
Harding, J. P. (1 Feb 1915)	Frizell, R. A.	Collins E. F.
Harrison, F. *Adjutant* (13 Dec 1915)	Harding, J. P.	Cregan, M. D.
Hayter, C. N. C. (4 Feb 1915)	Mahony, E. J. (19 Oct 1915)	Fitzgerald, M. H.
Quare, H. A. B. (11 Jan 1915)	McVeigh, W. J. (19 Oct 1915)**	Furney, F. E.**
Sheehan, D. D. (4 Jan 1915)	Moran, E. W. (19 Oct 1915)**	Mahony, E. J.
Shildrick, L. R. (4 Dec 1914)	Morell, C. M. (15 Apr 1915)	McVeigh, W. J.**
Watts-Russell, J. C. (6 Jan 1915)	Uzielli, E. N. (1 Jul 1915)	Moran, E. W.**
	Watts-Russell, J. C.	Morell, C. M.
		Uzielli, E. N.
2nd Lieutenants	**2nd Lieutenants**	**2nd Lieutenants**
Collins E. F. (26 Sep 1914)	Bourke, J. J. (28 Jul 1915)**	Bailey, D. J. (5 Apr 1915)
Cregan, M. D. (28 Sep 1914)	Casey, L. J. H. (25 Sep 1915)**	Beevor, H. S. (5 Mar 1915)
Fitzgerald, M. H. (20 Mar 1915)	Colfer, J. R. (7 May 1915)**	Bourke, J. J.**
Furney, F. E. (20 Mar 1915)**	Fitzgerald, M. H.	Casey, L. J. H.**
Mahony, E. J. (29 Oct 1914)	Furney, F. E.**	Gleeson, J. F.
McCormick, H. (10 Oct 1914)	Gleeson, J. F. (7 Oct 1915)	Holland, E.
McVeigh, W. J. (27 Feb 1915)**	Hogan, J. (16 Jul 1915)	Holmes, S. B. (9 Dec 1915)**
Moran, E. W. (11 Nov 1914)**	Lyne, P. J. (28 Aug 1915)**	Lyne, P. J.**
Moran, F. (4 Nov 1914)	O'Callaghan, D. J. (16 Nov 1915)	Murphy, C. J. (6 Apr 1915)
Morrell, C. M. (28 Sep 1914)	O'Callaghan, E. (28 Aug 1915)**	O'Callaghan, D. J.
Robinson, J. (23 Feb 1915)**	O'Flynn, F. J. (6 Nov 1915)**	O'Callaghan, E.**
Uzielli, E. N. (5 Oct 1914)	Power, J. A. (28 Aug 1915)**	Roche, G. P.**
Wilkinson, W. V. (22 Mar 1915)	Roche, G. P. (23 Jul 1915)**	Scanlan, M. J.**
	Scanlan, M. J. (28 Aug 1915)**	Sheehan, M. J. A.**
	Sheehan, M. J. A. (25 Sep 1915)**	
	Walsh, J. F. (7 May 1915)**	
Quarter-master	**Quarter-master**	**Quarter-master**
Osborne, J. J. (5 Oct 1914)	Osborne, J. J.	Osborne, J. J.

(Sources: Army Lists for April and December 1915 and July 1916; list of names of men commissioned through the cadet company [Parsons Papers, MD1111, Woolwich])

SOURCES AND BIBLIOGRAPHY

A. *Unpublished manuscripts and other archival material*

British Museum

Paget Papers (Ref 51250)

Imperial War Museum (IWM)

Beater (Captain O. L.) Papers (86/65/1)
Colyer (Captain W.T.) Papers (76/51/1)
Lyon (Lieutenant-Colonel W. A.) Papers (80/25/1)
Roworth (J. W.) Papers (80/40/1)
Staniforth (J. H. M) Papers (unreferenced)
Sulman (Captain P. L.) Papers (82/29/1)
With the Irish at the Front (Film Archives Ref. 212/1–2)

Liddell Hart Centre for Military Archives (King's College)

Parsons Papers

National Archives of Ireland (Four Courts)

Census returns (1901 and 1911) completed by, or on behalf of, the residents of Thomas's Avenue (Wheelbarrow Lane)

National Army Museum (NAM), London

Army Small Book (6404–96–8)
Hickie file. Papers relating to Major-General W. B. Hickie (50904–116)
Holt (Lieutenant-Colonel H. B.) Papers (7603–69–1)
Lord Roberts Papers (8310–162)

National Library of Ireland (NLI)

Hickie Papers (Call no. 8095)
Letter from Michael Davitt to Miss Mander (24,531)
Letter from Michael Davitt to P. M. Egan (13,157)
Maurice Moore Papers (10561)
Newspaper cuttings (Ref ILB 94141)
Nora Robertson Papers (P7476)
Papers relating to Father Crotty (13,100)
Redmond Papers (15,172; 15,201 [1]; 15,227; 15,238 [7, 8, 10 and 11]; 15,245 [6, 7 and 10]; 15,259; 15,261 [4, 6 and 7])

Public Record Office (PRO), Kew

Kitchener memorandum (WO 162/20)
Lists of War Badges and Certificates issued to men discharged with wounds or through illness, 1914 to 1918 (WO 329/3006–3009)
Maps (WO series 78/2540, 78/3021, 78/3425, 78/4706 and 78/4728)
Munitions (MUN series 5/11/200/13, 5/142/1121/22, 5/146/1122/5, 5/146/1122/10)
Plan, Waterford Artillery Barracks (WO 78/3085)
Printed War Office Circulars (WO 162–3)
Recruiting figures (NATS 1/398)
War Diaries (WO series 95/160–1, 95/713, 95/1955, 95/1969, 95/1970–5)
Wellington Paper (WO 30/113)

Royal Artillery Institution Library (Woolwich)

Newman (R. H.) Papers (MD 1169)
Parsons (Lieutenant-General Sir L. W.) Papers (MD 1111)

Trinity College, Dublin

Davitt Papers (9323–4; 9330; 9338–9; 9367; 9403; 9471; 9621)

B. *Newspapers and journals*

Irish:

Cork Constitution
Cork Examiner
Daily Express (Dublin)
Evening Echo (Cork)
Evening News (Waterford)
Freeman's Journal
Honesty
Irish Builder

Irish Industrial Journal
Irish Times
Munster Express
United Irishman
Waterford Mail
Waterford News
Waterford Standard

British:

Aldershot News
Camberley News
Daily Chronicle
Southern Daily Echo
Times, The

Number of Votes polled in each Constituency, 1910 (283)
LXXIII.673
Scheme for Allowances to Dependants of Deceased Sailors
and Soldiers, 1914–16 [Cd. 8183] XL.15
The Third Report of The Royal Commission for Enquiry into
the Housing of the Working Classes, Minutes of Evidence,
Ireland, 1884–5 [Cd. 4547] XXXI.187

Other

Hansard (House of Commons)
Standing Orders–9th (Service) Battalion The Royal Munster Fusiliers (Aldershot, 1914). Reference was made to
a copy in the personal possession of Martin Staunton,
Dublin.

C. Official publications

British Parliamentary Papers

Allowances and Pensions in Respect of Seamen, Marines,
and Soldiers, and their Wives, Widows and Dependants,
1914–16 [Cd. 7662] XL.15
Approximate cost of the hutting provided, or being provided,
for the accommodation of troops (including hospital
patients) and horses in the United Kingdom in the years
1914 to 1916, Aug. 1916 [Cd. 8193] XVII.559
Census of Ireland 1881 (Munster Province), 1882 [Cd.
3148] LXXVII.1
Census of Ireland 1891 (Munster Province), 1892 [Cd.
6567] XCI.1
Census of Ireland 1901 (Munster Province), 1902 [Cd.
1058] CXXIV/CXXV.1
Census of Ireland 1911 (Munster Province), 1912–13 [Cd.
6050] CXV.1
Census of Ireland 1881 (All Ireland), 1882 [Cd. 2931]
XCVI, [Cd. 3365] LXXVI, and [Cd. 3379] LXXIX
Census of Ireland 1891 (All Ireland), 1892 [Cd. 6782] XC
Census of Ireland 1901 (All Ireland), 1902 [Cd. 613]
XC.179 and [Cd. 1190] CXXIX.1
Census of Ireland 1911 (All Ireland), 1912–13 [Cd. 6663]
CXVIII.1
Report of the Royal Commission on the Rebellion in Ireland,
Evidence and Appendix, 1916 [Cd. 8311] XI.185
Report of an Enquiry by the Board of Trade into Working
Class Rents, Housing, Retail Prices and Standard Rate
of Wages in the United Kingdom, 1913 [Cd. 6955]
LXVI.393
Return Showing Number Voting as Illiterates in the 1895
General Election, 1896 (84) LXVII.307
Return Showing the Number of Persons who Voted as
Illiterates in each Constituency of the United Kingdom at
the General Election of January, 1910, and the Total

D. Bibliography (Published books, reference works, pamphlets and articles, and unpublished articles and theses)

Adelman, P. (1986), The Rise of the Labour Party
1880–1945, Harlow.
Akenson, D. H. (1970), The Irish Education Experiment,
London.
Allen, K. (1990), The Politics of James Connolly, London.
Anderson, E. B. (1951), Sailing Ships of Ireland, Dublin.
Anonymous (1871), 'A visit to Waterford', The Irish
Builder (15 Sep.), pp. 236–37.
Anonymous (1917), 'Catholic army chaplains: a diary',
Catholic Bulletin, VII, pp. 250–57.
Anonymous (1918), 'A British cardinal's visit to the
western front', The Universe, London.
Anonymous (1978), 'Conditions of employment a
century ago', The Past, 12, 31–32.

Bates, M. D. (1965), 'The barracks and posts of Ireland
—1', An Cosantoir, XXV, 19–27.
Becke, A. F. (1939), Order of Battle of Divisions; Part 2A
(9th–26th Divisions), London.
Beckett, I. F. W. (ed.) (1986), The Army and the Curragh
Incident, 1914, London.
—— and Simpson, K. (eds.) (1985), A Nation in Arms—
A Social Study of the British Army in the First World
War, Manchester.
Beckett, J. C. (1976), The Anglo-Irish Tradition, London.
—— (1981), The Making of Modern Ireland, London.
Bence-Jones, M. (1988), A Guide to Irish Country Houses,
London.
Bew, P. (1987), Conflict and Conciliation in Ireland
1890–1910, Oxford.

Bewley, C. (1989), *Memoirs of a Wild Goose*, Dublin.

Boyle, J. W. (ed.) (1978), *Leaders and Workers*, Dublin.

Brown, M. (1978), *Tommy Goes to War*, London.

Bull, P. J. (1972), 'The reconstruction of the Irish parliamentary party movement 1895–1903: an analysis with special reference to William O'Brien' (PhD thesis), Cambridge University.

Burke's Peerage and Baronetage (1980), London.

Callan, P. (1984), 'Voluntary recruiting for the British army in Ireland during the First World War' (PhD thesis), University College Dublin.

—— (1987), 'Recruiting for the British army in Ireland during the First World War', *Irish Sword*, XVII, 42–56.

Carroll, J. S., 'Waterford ships and shipping in the 19th century', *Decies*, 6 (1977), 11–16; 7 (1978), 5–9.

Carrothers, J. S. (compiled by D. S. Carrothers) (*c.* 1992), *Memoirs of a Young Lieutenant 1898–1917* (privately published and distributed), Enniskillen.

Chapple, M. (1986), *British Battle Insignia (1): 1914–18*, London.

Clark, H. (1989), *Sing a Rebel Song: The Story of James Connolly*, Edinburgh.

Clarkson, J. D. (1970), *Labour and Nationalism in Ireland*, New York.

Combined Area Residents Association (CARA) (1991), *Ballybricken and Thereabouts*, Waterford.

Commonwealth War Graves Commission (1961), *Their Name Liveth*, vol. v.

Connolly, J. (1987; 1988), *Collected Works*, 2 volumes, Dublin.

Coogan, T. P. (1980), *The I.R.A.*, Fontana ed.

Coppard, G. (1986), *With a Machine Gun to Cambrai*, London.

Cowman, D. (1988), *The Role of Waterford Chamber of Commerce 1787–1987*, Waterford.

Coyne, W. P. (ed.) (1902), *Ireland, Industrial and Agricultural*, Dublin.

Cronin, S. (1983), *Young Connolly*, Dublin.

Curriculum Development Unit (1978), *Dublin, 1913—A Divided City*, Dublin.

Curtis, L. (1984), *Nothing But the Same Old Story: The Roots of Anti-Irish Racism*, London.

D'Arcy, F. A. and Hannigan, K. (eds.) (1988), *Workers in Union*, Dublin.

Dallas, G. and Gill, D. (1985), *The Unknown Army: Mutinies in the British Army in World War One*, London.

Daly, M. and Dickson, D. (eds.) (1990), *The Origins of Popular Literacy in Ireland*, Dublin.

Daly, M. E. (1981), *Social and Economic History of Ireland Since 1800*, Dublin.

Dangerfield, G. (1977), *The Damnable Question*, London.

Davis-Goff, A. (1990), *Walled Gardens—Scenes from an Anglo-Irish Childhood*, London.

de Courcy, I. (*c.* 1965), 'Some aspects of Waterford in maritime history' (lecture paper), Waterford Municipal Library.

De Montmorency, H. (1936), *Sword and Stirrup: Memoirs of an Adventurous Life*, London.

Dearle, N. B. (1929), *The Economic Chronicle of the Great War for Great Britain and Ireland*, London.

Denman, T. (1987), 'The 10th (Irish) Division 1914–15: a study in military and political interaction', *Irish Sword*, XVII, 16–25.

—— (1987/1988), 'Sir Lawrence Parsons and the raising of the 16th (Irish) Division, 1914–15', *Irish Sword*, XVII, 90–104.

—— (1989), 'An Irish battalion at war: from the letters of Captain J. H. M. Staniforth 7th Leinsters, 1914–18', *Irish Sword*, XVII, 165–217.

—— (1991), 'The Catholic Irish soldier in the First World War: the racial environment', *Irish Historical Studies*, XXVII, 352–65.

—— (1992a), '"A voice from the lonely grave": the death in action of Major William Redmond MP, 7 June 1917', *Irish Sword*, XVIII, 286–96.

—— (1992b), *Ireland's Unknown Soldiers: The 16th (Irish) Division in the Great War*, Dublin.

Devine, T. M. and Dickson, D. (eds.) (1983), *Ireland and Scotland 1600–1850*, Edinburgh.

Dictionary of National Biography (1917), Oxford.

Dolden, A. S. (1980), *Cannon Fodder*, Poole.

Dooley. T. P. (1991), 'Politics, bands and marketing: army recruitment in Waterford city, 1914–15', *Irish Sword*, XVIII, 205–19.

Douglas, R. (1976), *Land, People and Politics—The Land Question in the United Kingdom 1878–1952*, London.

Dunne, S. (1991), *In My Father's House*, Dublin.

Edmonds, J. E. (1986), *The Official History of the Great War: Military Operations, France and Belgium Dec 1915–July 1916*, Woking.

Edwards, O. D. (1986), 'Patrick MacGill and the making of a historical source: with a handlist of his works', *Innes Review*, XXXVII, 73–99.

—— and Pyle, F. (eds.) (1968), *1916: The Easter Rising*, London.

—— et al. (eds.) (1968), *Celtic Nationalism*, London.

Egan, P. M. (1894), *Egan's Guide to Waterford*, Kilkenny.

Ellis, P. B. (1985), *A History of the Irish Working Class*, London.

Englander, D. and Osborne, J. (1978), 'Jack, Tommy and Henry Dubbs; the armed forces and the working class', *Historical Journal*, 21, 593–621.

Evans, J. (ed.) (1978), *Social Policy 1830–1914*, London.

Fisher, J. R. (1916), 'The Irish enigma again—what is wrong in Ireland', *Nineteenth Century and After*, LXXIX, 1184–89.

Fitzpatrick, D. (1977), *Politics and Irish Life 1913–1921*, Dublin.

—— (1978), 'Geography of Irish nationalism 1910–1921', *Past and Present*, 78, 113–44.

—— (1980), 'Strikes in Ireland, 1914–21', *Soathar*, **6**, 26–39.

—— (ed.) (1988), *Ireland and the First World War*, Dublin.

Foot, M. R. D. (ed.) (1973), *War and Society*, London.

Foster, R. F. (1988), *Modern Ireland 1600–1972*, London.

French, D. (1982), *British Economic and Strategic Planning 1905–1915*, London.

Fuller, J. G. (1990), *Troop Morale and Popular Culture in the British and Dominion Armies 1914–1918*, Oxford.

Fussell, P. (1975), *The Great War and Modern Memory*, Oxford.

Gailey, A. (1984), 'Unionist rhetoric and Irish local government reform 1895–9', *Irish Historical Studies*, **24**, 52–68.

Galbraith, J. K. (1980), *The Nature of Mass Poverty*, Harmondsworth.

Garvin, T. (1981), *The Evolution of Irish Nationalist Politics*, Dublin.

Germains, V. W. (1930), *The Kitchener Armies*, London.

Gough, H. (1954), *Soldiering On*, London.

Gourvish, T. R. and O'Day, A. (eds.) (1988), *Later Victorian Britain 1867–1900*, London.

Graves, R. (1960), *Goodbye to All That*, Harmondsworth.

Greaves, C. D. (1961), *The Life and Times of James Connolly*, London.

Griffiths, A. (ed.) (1916), *Meagher of the Sword, Speeches of Thomas Francis Meagher in Ireland 1846–1848*, Dublin.

Gwynn, D. (1932), *The Life of John Redmond*, London.

Gwynn, S. (1919), *John Redmond's Last Years*, London.

—— (1926), *Experiences of a Literary Man*, London.

Hachey, T. E. and McCaffey, L. J. (eds.) (1989), *Perspectives on Irish Nationalism*, Kentucky.

Hammerton, J. A. (ed.) (*c.* 1930), *The Great War, I Was There*, Vol. 1, London.

Hannay, J. O. (1915), 'Ireland and the war', *Nineteenth Century and After*, **LXXVIII**, 393–402.

—— (1916) 'Ireland in two wars—recruiting in Ireland today', *Nineteenth Century and After*, **LXXIX**, 173–80.

Harris, H. (1968), *The Irish Regiments in the First World War*, Cork.

Harris, R. G. (1989), *The Irish Regiments: A Pictorial History 1683–1987*, Tunbridge Wells.

Hay, I. (1915), *The First Hundred Thousand*, London.

Hechter, M. (1974), *Internal Colonialism*, California.

Hickey, D. J. and Doherty, J. E. (1980), *A Dictionary of Irish History Since 1800*, Dublin.

Higgins, G. (1912), *Cardinal Bourne—A Record of the Sayings and Doings of His Eminence Francis 4th Archbishop of Westminster*, London.

Hiley, N. P. (1984), 'Making war: the British news media and government control 1914–16' (PhD thesis), Open University.

Holding, N. (1982), *World War I Army Ancestry*, Solihull.

Howell, D. (1986), *A Lost Left: Three Studies in Socialism and Nationalism*, Manchester.

Hynes, S. (1990), *A War Imagined: The First World War and English Culture*, London.

Irish Catholic Directory, 1914 and 1915.

Jalland, P. (1986), *The Liberals and Ireland*, Brighton.

James, E. A. (1978), *British Regiments 1914–1918*, London.

Jeffery, K. (ed.) (1985), *The Military Correspondence of Field Marshal Sir Henry Wilson 1918–1922*, London.

Jervis, H. S. (1922), *The 2nd Munsters in France*, Aldershot.

Johnson, D. (1989), *The Interwar Economy in Ireland*, Dublin.

Joll, J. (1984), *The Origins of the First World War*, London.

Karsten, P. (1983), 'Irish soldiers in the British army, 1792–1922: suborned or subordinate?', *Journal of Social History*, **XVII**, 31–64.

Keegan, J. (1978), *The Face of Battle*, Harmondsworth.

Kerr, S. P. (1916), *What the Irish Regiments have done—with a Diary of a Visit to the Front by John Redmond*, London.

Kipling, R. (1915), *The New Army in Training*, London.

Knightly, P. (1975), *The First Casualty*, London.

Lankford, S. (1980), *The Hope and the Sadness*, Cork.

Larkin, E. (1989), *James Larkin, Irish Labour Leader*, Winchester.

Lavery, F. (ed.) (1920), *Great Irishmen in War and Politics*, London.

Lee, J. (1973), *The Modernisation of Irish Society 1848–1918*, Dublin.

Levy, C. (ed.) (1987), *Socialism and the Intelligentsia 1880–1914*, London.

Lloyd, A. (1976), *The War in the Trenches*, St Albans.

Lloyd George, D. (1938), *War Memoirs*, 2 volumes, London.

Luanaigh, D. (1983), 'Suspected importation of fenian guns through the port of Waterford', *Decies*, **22**, 29–32.

Lucey, D. J. (1972), 'Cork public opinion and the First World War' (MA thesis), University College, Cork.

Lucy, J. F. (1992), *There's a Devil in the Drum*, Dallington.

Lyons, F. S. L. (1973), *Ireland Since the Famine*, London.

—— (1975), *The Irish Parliamentary Party 1890–1910*, Connecticut.

—— (1979), *Culture and Anarchy in Ireland, 1890–1939*, Oxford.

Lysaght, E. E. (1918), 'Four years of Irish economics 1914–1918: Irish agriculture', *Studies*, 314–19.

Mac Giolla Choille, B. (1966), *Intelligence Notes 1913–16*, Dublin.

MacDonagh, M. (1916), *The Irish at the Front*, London.

MacDonagh, O. and Mandle, W. F. (eds.) (1986), *Ireland*

and Irish Australia: Studies in Cultural and Political History, Beckenham.

MacGill, P. (1915), The Amateur Army, London.

—— (1984a), The Red Horizon, Kerry.

—— (1984b), The Great Push: An Episode of the Great War, Kerry.

MacLysaght, E. (1982), More Irish Families, Dublin.

MacMahon, J. A. (1981), 'The Catholic clergy and the social question in Ireland, 1891–1916', Studies, LXX, 263–88.

Macmillan, H. (1966), Winds of Change 1914–1939, London.

MacSweeney, A. M. (1915), 'A Study of Poverty in Cork City', Studies, 93–104.

Malone, A. E. (1918), 'Four years of Irish economics, 1914–1918: Irish labour in wartime', Studies, 319–27.

Marks, T. P. (1979), The Laughter Goes from Life, London.

Marshall, T. H. (1970), Social Policy, London.

Marwick, A. (1965), The Deluge: British Society and the First World War, London.

McCance, S. (1927), History of the Royal Munster Fusiliers, 2 volumes, Aldershot.

McCarthy, M. J. F. (1902), Priests and People in Ireland, London.

McCartney, D. (1976), 'Sean O'Faolain: a nationalist right enough', Irish University Review, 6, 73–86.

McConville, M. (1986), Ascendancy to Oblivion, London.

McElwee, R. (1992), The Last Voyages of the Waterford Steamers, Waterford.

McGinley, N. (1987), Donegal, Ireland and the First World War, Letterkenny.

McNeill, D. B. (1971), Irish Passenger Steamship Services, Vol. 2, Newton Abbot.

Miller, D. W. (1973), Church, State and Nation in Ireland 1898–1921, Dublin.

Morton, G. (1980), Home Rule and the Irish Question, Harlow.

Moynihan, E. (ed.), People at War 1914–18, Newton Abbot.

Muenger, E. A. (1981), 'The British army in Ireland, 1886–1914' (PhD thesis), University of Michigan.

Murphy, M., 'The working classes of nineteenth-century Cork', Cork Historical and Archaeological Journal, 85, Part 241–2, 26–51.

Murray, R. H. (1916), 'The Irish enigma again (III)—the Sinn Fein rebellion', Nineteenth Century and After, LXXIX, 1203–20.

Nelson, J. E. (1973–74), 'Irish soldiers in the Great War, some personal experiences', Irish Sword, XI, 163–79.

Newspaper Press Directory, 1874 to 1915, London.

Nolan, W. and Power, T. P. (eds.) (1992), Waterford: History and Society, Dublin.

O'Brien, C. C. (1985), A Concise History of Ireland, London.

O'Brien, J. (1982), Dear, Dirty Dublin, California.

O'Connor, E. (1979), 'The influence of Redmondism on the development of the labour movement in the 1880s', Decies, 10, 37–42.

—— (1989), A Labour History of Waterford, Waterford.

O'Day, A. (ed.) (1987), Reactions to Nationalism, London.

O'Donnell, M. (1988), 'The Waterford Steamship Company in the 1880s', Decies, 37, 30–33.

O'Faolain, S. (1976), 'A portrait of the artist as an old man', Irish University Review, 6, 10–18.

—— (1985), Bird Alone, Oxford.

O'Flanagan, N. (1985), 'Dublin city in an age of war and revolution 1914–24' (MA thesis), University College, Dublin.

O'Neill, J. (1984), 'The sights, the sounds and the smells of Waterford', Waterford News and Star (Christmas supplement).

—— (1986a), 'Waterford's five railways', Irish Railway Record Society, 16, no. 101, 106–19.

—— (1986b), 'Waterford, 1913 and now', Waterford News and Star (Christmas supplement).

O'Rahilly, A. (1925), Father William Doyle, S. J., London.

O'Shea, J. (1982), Priest, Politics and Society in Post-famine Ireland, Dublin.

Oldmeadow, E. (1940), Francis Cardinal Bourne, 2 volumes, London.

Pankhurst, E. S. (1984), The Home Front, London.

Parmiter, G. de C. (1936), Roger Casement, London.

Pelling, H. (1965), The Origins of the Labour Party, Oxford.

—— (1987), A History of British Trade Unionism, Harmondsworth.

Perry, N. (1994), 'Nationality in the Irish infantry regiments in the First World War', War & Society, 12.

Philpin, C. H. E. (ed.) (1987), Nationalism and Popular Protest in Ireland, Cambridge.

Porter, F. (ed.) (1910), Thom's Directory of the City and County of Waterford 1909–10, Dublin.

Pratt, E. A. (1921), British Railways and the Great War, Vol. 1, London.

Ranelagh, J. O. (1983), A Short History of Ireland, Cambridge.

Read, D. (1979), England 1868–1914, Harlow.

Redmond, J. E. (1902), Mr Redmond's Speech (pamphlet printed for private circulation).

— (1915), Speech delivered by J. E. Redmond at Waterford City and County Convention 23 August 1915, London.

——, Kettle, T. M. and Furlong, Canon (1907), The Irish Party and its Assailants—its Policy Vindicated: A Record of Achievement.

Redmond, W. H. (1917), Trench Pictures from France, London.

Report of Standing Committee of the United Irish League (1915), Dublin.

Riordan, E. J. (1915), 'Chronicle: Irish industries—after twelve months of war', Studies, 463–70.

—— (1918), 'Four years of Irish economics 1914–1918: restraint of industry', *Studies*, 306–14.

—— (1920), *Modern Irish Trade and Industry*, London.

Robertson, N. (1960), *Crowned Harp*, Dublin.

Ryan, W. P. (1910), *The Plough and the Cross*, Dublin.

—— (1912), *The Pope's Green Island*, London.

Seaman, L. C. B. (1966), *Post-Victorian Britain 1902–1951*, London.

Shannon, C. B. (1973), 'The Ulster Liberal Unionists and local government reform, 1885–98', *Irish Historical Studies*, 18, 407–23.

Sheehan, D. D. (1921), *Ireland Since Parnell*, London.

Simkins, P. (1988), *Kitchener's Army: The Raising of the New Armies, 1914–18*, Manchester.

Snow, C. P. (1969), *The Two Cultures and a Second Look*, Cambridge.

Staunton, M. (1986a), 'The Royal Munster Fusiliers in the Great War 1914–19' (MA Thesis), University College, Dublin.

—— (1986b), 'Ginchy: nationalist Ireland's forgotten Battle of the Somme', *An Cosantoir*, XLVI, 24–26.

—— (1986c), 'Kilrush, Co. Clare and the Royal Munster Fusiliers—the experience of an Irish town in the First World War', *Irish Sword*, XIV, 268–70.

—— (1989), 'Soldiers died in the Great War 1914–19 as historical source material', *Stand To*, 27, 6–8.

Stone, L. (1969), 'Literacy and education in England 1640–1900', *Past and Present*, 42, 69–139.

Swinson, A. (ed.) (1972), *A Register of the Regiments and Corps of the British Army*, London.

Taylor, R. (1961), *Assassination: The Death of Sir Henry Wilson and the Tragedy of Ireland*, London.

Terraine, J. (1992), 'Understanding', *Stand To*, 34, 7–12.

The Times (1916), *The Times History of the War*, Vol. 6, London.

Thompson, E. P. (1980), *The Making of the English Working Class*, Harmondsworth.

Thompson, P. (1975), *The Edwardians*, London.

Tosh, J. (1984), *The Pursuit of History*, Harlow.

Townshend, C. (1983), *Political Violence in Ireland—Government and Resistance Since 1848*, Oxford.

Turner, J. (ed.) (1988), *Britain and the First World War*, London.

—— (1992), *British Politics and the Great War: Coalition and Conflict 1915–1918*, London.

Union Defence League (1912), *Irish Facts*, London.

Vane, Sir F. F. (1929), *Agin the Governments*, London.

Walker, B. M. (1973), 'The Irish electorate, 1868–1915', *Irish Historical Studies*, XVIII, 359–406.

Walker, G. A. C. (1920), *The Book of the 7th (Service) Battalion Royal Inniskilling Fusiliers*, Dublin.

Walsh, J. J. (1968), *Waterford's Yesterdays and Tomorrows*, Waterford.

Ward Lock & Co. (1904), *A New Practical, Descriptive and Pictorial Guide to Waterford and Wexford*, London.

Warner, P. (1976), *Battle of Loos*, London.

Waterford Central Technical Institute, *Central Technical Institute, Prospectus of Classes, Session 1907–08* (Ref. Ir 370 p. 23), NLI.

Waterford Corporation, A Municipal Directory, 1955 (1955), Waterford.

Weller, K. (1985), *Don't be a Soldier—The Radical Anti-War Movement in North London 1914–1918*, London.

Westlake, R. (1989), *Kitchener's Army*, Tunbridge Wells.

Wheatley, J. (1909), *The Catholic Workingman*, Glasgow.

Whitaker's Almanack, 1874 to 1916, London.

Who Was Who, 1929–1940.

Winstanley, M. J. (1984), *Ireland and the Land Question 1800–1922*, London.

Winter, D. (1978), *Death's Men*, Harmondsworth.

Winter, J. M. (1986), *The Great War and the British People*, Basingstoke.

Woods, C. J. (1968), 'The Catholic Church and Irish politics 1879–1892' (PhD thesis), Nottingham University.

Wymberry, E. (c. 1989), *Well!: Recollections of Waterford in the 1940s and 50s*, Waterford.

—— (c. 1991), *Well! Well!: Memories of Waterford in the 1950s*, Waterford.

Young, P. (ed.) (1984), *World War 1 (1915–16)*, Vol. 4, New York.

INDEX